Amy Tan

MCFARLAND LITERARY COMPANIONS
BY MARY ELLEN SNODGRASS

1. *August Wilson* (2004)

2. *Barbara Kingsolver* (2004)

3. *Amy Tan* (2004)

Amy Tan

A Literary Companion

MARY ELLEN SNODGRASS

McFarland Literary Companions, 3

McFarland & Company, Inc., Publishers
Jefferson, North Carolina, and London

LIBRARY OF CONGRESS CATALOGUING-IN-PUBLICATION DATA

Snodgrass, Mary Ellen.
Amy Tan : a literary companion / Mary Ellen Snodgrass.
    p.   cm. — (McFarland literary companions ; 3)
Includes bibliographical references and index.

ISBN 0-7864-2013-8 (softcover : 50# alkaline paper) ∞

1. Tan, Amy — Criticism and interpretation.   2. Women and
literature — United States — History — 20th century.   3. Chinese
American women in literature.   4. Chinese Americans in literature.
    I. Title.   II. McFarland literary companion series ; 3.
PS3570.A48Z885   2004   813'.54 — dc22   2004014713

British Library cataloguing data are available

©2004 Mary Ellen Snodgrass. All rights reserved

On the cover: Photograph of Amy Tan by Robert Soothorap;
background ©2004 Image Source

Manufactured in the United States of America

*McFarland & Company, Inc., Publishers
Box 611, Jefferson, North Carolina 28640
www.mcfarlandpub.com*

Acknowledgments

I owe thanks to Elise Capron at the Sandra Dijkstra Agency for the photographs of Amy Tan. Also, I acknowledge the advice and research assistance of the following people and institutions:

Avis Gachet, Book Buyer
Wonderland Books
Hickory, North Carolina

Hannah Owen, deputy director
Hickory Public Libraries
Hickory, North Carolina

Wanda Rozzelle and Amy Jew, reference
  librarians
Catawba County Library
Newton, North Carolina

Mark Schumacher, reference librarian
Jackson Library, UNC-G
Greensboro, North Carolina

Contents

The oppressed without hope are mysteriously quiet.
When the conception of change is beyond the limits of the possible,
there are no words to articulate discontent
so it is sometimes held not to exist....
But the fact that we could not hear does not prove that no pain existed.
Sheila Rowbotham
Women's Conscious, Man's World, 1973

You are beauty, and love is beauty and we are beauty.
We are divine, unchanged by time.
Amy Tan
The Bonesetter's Daughter, 2001

Preface

For readers seeking a greater knowledge or understanding of Amy Tan's contributions to feminist, American, and Amerasian literature, *Amy Tan: A Literary Companion* offers an introduction and overview. It equips the reader, feminist, historian, student, researcher, teacher, reviewer, and librarian with analysis of characters, plots, allusions, literary motifs, and classic themes from the works of one of America's most lauded writers. The text opens with an annotated chronology of the author's life, Chinese heritage, works, and awards, followed by a family tree of the Tans. The 97 A-to-Z entries combine analysis from reviewers and critics along with generous citations from primary and secondary sources. Each entry concludes with a selected bibliography on such subjects as yin and yang, suicide, China, the historical milieu, autobiography, men, dismemberment, superstition, humor, and wisdom. Charts elucidate the convoluted genealogies of the Bonesetter Gu, Hsu, Jong, Kwong, Louie, St. Clair, Woo, Yee, and Young clans. In addition to clearing up confusion about Chinese names, these family trees account for connections between kinship lines, as with the link between the Youngs and the family of Dr. Gu, evidence that Winnie Louie and Helen Kwong are not related by blood or marriage, and the recovered sisterhood that joins Jack Yee's two daughters with the prestigious Bishops of Hawaii. Generous cross references point to divergent strands of thought and guide the reader into peripheral territory, e.g., from violence to the Taiping Rebellion of 1864, abortion to spousal abuse, journeys to diaspora and reunions, patriarchy to disillusion and polygyny, and storytelling to talk-story, the female outlet for repressed memory and an antidote to the patriarchal silencing of women.

Back matter is designed to aid the student, reviewer, and researcher. Appendix A orients the beginner with a time line of historical events in China and during World War II and their intertextual importance to crises in the lives of fictional characters, for example, the approach of Communists to Shanghai and Wen Fu's rape at gunpoint of his ex-wife. The entries contain abbreviated reference and page numbers of the works from which each event derives.

A second appendix compiles a glossary of foreign terms and idioms, such as multiple meanings of *chang* and mathematical descriptions of *li* and *yuan*, along with parts of speech, translation, and the appearance of the terms in Tan's published works.

A third appendix provides forty-five topics for group or individual projects, composition, analysis, background material, enactment, and theme development, notably, cross-cultural mythology, motifs of matriarchy and marital discord, character attitudes toward materialism and spirituality, the author's choice of narrative modes, and the use of medical terms as character motivation.

Back matter concludes with an exhaustive chronological listing of primary sources and reprints followed by a general bibliography. Many entries derive from journal and periodical articles and reviews of Tan's essays, novels, short fiction, and memoirs in the newspapers of major cities in the United States, Great Britain, Canada, China, and Australia. Secondary sources, particularly those by experienced reviewers, are useful for the study of works that have yet to be analyzed thoroughly in academic journals.

A comprehensive index directs users of the literary companion to major and minor characters, peoples, diseases, belief systems, deities, movements, events, eras, historical figures, place names, landmarks, traditional rituals and holidays, published works, sources, authors, and issues, e.g., Precious Auntie, Lao Lu and Buncake, Hakka, multiple sclerosis and Alzheimer's disease, Taoism, Amitaba and Buddha, God Worshippers, Boxer Rebellion and Sino-Japanese War, Sung dynasty and Ching dynasty, Chiang Kai-shek and Claire Chennault, Kweilin, Chinatown, herbalism and Chinese New Year, *The Color Purple* and "Fish Cheeks," calligraphy, Maxine Hong Kingston and Michael Dorris, and foot-binding, bride price, and matchmaking.

Introduction

Amy Tan's writings are a model of the writer's truism that the best subject lies close to home. Her domestic scenarios have the ring of authenticity, in part because she draws material from anecdotes and events that impact her own family. From closeness with her mother, Daisy Tan, the author absorbed a subjective appreciation of Chinese traditions, rituals, and history. Without apology, the author mined from talk-story a lifetime of oddments and topical strands to flesh out the attack of Manchu mercenaries on a Christian enclave, the terror of a refugee fleeing Japanese invaders, a despairing concubine's death from deliberate opium consumption, an inkmaker's loss from fire at a Peking shop, and an industrial magnate's face-off against occupation forces. Flashes of realism leap from the pages as a teenager salts her diary with cruel taunts to her mother, a banner collapses on the elaborate funeral banquet honoring a Chinese matriarch, an apartment dweller eavesdrops on the intimate conversations of neighbors, a rebel child humiliates her parents by botching a piano recital, first-generation Chinese-American daughters distance themselves from their partially assimilated Chinese mothers, and a concubine lops off her hair as a gesture of defiance to patriarchy.

It is no accident that Tan's works are filled with engaging images of strong girls and women. The self-liberation of Daisy Tan impressed the author with the instinctive growth of feminism from centuries of feudal repression. Without politically correct cant or subtextual intent, Tan expresses the yearnings and risk-taking of Chinese women who seize freedom by accepting the consequences of overturning anti-female Confucian principles and of battling the misogyny of the lapsed Ching dynasty. It is no accident that their rage at gender disparity and attendant cruelties erupts simultaneously with military threats to China's survival. At a time when black American soldiers in Europe rid themselves of plantation racism during World War II and the contributions of female soldiers and nurses and of Rosie the Riveter prophesied the expansion of opportunities for women in the post-war United States, China's women threw off the shackles of paternalism, a horror worsened by arranged marriages, marital rape, and the foot-binding of little girls.

Valor and pride flourish in Tan's female characters. The laundress Nunumu rescues her friend Nelly Banner from slaughter. Sister Yu champions in Communist doctrine the concepts of Christianity that promise an equal distribution of food to hungry peasants. Drawing courage from the example of the feminist martyr Little Yu, Peanut extends a network of shelter and encouragement to refugees from patriarchal marriage. Lindo Jong concocts a nightmare so real that her in-laws gladly release her from a doomed union with a child-husband and pay her way to America. Suyuan Woo makes a new home in California while searching China nearly a half century for her lost twins. LuLing Liu Young earns renown and a comfortable living for brushing on parchment the artful pictograms of the Chinese alphabet she learned in childhood. Winnie Louie ends the torment and slow murder of children by aborting the fetuses sired by a monster husband. In each case, heroines confront self-doubt while remaining true to gut instinct.

To assure realism in characters, Tan avoids the easy out. Her fictional women bear their share of faults—materialism in Lindo Jong, gluttony and treachery in Helen Kwong, arrogance in Waverly Jong, spinelessness in Lena Livotny, mania in Precious Auntie, and meddling in Kwan Li. Eluding the tyranny of political correctness, Tan's characters abide by idiosyncratic principles. Old Aunt teaches female compliance and obedience to her motherless niece. Big Ma turns foster daughter Kwan Li into a child slave. Olivia Yee Bishop scapegoats her husband's old lover as the cause of marital failure. Rather than develop creativity, Ruth Luyi Young chooses an auxiliary role as ghostwriter and nurturer of mediocre talents. Winnie Louie swallows her sorrow and wears a brave face among the pilots' wives living at a makeshift billet in a monastery. For these characters, false values precede a soul-salving turnabout.

To emphasize redemption and grace, Tan offers her characters life-altering opportunities, some of which derive from hardship and heartbreak. GaoLing Young abandons Reagan era materialism by caring for her aged sister. Rose Hsu Jordan battles post-separation despair by defying her manipulative husband and rejecting his bribe. During wartime occupation, San Ma and Wu Ma cast off subservience by rescuing Jiang Sao-Yen from penury, illness, and neglect. Olivia Yee Bishop outgrows self-absorption and honors her martyred sister Kwan by taking her surname and passing it on to Samantha "Sammy" Li, Olivia's miracle child. June Woo adds depth to her two-dimensional life by retracing the Chinese diaspora to convey her deceased mother's love to adult children, Chwun Hwa and Chwun Yu, whom Suyuan left behind during a national panic. These extraordinary examples of devotion and fortitude elevate women in a society that traditionally overlooks their potential and negates their contributions.

In amassing women's stories, Tan chooses candor over artifice. She refuses to whitewash China's abysmal record of child endangerment, wife enslavement, and dehumanizing of the poor, aged, and handicapped; she chooses not to exonerate a motherland that allows Machiavellian politics to spawn a mass diaspora of its citizenry. Against a deluge of criticism from author Frank Chin and other writers espousing a pro–China stance, she opts for a forthright examination of feudal misogyny and praise for the pace-setters who led Chinese women toward equality. Without fear of reprisal from angry Amerasian males, Tan follows her staunchest heroine, Winnie

Louie, from teen engagement and dowry arrangements through a hellish marriage to a sexual deviate and child batterer. Over a cycle of brutality, Winnie develops guile and backbone. After the deaths of her infant daughters Mochou and Yiku, she rescues Danru, her first son, from the dominance of Wen Fu and accepts imprisonment rather than resumption of a domestic nightmare. Tan turns Winnie's experiences into grist for talk-story to affirm her daughter, Pearl Louie Brandt, during a battle with multiple sclerosis. The transformation of tragedy into instruction illustrates the author's belief that secrets and silence are insidious enslavers of women.

Tan's pro-female scenarios bear humanistic touches of grace. Suyuan Woo alleviates insecurity in her daughter June May by giving her a jade necklace and a nudge toward self-esteem. Ying-ying St. Clair urges her daughter Lena to protest the devaluation that the egotistical Harold Livotny heaps on her through petty list-making. The clairvoyant Kwan Li releases pent-up hurts by talking over the past with the ghost of Big Ma. Ruth Luyi Young acquires respect for her grandmother, Precious Auntie, by having a biographical manuscript translated from Chinese into English. Auntie Du remains in Shanghai to be near Winnie Louie during her fifteen months in women's prison while Winnie turns incarceration into a chance to help female inmates find their own way in a man's world. The woman-to-woman spread of hope and uplift epitomizes Tan's optimism and justifies self-liberating trickery among women who have nothing to lose.

While elevating the efforts of women to survive and prevail, Tan pairs them with equally admirable males. Bonesetter Gu loves his daughter enough to spare her foot-binding and to defy convention by teaching her medical and herbal skills. Geologist Pan Kai Jing convinces his bride LuLing that family curses are outdated superstitions. Jimmy Louie cradles his lover Winnie and tenderly frees her from flashbacks of trauma. Canning Woo comforts his daughter June by supplying details of his late wife's heroism and devotion to motherhood. Long Jiaguo redeems himself from female batterer to loyal husband by marrying Helen, his victim's sister. Gan, a young pilot, offers Winnie Louie a male-female friendship that boosts her morale at a low point in her marriage. Photographer Simon Bishop agrees to a journey to China with his estranged wife to further their career and restore their former intimacy. When measured against the sybaritic Wu Tsing, aristocratic Jiang Sao-yen, womanizing Lin Xiao, and demonic Wen Fu, Tan's supportive males coordinate well with the women they admire and refute charges of critics that Tan uses fiction as a form of male-bashing.

Tan's skill at fiction extends from plot and character to the intricacies of literary devices. She uses a whimpering fish as a metaphor for the coerced concubine, a bursting watermelon as a symbol of the opportunist's conquest of a virgin, scattered pages of "The Good News" as evidence that Christian missions made little change in the people they evangelized, and a legless crab as a parallel of damaged goods that a self-defeating daughter willingly settles for. Tan's frequent recitations of Chinese aphorism bear insights into attitudes, as with the reminder that raising a female child is as profitable as feeding the neighbor's pig. The judicious placement of fables and exempla offers insight into dilemmas and predicaments, for instance, the cautionary tale about a woman who buys a swan feather to pass on to her daughter and the myth of farmer Zhang, the ungrateful husband whom the Jade Emperor of Heaven turns into the judgmental Kitchen God. Tan's tweaking of the latter story results in Lady Sorrowfree, a nameless deity whom the author turns into a spokeswoman for beleaguered women. These deft touches elevate Tan from a writer of popular ethnic fiction to a masterful contributor to world and feminist literature.

The huge following for Amy Tan's writings attests to her success at feminist and universal themes. Her novels, stories, and essays brim with support for strong mother-daughter and woman-to-woman relations. She fills her plots with praise for female characters who accept near-impossible tasks— a pregnant bride traveling by wartime conveyance over much of China to reach safety in Kunming, a mother searching a California beach for the body of her drowned son, a friend who steals a pedicab to escape falling bombs, and a Chinese ghost-seer who retreats into a past life to offer her Amerasian sister another chance at domestic happiness. Fans greet Tan at book-signings and campus lectures with thanks for her sincerity. Awards and photo ops picture her as a rising star whose light springs from inner truth.

Chronology of
Tan's Family History,
Life and Works

1924 Author Amy Tan was influenced by the discord and tragedy in her maternal family line. Her mother, Daisy Du Ching, was born into what one reviewer called the "florid decay of imperial China" (Walsh). Tan's maternal grandmother, Gu Jingmei, was widowed after her scholarly husband died of influenza. In an insidious example of polygyny, in 1924, a wealthy industrialist raped Jingmei and added her to his household of three wives. She was known as the Replacement Wife for Divong, a previous wife whose death Jingmei helped to mourn.

New Year's Day, 1925 Out of despair at being a concubine of lowly rank, in 1925, Jingmei swallowed raw opium concealed in New Year's rice cakes. Her death took place in front of her nine-year-old daughter, Amy's mother, who became a vocational nurse and hospital technician in Shanghai. Of the social implications of parental suicide, Daisy later confided, "We had no face! We belonged to nobody! This is a shame I can never push off my back" ("Lost Lives of Women," p. 90).

1935 Daisy grew up pampered by servants and grandmother and showered with privileges. At age nineteen, she married Wang Zo, an abusive womanizer and pilot for the Kuomintang air force, whom she barely knew.

1941 During the Sino-Japanese War (1937–1945), Daisy met John Yuehhan Tan and his brother on a lengthy boat trip on a southwestern Chinese river to Wang Zo's new billet. Tan, a translator for the U.S. Information Service and amateur photographer from Beijing, recurs in his daughter's fiction as Jimmy Louie, the *bon vivant* suitor in *The Kitchen God's Wife* (1991).

1945 While John Tan was working in Tientsin, he encountered Daisy on the street and discovered that their love-at-first-sight had endured a four-year separation.

1947 After a wretched marriage to a batterer and the deaths of a son and daughter in infancy, Daisy blamed her husband Wang Zo and ran away, leaving behind three daughters, ranging in age from four to eleven. He retaliated by refusing her visitation rights with the girls. The Shanghai tabloids ballyhooed the events of her twelve-year marriage to Wang, who had her apprehended by the police and put on trial.

Daisy served a prison sentence for adultery with John, the man she eventually married. At age thirty-four, he rejected a scholarship to study electrical engineering at M.I.T. to pursue theology at the Berkeley Baptist Divinity School. He become a Baptist evangelist, as had his eleven younger siblings.

Summer, 1949 After two years in prison, Daisy gained her freedom and immigrated to the United States to marry John Tan. The couple spoke different dialects — Daisy fluent in Mandarin and Shanghaiese and John more conversant with Cantonese. During a period of civil war preceding the Communist takeover, she was wise to flee her homeland only five days before the frontiers closed to emigrants. Because Chinese law favored the father's rights to children, she left behind the three daughters sired by Wang Zo. In California, John found work building tiny electromagnetic transformers at home. Amy Tan later clarified her parents' intent in starting anew in America: "Immigrant parents come to America with the idea that they're going to lose ground, economically and socially, but that their children will eventually benefit from what they've done" (Chatfield-Taylor, p. 178).

February 19, 1952 A native Californian, An-mei Ruth "Amy" Tan was born in Oakland. The Tans named their middle child and only daughter for two missionaries; her Chinese name means "blessing from America." Reared in an insular home, she valued her family lineage, "the tapestry of who created us in our past, our parents, our grandparents, and beyond" (Kanner, p. 3). Up close, the family circle was less amiable. Her off-center relationship with Daisy began in toddlerhood with listening in Mandarin and replying in English. Tan remarked, "She raised me with all her fears and regrets. She hinted at great tragedies. She had so much advice ... and I didn't want to listen" (Kropf, p. E2). The author later revealed that assimilation required her to reject Chinese culture and embrace the American milieu as her home culture. The violation of her mother's viewpoint and values caused constant clashes, particularly her insistence that Amy was unattractive. Education in history classes that excluded the Chinese role in World War II increased the distance that grew between Amy's Amerasian generation and their immigrant parents.

The author described her mother as small, but combative — "just determined as hell" (Somogyi & Stanton, p. 24). Daisy's feisty public behaviors caused Amy to long for a mother "like Donna Reed in the 'Donna Reed Show' or Jane Wyman in 'Father Knows Best'" (Fong, p. 123). Throughout Amy's early life, her father offered comfort and sanctuary during Daisy's volatile displays: "She was very dramatic in her depression — she would throw the furniture upside down, things would be smashed. She always threatened to commit suicide. Once when the family traveled a California freeway, she opened the door of the car and threatened to jump out" (Singh Gee, p. 85). Daisy kept the family in constant suspense and demanded frequent moves to new quarters to escape disruptive spirits. The nomadic shifts placed Amy in eleven districts before she graduated from high school.

1955   Reared in the coastal cities of Oakland, Hayward, Santa Rosa, Palo Alto, and Sunnyvale before the final move to Santa Clara, Tan was the perpetual loner and new kid on the block. She struggled to harmonize American roots with her parents' Asian customs and with being the only Asian face in her class. She admitted to *Bookpage* interviewer Ellen Kanner that life with Daisy was difficult because of her belief in ghosts and her imaginative storytelling in fractured English. Daisy erroneously assumed that Amy communed with the spirit world from age three. Daisy regretted not having the powers of otherworldly communication, but insisted that Amy was able to move between the two dimensions and to relay messages from the dead. Amy commented, "She's always asking did you talk to your father today" (*Ibid.*).

Despite Daisy's quirks, Tan grew up in a loving matrix of strong women. Her mother actually organized a female gathering like the Joy Luck Club. Amy recalls, "It was named by my father — a group of people I grew up with and met regularly for their game of [mah jong]" (Taylor, p. F1). Integral to a strong womanly support system were the players "whom I called aunties, though they were not related" (*Ibid.*). With an impish drollery, in adulthood, Tan started her own club, Fool and His Money, an investment group.

1957   Amy's parents held high behavioral and intellectual standards for their three bilingual children. From their father came devotion to God. To a BBC interviewer, Tan reminisced about home worship: "We prayed at every meal, we asked for God's guidance, there were certain rules of behavior that we followed; no drinking, no swearing, no even using any partial words that might allude to blasphemous terms" ("Amy Tan"). The author summarized twenty years of her mother's instructions in three sentences: "First, if it's too easy, it's not worth pursuing. Second, you have to try harder, no matter what other people might have to do in the same situation — that's your lot in life. And if you're a woman, you're supposed to suffer in silence" (Kepner, p. 59). Taken together, the three precepts produced a no-win situation that left the mother in complete charge. As a result, Amy developed into a worrier, a pattern of insecurity and irrational fears that followed her into adult life.

Daisy demanded straight A's from kindergarten onward and forced Amy to practice piano daily. The author told Esther Wu of the *Dallas Morning News* how her parents coveted other children's success: "When I was growing up, my parents used to point to Ginny Tiu [a child pianist who performed often on "The Ed Sullivan Show"], and say, why can't you be like her?" (Esther Wu). In adulthood, Tan met Tiu and confessed to hating her in childhood for being a prodigy.

Daisy was aware that Amy lacked concentration and that she chose autonomy over obedience: "She always wanted independence, never did what I told her, didn't do the schooling she could have" (Goodavage, p. 12D). Amy suffered pressure exacerbated by fear that she might fail her mother and father. She did poorly on standardized tests because she bypassed easy answers to multiple choice questions in search of more complex solutions. She escaped mental unrest through reading, especially Grimms' fairy tales, Aesop's fables, fairy tales, bible stories, and the prairie memories of Laura Ingalls Wilder. In 1996, Tan reflected, "Books were my salvation. Books saved me from being miserable" ("Interview"). In *The Opposite of Fate: A Book of Musings* (2003), she identified books as "windows opening and illuminating my room" (p. 1).

1958   As early as age six, Tan felt the effects of depression, a serious mental debility that caused her mother to erupt in self-destructive tantrums, prophecies of death, threats of suicide, and object-hurling that the author described as "emotional terrorism" (Longenecker). She explained in *The Opposite of Fate*, "She had a need to cling to and then reject everyone she loved" (p. 340). In the chaotic household, Amy kept personal unhappiness to herself. At a breaking point, stress caused her to attempt suicide by cutting her wrist with a butter knife. Reflecting in adulthood on the high number of female suicides in her family, she admitted to irrational moments: "The urge was always to destroy myself violently. Like crashing my car into a tree" (Singh Gee, p. 86). She reflected on the "slippery slope" of self-annihilation and observed with wry wit, "I consider depression my legacy" (*Ibid.*).

1960   In third grade at Matanzas Elementary School, eight-year-old Tan joined her father in a weekly library visit. She was bright enough to skip a grade, but remained with her class. The teacher, Miss Grudoff, encouraged her to express herself through art and imagination, a suggestion that influenced Amy's fiction. She won a transistor radio and publication in the *Santa Rosa Press Democrat* for an essay on the subject of "What the Library Means to Me." She developed the thought with a pulpit minister's eye to the collection plate, by beginning with what good friends books are to readers and concluding with support for the Citizens for the Santa Rosa Library. Her own contribution was her life's savings of seventeen cents.

1962   While living the standard American childhood, Tan maintained a double life by following Chinese customs at home. At night, she slimmed her broad Asian nose by clipping it with a clothespin. Her father shared his sermons with her by reading them aloud and asking if there were any words that needed explaining. She profited from her father's storytelling ability, Chinese fables and fairy tales, and the gossip and family anecdotes that circulated in Shanghaiese between her mother and aunties while they shelled peas, snapped beans, chopped vegetables, or pounded dough.

Although living with a family that spoke English poorly and owned no mentally challenging books, Amy began reading more intellectual library books, including Harper Lee's *To Kill a Mockingbird* (1960), and two forbidden books, J. D. Salinger's *The Catcher in the Rye* (1951) and Richard von Krafft-Ebbing's *Psychopathia Sexualis* (1886). Tan later developed a strong love of free speech and intellectual liberty and a hatred of book banning. Free perusal of books contributed to her skill as an analyst of human secrets. She commented that conflicting ideas raised serious questions that enabled her to judge experiences from different perspectives. "That's what I think that a storyteller does, and underneath the surface of the story is a question or a perspective or a nagging little emotion, and then it grows" (Giles).

July, 1967   Daisy's sixteen-year-old son Peter fell into depression, then lapsed into a coma in May 1967 before he died of a brain tumor two months later. After his diagnosis, Daisy Tan blamed his decline on a failing grade for the semester in an English course after another pupil copied his report on Evelyn Waugh's *The Loved One* (1948), a satiric novel on the theme of death. Peter's loss occurred at an uncomfortable phase of Amy's adolescence, when she rebelled against her bicultural background and resented the Tans' contributions to poor cousins in Taiwan.

1968   The death of Peter Tan preceded a sudden paralysis on one side of her father's body. John Tan's death from brain tumor at age fifty-four exaggerated Amy Tan's teen funk and her expectations of failure. She told a BBC interviewer, "I was rebelling against any kind of hope in the world" ("Amy Tan"). She reminisced in *The Opposite of Fate* that she watched two members of her family "waste away to skeletons" (p. 369). Her uncle worsened family gloom by blaming John Tan for marrying a divorcee. Contributing to Amy's unhappiness was her job as Daisy's translator and scribe for personal letters and thank-you notes to friends and well-wishers. Another ill omen was Daisy's loss of religious faith. Ironically, the family learned in 1993 that she developed a benign meningioma of the brain about the time that Peter and John died.

Daisy's explanation of family turmoil was typical of her Chinese upbringing — the Tans and their neighborhood labored under a curse. To identify the forces that harried her family, she began visiting mediums and faith healers and instructed Amy to consult a Ouija board in hopes of contacting the spirits of her son, husband, mother, and grandmother. Amy recalled in an interview over National Public Radio: "She exhorted the doctors to try new chemotherapies and she spoke in tongues, went to religious groups. She hired geomancers to check out the *feng shui* [the Chinese concept of harmonious arrangement] in our house to see if we could change things and that would cure them" (Hansen). On a more practical level, Daisy also considered sending Amy to a Taiwanese school for wayward girls.

Meanwhile, Amy sought counsel from the family minister, who tickled, then sexually abused her. On her family's sufferings, Daisy remarked, "You have to have strength to survive that. I learned all my strength in China and I survived" (Goodavage, p. 12D). She used the opportunity to reveal that she had two deceased children and three living daughters from a first marriage and that she and John left them in China to flee to America. Amy, shocked by the disclosures, rebelled at revelations that altered her position in Daisy's life and became a hip, wise-mouthed rebel. She later reflected, "At age fifteen, I was busy finding my own identity. I didn't want to be connected to all this family stuff in China" (Doten, p. 63). In secret, Tan worried that Daisy might prefer children who spoke Chinese and who might abide by strict Chinese deportment codes.

August, 1968   After viewing a can of Old Dutch cleanser as a divine directive, Daisy secretly decamped with her son and daughter aboard the S.S. *Rotterdam*, then drove from Werkhoven, Holland, south across Germany by Volkswagen Beetle. In September, she made a home in Switzerland in a chalet and enrolled Amy and her surviving brother John at the Institut Monte Rosa Internationale, a private language-centered boarding school in Territet-Montreux founded in 1874 and housed in a turreted stone building. To interviewer Catherine O'Brien of the London *Times*, Amy described life at a new school: "In America I had been a dateless dork; in Switzerland I was exotique. My first infatuation was with Franz, a frizzy-haired hippie who wrote me love letters and threw himself on a rail track when I said that I wanted to break up" (O'Brien). She was no safer in the new setting, where a school janitor confined her in a closet and threatened rape. Her teachers transferred blame to the victim.

In distress from single-mothering and unresolved grief for her son and husband, Daisy lost control of her emotions. For twenty minutes, she threatened to slit the throats of Amy, John, and herself with a meat cleaver. The author reprised her terror in *The Opposite of Fate: A Book of Musings* (2001). In retrospect, she exonerated her mother from seeming like a crazed child-killer: "Who wouldn't crack? A son and a husband had died seven months apart. You're in a strange country with no support system, you don't speak the language, your kids are out of control, it seems like you're cursed anyway" (Bertodano).

Amy disliked history and scored in the 400s on the verbal half of the SAT, but flourished in math and science classes and at classical piano. Her mother arbitrarily selected neurosurgery and classical music as Amy's career goals. Daisy chose the brain as her daughter's focus as the most important part of the body and as the source of her son's and husband's deaths. In rebellion, Amy asserted her autonomy: "I wanted to prove that I could be the baddest of the bad. I couldn't wait until I could leave the house" ("Bestselling"). She discovered that Franz was a twenty-four-year-old army deserter and former mental patient who befriended Canadian hashish dealers and career thugs. Daisy Tan protected her daughter by hiring a private detective to observe the relationship and by reporting criminal behavior to the police.

1969 After graduating from high school in her junior year, Amy moved back to the Pacific coast and vowed to distance herself from everything Asian. In 1992 in a speech to the Novel of the Americas Symposium at the University of Colorado at Boulder, she echoed some of her teen sentiments by rejecting the label of Asian writer: "There is no unified racial description. Nobody can define cultural identity. There is no consistency in race" (Carlin, p. E1).

1970 On an American Baptist Scholarship, Amy Tan enrolled in pre-med courses at Linfield, a Baptist college in McMinnville, Oregon, and earned spending money working part-time at a pizzeria. She admitted in *The Opposite of Fate* that, like others of her generation, she bought Cliffs Notes on *Hamlet*, *Lord Jim*, and *Ulysses* to help her through honors English coursework. She had no inkling that two of her own novels would one day be analyzed in Notes.

While pursuing a career in neurosurgery, Tan gradually outgrew adolescent rebellion, gave up hippie clothes, and began seeing Louis M. DeMattei, an Italian-American law student, whom she met on a blind date. She related in an interview with *People* magazine: "I think my ghost-father was thinking, 'She's going to need somebody to take care of her — she's a bit out of control,' so he found Louis for me" (Singh Gee, p. 86). He offered her stability and affection, but his parents disapproved of their son's love match with an overall-wearing hippie. Daisy, an impressive combatant at four-feet-nine and eighty pounds, came to her daughter's defense by confronting the DeMatteis.

The experience toned down Amy's me-first attitude and even encouraged her to study Mandarin, her mother's primary language. Of this concession to Daisy, Tan explained the change that came with maturity: "It wasn't till I was older that I could let go of whatever rebellious streaks I had from childhood. Listening to [my mother], I find a lot of humor and wisdom and truth about myself" (Kanner, p. 3).

December 25, 1970　Wang Zo, Daisy Tan's first husband, died in China at Christmas, a fact she learned in 1989. The event served the novelist in *The Kitchen God's Wife*, in which she depicts Winnie Louie's anger that the evil Wen Fu's death at Christmas robbed her of the ability to sing holiday carols.

1972　To be near DeMattei, Amy Tan transferred to San Jose City College and changed majors from medicine to a double concentration in English and linguistics. The move angered her mother, who stopped speaking to Amy. Nonetheless, the author began acquiring a new respect for language: "For me language is both so rich and also impoverished. There's not a single word that can express completely a feeling" (Edwards).

1973　After a third college transfer, this time to San Jose State University, Tan graduated with a B.A. in English and began graduate work in linguistics at the University of California at Santa Cruz. The setting and graduate major influenced the creation of Olivia Yee Laguni, the protagonist of *The Hundred Secret Senses* (1995) who meets her future husband, Simon Bishop, in a linguistics class.

1974　Like novelists Maxine Hong Kingston and Fae Myenne Ng, Amy Tan came of age during the Pacific Coast's virulent anti–Vietnam War protests. After earning a master's degree, she enrolled in a doctoral program at the University of California at Berkeley. She supported herself on proceeds from her work at the Round Table pizzeria in San Jose. For fun, she backpacked into Yosemite National Forest.

February 19, 1976　On her twenty-fourth birthday, Tan abandoned post-graduate work after the torture and strangulation on Amy's birthday of a friend and flatmate named Pete, a bioengineering student and worker with disabled children. The loss left her badly shaken. After an ESP experience revealed the names of the two killer-thieves four days before the police apprehended them, she remained involved in the case, identified the body and items taken, and testified at the trial. The loss triggered ten annual bouts of psychosomatic laryngitis, a self-silencing at the thought of an unspeakable crime. She reprised the self-limiting silence in protagonist Ruth Luyi Young, the ghostwriter in *The Bonesetter's Daughter* (2001).

　　Tan married DeMattei and settled in urban San Francisco. He helped her cope with agoraphobia and bouts of depression, which eventually required the aid of a psychiatrist. Tan chose not to have children: "I was afraid that I would pass on a lot of the fears that I grew up with" (Donahue, p. 2D). To ease long-term depression, she began taking tranquilizers. She returned to her memories of college and the student upheaval of the 1970s in *The Hundred Secret Senses*, which also pictures protagonist Olivia Yee Bishop enjoying early marriage to a fellow student and working in public relations for medical groups.

1978 The DeMatteis settled in a two-bedroom flat in Danville, California. In the employ of the Alameda County Association for Retarded Citizens, Tan worked as speech pathologist for mentally disabled children. She was instrumental in helping a mute, blind two-year-old learn to speak. During this intense period, when Daisy Tan visited China and reunited with two of her daughters, Amy feared that she would lose out by comparison: "I thought she would see how great her other daughters were and think, 'I can get rid of the spare'" (Marbella, p. B11). To Amy's surprise, Daisy returned to San Jose and eased their tense relationship through talk-stories of her past. The author realized that her mother wanted a book written about her trials: "She not only wanted to give me her story but I think she was looking for a way to release the pain and the anger over 'that bad man,'" her mother's cloaked reference to Wang Zo, her first husband (Doten, p. 63).

1980 Tan directed MORE, a San Francisco project for developmentally handicapped children. To book reviewer George Gurley of the *Kansas City Star*, she divulged the importance of the job to her understanding: "I was meeting with families every day who'd just found out that their child had been diagnosed with a disability. That experience was a crash course about humanity, what hope means and the things that matter most. It was rewarding and sad and it helped me identify with many different kinds of people" (Gurley).

1981 Tan launched a journalistic career by publishing *Emergency Room Reports*. Her employer, according to Tan's description in the essay "Mother Tongue" (1990), lapsed into the American stereotyping of Asian students as more skilled in math and science than in language. He redirected her from writing to account management.

1983 Tan began a career in technical speech-writing for executives from such prestigious firms as Apple Computers, AT&T, and Pacific Bell. When she needed to conceal her ethnicity, she wrote under the Americanized, racially neutral pen name May Brown. For IBM, she completed a twenty-six-chapter monograph, "Telecommunications and You." The work fulfilled her familial obligation to succeed, but escalated to long hours and severe work stress, which extra income and psychotherapy failed to relieve.

Early 1985 Tan was in Hawaii on vacation when her mother suffered stress-related angina while squabbling with a fishmonger. With typical independence, she drove herself to Kaiser Hospital. Tan suddenly realized that Daisy was mortal and that the two had undergone a mother-daughter turnabout: "She was becoming more like the daughter and I was becoming more like the mother.... It was sad for me. It was sad I was the one to protect her" (Marbella, p. B11). The author took Daisy more seriously and vowed to Buddha and God to be a better daughter. When she learned that her mother was not seriously ill and had suffered no cardiac damage, she joked, "It was as though somebody had played a cosmic joke on me" (Ruiz).

Honoring her promises, Tan earned enough money from freelance work to buy Daisy a house. In addition, the author resolved to learn her mother's background and to take her on a three-week visit to China. The reason loomed in the author's subconscious: "I was cut off from Chinese society, and yet I was bound to it" (Rowland, p. 10).

1987   Tan began to worry about the toll that the writing of speeches for business executives was taking on her life. She faced a common midlife discovery, that success does not equate with happiness. In *The Opposite of Fate*, she admitted that her chosen field was "lucrative but meaningless" (p. 343). Discontent forced her to seek outlets playing jazz on the piano and shooting games of nine ball with her husband. Of billiards, she claimed that the concentration was similar to that required for writing. She also read the short works of Eudora Welty and the novels of Isabel Allende, Kaye Gibbons, Jamaica Kincaid, Maxine Hong Kingston, Alice Munro, and Flannery O'Connor. Tan was amazed at the richness of Louise Erdrich's *Love Medicine*, a suite of interlinking Native American stories drawn from a single family. It became the impetus to Tan's career in family-oriented fiction. She told interviewer Louise Naversen of *Harper's Bazaar*, "I just loved that book and thought, 'Hmm, maybe I can write a number of stories linked by community'" (Naversen, p. 116). Tan consumed other authors' fiction to jump-start her thinking—"to startle my mind, to tingle my spine, to take the blinders off. Fiction is my confidant and companion for life" (Clarey, p. B1).

Eager to write her own stories, Tan enrolled at the Squaw Valley Community of Writers workshop, taught by Oakley Maxwell Hall, author of *The Art and Craft of Novel Writing* (1989) and *How Fiction Works* (2000). Tan and other participants expected either to "be torn to pieces or ... be *discovered*" (Bennett, p. C2). Under fiction writer Molly Giles, author of *Iron Shoes* (2000), Tan learned about voicing and began composing short stories and historical fiction, which she published in *Atlantic Monthly, Canadian Reader's Digest, Elle Decor, FM Five, Glamour, Grand Street, Grazia, Harper's, Ladies' Home Journal, Lear's, Life, McCall's, New Yorker, Paintbrush, Publishers Weekly, San Francisco Focus, Seventeen, Short Story Review, Ski,* and *Threepenny Review*. From gradual understanding of honest narrative, Tan gained confidence. She exulted, "I had sort of found my religion" (Gupta, p. E4). Aiding her growth as a writer was the encouragement of Sandra Dijkstra, her literary agent in Del Mar, California.

October, 1987   The fear of the old country disappeared as soon as Amy arrived in the People's Republic of China, where she felt distinctly at home. She explained, "When you go to a country that's the home of your ancestors, there's more than the issue of birthplace, there's a geography that's in essence spiritual" (Kanner, p. 3). She hoped to blend in with other Asians, but stood out in bright-hued American fashions, jewelry, and makeup as well as self-assured carriage. For the first time, she visited her three half-sisters and created an instant family bond that changed her outlook. As the warring sides of her ethnicity made peace, she felt complete for the first time. The reunion served the closing chapter of *The Joy Luck Club* (1989), in which June Woo reunites with twin half-sisters, whom the family had not seen in forty-five years.

The intimacy of a first meeting with the Chinese side of the family reminded the author of how much the sisters owed to Daisy—her gestures, expressions, and sense of humor. The reunion helped Tan appreciate living in a free country and having a choice in career selection. Because her sisters enjoyed no such liberty, Tan mourned their creative incarceration during the Cultural Revolution: "They, too, once had imagination but it was pretty much stifled during that period. They were taught so long what to think. It was as if they lost the use of that muscle. The imagination rusted" (Gurley).

Tan empathized with her niece, who married in Shanghai. The couple, who shared her parents' three-room apartment, had no privacy because the waiting time for their own quarters was sixteen years. Traveling the Huangpu River, a route integral to the plot of *The Kitchen God's Wife*, the author was surprised to learn from a tour guide that Chinese citizens took the jobs that the government assigned them rather than choose for themselves. One of Tan's half-sisters chose to leave China rather than live apart from her husband, a surgeon posted a thousand miles from home. The two settled in Wisconsin to operate a Chinese eatery.

November, 1987 On return, Tan began listening to Daisy's life stories with renewed interest and sympathy: "She was so delighted; she wasn't so obsessed anymore! The fact that I wanted to hear these stories changed the way she was toward me" (Ruiz). Sandra Dijkstra surprised Tan with six offers for her stories, which formed a single book under the proposed title *Wind and Water*. Tan exclaimed, "It was like winning the lottery when I hadn't really bought a ticket!" (Bennett, p. C2). She admitted fears that the publisher chose her proposal merely to fill an ethnic quota.

January, 1988 After closing her freelance business, Tan became a full-time professional fiction writer. With a fifty-thousand-dollar advance from publisher G. P. Putnam & Sons, she aimed to complete a first novel by April 15.

May, 1988 Working in the basement by the fragrance of incense and recordings by Kitaro, a Japanese composer of spiritual New Age music, Tan completed the text by pretending that characters were visitors telling their stories. She later acknowledged that Waverly Jong, Rose Hsu Jordan, Lena St. Clair Livotny, and June Woo, the four daughters at the heart of the novel, reflect elements of her own personality and experience.

March 22, 1989 Tan issued *The Joy Luck Club*, a cross-cultural feminist novel endorsed on the dust jacket by Louise Erdrich, Alice Hoffman, and Alice Walker. It immediately moved in two directions, as popular women's fiction and ethnic literature. The interlaced text began as a short story, "Endgame" (1986), about a rebellious chess prodigy and, after galleys went out for initial readings, shifted into an atmospheric ethnic novel dedicated to Daisy Tan. A mathematically precise plot revealed in sixteen chapters contrasts the testimonials of seven women, three Chinese mothers and four Asian-American daughters, one recently bereaved by her mother's sudden death. Tan told the story in simple language to ease her mother's reading of English. Balanced by *feng shui*, the novel disencumbers the speakers from decades of family squabbles, regrets, envy, and grudges among the Hsu, Jong, St. Clair, and Woo families. In the author's summation, the novel describes "looking at balance, at what is lost and saved, finding peace" (Rowland, p. 10).

April, 1989 Within weeks, *The Joy Luck Club* was a bestseller and Tan a cross-cultural literary lion. In the words of her agent, the author was an anomaly, "but for some reason, society was ready. All of a sudden, they could see that this wasn't foreign, this was American" (Nguyen, pp. 48–49). Chang-Rae Lee, a creative writing teacher at the University of Oregon, stated that the bestseller altered the view that Asian-American writing is an automatic dud with consumers: "[Tan] proved to the publishing world that not only can Asian-American stories affect a mainstream general audience, but that it can make money" (Takahama).

According to reviewer Janice Simpson, the novel launched a cultural revolution by introducing readers to ethnic scenarios. A handful of exacting Asian-American critics dismissed the work as dumbed-down Orientalism suited to Caucasian readers. Sau-ling Cynthia Wong characterized the novel as "comforting [to whites] in its reproduction of stereotypical images and ... Orientalist fantasies of Old China" (Sau-ling Wong, p. 186). A militant critic of Asian-American feminists, Frank Chin, author of "Come All Ye Asian American Writers of the Real and the Fake" (1991), labeled Tan an outright phony prostituting her art for the white reader's dollars. He was most vocal in charges that Tan and other feminists exaggerated Chinese misogyny and emasculated Asian men through either insipid or ogreish male characters. Countering the sour notes of these critiques were the upbeat kudos of critic Elaine H. Kim, who referred to the novel as a "story of how women's lives flow through each other — whether mothers and daughters, friends and relatives, rich girls and beggar girls, or sisters across oceans and continent" (Kim, p. 83). Also impressive were actors' responses to playing stage and film roles from Tan's novels and the fervid fan letters to her, such as one from a Missouri teenager who realized that "some traits in the Oriental culture could never be traded for an American one" (Streitfield, p. F9).

Tan gave credit to serendipity because *The Joy Luck Club* was published at a time when baby boomer mothers had daughters of their own to understand. The story "hit a nerve because women had begun to think about themselves and their mothers" (Fry, p. C4). Because of the massive following, Ivy Books paid $1.23 million for the paperback rights. The novel remained on the *New York Times* bestseller list thirty-four weeks in hardcover, which passed through twenty-seven reprints before Holt purchased the soft-bound rights for $1.2 million. It flourished in paperback for nine months and abroad in twenty-five languages, but, to Tan's surprise, sold poorly in China. It won an American Library Association Best Book for Young Adults award, Bay Area Book Reviewers prize, and Commonwealth Club gold citation as well as nominations for the *Los Angeles Times* Best Book of the Year and a National Book Critics Circle's Best Novel. *Joy Luck* was also a finalist for the National Book Award and a literary selection for the 1992-1993 Academic Decathlon, a national scholastic competition for high school students.

Tan promoted her first novel with book signings, book club lunches, speeches, and lectures on college campuses. Of her notoriety among academics, she remarked in *The Opposite of Fate* that "the word *author* is as chilling as rigor mortis, and I shudder when I hear myself introduced as such" (p. 7). She learned to refuse requests for her time and talent, changed her telephone number, and moved from a first-floor address to a third-floor condominium in Presidio Heights, a building constructed in 1916 to overlook the Marin headlands, the Golden Gate Bridge, San Francisco Bay, and Tiburon. She blocked distractions by listening to soundtracks over earphones while laboring over seven false starts at her next project. In "Angst and the Second Novel" (1991), an essay issued in *Publishers Weekly*, she compared her quandary to "the rat who had taken the wrong turn at the beginning and had scrambled to ... a dead end" (p. 7). Among the pangs of celebrity were demands for Tan's opinions on global issues involving China. She wisely excused herself from political and social issues and retreated into her specialty — family.

August 9, 1989   Tan published an article in *Glamour* magazine, "Watching China" (1991), on the Tiananmen Square confrontation. A letter from a half-sister living in Beijing encouraged her not to worry about rioting and government retaliation. Reflecting on her sister's life during China's upheaval, Tan wondered how her life and art would have differed if John and Daisy Tan had not immigrated to California.

June, 1991   Daisy Tan's emotional freedom from an oppressive first marriage proved propitious to Amy's development as an author. In the words of *Boston Globe* literary critic Patti Doten, the collaboration of mother and daughter "unleashed the furies, the secrets, that had long been dormant" (Doten, p. 63). As a result of their synergy, Tan emerged as a major American novelist and spokeswoman for women's liberation. At her mother's request, Tan decided to tell Daisy's story about her disastrous twelve-year union with a bullying sexual deviate. The author confided to interviewer Jonathan Mandell, "I think one of my mother's great despairs was that she went through such a horrible life and nobody had compassion for her" (Mandell). Tan explained her mother's concept of storytelling as a form of disencumbrance from the past: "She wanted someone to go back and relive her life with her. It was a way for her to exorcise her demons, and for me to finally listen and empathize and learn what memory means, and what you can change about the past" ("Bestselling").

After walling herself off from interruptions, Amy produced an ambitious sequel to *The Joy Luck Club* in her framework novel *The Kitchen God's Wife*, a *roman á clef* that honors the author's parents and older brother Peter. Set during the chaos of the Sino-Japanese War, the episodic story of Jiang "Winnie" Weili Louie is a saga of hope that reprises the sufferings of Tan's grandmother Jingmei and mother Daisy. The mode is an intimate talk-story that the speaker offers as a gift to her daughter Pearl. Although a relative disapproved of the disclosure of family shame, Daisy disagreed and welcomed the opportunity to rid herself of a burden of guilt. Of the family's concealed past, the text remarked on the value of openness: "These secrets become the reason why we miss opportunities to connect with each other" (Tan, p. 114).

July, 1991   Often compared to the sweep of novels by Russian classic authors Feodor Dostoevsky, Boris Pasternak, and Leo Tolstoy, Tan's second novel captured the interest of readers from variant backgrounds. Of the book's presentation of the Asian-American community, critic Sheng-Mei Ma noted that "Tan may be the best-paid tour guide of Chinese America" (Ma, p. xiv). The novel rose to number one bestseller on the *New York Times* list in four weeks, remained for thirty-eight weeks, and appeared on similar lists in Australia, Canada, Denmark, England, Germany, Norway, and Spain. It won the *Booklist* 1991 Editor's Choice award, selection by Doubleday Book Club, and a nomination for a Bay Area Book Reviewers citation. By spring, *The Kitchen God's Wife* earned over two hundred fifty million dollars in hardcover before advancing to paperback. Literary Guild paid $425,000 for distribution rights as a main selection; Tan's agent worked out foreign rights with England, Germany, Holland, and Japan and translation into twenty languages. Perhaps its most significant honor is its choice as Tan's favorite book. In "Angst and the Second Novel," she explained: "How could it not be? I had to fight for every single character, every image, every word" (p. 7).

Part of the uniqueness of Tan's novel is the overly simple language that she chose so her mother could read it with no difficulty. She delighted her mother with stories of readers weeping over the main character's hardships. Daisy analyzed the successful narrative in her idiosyncratic way. According to Amy, "She thinks it's a balance.... She had bad luck in her family before, but now I'm part of her *good* luck" (Bennett, p. C2). The positive outlook boded well for Amy's ongoing detente with Daisy.

During discussions of film rights, the author worried that a script might be false to the real Daisy: "I'd want to be true to her intentions, her integrity, the passions she had.... I probably would be more protective not so much about the story line, but the character" (Moody, p. A7). Another situation, Daisy's attendance at one of Amy's speeches, made the author more aware of her educated vocabulary and sentence structure and the limitations of her mother's understanding. The situation introduces one of Tan's frequently anthologized essays, "Mother Tongue," a reflection on the silencing of immigrants who have not gained competence in the language of their second country. She revisited the idea of second-class citizenship in *The Opposite of Fate*, in which she warned: "Poor service, bad treatment, no respect — that's the penalty for not speaking English well in America" (p. 165).

1991   Tan developed a relationship with half-sister Jindo, a nurse married to Yan Zheng, a surgeon. The author helped them and their fourteen-year-old daughter relocate to Wisconsin. In this same period, Tan received an honorary Doctor of Humane Letters degree from Dominican College in San Rafael, California. She began writing about a Victorian missionary in *The Year of No Flood*, an unpublished historical novel set during the Boxer Rebellion. The story draws on the experiences of her paternal grandparents, whom missionaries converted. Elements of the manuscript foretold some of the drama of her third published work, *The Hundred Secret Senses*.

April, 1991   In "Angst and the Second Novel," Tan expressed determination that she would raise her aims for succeeding works, each one "increasing in scope, depth, precision of language, intelligence of form" (p. 4). In her fears that the first novel was a fluke and that the second would fail, she pictured "bar graphs of my literary career falling over like tombstones" (*Ibid.*). She developed psychosomatic hives, needed therapy for back and wrist pain, and developed TMJ and cracked three teeth from clenching her jaw during sleep.

Summer, 1991 After delivering a speech to the Chinese-American Student Association at the University of Wisconsin in April, the author undertook a grueling, month-long book tour across California and to England and Scotland. Her daily output included interviews, public readings, and television appearances on "Today" and "Larry King Live." She also contributed four essays to *A Closer Look: The Writer's Reader*, which anthologized works by Joan Didion, Annie Dillard, Jamaica Kincaid, Ursula Le Guin, Edward Said, John Updike, and Alice Walker.

1992 Tan ventured into children's literature with *The Moon Lady*. She teamed with a good friend, Gretchen Schields, a fashion and advertising illustrator who grew up in China and lived in other areas of the Pacific Rim. Shields illustrated Tan's story with Manchu-style images. An outgrowth of Ying-ying St. Clair's childhood mischief in *The Joy Luck Club*, the legend describes a spunky six-year-old who attends the annual Moon Festival, a night when wishes come true. In September, Tan began a book tour introducing her emergence as a children's author.

February, 1992 After Kathi Kamen Goldmark formed a band of authors in November 1991, Tan joined and sang at the 1992 American Booksellers Association convention, a vast meeting in Anaheim, California, of members of the book publishing and vending trades. She referred to the combo, called the Rock Bottom Remainders, as a "band of people who revert to being adolescents about once a year" (Ruiz). The group consisted at that time of Al Kooper directing, Roy Blount in Hawaiian shirt keeping order, lead guitarist Dave Barry, rhythm guitarist Stephen King, Robert Fulghum on mandocello, Ridley Pearson on bass, Barbara Kingsolver on keyboard, and Ted Bartimus, Louise Erdrich, Tan, and Goldmark doing vocals. The proceeds of their amateurish, but earnest musicales supported literacy campaigns and First Amendment rights.

May, 1992 Tan traveled from Boston with the band on a two-week tour. They performed "Chain of Fools," "Gloria," "Leader of the Pack," "Louie Louie," "Material Girl," "Money," "Nadine," "Teen Angel," and "These Boots Are Made for Walkin'," Tan's signature song. To get the most from Nancy Sinatra's hit, Tan devised a dominatrix costume — leather boots, red fringed or leopard skin costume, red wig, shades, studded cuffs, temporary tattoos, and choke chain. As a star Remainderette, she acted the S&M role by abasing men in the band. The performance relieved childhood injunctions against having fun. Of the experience, she admitted, "Singing in public is the closest I will ever come to a public execution" (Fenster).

May, 1993 Tan remained at the forefront of the book world's cultural revolution. She endorsed teacher efforts to put multicultural authors in school curricula and praised independent booksellers for displaying the latest titles. She described books as "frequent flyer miles" that allowed the reader full access to the world (Baker, p. 33). After giving up stodgy, male-dominated reading lists, she gravitated to books by female, gay, and minority authors and translated works from China and Japan. She felt drawn to the feminist and hyphenated–American slant of works by Michael Dorris, Charlayne Hunter-Gault, Gish Jen, Barbara Kingsolver, Terry McMillan, and Bharati Mukherjee. Through Tan's connections with these and other writers, she supplied speakers for literary lunches hosted by the National Kidney Foundation, which she co-chaired.

May, 1993   The author was hesitant to allow the filming of her first novel. She remarked on fearing "that if I sold myself to the devil Hollywood, it might turn into a movie which was another awful depiction of Asians" (Taylor, p. F1). The pre-filming jitters proved unfounded. She and Ron Bass co-authored the film version of *The Joy Luck Club*, co-produced by Tan and Oliver Stone for Disney Studios and filmed in Richmond, Virginia, and Guilin, China. Tan summarized the efforts as "a movie about all parents and children, because in all families, there are so many stories that never get told" (Fenster).

A source of authenticity was the perspective of director Wayne Wang, a native of Hong Kong and resident of San Francisco's Chinatown. He avoided crusading by concentrating on the complex story, which coordinated sixty speaking parts, fifty of them for women. He remarked, "I'm sure racism exists in the reluctance to make a good film about Chinese-Americans.... I just wanted to make them real people" (Taylor, p. F1). To fill the major roles, his staff interviewed possibilities in Chicago, Los Angeles, New York, San Francisco, Seattle, Toronto, and Vancouver. The result at the first casting call was a mob of four hundred women excited by the prospect of appearing in a movie depicting the long invisible Chinese woman. In July 1993, a second try-out at the Sheraton Hotel in Flushing, New York, brought two thousand Mandarin speakers as well as Filipinos, Japanese, and Koreans eager for roles. Many carried their personal copies of the novel as though it were sacred writ.

Tan credited Bass with devising and pacing a narrative method of stringing the four stories together at a family dinner. Bass even wrote a part that allowed Tan to appear as an extra in 1940s outfit and Betty Grable hair style. Contributing to authenticity was Daisy Tan, who visited the set to watch the filming and played in a party scene, along with her beau T. C. Lee. Use of family photos allowed Tan to include her deceased father and brother in the finished work.

Actress France Nuyen captured the screen version in a single image: "Joy Luck represents the fantasy of every misunderstood child" (Hajari, p. 32). The film's debut on Mother's Day pleased Daisy so much that she said, "What did I do to deserve such a daughter?" (Fenster). Amy was less exuberant about the hit movie: "I feel uncomfortable with success.... I don't trust it" (*Ibid.*). Reassuring her were a note from First Lady Hillary Rodham Clinton to Daisy Tan and an invitation to the author to view the White House screening of the film. Also uplifting were the profits, $32.8 million.

August, 1993–February, 1994   Northern Telecom and the Yale-China Association sponsored a stage version of *The Joy Luck Club* in Mandarin to debut in Asia. The play premiered in Shanghai with a three-week run and moved on to Hong Kong and Beijing, where the troupe played to a packed house. The six-month tour required the collaboration of the Shanghai People's Art Theater with the Long Wharf Theater of New Haven, Connecticut, where the play had one of the highest single ticket sales in the theater's history. Contributing to the trans–Pacific effort were the talents of Korean-American translator Susan Kim, director Tisa Chang, costumer Susan Tsu, artistic director Arvin Brown, deputy director Yu Luo-Sheng, and set designer Ming

Cho Lee, who managed locales for the eighteen scenes. An August review in the *Xinmin Daily News* noted a reluctance to accept the play's obviously pro–American bias in people who chose to remain in China rather than emigrate. In February 1994, the final performance was a featured event of the Hong Kong Arts Festival.

September, 1993 During the uproar following the demonstration in Tiananmen Square in 1989, Tan's identification with her half-sisters caused her worry that China's conservative backlash endangered the family. In "Watching China" (1993), she explained: "We did not imagine that the blood that is thicker than water would be running through the streets of Beijing. We did not believe that one Chinese would kill another" (p. 303). The events formed "an invisible great wall" that separated family members and ended their mail correspondence *(Ibid.)*.

At an emotional low point from these events, Tan began taking the antidepressant Zoloft, which helped her cope with fears of driving and of stalkers who might harm her. At first, she feared that any medication strong enough to combat stress would limit her scope as a writer. She corresponded with fellow sufferers by Internet and learned more about relief from a daily battle with an emotional abyss. She admitted to *People* magazine interviewer Alison Singh Gee, "I still have to wrestle with it, but I see where it fits in with my mother's life, my grandmother's life, my own life. For a long time, I think I didn't know how to be happy, and I didn't trust happiness—I felt that if I had it, I would lose it. But today, I am basically a happy person" (Singh Gee, p. 88).

1994 Tan teamed with Gretchen Schields again for *The Chinese Siamese Cat*, their second children's book. The story began as a dream that the author had about her cat Sagwa, which died three years later at age twenty-one. Tan read the text for an audio CD. At the end of a thirteen-week book tour, she returned to San Jose to address students at her alma mater for the *San Jose Mercury News* Modern Master Series. She entertained some one thousand fans with a response to the Cliffs Notes analysis of her motivations in *The Joy Luck Club*. Turning to more serious issues, she questioned the formation of educational syllabi: "I think American Lit. should be more diversified. Why can't Asian-American writers be included in all American literature, and not segregated on the ethnic multiculture lists?" (Gerrye Wong, p. 15).

October 30, 1995 Tan incorporated her half-sister in the plot of a third novel, *The Hundred Secret Senses*, a woman-centered tale about a ghost-seer. The work emerged in sixth place on the bestseller list and was short-listed for the Bay Area Book Reviewer's prize. The writing was more relaxed than her earlier fiction. She "felt carefree, kind of come what may, of letting go. There was a lot of serendipity" (Kanner, p. 3). The composition soothed the author with its view of sisterly love. To *Sonoma Independent* interviewer Gretchen Giles, the author confided: "As I was writing I realized that the kind of love that Kwan was providing was this unconditional love that felt very comforting to me, and I thought that part of me is always looking for that" (Giles). Her relaxed attitude toward the work brought complaints from critic Sheng-Mei Ma that the author panders to the casual reader with "a New Age ethnicity mongrelized with primitivism, that appeals to westerners' long-held Orientalist view of

Asians and Asia" (Ma, p. xxii). He lists as "Orientalist clichés" the profusion of mission scenes and exotic banditry from the Taiping Rebellion (*Ibid.*).

After an initial press run of 550,000 copies, Tan set out to visit forty-seven bookstores in thirty-three cities. As a token of luck she began touring at Elliott Bay Book Company in Seattle, where she had introduced *The Joy Luck Club*. She admitted a reluctant belief in the spirit world, based on a number of inexplicable coincidences: "I was worried that people would think I'd gone a little flaky, but there have been so many things like that in my life, that I felt compelled to write it…. Literally, the ghosts came and helped me" (Gurley). She added impishly that she relied on "a team of ghost researchers who'd go out and come back with what I needed, the more arcane the subject the better" (*Ibid.*). The admission did not surprise Daisy, who assumed that her daughter achieved bestselling fiction by communicating with the spirit world. The author disclosed that Daisy "thinks my writing comes through to me by people from the other world. My computer keyboard is a high-tech Ouija board" (Kanner, p. 3).

Thanksgiving Day, 1995   Daisy's erratic behavior reached a height of strangeness when she described seeing O. J. Simpson killing his wife. Shortly afterward, doctors diagnosed Daisy with Alzheimer's disease. She entered a nursing home near her daughter's house. During the long illness, Daisy began taking the antidepressant Paxil and shed some of her previous combativeness and grudge-holding. Her daughter was pleased: "She lost a lot of her worries. She would say words I had never heard her say—'I'm happy'" (Donahue, p. 2D).

March 30, 1996   The author experienced China's capricious censorship while preparing a speech to deliver to four hundred fifty international industrialists and ambassadors at a consortium raising funds for Chinese orphans and handicapped children. Because the gathering did not have the requisite permit to collect for charity, the Public Security Bureau cancelled the event only an hour before it was scheduled to begin. Forty police agents removed posters from the five-star hotel's ballroom. At the dinner, while a plainclothes officer looked on, the author spoke one-to-one with guests to explain the ban on speeches and on songs by Chinese children. That same year, she was inducted into the American Academy of Achievement and temporarily banned in China. During later appearances in China, authorities restricted her to the American Embassy.

Fall, 1996   Tan published "Required Reading and Other Dangerous Subjects" in *Threepenny Review*, commenting on her response to analyses of her works: "I am alarmed when reviewers and educators assume that my very personal, specific, and fictional stories are meant to be representative down to the nth detail not just of Chinese Americans but, sometimes, of all Asian culture." She used the essay as an opportunity to debunk scholarly analysis as applications of a particular authority's hobbyhorse.

Winter, 1997   After a five-day rain contributed to melting snow, a flood and mudslide menaced the DeMattei family cabin on the Truckee River near Lake Tahoe, Nevada. Five local sheriffs in wetsuits distributed helmets and life jackets and eased the strandees over the river by Zodiac raft. They floated Tan, her husband Lou, a houseguest, neighbors John and Nancy Leavitt, four dogs, and a cat to safety and rescued as well Tan's writing in her laptop, which she secured in a backpack. Six years later, the author described the event in *The Opposite of Fate: A Book of Musings*.

June, 1997 Tan continued her library boosterism begun at age eight. She joined U.S. Poet Laureate Robert Hass in co-chairing a gala for the San Francisco Public Library, which raised $100,000 to end a budgetary shortfall. After the reception and banquet, she expressed the importance of public libraries to her life.

1998 The two-and-a-half-hour stage version of *The Joy Luck Club* debuted on the West Coast at Theatre Works in San Francisco. Produced on a revolving stage by Margaret Brooker, founder of Seattle's Intiman Theater, the play featured authentic costuming from the 1920s, '60s, and '80s and starred Beijing-born film actor Lisa Lu as Lindo Jong, Bonnie Akimoto as Waverly, and Julie Oda as June Woo. Scenes included a Chinese opera stage, dragon-prowed pagoda boat, glowing red lanterns, and projected slides of Chinese villages and scenes from Chinatown in Oakland and San Francisco.

March 29, 1999 As a part of celebration of the short story, Tan presented a Broadway reading of excerpts by George Harrar, Sheila Kohler, and Tim Gautreaux from *The Best American Short Stories*, 1999, which Tan edited. The event, which was broadcast on National Public Radio, was the culmination of a project from October 1998 to February 1999 when she "read stories, manna from heaven" (p. 337).

November 22, 1999 Tan was relieved that her mother died of Alzheimer's disease rather than suicide, a threat that hung over Daisy since she had watched her own mother's suicide. In a final exchange between mother and daughter, Daisy offered an apology for past hurts that the author reprised on the last page of *The Bonesetter's Daughter*: "I just wanted to say that I hope you can forget just as I've forgotten. I hope you can forgive me, because if I hurt you, I'm sorry" (p. 308). Amy and her sisters discussed a pair of secrets from their mother's complex biography, that her birth name was Li Bingzi and that their maternal grandmother's birth name was Gu Jingmei. The author envisioned her grandmother chuckling, "At last! You idiots! None of you ever get it right!" (Ruiz).

In terms of grief, Tan underwent a feeling of insecurity. She told interviewer Jami Edwards, "For so many years she worried to the point of my aggravation and now that she's gone I feel that no one else in the world will worry as much about me. It makes me feel more vulnerable" (Edwards). With a new impetus, the author dismantled a fourth novel and restructured its chapters. She explained, "I just had to reassemble them in a new way. To find that heart and repair the bones, I had to break them into pieces, then start to dig" (Allen).

December 7, 1999 Increasing the author's grief was the death of her editor, Faith Sale, from a rare form of cancer caused by exposure to asbestos. Tan divulged her feelings about losing both mother and editor: "I felt that I had two people to help me, that I had a ghostwriter and a ghost editor. I mean that in the best of senses, that you carry on the memory and the intentions and the love of what that person would have wanted you to do" (Edwards). Unlike Western ghost lore, the Chinese concept of benevolent spirits was both comforting and supportive. At book readings, Tan sensed the presence of both her mother and grandmother, the two strongest females in her life.

June 23, 2000   Tan received honors at the World Trade Center sponsored by the Museum of Chinese in the Americas (MoCA), the Western hemisphere's first Asian museum. During the "Twentieth in 2000" Legacy Dinner at Windows on the World, Tan, Beijing-born actor Jackie Chan, and Hawaiian publisher William Yukon Chang, founder of the *Chinese American Times*, the first English-language newspaper in New York's Chinatown, accepted thanks for preserving Chinese-American history and for encouraging public programming that presents authentic Chinese-American experience and community.

August, 2000   In a second-floor office, Amy got started writing within an hour of completing *The Hundred Secret Senses* and turned the last chapter of her mother's life into the source for *The Bonesetter's Daughter*, in which the Daisy character is called LuLing Liu. The author based the new work on "the things we remember and the things that should be remembered" (Gray, p. 72). She chose November 22, the anniversary of her mother's death, for the novel's release.

February, 2001   After the debut of *The Bonesetter's Daughter*, Tan announced on an appearance on "Good Morning, America" that the novel was her most personal publication. Nancy Pate, book reviewer for the *Orlando Sentinel*, paid high compliments to the author: "When she gives herself over to the past, to where 'history is mystery,' she becomes an artist, her prose as fluid and lyrical as LuLing and Precious Auntie's calligraphy" (Pate). In its first week, the novel zoomed to second place on the bestseller list. New Millennium paid over a half million dollars for the audio rights. For the twelve-hour, eight-cassette unabridged version, Tan read the part of Ruth; a Shanghai native, actress and director Joan Chen, portrayed her mother Lu-Ling.

To promote the novel, Tan left her eight-room San Francisco condominium at Presidio Heights to launch a grueling twenty-two-city book tour in May, which included Adelaide, Melbourne, and Sydney, Australia. Accompanying her were two favorite travel companions, Yorkshire terriers Bubba Zo and Lilli, who eased the loneliness of hotel rooms. Even with pets, she expressed a distaste for unfamiliar settings: "When I'm in a hotel, I think of fires that could happen, where I should run to or what floor I'm on" (Gray, p. 74). She depended on the Yorkies for advance warning of danger.

May 2–3, 2001   Drawing on the experience of Yaddo, an artists' community in Saratoga Springs, New York, Tan joined Allan Gurganous and Rick Moody in an evening's entertainment at New York's The Park. The theme of their appearance was the relationship of memoir to fiction, the subject of compelling female stories in *The Bonesetter's Daughter*. Proceeds from the event aided some two hundred artists to take advantage of the Yaddo enclave.

June, 2001 At the end of a four-month world book tour, Tan recognized symptoms of inattention, visual and olfactory hallucination, memory loss, and unexplained vibrations that she described as "Dolby Digital syndrome" (Behe). At first, doctors diagnosed her mental vagaries as post-traumatic stress disorder. Eighteen months later, an MRI located fifteen lesions on her brain. A more accurate explanation of the anomalies was Lyme disease, which she had incubated since 1998 from the bite of a deer tick. Her laundry list of symptoms included a rash, stiff neck, fatigue, insomnia, achy joints, vertigo, tinnitus, and numbness.

Tan's illness halted her progress on a fifth novel. She noted, "I have a hard time with continuity, with segues and keeping pieces together. It feels like I have twelve pieces of fruit and vegetables being thrown in the air and trying to juggle them all. It's overwhelming" (MacDonald). Upon partial recovery, she began collecting short works, speeches, and essays under the title *The Opposite of Fate: A Book of Musings*, in which she thanked her doctor, Raphael Stricker, "for restoring my brain to sentence-writing strength" (n.p.). She recuperated enough to record the text on audio CD and to sing with the Rock Bottom Remainders at the Texas Book Fair.

The anthology answered a question she had posed earlier: "What in our lives is fate, the circumstances we're born into, and what are the things that we have really chosen at those important turns in our lives?" (Chiu, p. 7). The book's success earned her selection as one of *Esquire* magazine's "Women We Love." In an interview with the BBC, she predicted that her fifth adult work indicated a shift in direction: "This book comes at a time when I have already written about my mother's life and my relationship with her, and that probably, here on out, the fiction will be something different" ("Tan's Memoirs").

September, 2001 Tan and Gretchen Schields debuted a children's television series, *Sagwa: The Chinese Siamese Cat* (PBS), a daily half-hour program for Kids' Station. Set in ancient China, the episodes featured music, folk stories, fairy tales, and the animated adventures of a curious cat. Tan acknowledged that the series was an introduction to China for children lacking any other contact with Asia. Girl Scout troops in New York City used the televised programs as springboards for activities planned for the next Chinese New Year celebration.

July 29, 2002 Applebee's 1,300 restaurants distributed four million copies of an activity book derived from *The Chinese Siamese Cat*. Over a three-month period, the text introduced Amy Tan's cat Sagwa as a source of Chinese culture, particularly the lunar calendar. The free material promoted the Warner Home Video and DVD series of Sagwa, including the episodes "Firefly Nights," "Fu-Fu's Full Moon Flight," "Shei-Hu's Secret," "Explorer's Club," "Treasure Hunters," and "Sick Day!" A website, "Sagwa, the Chinese Siamese Cat" http://pbskids.org/sagwa/, offers characters from the series, songs and animated scenes, stories, games based on pictograms and tangrams, coloring and drawing activities, and data on how the show was produced.

January 9, 2003 Seventeen years after Amy Tan wrote "Endgame," the first episode of her first novel, playwright-director David Hsieh wrote a two-act stage version of *The Joy Luck Club*, the third adaptation of the original work. With Amy

Tan in attendance on opening night, the play had its world premiere with a five-week run at the Langston Hughes Theater in Seattle. To the nervous adaptor, Tan remarked, "I come with a sense of curiosity … an openness to any changes they want to make, knowing that I may not feel the same way about the book that they felt" (Jasmin).

Hsieh chose the novel, one of America's most popular and most successful Asian-American works, because of its epic story spanning seventy-five years. He exulted, "It's full of life, full of relationships, full of drama, full of history" (Bacalzo). His version of the novel required twenty-nine players and multi-level backlit screens for settings. Actors Shirley Oliver and Emjoy Gavino of the Repertory Actors Theatre, who appeared as Lindo and Waverly Jong, confided to *Post-Intelligencer* interviewer Gianni Truzzi that their stage roles revealed truths about their own lives as first-generation Amerasians.

March 4, 2003   Along with authors Bob Holman and Ishmael Reed, Tan received a Writer for Writers Award at a benefit dinner netting three hundred thirty-three thousand dollars for Poets & Writers. The honorarium extolled her assistance to new authors as well as to the National Kidney Foundation, PEN writers' fund, Squaw Valley Community of Writers, the University of California at Berkeley School of Journalism, and Yaddo artists' colony.

March 20, 2003   At a tense time in American politics, Tan joined Stephen King, Wally Lamb, and one hundred forty-four other protesters of the U.S.–led war in Iraq. In a full-page ad in the *New York Times*, the riposte declared that Iraq was not endangering the United States.

May 18, 2003   Tan was invited to deliver a commencement address at Simmons College in Boston, where she offered eighteen hundred graduating seniors sure-fire writing tips. Speaking from experience, she warned them, "No matter how much we've accomplished, we still feel inadequate, unprepared" (*The Opposite of Fate*, p. 294). Imbedded in her text was the kernel that became her next title, *The Opposite of Fate*. At the end of the presentation, President Daniel S. Cheever and Trustee Chair Anne Lincoln Bryant conferred an honorary doctorate of letters on Tan for exploring the elements of family and fate.

September 15, 2003   The publication of *The Opposite of Fate* offered Tan an opportunity to collect stray thoughts about the direction of her writing and life. She introduces the work by explaining that her writer's voice is perpetually attuned to fate and hope. As in previous publications, she acknowledges a debt to Daisy Tan, "who taught me the many permutations of fate" (p. 3). In an essay on the strength of matrilineage, the author describes herself as a woman who "makes her own living, doing what is important to her, which is to tell stories" (p. 103).

• *Further Reading*

Allen, Moira. "@Deadline." *Writer*, Vol. 114, No. 6, June 2001, pp. 12–14.
"Amy Tan (interview)." http://www.bbc.co.uk/religion/programmes/belief/scripts/amy_
   tan.shtml.

Bacalzo, Dan. "All Over the Map." http://www.theatermania.com/content/news.cfm?int_news_id=2976, January 9, 2003.

Baker, John F. "Fresh Voices, New Audiences." *Publishers Weekly*, August 9, 1993, pp. 32–34.

Bauers, Sandy. "*The Bonesetter's Daughter* Is Amy Tan's Best." *Philadelphia Inquirer*, March 20, 2001.

Behe, Regis. "Writer Amy Tan Relies on 'The Opposite of Fate' to Get By." *Pittsburgh Tribune-Review*, December 3, 2003.

"Beijing Determined to Censor Outside Voice." *American Libraries*, Vol. 27, No. 5, May 1996, p. 28.

Bennett, Elizabeth. "The Joy and Good Luck of Amy Tan." *Houston Post*, July 14, 1991, pp. C1–C2.

Bertodano, Helene de. "A Life Stranger Than Fiction." *Daily Telegraph*, November 11, 2003.

"Bestselling Author Amy Tan Is a Wonderful Storyteller." *Chinatown News*, Vol. 43, No. 8, February 18, 1996, pp. 22–23.

Bruckner, D. J. R. "For These Bonded Souls, Some Luck but Little Joy." *New York Times*, April 27, 1999.

Cardozo, Erica L. "The Spirits Are with Her." *Entertainment Weekly*, No. 298, October 27, 1995, p. 84.

Carlin, Margaret. "Writing for Herself." *Rocky Mountain News*, September 26, 1992, p. E1.

"Charity Ends at Home." *Economist*, Vol. 339, No. 7,960, p. 39.

Chatfield-Taylor, Joan. "Cosmo Talks to Amy Tan: Dazzling New Literary Light." *Cosmopolitan*, Vol. 207, November 1989, pp. 178–180.

Chin, Frank. "Come All Ye Asian American Writers of the Real and the Fake." *The Big Aiiieeeee!: An Anthology of Chinese American and Japanese American Literature.* New York: Meridian, 1991, pp. 1–92.

Chiu, Christina. *Lives of Notable Asian Americans: Literature and Education.* New York: Chelsea House, 1996.

Clarey, Kathey. "Amy Tan's Literary Concerns." *Fresno Bee*, October 5, 1994, p. B1.

Cujec, Carol. "Excavating Memory, Reconstructing Legacy." *World & I*, Vol. 16, No. 7, July 2001, pp. 215–223.

Donahue, Deirdre. "Tan's Books Excavate Life's Joy and Pain." *USA Today*, February 19, 2001, pp. 1D–2D.

Doten, Patti. "Sharing Her Mother's Secrets." *Boston Globe*, June 21, 1991, p. 63.

Edwards, Jami. "Amy Tan." http://www.bookreporter.com/authors/au-tan-amy.asp.

Fenster, Bob. "Singing Author's Luck Holds in Bringing Book to Film." (Phoenix) *Arizona Republic*, October 5, 1993.

Fong, Yem Siu. "Review: *The Joy Luck Club*." *Frontiers*, Vol. 6, No. 2–3, 1990, pp. 122–123.

Fry, Donna. "The Joy and Luck of Amy Tan." *Seattle Times*, July 7, 1991, pp. C3–C4.

Giles, Gretchen. "Ghost Writer." *Sonoma Independent*, December 14–20, 1995.

Goodavage, Maria. "'The Joy Luck Club' Is Born from Her Life of Hardship." *USA Today*, October 5, 1993, p. 12D.

Gray, Paul. "The Joys and Sorrows of Amy Tan." *Time*, February 19, 2001, pp. 72–74.

Gupta, Himanee. "Novelist's Efforts Led to Her Own True Voice." *Seattle Times*, January 10, 1991, p. E4.

Gurley, George. "Amy Tan: The Ghosts and the Writer." *Kansas City Star*, April 22, 1998.

Guy, David. "Wheel of Fortune: A Writer's Thoughts on Joy, Luck and Heartache." *Washington Post*, November 2, 2002, p. T4.

Hajari, Nisid. "Luck Is What You Make It." *Entertainment Weekly*, September 24, 1993, pp. 30–33.

Hansen, Liane. "Author Amy Tan Discusses Her Latest Book, Her Mother, Her Supposedly Cursed Life, and Her Participation in the Rock Bottom Remainders." *Weekend Edition Sunday* (NPR), November 9, 2003.

Holt, Patricia. "Amy Tan Hits the Jackspot with Her First Novel." *San Francisco Chronicle*, March 27, 1989, p. C3.

_____. "Between the Lines— Students Read a Lot Into Amy Tan." *San Francisco Chronicle*, August 18, 1996.

Hubbard, Kim. "*The Joy Luck Club* Has Brought Writer Amy Tan a Bit of Both." *People Weekly*, Vol. 31, April 10, 1989, pp. 149–150.

Hull, Akasha. "Uncommon Language." *Women's Review of Books*, Vol. 18, No. 9, June 2001, p. 13.

"Interview." http://www.achievement.org/autodoc/page/tan0int-1, June 28, 1996.

Jasmin, Ernest A. "Amy Tan Will See Play Based on 'Joy Luck Club.'" *Tacoma News Tribune*, February 13, 2004.

Kanner, Ellen. "From Amy Tan, a Superb Novel of Two Sisters, Two Worlds, and a Few Ghosts." *Bookpage*, December 1995, p. 3.

Kepner, Susan. "Imagine This: The Amazing Adventure of Amy Tan." *San Francisco Examiner Focus*, May 1989, pp. 58–60, 161–162.

Kester-Shelton, Pamela, ed. *Feminist Writers*. Detroit: St. James Press, 1996.

Keung, Nicholas. "Writer Found Role as 'Alienated Narrator.'" *Toronto Star*, June 10, 2003.

Kim, Elaine H. "'Such Opposite Creatures': Men and Women in Asian American Literature." *Michigan Quarterly Review*, Vol. 29, No. 1, pp. 68–93.

Kropf, Joan. "Finding Her Voice." (Longview, Washington) *Daily News*, January 11, 1991, p. E2.

Ling, Amy. *Between Worlds: Women Writers of Chinese Ancestry*. New York: Pergamon Press, 1990.

Longenecker, Donna. "Relationship with Mother Helped Tan Hone Writing Skills." *University of Buffalo Reporter*, March 27, 2003.

Ma, Sheng-mei. *The Deathly Embrace: Orientalism and Asian American Identity*. Minneapolis: University of Minnesota Press, 2000.

MacDonald, Jay. "A Date with Fate." *BookPage*, November 2003.

Mandell, Jonathan. "Interview." *New York Newsday*, July 15, 1991.

Marbella, Jean. "Amy Tan: Luck but Not Joy." *Baltimore Sun*, June 30, 1991, pp. B10–B11.

Maryles, Daisy. "Behind the Bestsellers." *Publishers Weekly*, Vol. 242, No. 44, October 30, 1995, p. 16.

Moody, Lori. "Culture Clash." *Los Angeles Daily News*, June 6, 1992, pp. A6–A7.

Naversen, Laurel, and Catherine Hong. "Write Guard." *Harper's Bazaar*, Vol. 134, No. 3,475, June 2001, pp. 116–117.

Nguyen, Lan N. "The Next Amy Tan." *A Magazine*, February/March 1997, pp. 46–51, 55.

"Obituary." *Washington Post*, November 26, 1999, p. B7.

O'Brien, Catherine. "What Does Life Tell Us About Love." *London Times*, December 24, 2003.

Palumbo-Liu, David, ed. *The Ethnic Canon: Histories, Institutions, and Interventions*. Minneapolis: University of Minnesota Press, 1995.

Pate, Nancy. "Review: *The Bonesetter's Daughter*." *Orlando Sentinel*, February 21, 2001.

Rowland, Penelope. "American Woman." *Mother Jones*, July/August 1989, p. 10.

Ruiz, Sophia. "Amy Tan." http://www.ireadpages.com/archive/marapr01/amytan/amytan.html.

"Sagwa, the Chinese Siamese Cat." http://pbskids.org/sagwa/.

"Scenes from a Distance: 'The Joy Luck Club' Tour Beijing." *TIME/ International Edition*, November 18, 1993.

Shilling, Jane. "What the Memory Box Holds." *Daily Telegraph*, November 17, 2003.

Simpson, Janice C. "Fresh Voices Above the Noisy Din." *Time*, Vol. 137, No. 22, June 3, 1991, pp. 66–67.

Singh Gee, Alison. "A Life on the Brink." *People*, Vol. 55, No. 18, May 7, 2001, pp. 85–88.

Smith, Craig S. "A Rare Shot at Screen Stardom for Asians." *Wall Street Journal*, September 1, 1992, p. 12.

Snodgrass, Mary Ellen. *Literary Treks: Characters on the Move*. Westport, Conn.: Libraries Unlimited, 2003.

Somogyi, Barbara, and David Stanton. "Interview with Amy Tan." *Poets & Writers Magazine*, Vol. 19, No. 5, September-October 1991, pp. 24–32.

Span, Paula. "The Lush Flowering of Asian American Drama." *Washington Post*, March 2, 1997, p. G1.

Streitfeld, David. "Authors Rock 'em at Booksellers Convention." *Washington Post*, May 27, 1992.

_____. "The 'Luck' of Amy Tan." *Washington Post*, October 8, 1989, pp. F1, F9.

Strohm, J. Elizabeth. "University of Pittsburgh: Author Tan Discusses Writing, Ouija Board Labors." *Pittsburgh Pitt News*, December 5, 2003.

Takahama, Valerie. "Riding Amy Tan's Success, Wave of Asian-American Writers Hits Mainstream." *Orange County Register*, June 14, 1995.

Talbot, Stephen. "Talking Story: Maxine Hong Kingston Rewrites the American Dream." *Image*, Vol. 24, June 1990, pp. 6–8.

Tan, Amy. "Excerpt: *The Kitchen God's Wife*." *McCall's*, July 1991, p. 114.

"Tan's Memoirs of a Tragic Life." *BBC News*, December 13, 2003.

Tauber, Michelle, et al. "A New Ending." *People*, Vol. 60, No. 18, November 3, 2003, pp. 89–90.

Taylor, Noel. "The Luck of Amy Tan." *Ottawa Citizen*, October 1, 1993, p. F1.

Truzzi, Gianni. "'Joy Luck Club' Mirrors Their Own Generational Conflicts, Actors Say." *Seattle Post-Intelligencer*, January 3, 2003.

Tseo, George K. Y. "The Perils of Transcultural 'Translation.'" *Literature/Film Quarterly*, Vol. 24, No. 4, 1996, pp. 338–343.

Tyler, Patrick E. "Joint Production Takes 'The Joy Luck Club' to China's Stages." *New York Times*, November 27, 1993.

Walsh, Bryan. "Family Phantoms." *Time Asia*, December 7, 2003.

Wang, Dorothy. "A Game of Show Not Tell." *Newsweek*, Vol. 113, No. 16, April 17, 1989, p. 69.

Warren, Tim. "Write-On Rock — Best-Selling Authors Put Their Talents to Another Sort of Creativity: Music." *Baltimore Sun*, May 27, 1993.

Wong, Gerrye. "Amy Tan Takes Her Book Tour to Old Hometown, San Jose." *Chinatown News*, Vol. 42, No. 5, November 3, 1994, pp. 15–16.

Wong, Sau-ling Cynthia. "'Sugar Sisterhood': Situating the Amy Tan Phenomenon," in *The Ethnic Canon: Histories, Institutions, and Interventions*. Minneapolis: University of Minnesota Press, 1995, pp. 174–210.

Woo, Elaine. "Interview." *Los Angeles Times*, April 17, 1989.

Wu, Esther. "In Latest Book Amy Tan Keeps Focus on Family." *Dallas Morning News*, February 26, 2001.

Wu, Kelvin, trans. "'Fabricated Chinese Culture' and the Continuation of Tradition." *Singtao Daily*, September 15, 2002.

Zura, Gregory. "Mahjong Epic." *The Stranger*, Vol. 12, No. 18, January 16, 2003.

Tan's Genealogy

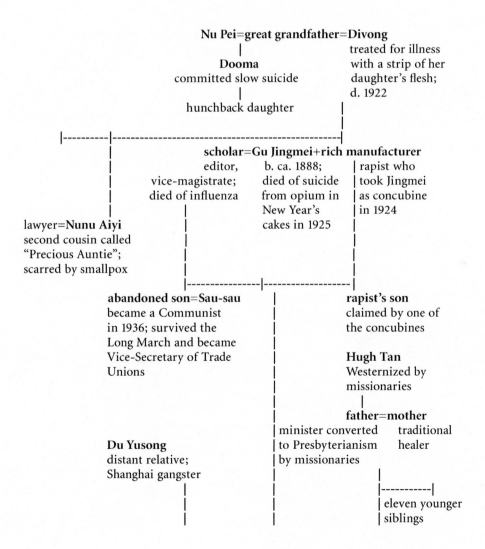

Nu Pei=great grandfather=**Divong**

Dooma
committed slow suicide

hunchback daughter

treated for illness
with a strip of her
daughter's flesh;
d. 1922

scholar=**Gu Jingmei**+rich manufacturer
editor,   b. ca. 1888;   rapist who
vice-magistrate; died of suicide   took Jingmei
died of influenza from opium in   as concubine
                  New Year's   in 1924
                  cakes in 1925

lawyer=**Nunu Aiyi**
second cousin called
"Precious Auntie";
scarred by smallpox

abandoned son=**Sau-sau**
became a Communist
in 1936; survived the
Long March and became
Vice-Secretary of Trade
Unions

rapist's son
claimed by one of
the concubines

Hugh Tan
Westernized by
missionaries

father=**mother**
minister converted   traditional
to Presbyterianism   healer
by missionaries

Du Yusong
distant relative;
Shanghai gangster

eleven younger
siblings

31

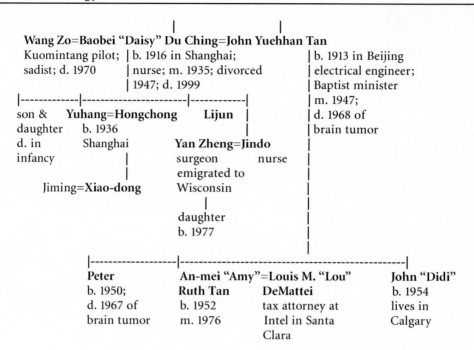

```
                    |                    |
     Wang Zo=Baobei "Daisy" Du Ching=John Yuehhan Tan
     Kuomintang pilot; | b. 1916 in Shanghai;        | b. 1913 in Beijing
     sadist; d. 1970   | nurse; m. 1935; divorced    | electrical engineer;
                       | 1947; d. 1999               | Baptist minister
     |------------|----------------------|-----------|   | m. 1947;
     son &      Yuhang=Hongchong      Lijun  |         | d. 1968 of
     daughter    b. 1936                      |         | brain tumor
     d. in       Shanghai       Yan Zheng=Jindo         |
     infancy              |      surgeon    nurse        |
                          |      emigrated to            |
         Jiming=Xiao-dong        Wisconsin               |
                                      |                  |
                                  daughter               |
                                  b. 1977                |
                                                         |
           |------------------|------------------------------------------------|
           Peter              An-mei "Amy"=Louis M. "Lou"       John "Didi"
           b. 1950;           Ruth Tan      DeMattei            b. 1954
           d. 1967 of         b. 1952       tax attorney at     lives in
           brain tumor        m. 1976       Intel in Santa      Calgary
                                            Clara
```

Amy Tan:
A Literary Companion

abortion

Amy Tan's fiction depicts reproductive rights and abortion as means of preserving the self and protecting the bodies of otherwise powerless women. Her first example in *The Joy Luck Club* (1989) is a victim of feudal marriage, Ying-ying St. Clair, the wife of Lin Xiao, an overbearing vulgarian. As a long-term comeuppance to a philanderer, she aborts his son, thereby depriving Lin Xiao of a male heir to perform ritual ancestral honors for his father. In *The Kitchen God's Wife* (1991), two of womanizer Wen Fu's paramours, the nameless fourteen-year-old servant girl and Min, the vaudevillian, choose to end pregnancies rather than carry them to term without a loving husband to welcome the children into life. The procedure kills the servant, who uses a folk method of self-abortion by dislodging the fertilized egg with a dirty broom straw. Min survives to establish a more satisfying relationship with another man.

Tan uses the ménage as evidence that mistresses and wives resorted to abortion as methods of controlling their lives. As desperate as Wen Fu's cast-off women, Winnie Louie, the battered wife, chooses abortion rather than perpetuate the illusion of a normal family. In Winnie's words, "That bad man was using my body ... as if I were — what? — a machine!" (p. 398). Living in military quarters in Kunming at the beginning of the Sino-Japanese War (1937–1945), she realizes the hopelessness of patriarchal marriage and grieves over her husband's role in the deaths of their baby daughters Mochou and Yiku. While rearing son Danru, Winnie aborts three subsequent children in the first five months of 1942. She considers the procedure a form of self-protection, a reclamation of her dignity, and maternal love for the unborn children: "In my heart, I was being kind" (*Ibid.*). Death before birth protects them from their psychopathic father, who precipitates emotional maladjustment in the toddler Yiku with slaps and yelling and terrorizes Danru into avoiding his parent.

With fewer details, Tan introduces abortion as a topic of interest in *The Hundred*

Secret Senses (1995). While approaching a cross-country skiing trailhead in Little Cottonwood Canyon, Utah, during winter break, Simon Bishop outrages his girlfriend, Elza Marie Vandervort, by failing to follow her train of thought concerning the emotional ramifications to pregnant women of abortion. Hysterical from debating an end to her own unplanned pregnancy, Elza becomes disoriented and dies of suffocation in an avalanche. Her death actualizes the recurrent theme of silencing, a mental torment that women suffer when facing unwanted or unexpected motherhood.

Tan uses spiritualism to link the father with his unborn child. Through a séance with the dead, ghost-seer Kwan Li learns that the spirit of Elza's baby passes successfully into another person. She explains the process of reincarnation: "He have only small waiting time, now already born someone else" (p. 118). In the novel's falling action, Olivia Yee Bishop, Simon's wife, realizes that she is Elza's daughter from an earlier existence, Tan's far-fetched resolution to Olivia's fear that Simon still adores his former love and compares Olivia unflatteringly to the brilliant, energetic Elza. The passage serves to reassure believers in the yin world that human spirits are immortal.

See also **Winnie Louie, spousal abuse, wisdom**

• *Further Reading*

Hamilton, Patricia L. "Feng Shui, Astrology, and the Five Elements: Traditional Chinese Belief in Amy Tan's *The Joy Luck Club*." *MELUS*, Vol. 24, No. 2, Summer 1999, pp. 125–145.

"Interview: Amy Tan." http://www.achievement.org/autodoc/page/tan0int-1, June 28, 1996.

assimilation

The pressure on immigrants to assimilate to Western culture informs much of Chinese-American literature, including Amy Tan's fiction, but the process is neverending. It is the contention of critic Amy Ling that an overriding subtext of these works is "the feeling of being between worlds, totally at home nowhere" (Ling, p. 105). Illustrating her point is the short-short story "Fish Cheeks" (1987), which Tan published in *Seventeen*. It describes a Chinese family's invitation to Caucasian guests to share a homey Christmas Eve dinner. Because the teenage speaker has a crush on the visitors' son Robert, she looks at the menu from his point of view and wishes that her family ate turkey and sweet potatoes rather than steamed cod, tofu, dried fungus, and squid. The crux of the story is the Chinese mother's awareness that the daughter disdains her favorite foods out of shame for her Asian heritage. Tan stresses the paradox of the first generation Chinese-American's assimilation while following the foodways of the old country: the family's enjoyment of native dishes appears exotic and distasteful to Caucasian viewers, who are unfamiliar with ethnic foodstuffs, preparation methods, and table courtesies calling for a belch of appreciation as thanks to the cook.

More serious to the acceptance of Asian newcomers is the ability to communicate in the language and alphabet of the new land. The author reveals in a personal essay, "Mother Tongue" (1990), that the immigrant Tan family's failure to comprehend, speak, and write standard English limits the children's relationships with their parents, particularly their mother. To Dorothy Wang, an interviewer for *Newsweek*, Tan confessed both humiliation and self-loathing because of the family's reliance on pidgin English. She characterized the stereotype of the American melting pot as an illusion of equality. In reality, newcomers "end up deliberately choosing the American things — hot dogs and apple pie — and ignoring the Chinese offerings" (Wang, p. 69). Thus, an arbitrary, pro–American prioritizing implies that United States culture is superior. As Asian customs and diet become the victims of full assimilation, their denigration drives a wedge between Amerasian children and their more conservative and sometimes homesick Chinese parents.

Vital to a successful transition to American ways is the issue of women's liberation, which most prominently affects husband-wife and parent-daughter alliances. In *The Kitchen God's Wife* (1991), Tan creates a fictionalized biography of her mother Daisy and her difficult relationship with Amy by focusing on the lingering emotional trauma of Daisy's feudal marriage. As author Gish Jen reveals in the excerpt "In the American Society" from *Typical American* (1991), assimilation requires a willingness to abandon old-world patriarchy before Asian newcomers to the United States can pursue the American dream. Unfortunately for Winnie Louie, the fictional version of Daisy Tan, the lingering doubt about daughter Pearl's paternity keeps the mother in suspense from constantly observing attitudes and behaviors for signs of the evil that threatened Winnie before she married Jimmy Louie, a Chinese male with American ideas about women and romantic love.

To apply a similar disconnect between siblings, Tan contrasts half-sisters Olivia Yee Bishop and Kwan Li in *The Hundred Secret Senses* (1995), in which the uneven acculturation of Kwan to American life clashes with Olivia's attempts to embrace a hip, culturally inclusive San Francisco lifestyle. Olivia's emotional distancing from Kwan extends for forty-four years until the two visit China, where Olivia observes the source of her sister's attitudes and beliefs. The full loop begun by the diaspora and completed by their return to Kwan's native village illustrates the importance of the Amerasian's personal experience with the old country.

See also **communication, diaspora, journeys, mother-daughter relationships, "Mother Tongue," otherness, pride, Ruth Luyi Young**

• *Further Reading*

Ling, Amy. *Between Worlds: Women Writers of Chinese Ancestry*. New York: Pergamon Press, 1990.

Ma, Sheng-mei. "'Chinese and Dogs' in Amy Tan's 'The Hundred Secret Senses': Ethnicizing the Primitive à la New Age." *MELUS*, Vol. 26, No. 1, Spring 2001, pp. 29–44.

Wang, Dorothy. "A Game of Show Not Tell." *Newsweek*, Vol. 113, No. 16, April 17, 1989, p. 69.

autobiography

In numerous interviews, Tan singles out people, events, and talk-stories in her life and family history that serve as elements of her historical fiction and short stories, particularly the short-short story "Fish Cheeks" (1987) and personal essay "Mother Tongue" (1990). She suffered under her mother's pithy, didactic aphorisms, gave up on psychiatry, endured comparisons to another girl, and played piano poorly at a recital, all facets of *The Joy Luck Club* (1989), which features a character bearing Amy's real name, An-mei. The story of the rape and forced concubinage of An-mei Hsu's mother actually occurred to the author's maternal grandmother, Gu Jingmei, the widow of a scholar. The grandmother also donated a strip of flesh to heal a dying mother, an act that An-mei's mother performs for Popo to honor mother-daughter tradition. In each example, Tan searches out the woman-centered events that draw her to a Chinese genealogy replete with undeniable horrors from China's patriarchal past.

After the success of the first novel, Tan mined her matrilineage for *The Kitchen God's Wife* (1991). In defining the novel's purpose, she expressed curiosity about family genealogy: "I wanted to write something deeper and wider this time, something that examines many of the toughest issues in my life" (Tan, p. 114). She followed with a personal essay for *Life* magazine, "Lost Lives of Women" (1991), a study of an old family photo. In the text, she tells the story of the wealthy man who raped her grandmother and of a haughty uncle who spilled soup that scarred his daughter's throat, two episodes incorporated in the second novel. She concludes that the novel is "a picture of secrets and tragedies, the reasons that warnings have been passed along in our family like heirlooms" (p. 90). Her statement indicates that talk-story, emotions, and verbal cautions comprise a valuable matrilineal legacy.

Through a mother-to-daughter talk-story about the war years, Tan disclosed a difference of perspective between her own and Daisy Tan's generations. Upon questioning Daisy about the Sino-Japanese War (1937–1945), Amy was surprised by her mother's comment that combat didn't affect her. Knowing otherwise, the author probed for justification of so cavalier a claim. Daisy's reply was unnerving, "I wasn't killed" (Vogel, p. C14). The difference in perception illustrates dissimilar mindsets between mother and daughter, each of whom applies a personal measuring stick to the nature and threat of national cataclysm. The variance in outlook on war was one of the reasons that Tan wrote her second novel and focused on the attitudes of Chinese wives and mothers.

Chinese-Americans criticize the author's attempts to recreate Chinese tradition and to explicate Asian expressions, which she acquired secondhand from her mother, particularly eye-witness accounts of a mother's suicide from opium-laced cakes to escape polygyny. Tan refuses to present herself as an apologist for all things Chinese and has admitted the importance of personal experiences to her works as well as her mother's talk-stories. Tan commented, "I never expected the need to take up the responsibility of introducing Chinese culture to the Western world. In addition, I feel that no single person could write enough to describe all of China and Chinese culture; it's a huge country inhabited by plenty of ethnic groups; how can one book possibly encompass all of it?" (Wu).

Undeterred by criticism, Tan continued drawing on personal experience in the writing of *The Hundred Secret Senses* (1995). Her ethnic mix of a Chinese face and hair and the Italian surname of Lou DeMattei serves fiction in the creation of

Amerasian protagonist Olivia Yee, who adopts Laguni, the Italian surname of her stepfather. Ironically, the name is a made-up, heritage-bereft patronym taken by orphans. Tan's linguistics study at the University of California at Berkeley and her early marriage and freelance business, which serves the National Kidney Foundation, influenced the adult life of the protagonist, who is initially content in her marriage to Simon Bishop and to their home office, where they write and illustrate articles. Like June Woo in *The Joy Luck Club* (1989) and like the author herself, who reunited with Chinese half-sisters as a means of understanding the loss that a trans–Pacific separation caused her family, Olivia visits the motherland and see firsthand the culture that refuses to die in the offspring of Chinese parents.

The author supplied *The Bonesetter's Daughter* (2001) with new views of her past, including Art Kamen's work as a linguistic consultant and Ruth Luyi Young's career as a "book doctor" freelancing corporate correspondence (p. 27). A poignant memory of her childhood rings true to the author's girlhood insecurities: "Moving to a new home eight times made her aware of how she didn't fit in" (p. 54). Contributing to the aura of autobiography are LuLing Liu's threats of suicide, a childhood trauma that Tan suffered with her own mother. The closing scenes move into emotional territory as the author describes introducing LuLing to a retirement community capable of handling the quirks and confusion brought on by Alzheimer's disease. The tender exchange between mother and daughter is virtually word-for-word a telephone apology that Daisy Tan made to Amy. A final touch is Ruth's move from ghostwriting to original fiction and her dependence on the spirit of her grandmother, who, like Tan's grandmother Gu Jingmei, nurtures the flow of healing words.

See also **The Bonesetter's Daughter, The Kitchen God's Wife**, names, LuLing **Liu Young**

- *Further Reading*

Fenster, Bob. "Singing Author's Luck Holds in Bringing Book to Film." (Phoenix) *Arizona Republic*, October 5, 1993.

Heung, Marina. "Daughter-Text/Mother-Text: Matrilineage in Amy Tan's Joy Luck Club." *Feminist Studies*, Vol. 19, No. 3, Fall 1993, pp. 597–616.

Ling, Amy. *Between Worlds: Women Writers of Chinese Ancestry*. New York: Pergamon Press, 1990.

Longenecker, Donna. "Relationship with Mother Helped Tan Hone Writing Skills." *University of Buffalo Reporter*, March 27, 2003.

Tan, Amy. "Excerpt: *The Kitchen God's Wife*." *McCall's*, July 1991, p. 114.

Taylor, Noel. "The Luck of Amy Tan." *Ottawa Citizen*, October 1, 1993, p. F1.

Vogel, Christine. "A Remarkable Life Controlled by Gods' Whims." *Chicago Sun Times*, June 30, 1991, p. C14.

Wu, Kelvin, trans. "'Fabricated Chinese Culture' and the Continuation of Tradition." *Singtao Daily*, September 15, 2002.

autonomy

Aside from suicide, the ultimate liberation, Amy Tan considers personal, social, and financial independence the only route for freeing women from patriarchy. In her first novel, *The Joy Luck Club* (1989), she depicts four first-generation Chinese-American women seeking freedom from Chinese customs and from the meddling of their old-style mothers. The shift in social mores actually begins during the upheaval following the fall of the Ching dynasty (1644–1912), China's last feudal dynasty, when Western values began their encroachment on feudal marriage and strict male-centered family life. The first wave of liberated women paid the price of the pioneer, a motif the author characterizes in the life of immigrant matriarch Lindo Jong, who lived in poverty before leaving the motherland for a freer life in America.

A valuable model for women seeking autonomy is Lindo's feminist exemplum, "The Red Candle," a story blending folk traditions of betrothal and marriage with the determination of a new woman, the post-feudal Chinese female. Looking into a mirror, she promises to honor her parents' arrangement of the union, "but I would never forget myself" (p. 58). Applying shrewd intuition about her in-laws' superstitions, Lindo is able to break the power of the red wedding candle by blowing it out on her wedding night and substituting strategy for folklore. By manipulating her mother-in-law's fear of nightmares, Lindo pretends that her marriage to Tyan-yu is doomed. When the mother-in-law sees a chance to wed her son to a rumored royal wife, the yearning for social position and children proves stronger than her intent to force Lindo's obedience to nuptial vows. Thus, Lindo's story conveys to her daughter Waverly proof that strategy can outflank traditional social expectations and end a coercive union without scandal.

The turmoil that turns China from its feudal past into a Communist nation rapidly alters lifestyles as it shatters folk customs. In Amy Tan's *The Kitchen God's Wife* (1991), female characters abandon learned helplessness and reach for self-fulfillment as they view the chaos of China and the emergence of a serendipitous freedom for women. One of the most eager for liberation is Peanut, Winnie Louie's cousin and sugar sister, who rejects polite gentrification in favor of a tough, no-nonsense women's liberation for herself and other refugees of brutal patriarchal marriages. To protect women and children suffering the tyranny of feudal unions, during the Sino-Japanese War (1937–1945), Peanut opens a shelter in the Japanese sector of Shanghai that welcomes the remnants of shattered families. By seizing Communist-inspired autonomy for herself, she sets an example for others, notably Winnie, who seeks the courage to leave Wen Fu, a violent husband who develops into a psychopath. The familial situation proves that women without hope are the ones most likely to make drastic changes in their attitudes toward obedience and to flee a death-in-life home situation.

The change in Winnie illustrates the value of networking as women, one at a time, share their woes and encourage their peers to extricate themselves from misery rather than swallow sadness in silence or wait for rescue. Following Peanut's example, Winnie is uncertain how to flee her father's mansion and make a new life for herself and son Danru. With the aid of Peanut, Auntie Du Ching, and Helen Kwong, Winnie manages to establish a new life with Jimmy Louie, her Amerasian lover. The cost is high—the death of Danru during his residence in Harbin with Helen and Long Jiaguo, a loss that heaps Winnie with guilt. To survive, she locates resolve in her inner self. She recovers from grief, endures fifteen months in a women's prison for escaping from Wen Fu, and continues plotting a flight to America. Her determination, telegrams to Jimmy, and careful purchase of visas and three airplane tickets prove successful just in time to save her from the Communist ousting of the Kuomintang in 1949. As an American living in a stable California home, she enjoys equal partnership in marriage to her second husband and a lengthy widowhood in which she lives independent from male authority.

See also **Jiang Sao-yen, mother-daughter relationships, obedience, polygyny, women, LuLing Liu Young, Ruth Luyi Young**

• *Further Reading*

Heung, Marina. "Daughter-Text/Mother-Text: Matrilineage in Amy Tan's Joy Luck Club." *Feminist Studies*, Vol. 19, No. 3, Fall 1993, pp. 597–616.

Ling, Amy. *Between Worlds: Women Writers of Chinese Ancestry*. New York: Pergamon Press, 1991.

Nadeau, Frances A. "The Mother/Daughter Relationship in Young Adult Fiction." *ALAN Review*, Vol. 22, No. 2, Winter 1995.

Su, Suocai. "Orientalism in Popular Culture and New Orientalism in Asian American Literature." *Jouvert*, Vol. 7, No. 1.

Bishop, Olivia Yee Laguni

For *The Hundred Secret Senses* (1995), Tan created protagonist Olivia Yee Laguni Bishop, a self-centered commercial photographer and half-sister to Kwan Li. *Book-page* reviewer Ellen Kanner characterized Olivia as a young, headstrong Amerasian who "[poses] identity questions in terms not just of cultures, but who do we belong to and why" (Kanner, p. 3). Eight years after the book's publication, Tan described the character in *The Opposite of Fate: A Book of Musings* (2003). Taking her cues from a friend who wanted to change a misspent life, she depicted the protagonist as a victim of "spiritual malaise, a common unease that plagues many from time to time, the longing to be special, the fear that one is not" (p. 257).

In an American family in Daly City, California, Olivia survives a brittle home life with a hip, self-absorbed Caucasian mother who is careless with her love. In 1960, when Olivia is four years old, her world takes a serious tumble after her Chinese father, Jack Yee, dies of renal failure. Two years later, the appearance of his first-born daughter, eighteen-year-old Kwan, begins a peculiar sibling relationship that brings joy to Kwan and guilt to Olivia for teasing and insulting the outsider. To account for the difficulty of maintaining a rational world view against Kwan's constant commu-nion with ghosts, Olivia explains, "I was a kid, I didn't have strong enough bound-aries between imagination and reality" (*The Hundred Secret Senses*, p. 57).

Tan uses Olivia as the butt of anti–California humor. The author depicts her as a fatherless, desensitized loner with an airhead mother, whom Olivia describes as "the quintessential social worker, totally obsessed with helping strangers and ignoring the homefront" (p. 76). As a result, Kwan assumes much of the role of parent, protec-tor, and spiritual guide. Even though Olivia is snide, dismissive, and contemptuous of the intruder, Kwan takes her mothering seriously. During the Vietnam War era,

Olivia blossoms as a teen rebel. She attends the University of California at Berkeley, she talks in slang, cases potential beaux, and indulges in the passions of the 1970s—pot-smoking, self-ennobling intellectualism, all-night carouses, and casual sex.

From the beginning, the intercultural relationship of Jack Yee's daughters is problematic and more like a mother-daughter relationship than a more mundane sibling rivalry. Anchoring Olivia within a dysfunctional family is the loving, loyal Kwan, who pronounces her sister's name "Libby-ah" and showers her with constant attention, advice, and cautions. Olivia's disappointment in her older sister derives from Kwan's otherness as a poorly assimilated immigrant to California: "Sometimes it irritates me. More often I become upset, even angry" (p. 21). The antagonism suggests Olivia's own doubts about her place among Caucasians, who voice racism through teasing and cruelty.

At the core of Olivia's differences with Kwan is an internal struggle over whether to accept superstitions about seeing and talking to ghosts. Kwan, a self-assured ghost-seer, introduces her to the spirit world through narratives in Chinese, an ongoing talk-story in the native language that helps to legitimize Kwan's Asian superstitions to an American mind. In adulthood, Olivia battles her own professional concerns over realism vs. edited realism. She supplies her clients "bucolic images of third world countries ... pre-edited into safe dullness" (p. 236). Her reasons are pragmatic rather than philosophical: "There's no market for [realism], and even if there were, hard realism would give the people the wrong impression, that *all* of China is this way, backward, unsanitary, miserably poor" (*Ibid.*). After Olivia develops her own hundred secret senses to perceive the yin world, the absorption of Kwan's spirit lore disorients Olivia. Most vivid are visions of past lives and her own death, which she shuts out by closing her eyes, much as editors strip her writing of hard truths.

Tan turns Olivia's muddled thinking into an opportunity to contrast Chinese and American points of view. At a crux in her emotional life, she suffers marital regrets and realizes how much her discounting of Kwan has hurt the blameless older sister. During a mid-life crisis triggered by the breakup of Olivia's relationship with Simon, her lover and business partner, she gives up scapegoating others for her troubles and looks inward. At this turning point, the author describes Olivia's ambivalence toward divorce and depicts her as "cut loose, untethered, not belonging to anything or anybody" (p. 171).

Aside from their national origins, Tan contrasts Olivia and Kwan in terms of outlook. Whereas Kwan views living and deceased human friends and relatives with a caring eye, Olivia looks through a camera lens to make exacting photos. While photographing the corpse of Big Ma at the Changmian funeral, Olivia contrasts the two approaches to truth: the camera "sees a million present particles of silver on black, not the old memories of a person's heart" (p. 274). Her admission of the plasticity of snapshots suggests that she envies Kwan the ability to converse with Big Ma's spirit and to learn the emotions and issues that concerned the maternal figure at the time of her death.

Tan forces Olivia to adopt Kwan's world view at a tense point in their visit to China, when Simon disappears in a labyrinth of caves. Because Kwan knows the cave from personal experiences in a former life as Nunumu, companion to a missionary during the Taiping Rebellion in 1864, she passes on to her sister the essential clues to reunite Olivia with her estranged husband. The author's handling of the couple's reunion leaves loose ends, but suggests a more stable future after the birth of Samantha Li, a "gift from Kwan," and the tentative inclusion of Simon in their family circle (p. 398). In a final embrace of Kwan's belief in reincarnation and the transmigration of souls, Olivia views the petty snipes of the past as obstacles that "shrink the heart and make life small" (p. 399). In token of the importance of Kwan and her ghost-seeing to Olivia's maturation, she admits that "believing in ghosts—that's believing that love never dies" (p. 399).

See also **Simon Bishop, Kwan Li, sisterhood, Yee genealogy**

• *Further Reading*

Fortuna, Diana. "Review: *The Hundred Secret Senses.*" *America*, Vol. 174, No. 14, May 4, 1996, pp. 27–28.
Kanner, Ellen. "From Amy Tan, a Superb Novel of Two Sisters, Two Worlds, and a Few Ghosts." *Bookpage*, December 1995, p. 3.
Shapiro, Laura. "Ghost Story." *Newsweek*, Vol. 126, No. 19, November 6, 1995, pp. 91–92.

Bishop, Simon

The husband of Olivia Yee Laguni in *The Hundred Secret Senses* (1995) is a curious blend of character traits. Seen through his wife's eyes, he entrances her in their college years at the University of California at Berkeley by avoiding the carnal to stress the philosophical. Stymying their relationship is his obsession with Elza Marie Vandervort, a childhood friend whom he loved until her death in a cross-country skiing accident, which also killed their unborn child. The development of his love for Olivia causes her to see herself as one of Simon's love objects rather than an equal marital partner. She is dismayed to feel like an addition to "an emotional harem," a mental form of polygyny that discounts her worth (p. 96).

Simon is one of Tan's more realistic males. Of his many qualities, Olivia recalls a down-to-earth outlook, sense of adventure, and attention to domestic details, including a delight in stretching clean sheets on the bed. He shares her freelance work in their home office, participates in the diagnosis of their childlessness, and helps to make their San Francisco co-op a pleasant residence. Eventually, their workday camaraderie outranks their withering marital union, spurring Olivia to complain, "We were partners, not soul mates" (p. 112). When the marriage founders in its seventeenth year, Simon is unable to bridge the gap solely on the couple's satisfying sexual relationship. It takes an outsider, Olivia's ghost-seeing sister Kwan Li, to bring the couple together for a two-week professional tour of a Chinese village, Changmian, a journey that Simon whole-heartedly enjoys.

Through Simon's observations, Tan undergirds the novel with stark contrasts between life in a remote Chinese village and the Bishops' California co-op. In Changmian, he surveys the peasant market system and takes notes on foodstuffs and cooking methods, which Olivia photographs to satisfy the client's assignment. The two are forced into intimacy when they board at Big Ma's house and share the only guest bed with Kwan. Although the physical side of the Bishops' love match resumes, Simon must work at relieving Olivia's doubts about their ability to survive as a couple.

Tan produces the rabbit out of the hat on the Bishops' return home with the birth of their miracle baby, Samantha Li. Simon flourishes as a father and continues to work out the snarls of marriage to Olivia. As opposed to womanizer Wu Tsing in *The Joy Luck Club* (1989), the psychopathic Wen Fu and cold Jiang Sao-yen in *The Kitchen God's Wife* (1991), and the evil Chang the coffinmaker, drug-addicted stalker Fu Nan, and mercenary General Warren Cape in *The Bonesetter's Daughter* (2001), Simon possesses both positive and negative qualities that allow him to be fully human and vulnerable.

See also **Olivia Lee Laguni Bishop, men, Yee genealogy**

• *Further Reading*

Ma, Sheng-mei. "'Chinese and Dogs' in Amy Tan's 'The Hundred Secret Senses': Ethnicizing the Primitive à la New Age." *MELUS*, Vol. 26, No. 1, Spring 2001, pp. 29–44.

Pavey, Ruth. "Spirit Levels." *New Statesman & Society*, Vol. 9, No. 390, February 16, 1996, p. 38.

Wilkinson, Joanne. "Review: *The Hundred Secret Senses*." *Booklist*, September 15, 1995.

The Bonesetter's Daughter

Amy Tan's fourth novel parallels two narrators, mother and daughter, in a story of skewed family dynamics and recovered memory. The author explained the biographical elements that reflect the life of her mother, Daisy Tan, who died of Alzheimer's disease before the work was complete: "The regrets are hers, the fear of the curse, the sense of danger she instilled in me while wanting me to have a better life. Asking forgiveness is in the book as well. That was part of our saying goodbye" (Cujec, p. 215). Tan bases the novel on the difficult lives of immigrants coping with first-generation American children. She earned high marks from *New York Times* reviewer Nancy Willard, who praised the author for valuing family histories and their preservers and transmitters.

Tan opens her novel with a chapter entitled "Truth," a dominant issue in confluent accounts of past lives and events. The search for the cause of LuLing Liu Young's confusion produces startling developments. Her daughter, Ruth Luyi Young, learns that the peculiar answers that her mother gives the physician reveal the onset of dementia as well as secrets from LuLing's past that have haunted her from girlhood. The author imposes the literary convention of the recovered manuscript, the first produced in impeccable calligraphy, the skill of Precious Auntie, LuLing's real mother. Through the translation of Mr. Tang, Ruth accesses a second recovered narrative, the story of LuLing's first marriage, widowhood, escape from a besieged orphanage, and emigration to California to marry pre-med student Edwin Young. The lengthy second widowhood turns into a miserable battleground with Ruth, a disobedient child who resents her Chinese mother's otherness and longs for independence.

The use of bones as a controlling image replaces abstractions with a sturdy metaphoric structure. Bones provide the healing powder that the Bonesetter Gu or Dr. Bone, Ruth's great grandfather, uses to bind the shattered limbs and splayed joints of quarrymen. The treatments restore the men to health, thus rescuing mining families from starvation. A generation later, the skeletal remains of Peking Man lure scientists to Dragon Bone Hill and bring together Bonesetter Gu's granddaughter LuLing and her first husband, Pan Kai Jing, a geologist and Communist collaborator martyred by the invaders during the Sino-Japanese War (1937–1945). A precious heirloom, the oracle bone, allows seekers to address questions of the gods and provides protagonist LuLing with a lone keepsake of her beloved nursemaid and tutor Precious Auntie. Beyond the concrete images lies a more revealing meaning of bones as ancestry, the heritage that affirms Chinese victims during the civil war of 1949.

The excavation of bones and old relationships and the unearthing of secrets and old loves, a dominant theme in *The Joy Luck Club* (1989), *The Kitchen God's Wife* (1991, and *The Hundred Secret Senses* (1995), equips Tan's fourth novel with suspense and a satisfying conclusion. The author extends the theme of communication to renew Ruth's romance with Art Kamen and to provide LuLing with an elderly suitor, Mr. Tang, who renders her memoir in English. The translator clarifies Ruth's questions about her mother's early life and offers a future for a woman rapidly slipping away into the past. In Art's assessment of their romance, "He's been in love with her since she was a little girl" (p. 303). Affection and forgiveness are the dominant images in the epilogue, in which LuLing lets go the sorrows of her youth and remembers only that she was once loved.

See also **the Bonesetter's genealogy, Peking Man, Precious Auntie, suicide, LuLing Liu Young, Ruth Luyi Young**

• *Further Reading*

Cujec, Carol. "Excavating Memory, Reconstructing Legacy." *World & I*, Vol. 16, No. 7, July 2001, pp. 215–223.
Donahue, Deirdre. "Tan's Books Excavate Life's Joy and Pain." *USA Today*, February 19, 2001, pp. 1D–2D.
Willard, Nancy. "Talking to Ghosts." *New York Times*, February 18, 2001.
Zipp, Yvonne. "A Life Recalled from China." *Christian Science Monitor*, Vol. 93, No. 57, February 15, 2001, p. 20.

the Bonesetter's genealogy

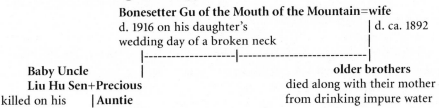

Bonesetter Gu of the Mouth of the Mountain=wife
d. 1916 on his daughter's | d. ca. 1892
wedding day of a broken neck |

Baby Uncle   older brothers
Liu Hu Sen+Precious   died along with their mother
killed on his | Auntie   from drinking impure water

wedding day by | Gu Liu Xin
a blow from his | b. ca. 1901
horse, 1916 | d. 1931 by
                  | suicide

        LuLing Liu = Pan Kai Jing

b. 1916 illegitimate;   geologist from
fostered by Liu Jen   Yenching University;
Sen and his wife, who   killed by invaders
pose as her parents   in the mid–1940s
until she enters an
orphanage

    See also **Young genealogy**

Brandt, Pearl Louie

Pearl Louie Brandt is a complex secondary figure in Tan's second novel, *The Kitchen God's Wife* (1991). In childhood, Pearl, like the author, was willful and proud. Her mother, Winnie Louie, recalls that she concealed the reading of J. D. Salinger's controversial novel, which Winnie misidentifies as *Catch Her in the Ride* (*The Catcher in the Rye* [1951]). After the death of her father, Jimmy Louie, from stomach cancer, Pearl grieves in private and rages at his loss, a fact she reveals with scribbles on a funeral card hidden in her jewelry box. The heirloom becomes a metaphor for the value she places on her father as well as for the enclosed nature of her emotions, which she refuses to expose to her bossy, intrusive mother.

From the exposition until dramatic revelations later in the novel, Pearl juggles secrets and lies. She maintains false assumptions about the Louie family's kinship with the Kwongs, her aunt and uncle. The misunderstanding of family ties bubbles to the surface after Winnie Louie complains about taking care of Helen's great aunt, Auntie Du Ching. Pearl, believing her mother is nurturing a martyr complex, proposes reality therapy — confront Helen with the charge that she is not doing her share for her own aunt. Pearl's direct method of confronting life's vicissitudes fails her when she suppresses thoughts of multiple sclerosis and a possible shortened life span. For good reason, she rages that the San Francisco physician who diagnosed the disease divulged personal information to Mary, an intrusive cousin, who passed the news on to her mother Helen Kwong. In self-defense, Mary challenges Pearl for not revealing the diagnosis to Winnie. The widening web of deception and secrecy sets the tone and theme of the remainder of the novel, which Tan unfolds through talk-story.

Like her nit-picking mother, Pearl compensates for fear of crippling and death by managing aspects of life that are controllable, such as the attendance at family functions and the arrangement of her underwear drawer. To deny worries of weakness and wheelchairs, she joins Phil in celebrating "small victories over the mundane irritations of life" (p. 25). To the blessing of remission of symptoms, she responds with nagging worry by visualizing herself in limbo and fretting that she hasn't been able to discuss the disease with her mother. The next day, at Auntie Du's funeral, Pearl experiences a catharsis that assuages the grief for her father that she has held back since she bolted from his funeral a quarter century before. In dreams, she pictures herself as Jimmy Louie's rescuer in a hospital terminal ward that they both occupy. The dreamscape suggests an overriding truth that all humanity is mortal.

Reviewer Cyra McFadden of the *San Francisco Examiner* is correct in her complaint that Tan leaves her readers wanting a worthier, fuller character for Winnie's daughter. Pearl faces a drama of her own that remains incomplete at novel's end. McFadden complains, "Her voice is angrier, wittier, and less long-suffering than Winnie's, and her perils aren't behind her but in front of her" (McFadden, p. C8). Tan implies that, like Winnie, the daughter possesses the moxie to live through whatever challenges come her way, even crippling and an early death that will leave her daughters motherless. Perhaps the author intends the reader to assume that a closer relationship with Winnie will arm Pearl against future obstacles at the end of her long remission.

See also **China, Louie genealogy, mother-daughter relationships, secrets**

• *Further Reading*

Bard, Nancy. "Adult Books for Young Adults." *School Library Journal*, Vol. 37, No. 12, December 1991, p. 149.
Barras, Jonetta Rose. "'Kitchen' Provides Complex Look at Relations of Women." *Washington Times*, July 15, 1991, pp. C6–C7.
McFadden, Cyra. "Amy Tan's Second Novel Is Rich and Satisfying Tale." *San Francisco Examiner*, June 17, 1991, p. C8.

Brandt, Phil

A San Jose pathologist and husband of Pearl Louie in *The Kitchen God's Wife* (1991), forty-seven-year-old Phil Brandt is one of Amy Tan's stronger male characters. At a family funeral for Auntie Du Ching, he becomes a long-suffering Anglo and permanent outsider in the verbal set-tos of his daughters Cleo and Tessa and between his wife and pushy mother-in-law, Winnie Louie. He attempts to make sense of the Chinese concepts of duty and family, the sources of most of the couple's marital spats, which escalate after Pearl is diagnosed with multiple sclerosis. To protect her from stress that might exacerbate the illness and end a long remission, he keeps tabs on her strength and reflexes.

In the novel's falling action, Phil becomes the same comforting paterfamilias that Tan creates in widower Canning Woo in *The Joy Luck Club* (1989), husband and father Simon Bishop in *The Hundred Secret Senses* (1995), geologist Pan Kai Jing in *The Bonesetter's Daughter* (2001), and Jimmy Louie, Winnie's deceased husband. Phil implies that the Brandts should decline the family invitation to Bao-bao Kwong's engagement party, in part to protect his wife from over-exertion and family squabbles. When the couple and their daughters attend over his objection, he provides the sense of humor and protection to guide Pearl through an awkward moment when she catches her heel and trips. Tan implies that Phil is a worthy mate for a wife facing a serious handicap.

See also **Louie genealogy, men**

China

Much of the drama of Amy Tan's fiction echoes the multiple cataclysms that forced China to abandon feudal principles at the fall of the Ching dynasty (1644–1912) and to accept the encroachment of Christianity, modern dress, Western customs, and democratized marriage. In "Watching China" (1989), a personal essay for *Glamour*, she calls herself "an ignorant observer" of demonstrations in Beijing, but declares the country her motherland (p. 302). She speaks an ethnic truism through Lindo Jong in *The Joy Luck Club* (1989), who is annoyed with her daughter Waverly for a major fault—confusing Taiwan with mainland China. Lindo snaps, "If you are Chinese you can never let go of China in your mind" (p. 203).

In a failed attempt to give daughter Waverly American circumstances and Chinese character, Lindo tries to teach five basic principles. First, obedience to parents, particularly the mother, is the beginning of Asian values. Second comes concealment of thoughts until the right opportunity for revealing them. Third, Lindo instructs her daughter on pursuing only difficult aims, a catechism that the author absorbed from her own mother. In this same vein is the fourth principle, valuing self-worth and treasuring it in secret. The fifth and last precept calls for embracing the Chinese mindset as the best. The purpose of strict home training in homeland traditions is meant to bridge the cultural, historical, and geographical gulf that separates the Chinese mother from her Amerasian daughter.

In the story of An-mei Hsu, Tan describes a more dramatic difference in customs, the coercive social order that forces An-mei's unnamed mother to commit suicide to liberate herself from a wretched situation as fourth wife of the womanizer and rapist Wu Tsing. The tyranny of feudal marriage and polygyny is the wife's undoing. An-mei describes her mother's decision to commit suicide as inevitable: "That was China. That was what people did back then. They had no choice. They could not speak up. They could not run away" (p. 272). The dramatic death from opium-poisoned rice cakes condemns the gender preferences of imperial China and contrasts less dire escapes for subsequent feudal wives. One example, Ying-ying St. Clair, accepts a convenient marriage proposal as her ticket out of China. A second, Lindo, deceives her in-laws into allowing her to divorce their son Tyan-yu and supplying her the money to start a new life.

American settings and the criticisms of first-generation Asian-Americans provide additional methods for the author to compare Western and Asian ideals. As Amerasian daughter Pearl Louie Brandt makes her way to her mother's flower shop in Chinatown in *The Kitchen God's Wife* (1991), she observes that the offerings of Ross Alley suit Chinese-American tastes. She passes trade and family associations, a dealer in ancestor memorials, and the defunct shop of a fortune-teller who promises lucky numbers and advice on prosperity. A Chinatown landmark, Sam Fook Trading Company, sells good luck tokens, statues of gods, incense, and spirit money for Buddhist funerals, all elements of the motherland's end-of-life ritual. Although Pearl lives outside the superstitions and customs of Ross Alley, she allows her mother to provide a new statue to replace the Kitchen God, whom Auntie Du left as a gift for Pearl. In place of the patriarchal myth, protagonist Winnie Louie restructures the story to exalt the Kitchen God's unnamed wife, a mate more deserving of honor for her loyalty and kindness. The switch of deities mirrors the willingness of immigrants to alter the arbitrary patriarchal standards of the old country to suit American equality.

Among the customs that deviate from Western behaviors are expressing parental love through cooked tidbits rather than hugs, consulting fortune-tellers, saving the best bedroom for guests, sleeping cocooned in quilts rather than on sheets, and the obligation of guests to attend social functions, the situation that opens Tan's second novel. She introduces additional glimpses of Chinese culture through memories of social caste, family gatherings and meals, worship and holidays, matchmaking, weddings, births, funerals, and memorials to ancestors. Through talk-story of girlhood memories, Winnie paints an extensive picture of traditional New Year celebrations. She includes an open-air market, travel by pedicabs, a visit to a fortune-teller's booth, and attendance at a rambunctious holiday play featuring a dragon and dedicated to the local god.

Literary critic Rocio G. Davis points to an irony of transcultural settings in *The Kitchen God's Wife*. Although Winnie eventually emigrates from her homeland, she achieves liberation and the beginnings of happiness in post-war China, which she honors with positive commentary. During her flight from the enemy at the height of the Sino-Japanese War (1937–1945), she describes the countryside, peasant lifestyle, and humble meals at wayside inns. After long days of a bumpy truck ride into the mountains, she and others in the party adapt to whatever food and lodging they can find among simple country folk, even sleep on mattresses infested with bedbugs. Winnie considers the group's toughness a natural element of the Chinese mindset. Her survival instinct takes charge as she formulates plans to flee Wen Fu, her sadistic husband. She admits to being directionless: "If I had known I was running away to something better, that would have been different. But I had no such hope to run to" (p. 273). Although enamored of American liberalism that she encounters at the Christmas victory dance, Winnie is still thoroughly Chinese in deportment, outlook, and strategy.

In the latter half of *The Hundred Secret Senses* (1995), Tan provides a late twentieth-century view of rural China through the eyes of visiting Californians, photographer Olivia and writer Simon Bishop, and one former Chinese resident, ghost-seer Kwan Li, Olivia's sister and surrogate mother. Through the myriad other-worldly stories and fables that Kwan has narrated over the past forty-four years, Olivia has acquired a ready knowledge of the land, which she pictured during Kwan's nightly storytelling. On the drive from Guilin to the outskirts of Changmian, Olivia and her estranged husband admire the outsized hopes of a line of waitresses squatting outside one-room restaurants offering an identical menu, bleak meals of noodle soup and orange soda. Closer to the poverty-stricken village, similar lines of entrepreneurs offer haircuts, boil surgery, and earwax removal. Although the demand is low for these services, Olivia concludes, "You can't stop people from wishing" (p. 225). After passing a car-bus accident, Rocky, their cab driver, remarks that such traffic disasters are common in China because of overcrowded conditions.

At Big Ma's house, the contrast in American and Chinese lifestyles takes on dismaying ramifications for the two outsiders. Olivia dreads sharing the only guest bed with Kwan and Simon. Both wince at Du Lili's slaughter of a chicken and the capture of its blood in a bowl as the basis of a broth. Simon receives a delicacy, one chicken foot, which he finds surprisingly tasty. The family polishes off their chicken dinner with pickle-mouse wine, a foul-tasting, but rejuvenating after-dinner drink. Other problems crop up when Olivia avoids the outdoor toilet and community bathhouse and when Kwan describes an American birthday party, which Du Lili considers decadent. At the sight of poverty and limited medical care, Olivia realizes that she could have had the same unpromising life that Kwan once knew if she had not been born in the United States.

With a fourth novel, *The Bonesetter's Daughter* (2001), Tan turns to ancient customs and medical precepts dating to the Sung dynasty (960–1279), a difficult era for China's poor. Precious Auntie, a mute nursemaid to LuLing Liu, introduces her charge to a secret cave, a source of dragon skeletons that bonesetters depend on for grinding into a healing powder. She describes her father, Bonesetter Gu, as a lifesaver of local quarrymen, who had to use stout limbs to work. Without earnings from the mines, families starved. With each miner's death came a family's demise and an eclipse of peasant lineage. In desperation, the poor clung to traditional bonesetters to restore shattered bodies to wholeness. Tan's admiration of an ongoing family tree suggests the transmission of China's past through talk-story, statuary and art, calligraphy, song, and folklore.

Contrasting the drab lives of the laboring class are the opulent wedding preparations of Precious Auntie's father, who spends his fortune to deck his daughter with the best. Tan characterizes the joy of the occasion in the red bridal costume and headdress, mule carts piled with gifts for the groom's family, and an enclosed sedan chair for the bride as she is ferried to the home of her in-laws, the Lius. Epitomizing the best the Bonesetter is able to afford are two jars of curatives, one of opium and one of dragon bones, which the coffinmaker Chang and his bandits steal during their raid on the wedding party. When joy gives way to sorrow, the bride, suddenly widowed and orphaned before an official marriage, lies brokenheartedly on her fiancé's k'ang, a heated bed built atop bricks, a symbol of the warmth of love and the heat of passion that die with him.

In a subsequent generation, Tan turns from rural China to Peking, a city of contrasts with pedestrians in traditional padded jacket and pants and others in Western suits and Hollywood hairstyles. Upon LuLing Liu's arrival, she admires gold lettering on a massive arch, hordes of rickshaws hurrying passengers to their destinations, even automobiles, which are a rarity in the early 1930s. On her walk through fast-paced shoppers in the market, she anticipates treats from the dumpling stall and rests from the heat at a park cooled by weeping willows surrounding a pond, a common form of Chinese landscape. At a pavilion, she hears birds singing in a cage and observes the various visitors to the park. The author characterizes the journey to Peking as the turning point in LuLing's fortunes. After a failed marriage proposal from Chang the coffinmaker brings catastrophe on the Liu family, she takes up residence in a Christian orphanage. Through her eyes, Tan surveys the shameful side of China's history—foot-binding, female suicide, opium dens, incest, beggary, slavery, the corruption of the Ching dynasty (1644–1912), and ignorant superstitions about charms, ghosts, and curses.

See also **patriarchy, polygyny, religion, Sino-Japanese War, Taiping Rebellion, yin and yang**

- *Further Reading*

Davis, Rocio G. "Amy Tan's *The Kitchen God's Wife:* An American Dream Come True — in China," in *Notes on Contemporary Literature,* Vol. 24, No. 5, 1994, pp. 3–5.
Fortuna, Diana. "Review: *The Hundred Secret Senses.*" *America,* Vol. 174, No. 14, May 4, 1996, pp. 27–28.
Ling, Amy. *Between Worlds: Women Writers of Chinese Ancestry.* New York: Pergamon Press, 1990.

The Chinese Siamese Cat

With her second illustrated children's story, *The Chinese Siamese Cat* (1994), Tan explores Asian myth with an explanation of why the term "Siamese cat" is a misnomer. In a description of Sagwa, an exuberant Chinese cat, the author incorporates information about brush writing on scrolls, public reading of new laws, and the themes of greed and cruel totalitarianism as deterrents to civil contentment. The story reaches a pleasant compromise after the grumpy magistrate hears people singing his praises. The reward to the cat Sagwa for changing laws in the people's favor is the singular honor of being known as the greatest of Chinese felines.

The story, Tan's second collaboration with artist Gretchen Schields in children's publications, brought mixed reviews for overdone, Crayon-bright illustrations. The most frequent critical descriptor of the drawings was "garish." Margaret A. Chang, a reviewer for *School Library Journal,* found fault with emotive facial expressions and hackneyed borders and art forms, a complaint echoed by veteran *Booklist* reviewer Janice Del Negro. Conversely, critic Sheng-Mei Ma credits both author and illustrator with "updating for our times the chinoiserie tradition and ethnic stereotypes of Chinese" (Ma, p. xxi). In the absence of drawings reprising the decorative art that Europeans of the 1600s and 1700s considered authentic Chinese, the audiocassette version pleased the public. Tan's performance against a background of Chinese music won the appreciation of *School Library Journal* for its expression of an animal myth in a pleasant, nonviolent narrative.

- *Further Reading*

Chang, Margaret A. "Review: *The Chinese Siamese Cat.*" *School Library Journal,* Vol. 40, No. 11, November 1994, p. 91.
Del Negro, Janice. "Review: *The Chinese Siamese Cat.*" *Booklist,* Vol. 91, No. 3, October 1, 1994, p. 335.
Ma, Sheng-mei. *The Deathly Embrace: Orientalism and Asian American Identity.* Minneapolis: University of Minnesota Press, 2000.
Mandell, Phyllis Levy, and Leah Hawkins. "Review: South Recording of *The Chinese Siamese Cat.*" *School Library Journal,* Vol. 41, No. 5, May 1995, p. 66.

Ching, Auntie Du

Grand Auntie Du Ching, a useful secondary character in *The Kitchen God's Wife* (1991), provides the ties that elevate networking as a means of female survival in a patriarchal society. Auntie Du lives a full, generous life and dies at age ninety-seven after surviving the social upheaval created by the fall of the Ching dynasty (1644–1912) and the Sino-Japanese War (1937–1945). Bearing a tenuous kinship to the Kwongs through Helen's father's family, Auntie Du is injured in a bus accident and dies of an undetected brain contusion after calmly dictating her will to old friend Winnie Louie. Winnie, who applies Chinese thinking to the loss, computes the deceased's goodness in the number of paid mourners and funeral wreaths that mark her passing.

Tan introduces Auntie Du to Winnie late in the story after the birth of Winnie's son Danru in 1940, a low point in her feudal marriage to Wen Fu, an evil womanizer. Auntie Du's arrival at Helen's quarters in Kunming requires seven years of travel across China's heartland. Like a grandmother to Danru, she plays an important part in bolstering Winnie against a miserable home life with the wisdom of the older generation. At the first parting of friends at war's end in August 1945, Winnie rewards the older woman with a gift, the blue perfume bottle that Winnie treasures because it once belonged to her mother. The present implies Winnie's mother-daughter relationship with the older woman, who deserves the honor.

Tan illustrates a sterling trust in Auntie Du after Winnie sends Danru to her in Harbin to protect him from Wen Fu's goons. As Winnie's fortunes decline, the older woman remains loyal, bringing news of Danru and Long Jiaguo's deaths from an epidemic and confronting Wen Fu at the Jiang mansion about Winnie's disappearance. When Winnie arrives at the provincial court building to be judged for stealing from her husband, Auntie Du appears with Peanut and Jimmy Louie and testifies that she witnessed Wen Fu's divorce from Winnie during the war. On a visit to Winnie in the women's prison, the old friend regrets that, along with toiletries and personal items, she bears the bad news that journalists have turned the divorce into a scandal and that Jimmy Louie must leave the country. Because her old friend is straightforward in transmitting the bad with the good, Tan suggests that she is more likely to deserve Winnie's trust.

Trust turns out to be warranted as Auntie Du continues to bolster Winnie during the fifteen-month incarceration. Because Jimmy Louie finances Auntie Du's stay in Shanghai, in his absence, she remains near the prison to uplift Winnie's morale and supply her with necessities, including newspaper and a piece of wood to cover a foul toilet bucket. Auntie Du brings the good news of Helen's remarriage and first pregnancy, intimidates officials into releasing Winnie, and greets her at the prison entrance in April 1949. To welcome her, Auntie Du trades a little jade bracelet for food that Helen cooks into a celebratory meal and insists that Winnie telegraph Jimmy immediately before Communists seize Shanghai. As a mother figure, Auntie Du earns love and respect; as a model of womanly pragmatism, she stands out alongside Peanut and Wan Betty as a mainstay of the Chinese network that helps Winnie to emigrate from her homeland to safety and a loving marriage in California.

See also **Kwong genealogy, men, religion**

• *Further Reading*

Chang, Joan Chiung-Heiu. *Transforming Chinese American Literature: A Study of History, Sexuality, and Ethnicity.* New York: Peter Lang, 2000.

Ma, Sheng-mei. "'Chinese and Dogs' in Amy Tan's 'The Hundred Secret Senses': Ethnicizing the Primitive à la New Age." *MELUS*, Vol. 26, No. 1, Spring 2001, pp. 29–44.

communication

The silences, squabbles, and misunderstandings of Chinese mothers and first-generation Chinese-American daughters are pervasive scenarios in Amy Tan's fiction, beginning with harsh mother-daughter competition in "Endgame" (1986), issued in *FM* magazine, and family shame in the short-short story "Fish Cheeks" (1987), published in *Seventeen*. While writing her first novel, *The Joy Luck Club* (1989), the author justified her choice of a daughter's perspective and her need to tell stories that would please her mother, Daisy Tan, a Mandarin speaker who knew limited English. Amy deliberately simplified the tone and diction, explaining, "I wanted those words to almost fall off the page so that she could just see the story, that the language would be simple enough, almost like a little curtain that would fall away" (Lew, p. 23). The visual image characterizes the pictorial quality of Tan's fiction, which adapted well to film and two stage plays.

In the novel's opening fable, a Chinese mother waits to tell her story until she has mastered English. Ironically, because the novel's daughters achieve the American dream of assimilation, they encounter a widening of the gap with the past as mothers feel more alienated, more out-of-date, and less able to embrace the children who make them proud. As the main plot takes shape, the author presents a makeshift Chinese-English patois as a border language, a cultural mix that allows Amerasian daughters to communicate with their Chinese mothers and to serve as go-betweens for the older women when they venture into American society and commerce. June Woo admits that she misunderstood her deceased mother, Suyuan Woo, and accounts for the lapse as a language problem: "I can never remember things I didn't understand in the first place" (p. 6). A subsequent explanation accounts in part for the lack of connection: Suyuan spoke in Chinese; June replied in English, a system that the author and her mother employed. June also acknowledges her mother's intuitive perceptions: "I seemed to hear less than what was said, while my mother heard more" (p. 27). The concept of truth suffers in translation from Chinese to English or to a hybrid language acceptable to both speakers. Reversions of mothers to Chinese suggests a way to express themselves more clearly to their daughters as well as a need for superiority of both motherhood and the Chinese motherland.

In *The Kitchen God's Wife* (1991), Tan advances communication as a central theme. She characterizes the relationship between Chinese pilots and General Claire Chennault's American Flying Tigers as riddled with misunderstanding from literal translations of idioms, such as sending the Japanese to "kingdom come" (p. 204). She extends a scene at a 1941 Christmas dance to indicate Jimmy Louie's skill as a linguist and his interest in Winnie. Their shared humor over the choice of the New Testament name "Judas" for Wen Fu survives Winnie's marital nightmare and remains a family joke after Winnie narrates her past troubles to daughter Pearl. Significantly, the talk-story encourages Pearl to inform her mother of Pearl's difficulties with multiple sclerosis, a life-threatening weakness that again places Winnie in the superior position of comforting parent.

In *The Hundred Secret Senses* (1995), the author employs an organic bilingualism. She depicts Olivia Yee Laguni as infected with Chinese words after her older sister, Kwan Li, talks each night in her childhood language. To Olivia, the learning is involuntary, an absorption into the brain of Chinese lore in the original language rather than in translation. Through Kwan's pidgin English and Mandarin, Olivia is able to communicate and to comprehend the oddities of Kwan's relationship with the spirit world. Olivia remains open to her sister's chats with ghosts, but doesn't fully believe in the powers of a ghost-seer until she experiences them personally. The text indicates that Olivia's knowledge of Chinese is essential to a conversion to Kwan's way of thinking.

Tan skillfully scrolls out the episodic story of Kwan's past existence as Nunumu, laundress for English missionaries in the early 1860s. Olivia and Kwan shelter near caves on Thistle Mountain and await Simon's return while Kwan tells the last of the story. The episodic narrative concludes with her death at the hands of Manchu soldiers who swarm over the village to exterminate God Worshippers. For months after the terrifying experience, Olivia pieces together Kwan's purpose in exposing her to China's turmoil during the Taiping Rebellion and in helping her locate Simon before Kwan disappears into the underground maze. The conclusion suggests that Kwan belongs to the labyrinthine episodes of her past while Olivia can thrive only in her Western existence as Simon's mate.

The use of silence vs. speech to create tension recurs in *The Bonesetter's Daughter* (2001), where incomplete communication overlays family understanding like the fog that rolls in from the Pacific to cloak San Francisco's harbor. After effectively silencing her mute nursemaid, Precious Auntie, by refusing to interpret for her within the family, LuLing Liu savors a moment of teen spite as she rebels against adult authority. The power game ricochets against her, causing a chain reaction of tragedies— Precious Auntie's suicide, the withdrawal of the Chang family's marriage offer to LuLing, and the terrible realization that she is not the older daughter of the prestigious Liu family, but the love child of her nursemaid. Tan's towering dramatic ironies illustrate the danger of perpetuating secrets until their revelation through personal disaster.

Significant to LuLing's recovery from multiple losses is the brush-and-paper communication method that she learned from Precious Auntie, her birth mother. Sequestered in a Christian orphanage, the girl makes a place for herself by applying the skill of calligrapher, which distinguished Precious Auntie during her miserable life as servant to the Lius. During her quality work for the staff as tutor and writing teacher, LuLing meets an educated man, Pan Kai Jing, a more suitable mate than the opium addict Chang Fu Nan, her original fiancé. LuLing and Kai Jing initiate courtship indirectly through praise of the sublime art of brush-writing, a beguiling exchange that conceals their love from nosy missionaries. After his bayoneting by Japanese executioners, LuLing clings to her husband's words that their love survives unchanged, immortal.

Upon LuLing's immigration to California, her dominant role gives place to dependence on her daughter Ruth Luyi Young, much as Precious Auntie once relied on LuLing as second-hand communicator. As a mother herself, LuLing takes pride in Ruth's bilingualism and values her as go-between to negotiate everyday business in San Francisco, including negotiations with demanding tenants. More intriguing is LuLing's effort to contact her mother in the spirit world through Ruth's scribbling on a sand tray. Whatever she offers as words from the spirit world, LuLing seizes as truth and applies to her life and to investments in the stock market. Ironically, Ruth learns in 1999 that years of deceiving her mother with the sand-writing trick produced shrewd advice that enriched her mother with blue chip stocks and treasury bills. Tan's metaphor for family enrichment serves as a coda to the family narrative, leading to an upbeat solution to paying the cost of LuLing's stay at a pricey retirement home. A double irony pictures her lovingly escorted by Mr. Tang, the eighty-year-old translator of her manuscript.

See also **disillusion, fables, ghosts, Kwan Li, Jimmy Louie, morality tale, Precious Auntie, secrets, silence, storytelling, talk-story, wisdom, June Woo, LuLing Liu Young, Ruth Luyi Young**

• *Further Reading*

Cujec, Carol. "Excavating Memory, Reconstructing Legacy." *World & I*, Vol. 16, No. 7, July 2001, pp. 215–223.
Heung, Marina. "Daughter-Text/Mother-Text: Matrilineage in Amy Tan's Joy Luck Club." *Feminist Studies*, Vol. 19, No. 3, Fall 1993, pp. 597–616.
Lew, Julie. "How Stories Written for Mother Become Amy Tan's Bestsellers." *New York Times*, July 4, 1989, p. 23.
Ling, Amy. *Between Worlds: Women Writers of Chinese Ancestry*. New York: Pergamon Press, 1990.

competition

Competition is a recurrent theme in the novels and stories of Amy Tan. In *The Joy Luck Club* (1989), games of mah jong relieve the tensions of war-time China. The women who wait, powerless and anxious about their soldier-husbands' survival, redirect their energies to the shuffling of tiles over the game table. The evening concludes with hopeful talk-story, a sharing of "good times in the past and good times yet to come" (p. 11). Competition is so valuable an outlet for their tensions that, after emigrating to California, Suyuan Woo and her women friends at the First Chinese Baptist Church resume their games with a mah jong club. They preserve its positive tone with the title Joy Luck. Lindo Jong characterizes the Chinese style of play as "very tricky," a competition requiring mental acuity and a good memory for what has been thrown away, a metaphor for the rejected lives left behind in China and the war era memories that refuse to die (p. 23).

Competitive skill becomes a matrilineal heritage adopted by Amerasian daughter from Chinese mother, but applied to American situations and ambitions. Lindo's assessment of game strategy passes to her daughter, tax attorney Waverly Jong. Her acumen in the business world becomes a way of life and a source of wealth, much as entrepreneurial savvy aids Olivia and Simon Bishop in *The Hundred Secret Senses* (1995) and enriches the Liu family, maker of high quality inksticks in *The Bonesetter's Daughter* (2001). Significant to an understanding of Waverly's mercenary behaviors and attitudes is her response to the game of chess. She learns the rudiments at age eight from her brothers, Vincent and Winston, both bearing names that imply winning. Thriving at tournament play, she brings honor to the Jong family and to San Francisco's Chinatown by snagging trophies and headlines. Tan develops Waverly's string of wins as a contrast to the inability to sidestep her mother's control. Ironically, it is Lindo Jong's adversarial relationship with Waverly that eventually tests the daughter's strategies and compromises her mastery of chess.

A more vicious form of competition erupts during the Sino-Japanese War (1937–1945) within the marriage of Winnie Louie and Kuomintang pilot Wen Fu, the evil first husband in *The Kitchen God's Wife* (1991). After she suffers the deaths of two daughters, she loses her naiveté about feudal marriage and plots methods of besting her cruel mate. Following night after night of degradation and sexual battery, she aborts their next three children to protect the unborn from the assaults that Wen Fu used to quiet daughter Yiku and son Danru. To defeat her smirking husband, who maintains before a judge that she left him, stole their son, and took valuables belonging to the Wen family, she plays a dangerous courtroom game. She retorts that she would rather serve time in women's prison than be his wife. As she plots immediate emigration from China, she makes one last stab at deflating Wen Fu's ego by tricking him into signing divorce papers before witnesses at the telegraph office. His vicious stalking, threats with a gun, and rape conclude their eight-year strife and sends Winnie on her way with a new anguish, her doubts as to the paternity of daughter Pearl.

See also **mah jong, pride, secrets**

• *Further Reading*

Ho, Wendy. *In Her Mother's House — The Politics of Asian American Mother-Daughter Writing*. Walnut Creek, Calif.: AltaMira Press, 1999.

confinement

The immurement of women at home or in institutions is a focal argument against feudal marriage in Amy Tan's novels. In *The Joy Luck Club* (1989), she cites the misery of Lindo Jong, who marries the child-husband to whom she was betrothed at age two. Her mother-in-law's insistence on a grandchild results in charges against the bride for refusing conjugal relations. Rather than exonerate herself and pass the blame onto Tyan-yu, Lindo accedes to his mother's rule that she not leave her bed. Confinement gives Lindo an opportunity to plot an exit strategy, a dream that reveals the woman whom Tyan-yu should have married and a prediction that the two will produce a child. Lindo gains not only release from house arrest but also renewed self-confidence and the opportunity to emigrate from China to America.

The confinement theme takes on new ramifications in *The Kitchen God's Wife* (1991), in which Winnie Louie goes to jail for fleeing a beastly husband. After stalking his wife and son Danru to the new quarters they share with Jimmy Louie, Wen Fu has her incarcerated for fleeing marriage to live with an American soldier, stealing from the Wen family, and taking Wen Fu's son Danru. After her sentence to two years in jail, she manages to turn the court's decision into victory by refusing an alternative to return to her husband. Tan depicts Winnie's character strength in the courtroom in her smile at Wen Fu's public humiliation. Sharing a cell with four other women is odious to Winnie, who recoils from a single mattress and a common toilet that does not flush. To her credit, she embraces the humanity of fellow inmates. As displayed in Isabel Allende's *The House of the Spirits* (1982), Nien Cheng's *Life and Death in Shanghai* (1986), Jeanne Wakatsuki Houston and James Houston's *A Farewell to Manzanar* (1973), and Malika Oufkir's *Stolen Lives: Twenty Years in a Desert Prison* (1999), such prison victories are small and abstract but meaningful to the inmate's self-esteem.

Tan's text illustrates the importance of a positive attitude during an enforced confinement. While female newspaper readers extol stories of Winnie's beauty and character, Wen Fu continues to degrade his jailed wife. The nonstop malice fails to demoralize Winnie, who uses the time for serious thought. She uplifts the inmates with lessons in reading and writing and joins them in manufacturing match boxes. She demonstrates personal cleanliness and the manners of a higher class than the other prisoners come in contact with. The inmates delight in her readings from Jimmy Louie's letters until she comes upon reference to his folk dancing lessons. Confinement exacerbates her doubts of his loyalty. Upon her sudden release in April 1949, she grasps her roommates' hands in farewell and leaves behind a treasured form of sisterhood.

Confinement returns to Tan's third novel, *The Hundred Secret Senses* (1995), in the historic flight of peasants during the Taiping Rebellion to the caves near Changmian, China. As Kwan Li narrates the lengthy story of her life as Nunumu and of her friendship with translator Nelly Banner, she completes the tale at a frightening moment after Olivia's husband Simon disappears. After Kwan volunteers to venture into a familiar cave to find him, her disappearance sets off a community alarm. Three days later, when Professor Po, assistant to the paleontologist who unearthed Peking Man, studies the interconnected passages, tunnels, and deliberate dead ends, he identifies the labyrinth as the retreat of local villagers during onslaughts of Mongols. Ironically, scientific and governmental interest in the ancient cave overruns Changmian with outsiders, ending its snug insularity as it opens itself to the Western world.

See also **Winnie Louie, polygyny, sisterhood**

• *Further Reading*

Solovitch, Sara. "Finding a Voice." *Mercury News*, June 30, 1991.

diaspora

Tan characterizes the Chinese diaspora through a limited portion of U.S. immigration history—the introduction of Chinese newcomers to California. She opens *The Joy Luck Club* (1989) in 1949 with the arrival of Canning and Suyuan Woo to San Francisco. A tongue-in-cheek suggestion of religious opportunism coats the family's welcome to the First Chinese Baptist Church, where members supply ill-fitting dresses and coerce the newcomers to join a bible study class and choir practice under the guise of teaching the Woos English. Suyuan recognizes in the numb faces of the Hsus, Jongs, and St. Clairs the sufferings that preceded their emigration from China. The subtext indicates that trauma from the Sino-Japanese War (1937–1945) follows emigrants to their new homeland. As critic Marina Heung explains, their individual stories express the disruption of families and re-alliances with outsiders in new definitions of kinship. The redrawing of clan lines constantly violates and diverges from the traditional model of the nuclear family into a pragmatic formation of the extended family.

Individual stories flesh out details. In a tortured memory of the war, Suyuan relives abandonment of twin infant girls, Chwun Hwa and Chwun Yu, during her flight from Japanese invaders from Kweilin west to Chungking. She is permanently separated from the children after they become the wards of Mei Ching and her husband Mei Han, illiterate Muslims living in a stone cave near Kweilin. The diaspora plagues Suyuan's mind until shortly before her death, when she learns the whereabouts of her daughters from a former schoolmate in Shanghai. Significantly, the girls are shopping for shoes, a common metaphor in stories of refugees and journeys that provides proof of rootlessness in traditional slave narratives and recurs in Alex Haley's *Roots* (1976) and *Queen* (1993) and Toni Morrison's *Beloved* (1987). Tan leaves up to June Woo, Suyuan's daughter, to arrange the reunion that introduces her to twin half-sisters and satisfies the wish of her dead mother. Ironically, the completion of the family circle requires that June retrace her mother's steps by returning to the motherland.

Tan reprises the terrors of the diaspora in *The Kitchen God's Wife* (1991), a novel that unites mother and daughter through talk-story. Winnie Louie's disclosure of escape from a psychopathic husband depicts her as one of many seeking exit from China in the closing days of the 1949 civil war. As Communists rapidly trounce Nationalists, the iron fist of Marxism begins limiting citizen movement. Winnie's clever self-rescue requires dealing with bureaucrats to obtain necessary visas. To cover multiple possibilities, she buys three airplane tickets and uses one within days of the Communist closure of China's borders to throngs of would-be emigrants. A similar instance of fast footwork resets the dynamics of Winnie's last-minute departure in *The Bonesetter's Daughter* (2001) with the escape of calligrapher LuLing Liu from a stalker, the drug-addicted Chang Fu Nan. She achieves a *deus ex machina* rescue after her sister GaoLing enables her to enter the United States as a guest artist, an elevation of emigration to the status of cultural exchange.

See also **disillusion, reunion, sisterhood, Suyuan Woo**

- *Further Reading*

Chang, Joan Chiung-Heiu. *Transforming Chinese American Literature: A Study of History, Sexuality, and Ethnicity*. New York: Peter Lang, 2000.

Heung, Marina. "Daughter-Text/Mother-Text: Matrilineage in Amy Tan's Joy Luck Club." *Feminist Studies*, Vol. 19, No. 3, Fall 1993, pp. 597–616.

Liu, Edward. "Chinese Supermoms." *Chinatown News*, Vol. 41, No. 10, February 3, 1994, p. 2.

Shear, Walter. "Generational Differences and the Diaspora in *The Joy Luck Club*." *Critique*, Vol. 34, No. 3, Spring 1993, pp. 193–199.

disillusion

Tan interweaves her fiction with scenarios of fragile illusions giving place to reality. A central motif of *The Joy Luck Club* (1989) is the failure of the American experience to satisfy the dreams and false hopes of emigrants from China. In the prefatory parable about a woman and her idealistic duck that wanted to have the long neck of a goose lie elements of the main text. Transformed beyond expectation into a swan, the bird accompanies her on a voyage to the United States, but is seized by authorities. The confused old woman abandons her original hopes, but keeps a single swan feather to pass along to her daughter after the mother learns to communicate in English. The story prefigures the anticipations of An-mei Hsu, Lindo Jong, Ying-ying St. Clair, and Suyuan Woo, the novel's four Chinese matrons. To their dismay, they never achieve the level of communication with their daughters that will allow them to bridge the continental divide that conceals from Chinese-American daughters their parents' Chinese motives, girlhood hopes, and dreams.

Two clear pictures of childhood innocence giving way to mature experience occur in the stories of An-mei and Ying-ying. The latter is the spoiled darling who stains her new outfit with kitchen muck, tumbles overboard from a holiday boat, and encounters a fantasy figure, Chang-o, the Moon Lady. The alluring myth of secret wishes coming true collapses as the child presses close to ask for her own heart's delight. On discovering that the magical lady is really a coarse male actor, Ying-ying loses self-assurance and begins to doubt her true identity. A more traumatic coming-to-knowledge assaults An-mei, the parentless child who reunites with her mother and lives among concubines in a rich man's house. The night that Wu Tsing demands conjugal rights from the girl's mother, An-mei begins to understand the high price of loveless polygyny. Both Ying-ying and An-mei carry into their adult lives the shock of disillusion.

Additional disenchantment afflicts other characters at dramatic moments in their growth as adults. For An-mei, it is the drowning of her young son Bing after he falls from a reef into the ocean. The sudden loss destroys her former trust that God will always bless the Hsu family with prosperity and contentment. For An-mei's peer, Waverly Jong, faith in unlimited success as a chess whiz dies after she spites her mother by refusing to compete. A succession of losses in tournament play teaches Waverly the hard lesson that fame is fleeting. For Rose Hsu Jordan, the departure of her husband Ted to another woman destroys her trust in their marriage and forces her to give up an accommodating personality. She turns loss into victory by developing resolve and refusing to give up her home. Most seriously wounded by disillusion is Suyuan Woo, who learns during the Sino-Japanese War (1937–1945) that a mother's best intentions can't hold together a family of four. For the remainder of her life, she attempts to reunite with her abandoned twin daughters Chwun Hwa and Chwun Yu, but dies without achieving her heart's desire. The resulting despair supplies Tan with a framework for the novel, which concludes with June's reunion with her adult half-sisters.

In *The Kitchen God's Wife* (1991), Tan perpetuates the theme of reality vs. illusion with multiple examples — the failure of Bao-bao ("Precious Baby") and his two failed marriages and broken engagement, Pearl Louie Brandt's pose of health to spare her mother worry, and Helen Kwong's pretense of a terminal brain tumor. Opening the text is a funeral for Auntie Du Ching, who dies from an undetected concussion. Contributing to the motif of illusion are the spread of a fake banquet, distribution of play money to accompany the deceased into heaven, and attendance at a Buddhist funeral at which paid mourners bewail the deceased. At the novel's crux, the author orders a series of rises and falls of fortune in the life of Winnie Jiang Louie as a contrast from how prosperous she is in childhood to how miserable she becomes after her mother disappears. A second rise and fall begins with her unpleasant life on Tsungming Island with Uncle Jiang's family. At the height of despair, she withdraws to the greenhouse and dreams of a flower bulb that turns into a fairy playmate. Her fantasy suggests the extreme disillusion that assails young girls ruled by patriarchy and condemned to feudal marriage.

Tan paces Winnie's story with cyclical hopes and defeats. Like the phoenix in the name of her father's business, she rises to prenuptial glory at her father's house on Julu Road, where he validates her worth with honor to her status and a sizeable dowry. After purchasing household furnishings and personal goods before marriage, she enters the home of the Wens expecting welcome from her prospective in-laws. The emotional high is short-lived when she realizes that they value her only as a source of pelf. They pillage her luggage, quilts, porcelain basins, mirror, and picture frames. As a token of self-preservation, she conceals in the lining of her suitcase the ten pairs of silver chopsticks once intended to grace her table. The act foretells her survival of a brutal patriarchal marriage, revival of self-esteem in the arms of a lover, and self-preservation through immigration to America.

For her third novel, *The Hundred Secret Senses* (1995), Tan depicts the maturation of six-year-old Olivia Yee, the beloved daughter of Jack Yee. After her father's death, the illusion of a functional family disintegrates when her mother marries, then discards, Bob Laguni and begins dating a series of unpromising suitors. Filling the gap in parenting is Kwan Li, Olivia's eighteen-year-old half-sister from Changmian, China, who arrives in California and accepts Olivia as a pseudo-daughter in need of affection and mentoring. Kwan's unusual outlook on the living and the dead permeates Olivia's thinking throughout her teens and continues to influence her after she weds Simon Bishop, a dream mate whose gentleness and loyalty bode well for her future.

Tan uses the youthful union as an example of a typically American illusion of happily ever after. At a nadir in Olivia's life, her seventeen-year marriage crumbles, leaving her unsettled and uncertain of how to proceed with home life and a freelance business, which she shares with Simon. Kwan's clever ruse of a trip to China restores the couple at the same time that it introduces Olivia to the truth of Kwan's belief in a past life that ended in 1864. Reality sets in for Olivia after Kwan uses knowledge gained during the Taiping Rebellion to rescue Simon from a labyrinthine cave. The retrieval comes at a high price — Kwan's disappearance and Olivia's sadness at losing her. Additional surprises alter the Bishops from their snug husband-wife office and co-op. Although medical opinions declare Simon infertile, Olivia gives birth to daughter Samantha Li, whom she conceived during the trip to Changmian. Tan concludes the novel with hope that the Bishop family will recover from disillusion and learn to live as a threesome.

A similar illusion of joy in mating lies at the core of *The Bonesetter's Daughter* (2001), in which Precious Auntie destroys her chance for happiness by allowing intimacies with Liu Hu Sen before their nuptials. The domino effect of a robbery of her wedding train, murder of her father, and death of her fiancé precedes a more damning fault, the birth of an illegitimate daughter. Precious Auntie seals her fate as a spurned household servant by drinking boiling resin, which melts half of her face and tongue and condemns her to silence. Tan supplants the ruined bride's despair with a favorite theme, joy in motherhood, even though Precious Auntie must conceal from LuLing their kinship. The author briefly relieves a life of silent suffering with a confessional, the manuscript that Precious Auntie gives her daughter. Salvaging LuLing from a lifetime of self-blame are memories of her beloved nursemaid, practice of Precious Auntie's skill at calligraphy, and the passage to LuLing's daughter of a memoir that rids the past of secrets and illusions. By elevating narrative as an antidote to past failures, Tan honors her own mother's disillusions and hardships, which the author used as source material.

See also **dismemberment, Winnie Louie, *The Moon Lady***

• *Further Reading*

Ho, Wendy. *In Her Mother's House — The Politics of Asian American Mother-Daughter Writing*. Walnut Creek, Calif.: AltaMira Press, 1999.

dismemberment

Truncation of people, things, and ideals is a powerful motif in Amy Tan's writing. Some of the dismembering is mundane, e.g., a mother's ripping veins from prawns and crosshatching squid before cooking in the short-short story "Fish Cheeks" (1987), an early effort published in *Seventeen* and reprinted in *The Opposite of Fate: A Book of Musings* (2003). At the holiday table on Christmas Eve, a significant moment arises when the father plucks a succulent tidbit with his chopsticks from under the eye of a steamed rock cod to feed his teenage daughter. The choice prefaces a glimpse of the bicultural divide. It portrays a Chinese parent catering to the delight of a child in her favorite food. To a Caucasian, on the other hand, eating fish cheeks on a day usually favored with turkey and cranberry sauce, the gesture loses its affectionate intent.

In a more serious vein, Tan pictures the lopping off of contact with China in *The Joy Luck Club* (1989) through the wartime emigration of survivors An-mei Hsu, Lindo Jong, Ying-ying St. Clair, and Suyuan Woo. Because Communist agents close the nation's borders to visits and communication with family caught up in the diaspora, newcomers to America cling to customs, language, folklore, and philosophies to preserve endearing memories of the motherland. Most serious of the separations is Suyuan Woo's loss of her twin daughters, Chwun Hwa and Chwun Yu, whom she abandons in 1944 amid refugee panic. The drive to find the girls impels her to write letters seeking information about them. In honor of Suyuan's loyalty to the missing family members, the author depicts June, her American daughter, in her mother's stead during a visit that reunites her children. Thus, the family's disjuncture ends in the next generation, as the Amerasian daughter embraces her Chinese sisters and finds in their faces a likeness of their mother.

On a personal level, the author incorporates dismemberment in a dramatic mother-daughter scene. When An-mei's outcast mother tries to return to oneness with her mother Popo, the scenario calls for a primitive sacrifice — the slicing of the daughter's flesh for cooking in soup to revive the dying mother. Tan adapted the riveting act from the experience of her grandmother, Gu Jingmei, which Tan learned from her mother Daisy. The text depicts the ritual through the eyes of An-mei, who bears the author's Chinese birth name. At age nine, An-mei is inexperienced and impressionable. She carries into adulthood a memory that the sacrifice did nothing to save Grandmother Popo or to restore her mother to a place of familial honor. To counter the abasement of her mother, An-mei shares the event with the next generation through talk-story, a narrative form that allows the teller to reclaim the degraded mother and to restructure her blood sacrifice from a positive, pro-woman viewpoint.

The trope of human dismemberment recurs in *The Kitchen God's Wife* (1991) in numerous scenarios. The death of Helen's sister in childbirth calls for dismembering the partially born child, but the family chooses to bury both without separating them. During the Sino-Japanese war (1937–1945), enemy bombardment generates more hideous corpses. One soldier, Winnie's friend Gan, is disemboweled and left to die slowly from irreparable injury during aerial combat. More serious to the plot is Wen Fu's loss of an eye in a jeep accident, a disability that exacerbates his barbaric nature at the same time that it gives him a visible scar and a reason to declare himself a combat hero of the Kuomintang. As he returns east to Shanghai with his family, visions of the symbolic dismemberment of society form a collage of loss and continued suffering by disoriented Chinese citizens. To Winnie's surprise, she finds her father, Jiang Sao-yen, partially impaired by stroke following his humiliation by manipulative Japanese officers. The prestigious house of Jiang collapses after Winnie flees with the last of her father's ingots, leaving her foolish husband to rip apart floors and walls in a hopeless search for concealed treasure. The savaged mansion and the demise of the Chinese industrial class symbolizes the lives of wartime survivors after Marxists oust Nationalists and impose their own dismemberment of traditional Chinese society, education, and government.

With *The Hundred Secret Senses* (1995), Tan extends the maiming and dis-memberment motif with memorable images of a merchant who self-destructs except for his feet and of a bus-car crash that kills Big Ma and of pigs screaming during Du Lili's killing of a chicken for dinner. The scenarios lead up to narration of the revolt-ing atrocities committed by the Manchu against God Worshippers in 1864 during the Taiping Rebellion. A dismayingly pictorial response to mercenary attacks is Nunumu's instinctive attempt to rejoin the head and body of Lao Lu, a friend and former mission gatekeeper whom the soldiers behead on their entrance to the com-pound. Contributing to horror is General Warren Cape's order that Lao Lu's leg be lopped off and roasted on a spit. Blood begets blood the next morning when Pastor Amen, crazed and raging, swings the roasted shank and splits Cape's skull. The images illustrate escalating horror as warriors attempt to exterminate God Worshippers from China.

Tan recovers Nunumu's pragmatism in the tender care of friend Nelly Banner, whose compound fracture from a blow by Pastor Amen's shank bone to her leg threat-ens her ability to escape. By turning a useless corset into a splint, Nunumu is able to coax Nelly hop by hop up Thistle Mountain to hiding places in a maze of caves. The selfless act offers the two women only a short reprieve from violence. Multiple slaughters of villagers proceed as mercenaries pursue them and burn out the caves. Tan's recall of an era in China's bloody past illustrates the value of personal narra-tive: rather than a sterile encyclopedic version of the Taiping Rebellion, Nunumu's eyewitness account describes massive social change through the experience of hap-less victims.

See also **abortion, suicide**

• *Further Reading*

Huntley, E. D. *Amy Tan, A Critical Companion*. Westport, Conn.: Greenwood Press, 1998.
Ma, Sheng-mei. "'Chinese and Dogs' in Amy Tan's 'The Hundred Secret Senses': Eth-nicizing the Primitive à la New Age." *MELUS*, Vol. 26, No. 1, Spring 2001, pp. 29–44.
Michael, Franz. *The Taiping Rebellion*. Seattle: University of Washington Press, 1971.

doppelgänger

To express duality in characters, Amy Tan employs the concept of character doubles. In the early short-short story "Fish Cheeks" (1987), which she issued in *Sev-enteen*, she pictures a teenage girl who is unable to perpetuate an all–American pose after a boy she likes eats Christmas Eve dinner with her family. Ironically, her par-ents, out of love for their daughter, expose her Chinese roots by serving succulent steamed rock cod, tofu, squid, and dried fungus, delicacies from the old country. Her shame emerges from Robert's dismay at the ethnic menu. The silent contretemps suggests that the girl lives a less conformative life at home than the assimilated per-sona she projects to American peers. The girl's discomfiture at the holiday meal repli-cates the ongoing duplicity of first-generation Amerasians in jettisoning native diet and customs in order to fit in with Caucasian Americans.

In *The Kitchen God's Wife* (1991), the author turns to more deadly duplicity during the onset of the Sino-Japanese War (1937–1945). She illustrates the mendacity in Wen Fu by his lying to the military and supplying graduation papers earned by his brother Wen Chen, an honor student at merchant seaman school who died of tuberculosis in 1935. The incident at first mystifies, then illuminates Winnie's perception of Wen Fu as husband and air force flier. She begins to see him as two people, the real man and the manipulative *poseur*. To protect herself from harm, she tries to segment her emotions by loving only his better half. The effort leaves her open to disillusion, identity loss, and battery from nightly spousal abuse.

As Wen Fu's comeuppance, Tan creates a spiritual double in the womanizing Kitchen God. Because time, distance, and circumstance prevent Winnie from wreaking vengeance on her former tormentor, she rips out the portrait of the Kitchen God and consigns it to the flames. A touch of situational humor pictures Winnie wincing at the squawk of the smoke detector as though the disembodied voice of Wen Fu/Kitchen God were scolding her. In the former deity's place, Winnie, a newly liberated woman, elevates a Chinese goddess, the nameless statue she dubs "Lady Sorrowfree" (p. 532). The naming confers blessing on Winnie's old age at the same time that it comforts Pearl during a remission of symptoms of multiple sclerosis. The boldness of Winnie's grasp at contentment illustrates the importance of abandoning the wifely duplicity of feudal marriage and embracing her real self.

Tan refers directly to the *doppelgänger* motif in *The Hundred Secret Senses* (1995) through Amerasian protagonist Olivia Yee Laguni. When she meets Simon Bishop, a Hawaiian student in a linguistics class at the University of California at Berkeley in 1977, she thinks of him as her male double — a person of Asian lineage who doesn't look the part. They maintain an intellectual friendship and discuss primitivism, racism, irony, satire, and parody. Before the pair become lovers, Olivia summarizes: "When I was with him, I felt as if a secret and better part of myself had finally been unleashed" (p. 75). The admission points to a fault in Olivia's public face, which conceals her true nature.

Tan builds the doubling of characters into a dizzying list. Through her half-sister Kwan Li, Olivia absorbs a lengthy narrative about Kwan's past life, which is based on Hakka and Buddhist notions of reincarnation. At length, Olivia accepts the fact that she and Kwan were faithful friends in the 1860s— Olivia as Nelly Banner, an interpreter for Christian missionaries, and Kwan as Nunumu, the mission laundress and Nelly's rescuer from marauding Manchus. Kwan delights in seeing Olivia marry Simon, who was her lost love, Yiban Johnson, in the past; Kwan's husband, grocery manager George Lew, was her pseudo-husband Zeng, who sold earthenware jars at the mission. The reunion of the two couples negates memories of a harsh period of Chinese history that saw the slaughter of God Worshippers during the Taiping Rebellion of 1864. The spiral of multiple identities typifies Kwan's concept of reincarnation as an opportunity for love to overcome death.

Tan elongates pairing with the villainous General Warren Cape, modeled on the Massachusetts-born mercenary Frederick Townsend Ward. To halt Cape's duplicity as a mercenary available to the highest bidder, the text reincarnates him as Olivia's dog. Subplots about Kwan's kinswoman Du Lili picture her as Du Yun, a foster mother who takes the name of her drowned daughter. Easing Olivia's worry about her husband's loyalty is Kwan's assurance that Elza, Simon's deceased girlfriend, was once Olivia's mother. A confusing addition to doubles is Kwan's confession that she fled a fragile body and reappeared in the child Buncake's sturdy form after her own drowning death. The lengthy strand of reincarnations expresses Kwan's belief that death is nothing to fear because it clears the way for additional returns to earth.

See also **heritage, Jiang Sao-yen, Ying-ying St. Clair**

• *Further Reading*

Frostchild, Daphne. "Reading the Past." *Wag*, March 2001.
Ma, Sheng-mei. "'Chinese and Dogs' in Amy Tan's 'The Hundred Secret Senses': Ethnicizing the Primitive à la New Age." *MELUS*, Vol. 26, No. 1, Spring 2001, pp. 29–44.

fable

The interweaving of anecdote, memoir, legend, and fable provides Amy Tan's fiction with a textured telling, a multi-layered revelation that validates insights about love, alienation, and loss. In "Feathers from a Thousand Li Away," a fable on the opening pages of *The Joy Luck Club* (1989), she sets the focus of her canon with the introduction of an elderly female recalling purchase of a swan feather. The story of gender differences in Shanghai contrasts the male and female digestive systems: significantly men earn prestige by their loud belches; women survive by swallowing their sorrows, a private act implying the beginnings of life-long secrets, silencing, and internal unrest. The feather, for all its delicacy, survives in the woman's keeping until the time is right for mother to tell daughter the source of the mother's ambitions. Subsequent stories illustrate virtues and sins, for example, Popo's tale of the little girl who swells up like a pregnant woman and dies with a white winter melon inside her as a symbol of her greed. The moral declares that the object of greed grows inside the spirit and makes it perpetually hungry.

In *The Kitchen God's Wife* (1991), Tan explains the title by relating the fable of farmer Zhang, who prospers and indulges his lust with a second wife named Lady Li. The trophy wife mistreats and impoverishes him, abandoning him to beg from door to door. Swooning from hunger and exertion, he collapses in the kitchen of a kind peasant woman who turns out to be his first wife, whom he dishonored by taking Lady Li to his bed. Out of shame, Zhang immolates himself on the cookfire. In an act of male preferment, the Jade Emperor of heaven rewards the farmer by naming him the Kitchen God, a deity who judges human fault and who selects people to receive good fortune. Tan uses the story as commentary on Chinese patriarchal mythos, which rewards the fallen husband instead of the charitable wife.

See also **Kitchen God, Kwan Li, morality tale, storytelling**

• *Further Reading*
Casey, Constance. "Amy Tan's Second Book Focuses on the Overlooked Woman." *San Diego Union*, June 16, 1991, pp. C4–C5.

Ling, Amy. *Between Worlds: Women Writers of Chinese Ancestry*. New York: Pergamon Press, 1990.

Romagnolo, Catherine. "Narrative Beginnings in Amy Tan's *The Joy Luck Club*: A Feminist Study." *Studies in the Novel*, Vol. 35, No. 1, Spring 2003, pp. 89–107.

fate and fortune

The Chinese view of fortune and fate is a dominant theme in Tan's novels. In *The Joy Luck Club* (1989), four immigrant women — An-mei Hsu, Lindo Jong, Ying-ying St. Clair, and Suyuan Wood — the dispossessed of wartime China, evade evil fortune with a touch of chutzpah, a weekly game of mah jong. Their laughter in the face of family separation, exile, unhappy marriage, and violent death characterizes powerless women as risk takers who have nothing to lose by grasping at joy and luck. Tan repeats the scenario in *The Kitchen God's Wife* (1991), in which pilots and their wives retreat to Kunming and play mah jong late into the night while the Sino-Japanese War (1937–1945) rages far to the east. Winnie Louie compares the need for amusement to the frenzied nightclubbing of Berliners during World War II to displace thoughts of war, rationing, and loss. Like the night-out scene between Commander Fred and his concubine Offred in Margaret Atwood's *The Handmaid's Tale* 1985), the social scenario echoes a human universal, the refusal to be overwhelmed by woes and a willingness to be frivolous and gamesome in the face of imminent danger.

Superstition and fear of bad fortune overwhelm Winnie, the protagonist. Before meeting her future husband, Wen Fu, she misses a chance to have her fortune told. In retrospect, she explains the difference between chance and fate, noting that chance equates with the human initiative to make the most of arbitrary fortune. After the retreat to Kunming, she and Wen Fu lodge in a room "facing a bad-luck direction" (pp. 301–302). Because of the placement of a closet, they are unable to move their bed into a more propitious location. In the ninth month of a first pregnancy, she drops scissors, which impale their points in the floor in the spread-eagle stance of a soldier. Instantly, her baby stops moving. She interprets the sign as an omen of her unborn child's death. These portents reinforce the evil of her husband's behaviors, which have already doomed their union.

The bifurcated image escalates to a major disaster after Winnie knocks to the ground a vendor's table display of local-made scissors. Because Wen Fu is injured in a jeep accident at the same time, she blames herself for generating ill fortune. The self-punishment proves unnecessary after Captain Long Jiaguo reveals that Wen Fu took an army jeep without permission for a joyride with a girl. The upset was his fault for speeding and turning recklessly, a move that killed his passenger. The author's insistence on human culpability overrides pervasive Chinese beliefs in predestined, immutable fortunes.

Tan continues to express fortune in terms of character volition. Winnie's salvation is Jimmy Louie, an Amerasian translator she feels fated to encounter at the victory dance on Christmas 1941. When she bumps into him in Shanghai five years later near the book and newspaper sellers in the Japanese sector, she convinces herself that she was meant to leave Wen Fu and marry Jimmy. Conversant with both Chinese and American concepts of luck, Jimmy considers the encounter destiny, a fate that cannot be avoided. He concurs with the author's viewpoint by believing that the couple's love is so strong from the beginning that their will causes them to reunite in Shanghai. Although wisps of caution color Winnie's thinking, e.g. the fate of the landlady whose Chinese-American husband deserted her for an American wife, Winnie clings to Jimmy's promises. After he becomes a Baptist minister, he alters his view of fate one more time by declaring their marriage God's will, a reflection of his abandonment of Chinese philosophy and his devotion to Christianity.

A backward view of fate in *The Hundred Secret Senses* (1995) allows Tan to frame ironies and unforeseen pitfalls in human lives. Through Kwan Li's episodic narration of her former life as Nunumu, laundress for a mission compound in Changmian, China, the author illustrates the random violence of the Taiping Rebellion of 1864, which cost the nation some thirty million deaths. General Warren Cape, an embodiment of mercenary villainy, perpetrates serial atrocities on peasants as he serves multiple forces in subduing the Chinese. His arrival at the mission results in the savage beheading of gatekeeper Lao Lu and an atavistic roasting of the victim's leg on a spit. As Manchu marauders sweep into the village, peasants take to the hills to shelter in a warren of caves, a natural shield against invasion. Fate turns on the victimizers after they set fires at the cave mouths to suffocate the concealed villagers. A tricky wind from Thistle Mountain engulfs the entire scene in flame and smoke. Only a few soldiers escape a conflagration that sweeps the region, ending protracted warfare with empty homes and a crumbling mission. Tan's post-war scenario implies that nature has the final word on a region's destiny.

Because Kwan has "yin eyes" and can look to distant past and present, she casts over catastrophe the dispassionate view of the historian (p. 3). Like the griot instructing a generation of listeners in the struggles of the past, she recalls unthinkable deaths— premature burial, wartime slaughter, the cracked skull of an enemy, a carbus crash, the drowning of children — yet moves on to peaceful times when souls return through reincarnation to enjoy more satisfying existences. By picturing herself as the loyal Nunumu reunited with Nelly Banner in the form of Kwan and her half-sister Olivia, Kwan rejuvenates a sisterhood unchanged by a century of separation. By rejoicing that Nunumu and lover Zeng return as Kwan and husband George Lew and that Yiban Johnson, Nelly's faithful wooer, lives once more as Olivia's husband Simon, Kwan expresses the value of love as an undying commodity in an uncertain world.

See also **religion, social class, superstition**

- *Further Reading*

Benedict, Kitty. "Mother to Daughter: Here Is the Truth of My Life." *Hartford Courant*, June 30, 1991, p. C10.
Marbella, Jean. "Amy Tan: Luck but Not Joy." *Baltimore Sun*, June 30, 1991, pp. B10–B11.
Vogel, Christine. "A Remarkable Life Controlled by Gods' Whims." *Chicago Sun Times*, June 30, 1991, p. C14.

food

Tan uses purchase of foodstuffs and the preparation and eating of ethnic dishes as a means of introducing Chinese ideals and manners. The selection of delicacies for a special Christmas Eve dinner is the theme of "Fish Cheeks" (1987), a short-short story issued in *Seventeen*. The family's teenage daughter is embarrassed that her Chinese mother serves steamed rock cod, tofu, dried fungus, and squid rather than the usual American turkey menu. Even though Chinese dishes are the girl's favorite, she regrets that Robert, a boy she admires, sees how unassimilated her family is and how Chinese her homelife must be. As usual in Tan's fiction, the mother speaks the wisdom of the moment by reminding her daughter that the real shame is feeling shame at her family's foodways.

Celebratory food and comfort meals also play an integral role in the author's first novels. In *The Joy Luck Club* (1989), Suyuan Woo begins the club as a means of sharing experiences, advice, and *dyansyin* or *dianxin* foods, the festive dumplings, rice noodles, boiled peanuts, and oranges that bring good fortune. The concept of a mah jong club counters the privations of the Sino-Japanese War (1937–1945), when players share friendly competition and tasty snacks as a respite from combat and limited rations. Food continues to express security and affection through what June Woo remembers as "stern offerings of steamed dumplings, duck's gizzards, and crab" (p. 227). As described by critic Amy Ling, each serving is a "gift that cannot be refused because it carries the weight of authority" (Ling, p. 134). After Suyuan's death, her daughter continues the tradition by treating Canning Woo to his wife's dishes, a wholesome example of womanly love and honor to Suyuan's memory.

In *The Kitchen God's Wife* (1991), Winnie Louie expresses maternal love for Pearl by offering noodle soup and tea during the lengthy narration of Winnie's wartime experiences. In both novels, food is a unifying agent, a reason to come together at table to relax, enjoy familiar recipes, and share conversation, a source of healing talkstory. At the novel's end, guests at Bao-bao's wedding reception sip the last of the chrysanthemum tea and scoop into take-away cartons the ample leftovers from platters of pork, chicken, and fish. The meat, intended for subsequent meals, symbolizes the lasting warmth and good will that the family generates at get-togethers. Table gleaning also resonates with the uncertainty that refugees bear as tokens of war and flight in their early lives.

Tan uses food as an element of plot motivation for her third novel, *The Hundred Secret Senses* (1995). An estranged couple, Olivia and Simon Bishop, accept a boost to their freelance career by agreeing to visit Changmian, China, to compose articles on home-raised animals and plants, peasant shopping, cookery, and home meal service. The jaunt occurs at a height of Olivia's disappointment in marriage and her unwillingness to reunite with Simon. Although the foods are unfamiliar and the hygiene primitive, the two American diners open themselves to a rural Asian experience at Du Lili's sparse table. By throwing themselves into taking pictures, observing herb beds and livestock, taking notes on poultry markets and broth preparation, and interviewing peasant cooks, the couple rediscover their mutual love of a challenging project and of each other. Tan suggests that food is a necessary nurturance of both body and spirit.

In *The Bonesetter's Daughter* (2001), the author maintains her depiction of ethnic customs and beliefs through scenarios centering on food. After Ruth Luyi breaks her arm and injures her lip by lurching haphazardly down a playground slide, her mother LuLing tempts her with an American hamburger patty, a food the mother rejects because of beef's resemblance to ground flesh. At Ruth's refusal to say "hamburger," LuLing shelves the patty in the refrigerator and turns to rice porridge, a more familiar Chinese comfort food (p. 66). Life reverses the order of giver and receiver after LuLing lapses into senile dementia. In addition to removing spoiled leftovers from her mother's refrigerator, Ruth treats her to dinner out twice a week and insists on Chinese dishes after LuLing enters a retirement home, Mira Mar Manor. The reciprocity of love characterizes Tan's vision of the ideal mother-daughter relationship. A brief echo of reciprocal affection accompanies Art and Ruth into a restaurant, where he pointedly orders the oysters with the most aphrodisiac power. His humor implies that he intends to revive his love relationship with Ruth, a support she needs during her mother's mental decline and Ruth's shift in careers. Thus, food maintains its place as a human necessity bearing more than nutritional value to cooks and partakers.

See also **love**

- *Further Reading*

Leonard, George, ed. *The Asian Pacific American Heritage: A Companion to Literature and Arts*. New York: Garland, 1998.
Ling, Amy. *Between Worlds: Women Writers of Chinese Ancestry*. New York: Pergamon Press, 1990.
Wong, Sau-ling Cynthia. *Reading Asian American Literature: From Necessity to Extravagance*. Princeton, N.J.: Princeton University Press, 1993.

ghosts

An element of Chinese outlook that Amy Tan retains from her family's Asian past, ghost lore invigorates her fiction in the guise of superstition, genealogy, and history. An-mei Hsu explains in *The Joy Luck Club* (1989) that a ghost is any forbidden topic of conversation, including her unnamed mother, who dishonored the family by becoming the third concubine of rich carpet manufacturer Wu Tsing. His second wife, a former sing-song girl in a Shantung teahouse, controls him by pretending to die from an overdose of opium after he refuses her more money. Thus, she turns superstition into one of the few weapons that women aim at patriarchal men. Out of fear of a suicide's ghost, Wu Tsing increases her allowance to more than she demanded. Subsequent pretended suicides illustrate the power of pre-death posturing, which nets the second wife a better room, private rickshaw, home for her parents, and cash to spend at temples for blessings.

In the novel's most poignant death story, Tan extends the psychological power of a suicide's ghost over polygyny. A staged death frees An-mei's mother from concubinage to her rapist, Wu Tsing. She chooses to swallow a lethal amount of bitter poison concealed in rice cakes, a metaphor that overturns the womanly offering of food as a love gift into a medium for self-murder. The slow poisoning occurs two days before the lunar New Year so her soul will return on the holiday, when debtors pay what they owe and settle outstanding grievances. To avoid disaster, Wu Tsing dresses in humble white mourning clothes, elevates his dead wife to the prestige of first wife, and promises to honor her children, An-mei and her brother Syaudi. An-mei directs her new-found authority against his tyranny and frees herself from maidenly silence, a self-liberation that enables her to "[learn] to shout" (p. 272). Ironically, in an example of female pragmatism, she, like Lindo Jong, liberates herself by using ancient superstition to her advantage.

In *The Kitchen God's Wife* (1991), Tan moves sure-footedly in and out of ghost lore with complete familiarity with supernatural otherness. Two female examples are the spirit of a fourteen-year-old servant girl who dies from a home abortion executed with a broom straw and Lady White Ghost, who induces memory loss in drivers facing the Twenty-four Turnarounds on their way up the mountain to Kunming. In the latter incident, the phantasm materializes in the form of thick clouds that envelop Old Mr. Ma's truck. Helen calms Winnie's jitters with the story of the Heavenly Cowherd Maiden, a female constellation that spills milk from the sky. Sensibly, Helen refuses to give in to fear and comes up with a practical plan to avert danger from driving in fog — she provides a red skirt that Captain Long Jiaguo flaps as he feels his way up the road and guides the driver safely through the clouds to an idyllic view of blue skies and a mountain retreat. Unlike her realistic friend, Winnie clings to fantasy and interprets their rescue from the clouds as a death and rebirth as deities. Her choice of fantasy over reality bodes ill for a failing marriage that refuses to bring blessing or safety to the young bride.

In its perusal of a period of drastic change in China, the text illustrates the difference between traditional and Christian views of the hereafter. The author develops an eerie presence from a smoky jack-o'-lantern that Pearl Louie Brandt sees at age five. In terror, she alerts her mother Winnie, an old-world believer who matter-of-factly searches the room for a ghost. In contrast to the superstitious mom, Jimmy Louie, a minister at the First Chinese Baptist Church, insists that the Holy Ghost is the only spirit and that it constitutes a benevolent rather than ominous presence. Despite her husband's acceptance of Christian dogma, Winnie keeps a foot in each tradition by honoring her husband's faith while still believing in ghosts. She recalls listing all the possibilities for her mother's disappearance in 1924 — reunion with her lover Lu, insanity, joining a convent, dying of an illness. One hypothesis is that the original second wife returned from the world of the dead to snatch the mother from her place in Jiang Sao-yen's family. By according spirits like Winnie's mother the opportunities to manipulate whole households, the speaker removes some of the fear of death and confers on the deceased limited power over the living.

In another view of ghosts, Tan concludes a would-be romance with a macabre ending. Gan, the vulnerable Kuomintang air force pilot whom Winnie befriends in Yangchow, explains why he fears the dark. Eleven years earlier, he saw a ghost that predicted his death in the next tiger year, which is only a few months away in 1938.

The spirit promised a painless demise and proved his knowledge of Gan's future by listing the nine bad fates that will precede his death. After incurring eight of those events, Gan is certain that the ninth will end his life. While he awaits a gruesome death from disemboweling after the crash of his plane, he addresses the harbinger, claiming to welcome death. Winnie notes that the ghost's promise of an easy death proves false. The overturning of truth suggests either that Gan imagined the spirit's prophecy or that he stripped terror from its message to rid him of fear of pain.

Superstition about the spirit world recurs in Tan's next two books. Her first children's publication, *The Moon Lady* (1992), describes a young boy who wears a chain and silver lock on his jacket to protect him from ghosts that steal young boys. Her third novel, *The Hundred Secret Senses* (1995), narrates a bi-level plot permeated with spirit lore in which Kwan Li, a ghost-seer, moves easily from the late twentieth century back to the Taiping Rebellion of 1864. Tan supplies a spiritual interpretation of Jack Yee's deathbed revelation of a Chinese daughter from his first marriage to Li Chen, whom he abandoned. Betty Dupree, taking the woman's point of view, insists that the ghost of Li Chen warned him that he must acknowledge his child or suffer torment in the afterlife. The arrival in the Yee household of eighteen-year-old Kwan Li, Jack's first child, introduces more ghostly secrets seen through her "yin eyes," which can view individuals in the spirit world (p. 3). The claim sets the tone and motifs of the rest of the novel.

Kwan's ghosts take a variety of poses. The wraith of a Punti merchant haunts the mission compound in Changmian. He terrorizes locals less by appearances than by the memory of his spontaneous combustion, a Gothic demise Tan may have adapted from Charles Brockden Brown's macabre novel *Wieland; or, The Transformation* (1798), in which a patriarch vanishes in a puff of smoke. Because the Chinese merchant's feet survive the immolation, folklore suggests that he has no means of departing from his former home to the afterlife. More appealing than dismemberment of a flaming merchant is the ghost of the mission gatekeeper Lao Lu, a jovial friend to Kwan in an earlier life. In the late twentieth century, he surprises her at Catholic mass by pretending to be Jesus, then by laughing at her for falling for his ruse. His good humor overrides the Western view of fearful and spooky haints by revealing a harmless trickster.

A more serious haunting is the spirit of Elza Marie Vandervort, a childhood sweetheart of Simon Bishop who dominates his thinking, causing him to compare other women and their actions and thoughts to his dead paragon. Because of her pursuit of Simon, Olivia Yee Laguni, Kwan's half-sister, remarks, "Foolish me, I didn't know I would have to pry Simon from the clutches of a ghost" (p. 84). The statement foretokens the remainder of the novel, during which Olivia hurls the disk of his novel about Elza out the window, a lame gesture intended to exorcise an obsessive love. In a later scene, he accuses Olivia of using Elza as an excuse for insecurity. As a result of the wedge the recurrent memories drives between them, Simon and Olivia part.

Tan inserts a sad moment in Kwan's return to Changmian with her recognition of the ghost of Big Ma, the mean-mouthed aunt who raised her. Their meeting after Kwan's lifetime of recriminations against her foster mother eases old heartaches at the same time that it proves that living people can be ghost-seers. Although the rural community is unaware of Big Ma's death, Kwan's knowledge of the loss is obviously correct, as corroborated by an official who reports her death in a car-bus accident that morning on the road to Guilin. The incident verifies Kwan's gift for communing with the spirit world and for delivering news from the afterlife to the living. A subsequent story about Kwan's childhood friend Buncake departs from poignance to ambiguity because of its implication of transmigration of souls after Kwan's spirit merges from her frail body into Buncake's plump frame. Tan illustrates how bodies can fail a resilient spirit. The transfer strengthens Kwan for her earthly search for old friend Nelly Banner, whom Manchus killed in 1864.

The novel's resolution completes the story of Kwan's life in the 1860s. She was known as Nunumu, a laundress for a Christian mission during the Taiping Rebellion of 1864, a terrifying upheaval in Chinese history. Through the final episodes of Nunumu's short life, Kwan clarifies the parting of lovers and their reunion after reincarnation, a Buddhist concept that Tan reprises in the vignette "How We Knew" (2003). In a tidy conclusion derived from what reviewer Claire Messud calls "eternal cosmic renewal," couples reclaim lost loves (Messud, p. 11). Tan indicates that Nelly finds a lasting romance with Yiban Johnson through the union of their twentieth-century incarnations, Olivia and Simon Bishop. At the same time, Kwan and her husband, grocery manager George Lew, requite the love of Nunumu and the potseller Zeng, who were never officially man and wife. Tan requires the sacrifice of Kwan in the falling action to assure that the Bishops have an opportunity to reunite and produce a daughter. Kwan's disappearance concludes with George's remarriage in 1994 to his cousin Virgie from Vancouver and the implication that Kwan returns to the yin world to enter the reincarnation cycle once more.

Tan contributes more ghost lore to *The Bonesetter's Daughter* (2001), another novel that attempts to settle old scores left raw-edged and dangerous in past generations. In the late twentieth century, Ruth Luyi Young recalls that her mother, LuLing Liu, warned her that shooting stars were actually "melting ghost bodies" (p. 11). Additional ghost messages come from broken crockery, barking dogs, and crank phone calls. More menacing are the ghosts of the early twentieth century. Great-Granny Liu fears maleficent spirits will attack her family if she fails to pity her dead grandson's bride, Precious Auntie, who tries to commit suicide after Liu Hu Sen's accidental death from the kick of a horse before their wedding. Double vengeance from a disgruntled bride and groom could condemn the family to a life of discontent from rancid smells and spoiled food, attacks of wild animals, and sleepless nights.

Tan retains ghost lore in family scenarios in which a member violates a trust or mistreats another relative. Requital for the Liu family's sins erupts after the nursemaid, Precious Auntie, kills herself in protest of LuLing's betrothal to Fu Nan, a son of the evil coffinmaker Chang, the murderer of Precious Auntie's father, the Bonesetter Gu. The servant's ghost, streaming tears and black gore, haunts LuLing's foster father and causes a disastrous fire that destroys his Peking headquarters and burns buildings on either side. Although the incident can be explained as a series of mishaps following a bad dream, the conflagration appears to be the work of a spiteful phantasm, a literary metaphor for Liu's guilty conscience. According to Chinese thinking, the Lius' rapid decline as magnates of the inkstick business proceeds directly from their mistreatment of Precious Auntie. Thus, Tan equates bad blood with emotional unrest that keeps a family at odds until animosities erupt in cataclysm.

Tan returns to ghost lore in *The Opposite of Fate: A Book of Musings* (2003), a collection of stories, essays, and memoirs. In the chapter entitled "Room with a View, New Kitchen, and Ghosts," she describes the second floor of the DeMatteis' San Francisco condominium as a reclaimed attic haunted by a noisy ghost. To curb its extreme misbehaviors, she calls in George, a Chinese engineer-psychic, to rid her house of the unwelcome phantom. After discerning that the ghost is female hiding in the eaves, he organizes a séance to nudge her along to the next dimension. A later segment, "The Ghosts of My Imagination," narrates the series of coincidences that gelled into *The Hundred Secret Senses* (1995). With pointed guilelessness, the author asks, "Did the ghosts of friends and family come and serve as my muses?" (p. 266). She shrugs off the obvious and reaches for an absolute, the fact that ghosts are the human need to know that love survives death and lives beyond day-to-day sensations.

See also **Kwan Li, love, suicide, superstition**

• *Further Reading*

Messud, Claire. "Ghost Story." *New York Times Book Review*, October 29 1995, p. 11.
Painter, Charlotte. "In Search of a Voice." *San Francisco Review of Books*, Summer 1989, pp. 15–17.

heritage

In describing family relationships, Tan anchors her views on self to ethnicity, language, and social milieu. In an early short-short story, "Fish Cheeks" (1987), published in *Seventeen*, she describes rock cod, tofu, squid, and dried fungus as the gustatory heritage of Asian families, even those living in the United States and celebrating Christmas Eve, a Christian holiday. To the chagrin of the family's teenage daughter, the choices reflect aspects of their new life in America that remain stubbornly Chinese. In *The Joy Luck Club* (1989), the author produces another face-to-face meeting between the Chinese past and assimilated youth. June Woo feels caught in a time warp as her mother and the other three Joy Luck Club members play mah jong in their formal silk dresses embossed over the heart with Chinese motifs. She views their garments as old-fashioned carryovers from the motherland. To reaffirm her link to a modern daughter, her mother, Suyuan Woo, asserts that, even though June was born and reared in the United States, she can't deny her Chinese traits: "Once you are born Chinese, you cannot help but feel and think Chinese" (p. 306).

Obviously, the promise of life in America is problematic for bicultural citizens. In the opinion of Lindo Jong, "In America, nobody says you have to keep the circumstances somebody else gives you" (p. 289). Contrary to Suyuan's thinking that ethnicity is undeniable, Lindo believes that opportunity in America allows for individual growth and creativity. Tan returns to this mode of thinking in *The Hundred Secret Senses* (1995), in which Olivia Yee Laguni, a Chinese-American from California, and Simon Bishop, an Amerasian from the prestigious Bishop family of Hawaii, prosper as young marrieds living in a San Francisco co-op and working out of their home as freelance photographer and writer. Ironically, as their marriage founders, the couple throw themselves into work by accepting a two-week assignment in China to cover peasant cookery. The journey acquaints them with the rudiments of rural poverty and convinces them of the joys of living in a close-knit community that shares hardships and celebrations.

In Tan's fourth novel, *The Bonesetter's Daughter* (2001), the legacy of a medical apprenticeship proves useless to Precious Auntie, a victim of her father and fiancé's deaths on her wedding day. Because women can't practice the bonesetter's art, she becomes a nursemaid. To her love child, LuLing Liu, Precious Auntie passes on a skill for reading and calligraphy that eventually offers LuLing an opportunity to immigrate to America as a guest artist. Tan illustrates the Zeitgeist, an interpretation of history that requires a pairing of the right person with a propitious point in time. Thus, LuLing outdistances her mother's frail hopes by riding the crest of women's liberation in the West. Heritage becomes a bonding agent for the next mother and daughter pair. Throughout her new life, LuLing works at painting signs with Chinese lettering, a skill that allows her self-actualization as an artisan. The meticulous job of brushing lettering onto paper creates anguish in her daughter Ruth Luyi, who never learns the knack. A mother-daughter art and writing project offers the two an opportunity for a fresh start after senile dementia begins to wither LuLing's memory. As the two work on Ruth's proposed children's book about animals, LuLing shares the matrilineal creative process with her daughter and once more feels useful. Their synergy, which emerges too late to allow the mother true satisfaction through art, restores a love that carries LuLing into old age.

See also **China, mother-daughter relationships**

• *Further Reading*

Lelyveld, Niva. "Mother as Muse: Amy Tan Had to Unravel the Mystery of Li Bingzi, Who Had Become the Voice of Her Novels." *Philadelphia Inquirer Magazine*, February 18, 2001.
O'Brien, Catherine. "What Does Life Tell Us About Love." *London Times*, December 24, 2003.
"Short Takes on Beliefs and Behavior." *San Diego Union-Tribune*, January 8, 2003, p. E3.

Hsu, An-mei

The San Francisco hostess for the pivotal mah jong game in *The Joy Luck Club* (1989), An-mei Hsu is pathetically incomplete from life without a real father and mother. Of her Chinese upbringing, she recalls, "I was taught to desire nothing, to swallow other people's misery, to eat my own bitterness" (p. 241). She pictures her scholarly father as the unsmiling visage of a large portrait that seems to stare and accuse her of wrongdoing. The past reduces her widowed mother to an anguished memory slandered by the little girl's aunt, uncle, and grandmother Popo, a bitter family motif that the author repeats in *The Kitchen God's Wife* (1991) in the story of

Winnie Louie's mother, another victim of polygyny and patriarchy. In the words of critic Amy Ling, Tan's ghosts are "what remains of a living person after her spirit has suffered the worst that it can endure" (Ling, p. 135).

Upon her unnamed mother's return in 1923 in foreign clothes, nine-year-old An-mei sees the family resemblance. The reunion generates harmful memories of being burned on the neck by hot soup at the table in 1919, when the mother abandoned An-mei. The scar symbolizes the harm done to the child's psyche before she was able to decide for herself how to relate to her absent mother. After the two travel to an uncle's house in Ningpo, he slaps his wayward sister and humiliates her for disgracing the family through concubinage to Wu Tsing. An-mei watches while her mother's ministering hands lay cool cloths on Grandmother Popo's face and serve up soup in which the mother has sliced her own flesh, a barbaric filial sacrifice demanded by the early twentieth-century Chinese concept of obedience.

An-mei chooses to leave the toxic family circle in Ningpo and follow her mother on a seven-day journey to Tientsin, leaving a little brother in tears. An-mei's makeover from dutiful Chinese reject to her mother's favored child begins with the gift of a new outfit — a Western-style white dress, stockings, shoes, and hair bow. The ensemble symbolizes her mother's liberation from old-style Chinese society, which regarded white as a mournful color and bound little girls' feet to keep them from straying from humility and submission.

Like a lavish prison, the three-story house of Wu Tsing, An-mei's new home, sits at a privileged spot near the British sector. An-mei's bed is a huge four-poster; her life is filled with luxuries, epitomized by piped-in hot water and modern plumbing. Later, she learns that Wu Tsing married her mother in 1919 after Second Wife lured her to the house to play mah jong and spend the night, when the host raped her. Because of the dishonor, Popo banned her from home, a scenario depicting a woman's betrayal of her own daughter as a show of collusion with patriarchy and of respect for male-dominated families.

Tan depicts the value of self-determination over destiny by picturing a grown-up An-mei working in San Francisco folding fortune cookies, a job she shares with Lindo Jong. Married to George Hsu, formerly a doctor in China, An-mei adopts the Baptist faith and carries a small bible to church each Sunday. After the drowning of her son Bing in the ocean at Devil's Slide, faith deserts her. She prays at length to God by the shoreline and blames herself for being careless with divine blessings. To restore balance to the family, she uses the bible as a wedge to stabilize a wobbly table, a gesture of disrespect toward the god who failed her.

Tan uses An-mei's life as a model of the completed circle, emigration followed by a return to the mother country. June Woo confides that An-mei traveled to China with two thousand dollars' worth of food and flashy California clothes as gifts for the family of her poor brother. The group from Ningbo grew so large with in-laws and cousins that An-mei impoverished herself by giving cash to twenty-six greedy people and by paying for their lodging. The costs mounted to nine thousand dollars. Tan implies that An-mei's use of American wealth to restore family relations is a waste of money and a squandering of the opportunity to reunite spiritually with her surviving kin.

See also **Hsu genealogy**

• *Further Reading*

Ling, Amy. *Between Worlds: Women Writers of Chinese Ancestry.* New York: Pergamon Press, 1990.

Tseo, George K. Y. "The Perils of Transcultural 'Translation.'" *Literature/Film Quarterly*, Vol. 24, No. 4, 1996, pp. 338–343.

Hsu genealogy

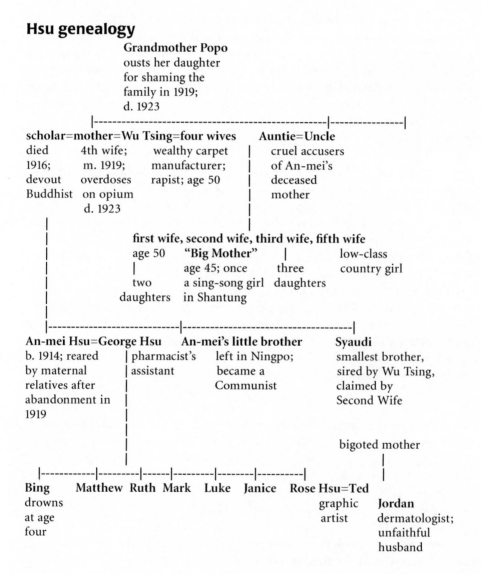

Grandmother Popo
ousts her daughter
for shaming the
family in 1919;
d. 1923

scholar=mother=Wu Tsing=four wives   **Auntie=Uncle**
died   4th wife;   wealthy carpet   cruel accusers
1916;   m. 1919;   manufacturer;   of An-mei's
devout   overdoses   rapist; age 50   deceased
Buddhist on opium   mother
          d. 1923

          first wife, second wife, third wife, fifth wife
          age 50   "Big Mother"   low-class
                     age 45; once   three   country girl
          two   a sing-song girl daughters
          daughters in Shantung

An-mei Hsu=George Hsu   An-mei's little brother   Syaudi
b. 1914; reared   pharmacist's   left in Ningpo;   smallest brother,
by maternal   assistant   became a   sired by Wu Tsing,
relatives after   Communist   claimed by
abandonment in   Second Wife
1919

                                                   bigoted mother

Bing   Matthew Ruth Mark   Luke   Janice   Rose Hsu=Ted
drowns   graphic   **Jordan**
at age   artist   dermatologist;
four   unfaithful
                                                             husband

humor

Tan's use of humor tends toward word association, situational incongruity, and dramatic irony. In *The Joy Luck Club*, the author turns phrases to her own advantage, e.g., the title "Rice Husband," a resetting of the aspersive "rice Christian" for a person who hangs out at missionary meetings in anticipation of a free meal (p. 161). Tan extends the humor of misheard phrases with Ying-ying St. Clair's malapropism of "so-so security" and the puzzling prophecies that Lindo folds into fortune cookies (p. 275). One racy pun in Suyuan Woo's misperception is her tenant's insult: "Call me worst Fukien landlady. I not from Fukien" (p. 224). One witticism illustrates Chinese chauvinism. During Waverly's toying with her mother, Lindo Jong, over the morning's tortuous hair-plaiting ritual, Lindo assures her daughter that the Chinese are the best at all endeavors—business, medicine, painting, and torture. At a serious point in Rose Hsu Jordan's divorce, Tan highlights a fortune-cookie aphorism offering a painful truth: a husband who neglects his garden is "thinking of pulling up roots," a true estimation of Ted Jordan's disloyalty to his wife (p. 215).

Similarly, in *The Kitchen God's Wife* (1991), Tan's humor accompanies some of the painful scenarios and tragedies that color the lives of two interconnected families, the Kwongs and the Louies. Among the verbal gaffes are Helen's misidentification of Pearl's disease as "multiple neurosis," Helen's "B nine" brain tumor, Cleo Brandt's interest in dingbats at the zoo, and Winnie's memories of luxuries during wartime, which she compares to a fractured version of an English adage, "Eat, drink, be married" (pp. 36, 523, 372). Winnie Louie corrects her daughter Pearl's question about a stroke as the cause of Auntie Du's death with a terse reply, "A bus" (p. 6). At Winnie's flower shop, Winnie uses the cash register to hold "ends and odds and evens," a splicing of idioms that reflects the jumbled understanding of a Chinese immigrant (p. 15).

Tan's skill at juxtaposition turns humor into a pair of bookends embracing the framework story's heinous conclusion. Winnie cleverly humiliates Wen Fu and his haughty wife at the telegraph office by forcing him to sign divorce papers before accepting a registered package of donkey dung. His retaliation is swift and evil—stalking Winnie to her apartment and raping her at gunpoint. To save her exit documents and plane tickets, she once more submits to his degrading sexual assault. The arrival of Helen, a bumptious *deus ex machina*, concludes with Wen Fu cowering half naked as Winnie holds him at gunpoint and Helen tosses his pants out the window to dissuade her from committing murder. Suitably abased, Wen Fu must depart degraded and whipped with his lower half disclosed, the part of his body that he has used to torment and abase Winnie and other female conquests. Although the villain suffers, Tan illustrates how Winnie's boldness costs her a lifetime of worry about the siring of her daughter.

In religious discussions between Kwan and Olivia Yee in *The Hundred Secret Senses* (1995), a cynical attitude toward the power of the Virgin Mary and toward the worshipper's ability to see Jesus creates a humorous undertone. Several remarks produce comic relief, particularly the choice of Dr. Too Late and Pastor Amen as names for white men at the mission compound. Contributing to the humor of services held in the Ghost Merchant's House is the minister's use of his house staff as claques, who shout "Amen" every time he raises his eyebrows. Chinese traditions are equally droll, for example, Lao Lu's belief that an angry God of War can drop horse manure from the sky. Instead of translating Pastor Amen's sermons to the Chinese congregation, Nelly Banner uses the opportunity to relate a fairy tale, episode by episode, which is more interesting than a dry Christian homily.

At a crucial moment in Kwan's relationship with her half-sister Olivia, Kwan explains the different sites in the next world. To quell Olivia's fear that the afterlife is segregated, Kwan explains that people reunite with what they loved on earth. Those loving Jesus or Allah spend eternity in either a Christian or Islamic heaven. For agnostics, she describes a Disney heaven where spirits can try out various heavenly options at no charge. Her litany continues with a heaven similar to a medical waiting room and with the Jewish Zion, which she compares to an upscale resort. She adds, "You love sleep, go sleep" (p. 111). Tan's flippant remark expresses her disdain for early missionary efforts to convert the Chinese to Christianity.

Kwan's continued quick thinking enables her to live as Nunumu among the foolish missionaries on her own terms. To steal salt for curing thousand-year-old duck eggs, she states to Dr. Too Late that she needs salt to remove stains from the laundry. To demonstrate, she embarrasses him by displaying Miss Mouse's panties, stained with menstrual blood. To Nunumu, "It was a Jesus miracle!" (p. 190). She presses on with curing eggs, using pages from "The Good News," a Christian pamphlet, to wrap the eggs for the drying process. The relegation of religious propaganda to culinary use confirms Tan's wry depiction of the lasting effect of Christian proselytizing in China.

Humor lightens the darker moments of *The Bonesetter's Daughter* (2001), which depict the mother's mental decline generating agitation in daughter Ruth Young. During Dr. Huey's examination of LuLing Liu Young, he asks her to name the last five presidents in reverse order. She sidetracks to welfare and mutters, "I don't get welfare. What so fair? No fair. Only make people lazy to work!" (p. 58). In addition to "non sequiturs, as free-floating as dust motes," her malapropisms continue with reference to layered Chinese bell tones as "Buddha-ful" (pp. 87, 298). In the epilogue, the layered memories of the past reunite LuLing with the spirit of Precious Auntie and offer an opportunity for atonement. While LuLing slides into deeper levels of dementia, Precious Auntie's upbeat ghost develops into the matrilineal voice that guides Ruth's career change from book doctor to novelist.

See also **mother-daughter relationships**

• *Further Reading*

Benedict, Kitty. "Mother to Daughter: Here Is the Truth of My Life." *Hartford Courant*, June 30, 1991, p. C10.
See, Carolyn. "Drowning in America, Starving for China." *Los Angeles Times Book Review*, March 12, 1989, pp. 1, 11.

The Hundred Secret Senses

Amy Tan draws on a prickly sisterhood between an Amerasian, Olivia Yee Laguni, and Kwan Li, her Chinese half-sister in *The Hundred Secret Senses* (1995), a hopeful tale of cultural legacies from disparate homelands. The third of Tan's novels, the book earned kudos from numerous reviewers. Gail Caldwell of the *Boston Globe* acknowledged the author's wisdom and skill at engrossing narration. Penelope Mesic, book editor for the *Chicago Tribune*, lauded the work's consistency of action and abundant detail. Their commentary focuses on Tan's most refined quality, her gift for complex storytelling.

To establish contrast in outlook, the author follows the clash between the two sisters from Olivia's viewpoint. The variance produces a rich source of conflict, irony, and humor. Unlike Tan's first two novels, which derive from simple memories, the third novel relies on spectacle and spiritualism that connect thoughts and experiences one hundred and thirty years apart. The author divulged to interviewer Gretchen Giles, "The word *ghost* itself is so very tainted with assumptions and negative connotations that you're whacked out if you believe that such things exist. But when I was about two-thirds of the way through writing this book, I really felt that I couldn't deny any longer that I get help from somewhere" (Giles). Whether wisps of family talk-story or actual ghosts, the outside help strengthens the author's double-layered story.

The amalgamation of late twentieth-century marital angst with the Taiping Rebellion of 1864 takes Tan far afield from the emotional territory of her first two novels. In counterpoint against the magical realism of Kwan's vivid spirit world and time-tripping across serious emotional geography, Olivia describes the growing-up years of a cynical Californian. She disdains Christianity, longs to appear on Art Linkletter's program *Kids Say the Darndest Things*, and connives with peers who ridicule Kwan. During the rebellion of West Coast youth against the Vietnam War, Olivia spends part of her college experience smoking pot with her future husband and discussing various beliefs about immortality while ignoring Kwan's intense mothering. Olivia's ongoing slight fails to alter Kwan's focus on the past or to dim her faith in teaching Olivia Chinese attitudes and values.

In a climactic chapter, Tan develops the purpose of the novel's title. Olivia, desperate to rid herself and her lover of Elza Marie Vandervort's ghost, acknowledges Kwan's expertise as an adviser by asking her help. In reply, Kwan explains that she must call on her hundred secret senses to locate the spirit of a Polish Jew. She describes the secret receptors as a human phenomenon, a divine natal gift in the style of William Wordsworth's lines from stanza five of *Intimations of Immortality* (1807): "Trailing clouds of glory do we come/From God, who is our home" (ll. 64–65, p. 588). As the poet indicates, these divine abilities erode in most people during maturation.

Kwan's reading of her senses is essential in passing messages between the living and dead. She illustrates inter-world communication by chatting with Elza, who identifies herself by her Polish birth name, Wakowski. Kwan furthers her sister's romance by telling Simon that Elza wants him to forget his former love. The moment establishes for Olivia that she, too, can see Elza's ghost, who pleads with Simon to wait until she returns. When the deceit from Kwan's séance follows Olivia and Simon to their wedding, a Pacific fog rolls over the gathering at Golden Gate Park, a metaphoric haze that threatens the survival of their union.

At the high point of the novel, Karmic retribution, a Gothic element, takes control of the narrative. To achieve sibling understanding, Olivia and Kwan visit Changmian village in China and probe past events. Tan chose the village from her experience while filming *The Joy Luck Club* at Bei Sa Po at an ingrown Hakka hamlet near Thistle Mountain outside Guilin. A Rip Van Winkle atmosphere derived from lack of plumbing, communication, and paved roads and the reliance of locals on their own dialect. Beyond lay rocky ruins and caves and signs of abandonment some centuries past. To Tan, it seemed "a forbidden realm [where] something terrible had happened" (p. 253).

Tan enlivens the setting with a meeting between the modern world and China's rural outback. In the plot, the unforeseen death of Kwan's aunt, Big Ma, prefaces a sad exchange between Kwan and her aunt's ghost. Their chat gives Kwan an opportunity to explain the hundred secret senses of the title, the human sensors that communicate in "heart-talk" (p. 237). The text identifies these mystic senses as "related to primitive instincts," a kind of intuitive transmission that links people who share the same family tree (*Ibid.*). Tan joins the abstract with the concrete in Kwan's return to the cave she sheltered in during her former life. The camaraderie of Kwan with Olivia at the site heals the sisters' differences of opinion about love and loyalty and opens Olivia's heart to her need for Simon. Tan explained the revelations of visiting a site long abandoned: "When we come back to a place, we have feelings of both nostalgia and chagrin. Sort of a sadness that things have changed, a pride in things that have become better" (Kanner, p. 3). The author noted that the alteration is internal rather than external: "It really is more a reflection of who we are and how our expectations and hopes have changed over time" (*Ibid.*). Gracing the reunion of husband and wife is their daughter Samantha Li, a miracle child born out of love and the martyrdom of Kwan, who disappears underground. The motif of buried or underground secrets supports the supernatural ending and returns even stronger in the author's fourth novel, *The Bonesetter's Daughter* (2001). In both novels, the act of retrieving a hidden past relieves characters of tensions and restores a wholeness of spirit that strengthens and affirms them.

See also **ghosts, Yee genealogy**

• *Further Reading*

Caldwell, Gail. "Review: *The Hundred Secret Senses*." *Boston Globe*, October 22, 1995, p. B37.

Fortuna, Diana. "Review: *The Hundred Secret Senses*." *America*, Vol. 174, No. 14, May 4, 1996, pp. 27–28.

Giles, Gretchen. "Ghost Writer." *Sonoma Independent*, December 14–20, 1995.

Kanner, Ellen. "From Amy Tan, a Superb Novel of Two Sisters, Two Worlds, and a Few Ghosts." *Bookpage*, December 1995, p. 3.

Ma, Sheng-mei. "'Chinese and Dogs' in Amy Tan's 'The Hundred Secret Senses': Ethnicizing the Primitive à la New Age." *MELUS*, Vol. 26, No. 1, Spring 2001, pp. 29–44.

_____. *The Deathly Embrace: Orientalism and Asian American Identity*. Minneapolis: University of Minnesota Press, 2000

Mesic, Penelope. "Review: *The Hundred Secret Senses*." *Chicago Tribune*, November 9, 1995, p. 16.

Wordsworth, William. *The Works of William Wordsworth*. Ware, Herts.: Cumberland House, 1994.

imbalance

The importance of balance to Chinese people recurs in Tan's fiction as a sub-textural yearning for peace and contentment. In *The Joy Luck Club* (1989), characters worry about the alignment of apartments and furniture, the two ends of a wedding candle, replacement of missing chessmen, leveling of uneven table legs, chic asymmetrical haircuts, a broken nose, a face marred on one side by a surgeon's scalpel, a pair of piano pieces by Robert Schumann, even the number of legs on a damaged crab. Ying-ying St. Clair dislikes her family's new apartment atop one of San Francisco's hills. Before the birth of the Cliffords' second child, Ying-ying repairs imbalances in her life by rearranging canned food, a mirror, and furniture as though *feng shui* can dispel danger and restore her lost confidence. The actions prove futile in preserving their doomed infant or reviving Ying-ying's enthusiasm for life.

The fear of imbalance recurs in the life of Ying-ying's daughter Lena. During a visit to Lena, the mother-in-law sizes up disparities in her husband, architect Harold Livotny, who remodeled a barn into their trendy home. The tipsy bedside table and wobbly vase collapse, causing Lena to rush upstairs to protect her mother. More threatening to family harmony is the off-kilter marriage that Harold thrusts on Lena. She despairs at his specious demands for splitting the rent, restaurant bills, and cost of incidentals. Ying-ying tries to strengthen her daughter to discard the shallow union and take what is rightfully hers.

A similar imbalance ends the marriage of Dr. Ted Jordan to Rose Hsu, a shy, self-effacing woman. Rose's constant ceding of will to her husband's tastes and choices foreshadows the demise of their relationship. After Ted moves out of their spacious home, Rose learns of his adultery and intent to remarry. A settlement check for ten thousand dollars illustrates how little she means to Ted, a wealthy dermatologist. With the help of her mother An-mei, Rose finds the courage to combat his coercive methods by allowing the meticulously manicured yard to grow wild and by demanding that he sign the house over to her. Her rebellion, which takes the form of advancing weeds in the flagstones, implies that she has acquired the backbone to fend for herself without the aid of a protective male.

The most significant imbalance in Tan's first novel is the separation of family that grieves Suyuan Woo, a war widow. Throughout her second marriage, she continues to write contacts in China concerning the twin girls she had to abandon as Japanese forces pressed south toward Kweilin, China. After her death, Canning Woo, her kind husband, assumes that the longing to reunite with the twins may have exploded in her brain, killing her instantly. To resolve multiple forms of imbalance, June agrees to sit at her mother's place at the mah jong table and to accept a gift of twelve hundred dollars in travel funds to return to China and meet her half-sisters, Chwun Yu and Chwun Hwa Wang. The reunion creates a tripartite image of Suyuan made up of the features of her three adult daughters. Tan suggests that family unity is the most valuable form of *feng shui* for its union of members, who draw strength from each other as they grieve for their dead mother.

A consistent struggle for familial balance grieves Winnie Louie, an autobiographical characterization of Daisy Tan in daughter Amy's *The Kitchen God's Wife*

(1991). Winnie comes of age on the cusp of social upheaval that releases Chinese women from feudal patriarchy. Battling an undertow that overvalues husbands and fathers, she realizes that responsibility to her children requires an end to a violent marital relationship based mainly on sexual and domestic servitude to Wen Fu, an unpredictable psychopath. To achieve safety and serenity, she has no choice but divorce him and accept the marriage proposal of Jimmy Louie, a sweet-natured American soldier.

Tan illustrates the pain that pioneering women undergo as they reestablish stasis in otherwise wretched lives. Several false starts precede Winnie's divorce, which concludes in 1949 with Wen Fu's vindictive return to rape and terrorize her at gunpoint. In her new life in California, she continues to battle him mentally late in widowhood, when she and daughter Pearl unknot the final snarl in Winnie's peace of mind. By acknowledging that Pearl was born of rape, Winnie relaxes from a lifetime of worry. As though exorcising Wen Fu from both their lives, she burns the picture of the wicked Kitchen God and substitutes a woman-made deity, whom she names "Lady Sorrowfree" (p. 532). The act elevates downtrodden females with the blessing of a divine authority who rules a womanly domain, Pearl's kitchen.

In 2003, Tan published *The Opposite of Fate: A Book of Musings*, in which she accounts for a series of coincidences that gave her details and focus for *The Hundred Secret Senses* (1995). After encountering an Asian man stacking rocks into spires on the beach, she learned from him that the pieces stayed erect because of balance. She realized that the plot she was creating needed the image of balance. In gratitude to the "collective unconscious," she thanked an unseen force for yielding "research, contacts, connections, images, and meanings" (p. 262).

Balance retained its importance in Tan's fourth novel, *The Bonesetter's Daughter* (2001). One of the clues to LuLing Liu's mental decline is her inability to write Chinese characters with a brush, a skill that earned her a sizeable reputation for accuracy and classic style. From childhood, Ruth remembers her mother's explanation of her tutor's philosophy of writing: "Each stroke has its own rhythm, its balance, its proper place" (p. 48). The philosophy extends to all aspects of life. After the onset of senile dementia, LuLing flounders in the present and scours the past for release from a terrible sin against her mother, a source of imbalance that fosters severe self-torment.

The restoration of balance in the mother-daughter relationship requires a major revamping of the extended family's lives. Tan depicts Ruth in the act of daughter-becoming-parent by selecting a retirement home, Mira Mar Manor, to care for Lu-Ling. For a shared activity in their idle hours, Ruth sets LuLing to drawing animals for a children's book. The picture of the two working together reprises memories of the matrilineal past: Just as Precious Auntie taught LuLing calligraphy, LuLing taught Ruth. At story's end, while LuLing gradually loses her memory of meticulous Chinese characters, Ruth encourages her to ink-brush simple animal shapes. The change in Ruth inspires a sweeping alteration of her career from book doctor for other people's self-help books to original family-inspired stories.

See also **Rose Hsu Jordan, mother-daughter relationships, Ying-ying St. Clair, Suyuan Woo, yin and yang**

• *Further Reading*

Hamilton, Patricia L. "Feng Shui, Astrology, and the Five Elements: Traditional Chinese Belief in Amy Tan's *The Joy Luck Club*." *MELUS*, Vol. 24, No. 2, Summer 1999, pp. 125–145.
Heung, Marina. "Daughter-Text/Mother-Text: Matrilineage in Amy Tan's Joy Luck Club." *Feminist Studies*, Vol. 19, No. 3, Fall 1993, pp. 597–616.

Jiang Sao-yen

The all-too-human father of Winnie Louie in *The Kitchen God's Wife* (1991), Jiang Sao-yen epitomizes the luxurious, self-indulgent lifestyle of the wealthy industrial class in the early twentieth century and its appeasement of the Japanese after their takeover of Shanghai in September 1937. He holds a prestigious place in the city and elevates his brother by establishing him in a sizeable mansion on Tsungming Island. Because Jiang fails to visit his daughter at boarding school, Winnie recalls few face-to-face encounters with him. The height of father-daughter interaction occurs after the negotiation of a bride price when the matchmaker betrothes her to Wen Fu. Jiang agrees to a ruinous marriage; however, his gift of four thousand yuan is a liberating force that keeps her solvent during the war years and allows her some autonomy in a society that tends to confine and depersonalize women.

National conflict alters community and familial relations, changing the fragile relationship of Winnie with Jiang. At the end of World War II, the Wen family's hopeful return east from Kunming to Shanghai causes Wen Fu to anticipate a home with a privileged family. Secretly, Winnie fantasizes Jiang's stern intervention against a monstrous husband. On arrival at the house on Julu Road, she realizes that Jiang has suffered direct contact with an enemy that forced him to capitulate emotionally. Weakened by a stroke, he bears the shame of having collaborated with the Japanese to keep his Five Phoenixes Textile Trading companies in business. San Ma, the third wife, fills in details of his defiant gesture of hurling tea at an heirloom painting to register a wordless rejection of the insidious Japanese. The servant characterizes Jiang's aphasia as duality — one side of his face maintains dignity; the other wears his defeat. Tan's empathy for his sufferings defies critical sneers that she fails to flesh out male characters.

After Japan's surrender in August 1945, the struggle for closure continues for men like Jiang. For accommodating the enemy, he earns the scorn of the Kuomintang, which returns to power with a vengeful agenda against collaborators. In forgiving her father, Winnie advances in compassion. She realizes that she can accuse Jiang of treachery only if she issues equal blame toward her mother for abandoning her. Out of sympathy for all parties in wartime, Winnie is able to suspend judgment on her parents as well as on herself. She ponders Jiang's mistreatment of her mother and his disinterest in his daughter and chooses to remain loyal to Jimmy Louie rather than protect her ailing, mentally foggy parent.

The late-in-life emergence of forgiveness and mercy in Jiang elevates him as a character and as a symbol of domestic justice for women. Although his son-in-law uses the past against Jiang by threatening to turn him over to the Kuomintang for execution as a turncoat, the old man quickly perceives Wen Fu's battery of his wife and sides with his beleaguered daughter, even if loyalty to her costs him everything. Jiang's gift of three gold ingots, hidden in the rod of an heirloom scroll, indicates what his wordlessness can't express. Symbolically, the wall hanging pictures spring, a vision of hope. Winnie, experiencing a springlike rejuvenation of family unity, allows herself to believe that Jiang loves her.

Tan creates in Jiang's recovery a hopeful gesture toward handicapped people. In 1948, a masterful self-control returns in his final hours, when he regains his voice, sits up in bed, even opens a window. Demanding and lordly, he complains that his room is shabby and stripped of paintings and rugs, elements of his opulent pre-war lifestyle that the Japanese stole. He refuses an invalid's pap and eats normal food. As proof of mental acuity, like a child pulling a string from a cat, he torments Wen Fu by claiming to forget where he stored gold in the house. Within three hours, Jiang is dead, leaving Wen Fu and his father in a tizzy to locate hidden treasure. The end-of-life joke elevates Jiang's final words to the last laugh on a parasitic son-in-law.

See also **Jiang genealogy, men, patriarchy, pride, wisdom**

• *Further Reading*

Chung, L. A. "Chinese American Literary War: Writers, Critics Argue Over Portrayal of Asians." *San Francisco Chronicle*, August 26, 1991, p. D4.

Huntley, E. D. *Amy Tan: A Critical Companion.* Westport, Conn.: Greenwood Press, 1998.

Jiang genealogy

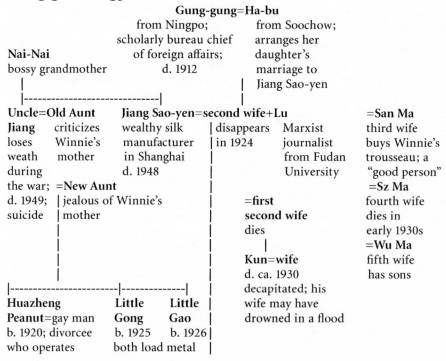

```
                          Gung-gung=Ha-bu
                    from Ningpo;        from Soochow;
                    scholarly bureau chief   arranges her
Nai-Nai             of foreign affairs;     daughter's
bossy grandmother       d. 1912            marriage to
  |                                      |  Jiang Sao-yen
  |----------------------------|         |
Uncle=Old Aunt    Jiang Sao-yen=second wife+Lu          =San Ma
Jiang   criticizes   wealthy silk     | disappears  Marxist    third wife
loses   Winnie's     manufacturer     | in 1924     journalist  buys Winnie's
weath   mother       in Shanghai      |             from Fudan  trousseau; a
during               d. 1948          |             University  "good person"
the war;  =New Aunt                   |                         =Sz Ma
d. 1949;  | jealous of Winnie's       |                         fourth wife
suicide   | mother                    |      =first             dies in
          |                           |      second wife        early 1930s
          |                           |      dies               =Wu Ma
          |                           |        |                fifth wife
          |                           |      Kun=wife           has sons
          |                           |      d. ca. 1930
          |                           |      decapitated; his
  |----------------------|-------------| |   wife may have
Huazheng        Little      Little  |       drowned in a flood
Peanut=gay man  Gong        Gao     |
b. 1920; divorcee b. 1925   b. 1926 |
who operates    both load metal     |
```

```
a Shanghai         on the docks    |
shelter for        after the war   |
battered women                     |
     |                             |
adopted son                        |
purchased to conceal               |
the husband's homosexuality        |
                                   |
```

        Wen Fu=**Jiang Weili "Winnie"**=**James Y. "Jimmy" Louie**
        m. 1937; divorced 1949   m. 1949

        See also **Louie genealogy**

Jong, Lindo

In *The Joy Luck Club* (1989), Tan characterizes Lindo Jong as cruelly competitive and brutally frank, two traits of people born under the sign of the horse. Lindo
suffers from the misery of a brokered betrothal, which selected her future husband,
Tyan-yu Huang, when she was two years old and her fiancé was only a year old. A
decade later, her marriage date is set by fate after the Fen River forces the family to
flee to Wushi. Her parents leave her behind with the Huang family. She accredits the
misery of wedlock with a selfish boy-child to rural customs in Taiyuan long out of
style in more up-to-date Chinese cities. Critic Ben Xu explains Lindo's mindset:
"Chinese Taoist culture helps to maintain this kind of victim mentality because it
reinforces a passive if not fatalist attitude toward life" (Xu).

On her wedding day, Lindo epitomizes the Chinese woman's clever fight against
silencing and coercion. She identifies with the wind, an invisible force that blows the
river and shapes topography. Using her own breath, she initiates autonomy by blowing out half of the two-ended nuptial candle, a symbol of her one-sided union with
Tyan-yu. With new faith in independence, she is able to accept the arranged nuptial
while guarding her true self. Tan intensifies Lindo's need to face a legalistic marriage
that can't be dissolved and that requires the groom's widow to remain unmarried
upon his death. To make the Huang family allow her a divorce, she chooses a propitious day on the Chinese calendar and fakes a prophetic nightmare. Her histrion-
ics trick them into thinking that their son must marry a divinely chosen servant girl,
who allegedly was born of royal blood. The divorce gives Lindo a second chance at
the same time that it feeds her illusion of autonomy and control.

Lindo retains duplicity as a means to many ends. After working twelve years as
a telephone operator, she lies about being a student of religion, becomes an American resident, and wears a suitable face for the demands of a new country. Ironically,
while defying destiny, she takes a cheap flat and works in a fortune cookie factory.
As the wife of Tin Jong and the mother of two sons and a daughter, she is demanding and self-adulatory. In *The Opposite of Fate: A Book of Musings* (2003), the author
reflects on Lindo's relationship with daughter Waverly as "double jeopardy" because
the mother functions as both ally and adversary (p. 109). After Waverly becomes a
national chess champion at age nine, Lindo takes the credit for thinking up winning
strategies. She pretends to complain to An-mei Hsu about having to dust all the

trophies, an unsubtle self-congratulation that annoys her old friend. Lindo continues to challenge her willful daughter and, at age sixty-nine, wears what Waverly describes as a "tight-lipped, pinch-nosed look," a description that characterizes a willful mother (*The Joy Luck Club*, p. 182).

The sneaky behavior that saves Lindo from her first marriage persists into old age. To outflank Suyuan Woo, Lindo and her friend "ceaselessly [torment] each other with boasts and secrets" (p. 194). Lindo plays a destructive game of comparing June Woo, a thirty-six-year-old ad copywriter, to her brilliant daughter Waverly, who is much more successful as a tax attorney. To belittle June, Lindo pretends to inquire about her education, which June left incomplete after two years of college. The badgering cruelly diminishes June, who lacks the psychological weapons to fight both Lindo and Waverly.

After Waverly grows up, Lindo's pride migrates from chess trophies to cookery. When she learns that Waverly's new love, Rich Schields, raved over Suyuan's dinner, Lindo immediately issues an invitation to outdo Auntie Su. The trial by food swings back to favor the mother as Waverly's fiancé makes gaffe after gaffe at dinner, climaxing in the addition of soy sauce to her prize pork dish. To save the mother-daughter relationship, she surprises Waverly and Rich by suggesting that she accompany them on a honeymoon to China, an opportunity for Waverly to survey her cultural roots and to appreciate her parentage. The gesture suggests a mellowing of Lindo's subtle maneuverings, but leaves opportunities for her to continue needling Rich and Waverly on the journey.

After Suyuan Woo's death, Lindo's manipulative ways resurge in a less sinister setting. When a letter from Chwun Yu and Chwun Hwa, Suyuan's grown twin daughters, arrives from Shanghai, Lindo replies as though Suyuan were still alive. Craftily, Lindo plots to send June Woo in her mother's place at the long-awaited family reunion. By engineering an emotional confrontation with June over the mah jong table, Lindo elicits the response she intended—June admits that she didn't appreciate her mother. Tan suggests that a triumph for one mother extends to all the aunties, who share concerns that they have lost influence over their daughters' behavior.

See also **fate and fortune, Waverly Jong, Jong genealogy, mother-daughter relationships, social class, yin and yang**

• *Further Reading*

Hamilton, Patricia L. "Feng Shui, Astrology, and the Five Elements: Traditional Chinese Belief in Amy Tan's *The Joy Luck Club*." *MELUS*, Vol. 24, No. 2, Summer 1999, pp. 125–145.

Miner, Valerie. "The Daughters' Journeys." *Nation*, Vol. 248, No. 16, April 24, 1989, pp. 566–569.

Tseo, George K. Y. "The Perils of Transcultural 'Translation.'" *Literature/Film Quarterly*, Vol. 24, No. 4, 1996, pp. 338–343.

Xu, Ben. "Memory and the Ethnic Self: Reading Amy Tan's *The Joy Luck Club*." *MELUS*, Vol. 19, No. 1, 1994 Spring, pp. 3–19.

Jong, Waverly

Waverly Jong, a hard-edged daughter in *The Joy Luck Club* (1989), excuses her thin-skinned nature as the result of birth in the year of the rabbit. She grows up in the confines of San Francisco's Chinatown at Waverly Place, a picturesque two-block expanse near what was once known as Tien Hau Miew Gai or the Temple of the Heavenly Queen, built in 1911. Affectionately called Meimei or Little Sister, Waverly belies the image of a tender child. She nurtures a lust for power at age eight, when she learns to play chess. To comprehend complex rules, she checks out books from the library that explain the uniqueness of each chess piece and its moves. As though preparing for her career as a tax attorney, she learns "why tactics between two adversaries are like clashing ideas" (p. 95). From chess strategies, she learns foresight, patience, and assessment of an opponent's weak and strong points as well as the ability to throw up invisible barriers to protect her position. The insidious nature of her chess-playing bears the traits that allowed her mother, Lindo Jong, to escape an unfulfilling first marriage and emigrate to America.

Even though Waverly acquires notoriety in Chinatown, skill at chess depersonalizes her relationships with others. Turning chess matches into mystic experiences, she becomes adept at getting out of jams by assessing all possible moves before committing herself to action. Within a year of competitive play, she becomes a national chess champion with her photo displayed in *Life* magazine. To friend June Woo, Waverly displays arrogance, a quality that follows her into adulthood. Conceit riddles her interpersonal exchanges with lacerating comments and self-serving observations that critic Wendy Ho describes as "self-erected psychological barriers" (Ho, p. 22).

Despite her power over June, Tan depicts Waverly as a failure at escaping an adversarial relationship with her overly proud mother, depicted as a yellow-eyed tiger. Critic Marina Heung characterizes Waverly's disaffection as matrophobia, the fear that she will absorb her mother's worst traits. Fleeing a fantasy pursuer into the back alleys of Chinatown, Waverly becomes a pawn on a life-sized board. She hates being the tool of her mother, yet echoes Lindo's exorbitant pride after June Woo's failed piano performance by muttering, "You aren't a genius like me" (pp. 151, 228). The statement still carries a sting in June's memory a quarter century later, after Waverly advances to the post of tax attorney at San Francisco's impressive Bank of America building. To salve the hurt, Suyuan Woo dismisses Waverly's clever putdowns as "always walking sideways, moving crooked" like a crab (p. 235). The simile is one of Tan's many unflattering comparisons between human and bestial behaviors.

The downfall of Tan's Chinese-American superwoman occurs in 1987, when Waverly hesitates to tell her overly critical mother about plans to marry a second husband, Rich Schields. Waverly recalls at age ten trying to outflank Lindo and stop her bragging by refusing to compete in chess tournaments. The ruse backfires on the perpetrator, who loses a national competition when she returns to play and fails to summon the confidence she calls her "magic armor" (p. 190). Ironically, she loses, not to a competitor, but to her mother. By age fourteen, Waverly quits the game in utter defeat. To Caucasian friend Marlene Ferber, Waverly is unable to explain the hold that Chinese mothers maintain over their daughters. The admission carries autobiographical significance from Tan's lengthy battles with Daisy, her mother and chief mentor.

Waverly appears to mature during the romance with Rich Schields. As he increases demands on their intimacies, she admits to herself a list of hidden faults— meanness, pettiness, and self-loathing. Most destructive to her happiness with Rich is the fear that Lindo will ruin the glow of a new love with her treacherous remarks and criticisms. Too late, Waverly admits, "In her hands, I always became the pawn" (p. 199). With mature eyes, she is able to look at the elderly form of her mother limp with sleep and envision her dead "when I was having terrible thoughts about her" (p. 200). The sudden making up after years of antipathy results in plans for Lindo to accompany her daughter and new son-in-law on a honeymoon journey to China. The scene concludes with the image of the three of them sharing a row of plane seats as the flight moves them from the West to the East, the reversal of the diaspora that brought Lindo to America.

See also **Lindo Jong, Jong genealogy, secrets, June Woo**

• *Further Reading*

Gates, David. "A Game of Show Not Tell." *Newsweek*, Vol. 113, No. 16, April 17, 1989, pp. 68–69.

Heung, Marina. "Daughter-Text/Mother-Text: Matrilineage in Amy Tan's Joy Luck Club." *Feminist Studies*, Vol. 19, No. 3, Fall 1993, pp. 597–616.

Ho, Wendy. *In Her Mother's House — The Politics of Asian American Mother-Daughter Writing*. Walnut Creek, Calif.: AltaMira Press, 1999.

Kim, Elaine H. "'Such Opposite Creatures': Men and Women in Asian American Literature." *Michigan Quarterly Review*, Vol. 29, No. 1, pp. 68–93.

Koenig, Rhoda. "Heirloom China." *New York*, Vol. 22, No. 12, March 20, 1989, pp. 82–83.

Wong, Sau-ling Cynthia. *Reading Asian American Literature: From Necessity to Extravagance*. Princeton, N.J.: Princeton University Press, 1993.

Jong genealogy

             Dr. Sun Yat-sen
             distant relative
                    •
                    •

             mother
             separated from
             her daughter by
             a flood
Huang Taitai |
a fierce mother-in-law |
whose weakness is |
social climbing |
      | |
      Tyan-yu=**Lindo Sun Jong**=**Tin Jong**
      Huang   b. 1918 | Cantonese immigrant

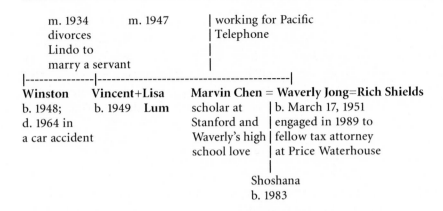

```
    m. 1934        m. 1947     | working for Pacific
    divorces                   | Telephone
    Lindo to                   |
    marry a servant            |
|--------------|---------------------------------------------|
Winston      Vincent+Lisa    Marvin Chen = Waverly Jong=Rich Shields
b. 1948;     b. 1949  Lum    scholar at   | b. March 17, 1951
d. 1964 in                   Stanford and | engaged in 1989 to
a car accident               Waverly's high| fellow tax attorney
                             school love  | at Price Waterhouse
                                          |
                                      Shoshana
                                      b. 1983
```

Jordan, Rose Hsu

The middle child of the seven children born to An-mei and George Hsu in *The Joy Luck Club* (1989), Rose Hsu lives in a confident family. They trust Christian faith until it fails them when Rose's little brother Bing drowns on the California coast. Rose feels so much guilt at not protecting him from slipping from a reef into the ocean that she frees herself from adult responsibilities by letting others make decisions for her. By repositioning herself as the helpless child, she takes Bing's place and remains open to rescue by mature, stronger-willed people.

A false self-image delays Rose Hsu's development as a whole person. At the University of California at Berkeley during her second semester of liberal arts study, she meets Ted Jordan, a pre-med student who frees her from adult demands arising from "too many choices" (p. 191). Tan characterizes the couple as a father-daughter relationship rather than an equal man-woman union. Ted's choice of dermatology as a major also implies that he relies on a surface-level understanding of his wife that remains only skin deep.

The Jordans' hasty wedding grows out of a rescue motif by which Ted saves Rose from his mother's disapproval of Asians. Willingly, Rose plays the part of victim in need of protection and lapses into a pattern of inaction. After settling into a Victorian house in Ashbury Heights, a symbol of the patriarchal English marriage, she opens a free-lance graphics studio downstairs, but defers household decisions to Ted. After his own self-confidence withers following a malpractice suit, he lacks a mature wife to lean on. He wearies of her wishy-washy nature and drifts into an affair. She has a child-like fear of confessing to her mother the dissolution of her union with Ted lest An-mei insist that she try harder to preserve the marriage. In the opinion of her mother, Rose's compliant nature lacks wood or stability, one of the five elements that promises balance to human life.

Ted's chief complaint of his wife is her shilly-shallying, yet he attempts to manipulate her by cancelling her choices. His divorce negotiations propose a lose-lose situation for Rose with a demand that she accept ten thousand dollars in exchange for relinquishing the house. Friend Waverly Jong applauds Rose for parting with "an emotional wimp" (p. 211). Lena St. Clair Livotny urges Rose to hire a lawyer to get even with Ted for belittling and exploiting her. Rose concludes that fate is created from equal portions of expectation and inattention, an element that shifts much of the blame to her. For the first time, she acknowledges her lack of volition and alters her thinking from victim to fighter. While in therapy, she undergoes an epiphany and confides to Lena that Chinese humility makes women feel undeserving.

Tan champions Rose's ability to abandon a lifetime of faulty thinking and of accepting other people's opinions of her. Like Winnie Louie in *The Kitchen God's Wife* (1991), Rose learns to make her own luck. A dream offers a new perspective on her mother-daughter relationship with An-mei. In the scenario, the mother seeds Rose's planter box with weeds, which spring up and wander in all directions. Rose interprets the dream as proof that her mother accepts her and her faults. After abandoning friendly advice and psychiatric evaluation, Rose asserts her own desires by allowing the over-manicured yard to flourish and by rejecting Ted's offer of cash for the house. Freed of the strict obedience expected of Chinese women, Rose makes a bold stand that befuddles Ted, who counts on his wife's spineless acceptance of whatever crumbs he offers.

See also **Hsu genealogy**

• *Further Reading*

Hamilton, Patricia L. "Feng Shui, Astrology, and the Five Elements: Traditional Chinese Belief in Amy Tan's *The Joy Luck Club*." *MELUS*, Vol. 24, No. 2, Summer 1999, pp. 125–145.
Huntley, E. D. *Amy Tan, A Critical Companion*. Westport, Conn.: Greenwood Press, 1998.

journeys

The journey motif dominates Amy Tan's fiction. Travels are a natural adjunct to motifs of the Chinese diaspora and expatriate life in California's Chinese-American enclave. Of trips to the motherland, critic Sheng-Mei Ma explains the need of Chinese-Americans to complete the loop, to "[revisit] in good time that which he or she took leave of" (Ma, p. xv). In *The Joy Luck Club* (1989), the wartime emigration of heroines An-mei Hsu, Lindo Jong, Ying-ying St. Clair, and Suyuan Woo to the Pacific Coast precipitates problems with assimilation in a Western land. As mothers, the four women attempt to guide and control their perplexing Amerasian offspring, who try to place symbolic feet in the United States while maintaining a toehold in their parents' homeland. The daughters' half-hearted loyalty to Chinese culture creates dissensions that form the novel's conflicts.

One satisfying personal story reverses the China-to-America journey and the emigrant's self-doubts by sending June Woo to China to meet relatives and to reunite Suyuan's divided family. The emotional trek to modern China introduces June not only to twin adult siblings but also to Canning and Suyuan Woo's motherland, the fount of the puzzling rituals and customs that Chinese-American girls learn out of context in their American homes. Hesitant to bridge the gap of years, miles, history, and cultures, June looks out at her sisters, Chwun Yu and Chwun Hwa, and sees instead Suyuan: "And now I see her again, two of her, waving" (p. 287). Without words, the three daughters, like mirror images from different angles, reconnect the fractured family and restore Suyuan as mother of them all. Critic Amy Ling describes the reunion as a reclaiming of Suyuan through surrogate mothers and "a trope for the lost motherland for the [novel's] daughters" (Ling, p. 132).

The brutal physical displacement of noncombatants in *The Kitchen God's Wife* (1991), Tan's second novel, presents a less sanguine view of travel as Chinese air force pilots take along their young wives, who attempt to make the best of wartime billets. Winnie, bride of the beginning Kuomintang pilot Wen Fu, has already endured departure in shame from her father's Shanghai mansion on Julu Road to her uncle's less sumptuous home on Tsungming Island. Invigorated by the promise of marriage and a new residence, Winnie returns to Shanghai to shop with San Ma, a kind surrogate mother. The fantasy of housewifery among all-new belongings fades immediately after the wedding, when the greedy Wen family rips through Winnie's treasures, selling some and keeping the rest for themselves. Tan illustrates that Winnie's internal journey to liberation must come from self rather than belongings.

Tan gives Winnie little time to moon over lost dowry purchases by dispatching the neophyte national air force on a labyrinthine war-time trek. A series of stopovers begins with a defunct monastery at Hangchow and a coarse environment that introduces Winnie to working-class existence. Tender and modest, she is most put out by the improprieties of women sharing a bathhouse and disrobing and washing in front of each other. Her sensibilities accede to more demands as the extended military family presses on to Yangchow and Nanking before setting out on a demanding four-month journey by boat and truck southwest to Kunming. The makeshift housing and dining facilities along the way reach a low during the early months of Winnie's first pregnancy. By the time that the entourage rises into the clouds topping the mountain peaks, she embraces an illusion of reaching into heaven for the constellations that she and Helen turn into myth. Their impromptu storytelling illuminates the young brides' lack of preparedness for the worst of the Sino-Japanese War (1937–1945).

Combat advances on two fronts toward Winnie. Kunming itself is the test of her maturity, patience, and self-reliance as Wen Fu escalates from wife abuser to a murderous one-eyed cyclops. No longer able to turn to older women for guidance, she relies on Helen, her countrified peer, for advice and for protection during an air raid by Japanese bombers. Departure from the foul, crowded mountain town in 1945 turns into a documentary of human sufferings as Winnie views the pitiful condition of Chinese peasants. Her hopes for a better life grow as she, her husband, and their son Danru approach Jiang Sao-yen's mansion. His fall from prestige and honor deflates her dreams of respite. Another trip to Tsungming Island reassembles the foster family that she grew up in, but pitiful scenarios prove to her that residents of China's eastern shore fared worse than she had expected. Tan illustrates that invidious comparisons do little to ease Winnie's mental unrest.

The author continues to test Winnie with additional eye-opening travel. Using the addresses provided by Old Aunt and New Aunt, Winnie locates the refugees' retreat that Peanut opens in Shanghai for downtrodden women and their children. A surprise coincidence reunites Winnie not only with her cousin but also with Jimmy

Louie, who visits the Japanese sector to buy the newspapers that constitute his daily assignment for military intelligence. After the joys of living in his apartment away from the vicious Wen Fu, Winnie quickly sinks into the despair of a childless mother after the death of Danru. An unforeseen arrest and plunge into women's prison suggests the harrowing of the underworld, the lowest points in the epics of Homer and Virgil and the last earthly days of Christ. Rather than feel sorry for herself, she uplifts the women who turn to her for reading, writing, and deportment lessons. Tan establishes that the new Winnie is capable of surviving, in part because she looks beyond her own tragedy to those of fellow inmates.

The final pages of the novel press Winnie into a whirlwind trans–Pacific journey. Returned to her empty Shanghai apartment, she ponders the next move toward Jimmy Louie, whom the government has recalled to the United States after the scandal his romance caused. To preserve her status of ex-wife, Winnie fends off Wen Fu once more and books a flight out of China just in time to avoid the Communist takeover. The restoration of her romance with Jimmy Louie offers her the original dream — marriage to an adoring husband who holds her at night and adores her as his "Baby-ah" (p. 469). In retrospect, Tan's lengthy woman-building journey produces a resilient adult capable of surviving even widowhood.

In another return-to-the-motherland motif, in *The Hundred Secret Senses* (1995), Tan builds character affection and excitement. Kwan Li employs a two-week return trip to her native village, Changmian, China, as a means of reinstating the love of her half-sister Olivia Yee Laguni for Olivia's estranged husband Simon Bishop. After thirty-two years in California, Kwan delights in reexamining her past with her co-travelers. Reflecting on Kwan's devious methods of convincing Olivia and Simon to go, Olivia declares wryly, "Fate is another name for Kwan" (p. 187).

Tan expands the journey in space and time. As the visit spools out, Kwan uses moments alone with Olivia to complete an episodic narrative of Kwan's existence as Nunumu, a laundress for a mission compound in the mid-nineteenth century. As Olivia envisions how Manchu mercenaries overran Changmian in 1864 during the Taiping Rebellion, she gains enough clues to convince her that Kwan actually recalls a past life and communicates with ghosts. The journey ends with Kwan's unforeseen disappearance in a maze-like cave and the Bishops' attempts to rescue her. The loss is a common motif in classic literature, the sacrifice of one character for the reclaiming of another. On return to San Francisco, the couple commemorates Kwan's importance in their lives by adding Li to the name of their daughter Samantha, whom they conceived on the journey. Significantly, the child's given name comes from the Hebrew for "listener," a gesture toward the importance of Kwan as a storyteller during the long trip.

Tan illustrates the eye-opening quality of travel to country folk in *The Bonesetter's Daughter* (2001). After fifteen-year-old LuLing Liu journeys on Mr. Wei's cart the thirty miles from the village of Immortal Heart to Peking, she abandons her rural upbringing and looks forward to a nuptial match that will free her from a bucolic home and the rule of Precious Auntie, her mute nursemaid. LuLing foolishly rejects her beloved servant and ignores her written manuscript, which explains LuLing's illegitimate birth. The sudden coming-to-knowledge, like the epiphany of a day's walk through Peking, conveys to the teenager that she has devalued the dearest person in her life and has precipitated multiple disasters on the Liu family, which ousts her and sends her to an orphanage.

Tan concludes her fourth novel with another haphazard emigration from China. Stalked by Chang Fu Nan, a sinister one-eyed, opiate-addicted brother-in-law, Lu-Ling, like Winnie Louie in *The Kitchen God's Wife*, must plot an exit strategy. After seeking the forgiveness of her father and Precious Auntie, LuLing sells a valuable oracle bone and fends off Fu Nan with enough cash to feed his habit until she can gain a visa. Traveling as a visiting artist, she achieves her freedom in California. Tan avoids any happily-ever-after illusions by picturing LuLing as bride, mother, and widow in short order. The rapid transition illustrates the continuing emotional journey, a universal trope in classic literature.

See also **diaspora, reunion**

• *Further Reading*

Chua, C. L. "Review: *The Kitchen God's Wife.*" *Magill's Literary Annual.* Englewood Cliffs, N.J.: Salem Press, 1992.

Heung, Marina. "Daughter-Text/Mother-Text: Matrilineage in Amy Tan's Joy Luck Club." *Feminist Studies*, Vol. 19, No. 3, Fall 1993, pp. 597–616.

Ling, Amy. *Between Worlds: Women Writers of Chinese Ancestry.* New York: Pergamon Press, 1990.

Ma, Sheng-mei. *The Deathly Embrace: Orientalism and Asian American Identity.* Minneapolis: University of Minnesota Press, 2000

The Joy Luck Club

Amy Tan's *The Joy Luck Club* (1989), which reviewer Carolyn See claims is a devotional *tour de force*, seized the Western world's imagination and contributed to the canon of feminist literature. The text gives voice to previously silenced Chinese women, some of whom were victims of patriarchal families and feudal marriages. Because Tan follows the philosophy and subtexts of Maxine Hong Kingston's landmark novel *The Woman Warrior* (1976), critic Amy Ling characterizes Tan's fiction as "an echo and response and in parts a continuation and expansion" of her predecessor's novel (p. 130). To honor Tan's individuality, Ling notes that she focuses on Mandarin speakers and produces a text less hostile and more lyrical than Kingston's.

After the diaspora following the Sino-Japanese War (1937–1945) sends Chinese emigrants to safer countries, the creation of a mah jong club in California suits the time and place by supplying a sense of community and welcome to outsiders. The symmetry of four mothers—An-mei Hsu, Lindo Jong, Ying-ying St. Clair, and Suyuan Woo—and their daughters—Rose Hsu Jordan, Waverly Jong, Lena St. Clair Livotny, and June Woo—allows the author a systematic focus by making two rounds of the table in stand-alone vignettes of women's interconnected lives. Because of the death of Suyuan Woo, the novel's voices are limited to seven—four daughters and three mothers—and the assumption of Suyuan's personal quest for her Chinese daughters, Chwun Yu and Chwun Hwa Wang. Contrasting the carefully brought-up mothers, the daughters, according to *New York Times* reviewer Orville Schell, are "upwardly mobile, design-conscious, divorce-prone and Americanized" (Schell, p. 28). The misunderstandings between generations derive in part from language difficulties and from daughters who have no clear understanding of how their Chinese mothers survived both a feudal culture and a national catastrophe.

Forty years earlier, Suyuan Woo, who created the original mah jong club during aerial bombardment of Kweilin by the Japanese, hungers for a bit of hope and joy. She wants some mundane activity to counter fear, retreats to caves, and the screams and smell of so many people packed into the city. She and others find their release in the shuffling of mah jong tiles and attendant storytelling, jests, and feasting on dumplings, noodles, boiled peanuts, and oranges, symbols of the sweet life. Her outlook parallels "Eat, drink, and be merry, for tomorrow we shall die," an adage that has grown from simpler statements in Ecclesiastes and Luke to express the Roman philosophy of "carpe diem"— seize the day, the advice of the poet Horace.

Tan illustrates the need for continuity in the lives of newcomers, who miss the camaraderie of the Chinese motherland. In 1949, Suyuan, safely emigrated to San Francisco, organizes a new club comprised of the three women she meets at the First Chinese Baptist Church, an enclave of first-generation Chinese-Americans and their families. Among friends, she encourages sisterhood, storytelling, tips on investing money in the stock market, and the sharing of Chinese food. Upon her death, June moves into the east seat, a metaphor for beginnings and China itself, the home soil of the older players. Thus, her position at the mah jong table foreshadows the lengthy plane trip to her mother's native land to meet with her missing half-sisters.

To reunite mothers with daughters, the setting departs from the rectangle of the mah jong table and embraces circles— the eternal linkage of female family members separated by the diaspora. The motif reaches its height in June Woo's reversal of the emigrant path to America and her meeting with her twin sisters at Shanghai airport. To critical comments that the author uses the stories as an apologia for the Asian-American experience, Tan retorted that her work is personal, not political or symbolic. She intended the novel as a human statement about "individual rather than collective awakening" (Rowland, p. 10).

See also **diaspora, An-mei Hsu, Hsu genealogy, Lindo Jong, Waverly Jong, Jong genealogy, Rose Hsu Jordan, journeys, Lena St. Clair Livotny, mah jong, Ying-ying St. Clair, St. Clair genealogy, June Woo, Suyuan Woo, Woo genealogy**

• *Further Reading*

Dooley, Susan. "Mah-Jongg and the Ladies of the Club." *Washington Post Book World*, March 5, 1989, p. 7.
Hamilton, Patricia L. "Feng Shui, Astrology, and the Five Elements: Traditional Chinese Belief in Amy Tan's *The Joy Luck Club*." *MELUS*, Vol. 24, No. 2, Summer 1999, pp. 125–145.
Heung, Marina. "Daughter-Text/Mother-Text: Matrilineage in Amy Tan's Joy Luck Club." *Feminist Studies*, Vol. 19, No. 3, Fall 1993, pp. 597–616.
Ling, Amy. *Between Worlds: Women Writers of Chinese Ancestry*. New York: Pergamon Press, 1990.
Rowland, Penelope. "American Woman." *Mother Jones*, July/August 1989, p. 10.

Schell, Orville. "Your Mother Is in Your Bones." *New York Times Book Review*, Vol. 26, March 19, 1989, pp. 3, 28.

See, Carolyn. "Drowning in America, Starving for China." *Los Angeles Times Book Review*, March 12, 1989, pp. 1, 11.

Snodgrass, Mary Ellen. *Literary Treks: Characters on the Move.* Westport, Conn.: Libraries Unlimited, 2003.

Kitchen God

The bewhiskered kitchen deity that adorns Auntie Du Ching's gift of a household altar in *The Kitchen God's Wife* (1991) resides in a central frame like a king or religious icon. The likeness, which writes with a quill on a tablet, results from a Chinese legend about farmer Zhang. Although he was prosperous and lucky to have Guo for a wife, he was discontented. When second wife Lady Li came to the house, she chased Guo away and, within two years, went through all of Zhang's money. After she left Zhang, he was reduced to beggary. The kind woman who seated him at her hearth turned out to be Guo. Out of shame, Zhang leaped into the fire and was reduced to three puffs of smoke. In heaven, the Jade Emperor named Zhang the Kitchen God, the warden of human behavior, who reports on wrongdoing every year a week before the new year. His elevation characterizes the superior value of males, even bad ones, over females in a patriarchal society.

The Taoist placement of a divine spy at every fireplace suggests the centrality of fire and warmth to human dwellings, where families fall under the eye of the celestial observer. Unlike Santa Claus, who brings gifts down the chimney on Christmas, the Kitchen God expects presents of tea and oranges, candy, cigarettes, whiskey, and honey to seal his lips, the bribes that net families a good report to the Jade Emperor. The legend depicts the Kitchen God as unpredictable — sometimes cranky, sometimes biased against a household. Winnie Louie recognizes the faulty logic of a patriarchal society — that Zhang, a selfish adulterer, bears a moral responsibility that he doesn't merit. It is Guo, the good wife, who deserves the honor for her faithfulness and generosity and who is more likely to report human flaws with mercy and understanding.

During Winnie's flight to Kunming with the pilots and Helen, the two women share stories of the Kitchen God and the constellation representing one of his seven daughters. After Wen Fu's car accident precipitates insane outbursts and unpredictable cruelties, Winnie compares herself to the Kitchen God's wife, whom nobody worshipped or credited with charity toward an evil husband. In old age, Winnie's purchase of the porcelain statue of a nameless goddess from the Sam Fook Trading Company brings tears to her daughter Pearl's eyes. With an appropriate move beyond Chinese lore, Winnie creates her own watchful deity, Lady Sorrowfree, and makes up a new story about the supernatural female who will protect Pearl.

• *Further Reading*

Vogel, Christine. "A Remarkable Life Controlled by Gods' Whims." *Chicago Sun Times,* June 30, 1991, p. C14.

The Kitchen God's Wife

Tan creates a Chinese *Gone with the Wind* in her second novel, *The Kitchen God's Wife* (1991), perhaps her best writing. Reviewer Constance Casey of the *San Diego Union* applauded the work as a page-turner "spanning decades and leaping oceans and all that goes with epicdom" (Casey, p. C5). Cyra McFadden of the *San Francisco Examiner* summarized the work's themes as "family relations, the unreliability of memory, the nature of secrets, Chinese history, customs and society, and the difficulties of assimilating into a new culture" (McFadden, p. C8). Maureen Harrington, writing for the *Denver Post*, characterized the overall effect as stunning, "full of power and fury, love and glory, pathos and revenge" (Harrington, p. C9).

Compared to the works of Leo Tolstoy, Tan's war novel, written from a noncombatant female's point of view and told in flashback, is a vigorous and complex personal narrative or confessional *Bildungsroman* that dramatizes the hardships of a country and a heroine under siege. As the author explains in *The Opposite of Fate: A Book of Musings* (2003), the key question is about hope: "How does it change, transform, endure according to life's quirky circumstances?" (p. 209). The text wedges the main plot line between the bookends of daughter Pearl Louie Brandt's relationship with her mother, a beginning and ending suggesting the *prologos* and *exodos* of Greek tragedy. Through clever shifts and insightful dialogue, Tan produces what reviewer David Guy refers to as an ambivalence that is simultaneously "comic and heart-wrenching" (Guy, p. T4). By bridging an intergenerational gap between Chinese mother and Amerasian daughter, the story relieves Winnie of guilt over Pearl's siring by a rapist and passes on hope as the gift of the older generation to their children.

With an alliance of Bao-bao's betrothal and Auntie Du's death, the text opens in San Francisco's Chinatown in January 1990 at a gathering at five tables of the Water Dragon Restaurant for the extended Kwong and Louie families. The symbiotic relationship between Helen Kwong and Winnie Louie blossoms in the weeks preceding Chinese New Year, when Helen wants to sweep her life clean of lies and secrets about the past. Because wartime events bind her to Winnie, Helen can't divulge only her share of the lies without laying bare the truth about the years she shared with Winnie. The problematic sisterhood forces the two women, like yoked oxen, to cooperate in the effort to enlighten Pearl about her mother's difficult first marriage.

When Winnie begins telling Pearl the whole truth about her young womanhood, she briefly describes a change that swept all of China during the Sino-Japanese War. A military wife's limited observation of the Rape of Nanking, a little-known episode to the outside world, reveals only a few details of the atrocities that killed some 260,000 Chinese peasants over a two-month period. In Winnie's estimation, the conflict alters the national morality standard, allowing people to behave out of character. Peripheral comment charges the British with closing the Burma Road, China's supply line to the southwest, and vilifies Americans for wartime profiteering by selling fuel and metal to the Japanese. As a result of upheaval, more compassionate people condoned the behaviors and morals of the peasant and servant classes, who did the best they could to stay alive. Shanghai citizens, represented by the turncoat

Jiang Sao-yen, developed a siege mentality and fended for themselves, regardless of how they had to grapple for food, warmth, and shelter.

Keeping a focus on women's lives, Tan's story equates Japan's opportunism against China with a husband's patriarchal crimes against the family. The shift in values from industrial-class gentility to survivalism serves as a backdrop to Winnie's determination to escape marital rape before it kills her or destroys her spirit. In his own defense, Wen Fu, like the Japanese, poses as a Kuomintang hero and disabled veteran of World War II and pretends to be the injured party. On the stand, he offers patriarchal testimony that presents his wife's sins as unthinkable acts of seduction, child stealing, and theft of family heirlooms. His lies marginalize Winnie to the status of concubine or sex slave, a modern-day Griselda whose longsuffering extends over twelve years of abuse and into her seventies with unspoken fears that Pearl, Wen Fu's daughter, bears genetic evil in her character.

Reviewers, particularly Amerasian critics, have accused Tan of tailoring historical fiction to suit Western expectations and to entice a trendy American readership. In literary scholar Sheng-mei Ma's *Immigrant Subjectivities in Asian American and Asian Diaspora Literature* (1998), the text classes Tan's novel along with Maxine Hong Kingston's *The Woman Warrior* (1975) and Amerasian playwright Dmae Roberts's drama *Mei Mei: A Daughter's Song* (1990) under the pejorative heading of ethnographic feminism. Ma charges that the loss of authenticity derives from the writers' choice of exotic incidents and politically correct treatment of women's issues as a means of appealing to book buyers.

See also **Pearl Louie Brandt, confinement, diaspora, Jiang Sao-yen, Jiang genealogy, journeys, Kitchen God, Helen Kwong, Kwong genealogy, Winnie Louie, Louie genealogy, Peanut, spousal abuse, violence, Wen Fu**

- *Further Reading*

Adams, Bella. "Representing History in Amy Tan's *The Kitchen God's Wife*." *MELUS*, Vol. 28, No. 2, Summer 2003, pp. 9–30.

Caesar, Judith. "Patriarchy, Imperialism, and Knowledge in *The Kitchen God's Wife*." *North Dakota Quarterly*, Vol. 62, No. 4, 1994-1995, pp. 164–174.

Casey, Constance. "Amy Tan's Second Book Focuses on the Overlooked Woman." *San Diego Union*, June 16, 1991, pp. C4–C5.

Ellison, Emily. "Tragic Story Dazzles and Awes." *Atlanta Journal*, June 16, 1991, pp. C12–C13.

Guy, David. "Wheel of Fortune: A Writer's Thoughts on Joy, Luck and Heartache." *Washington Post*, November 2, 2002, p. T4.

Harrington, Maureen. "Tan's Immigrant Tale Top Quality." *Denver Post*, June 23, 1991, p. C9.

Ma, Sheng-mei. *Immigrant Subjectivities in Asian American and Asian Diaspora Literature*. Albany: State University of New York Press, 1998.

McFadden, Cyra. "Amy Tan's Second Novel Is Rich and Satisfying Tale." *San Francisco Examiner*, June 17, 1991, p. C8.

Mendoza, Alice. "The Ink of Diverse Gods." *Quarterly Literary Review Singapore*, Vol. 2, No. 2, January 2003.

Wong, Sau-ling Cynthia. "'Sugar Sisterhood': Situating the Amy Tan Phenomenon," in *The Ethnic Canon: Histories, Institutions, and Interventions*. Minneapolis: University of Minnesota Press, 1995, pp. 174–210.

Kwong, Hulan "Helen"

The irritant in the mother-daughter relationship between Pearl Louie Brandt and her mother Winnie Louie, Helen Kwong is an energizer to the plot of *The Kitchen God's Wife* (1991). In the opinion of her friend Winnie, Helen was born to good luck. Because she has maintained an *ipso facto* kinship with Winnie from before the Sino-Japanese War (1937–1945), Helen has no compunction about intruding in private family matters. At a quiet moment with Pearl Brandt, Winnie's daughter, at Bao-bao Kwong's engagement party, Helen dramatically divulges that she has been diagnosed with a brain tumor and maneuvers Pearl into promising to report her own illness with multiple sclerosis to Winnie. At a fish dinner a week later, Helen further roils the waters by promising to reveal Winnie's secrets. The psychological blackmail suits a pair of women who grew up in China during the years when women who were silenced by patriarchy achieved limited autonomy through guile and lies.

The unveiling of truth is lengthy and painful. When Winnie accounts for her long-standing relationship with Helen, she begins at the makeshift bathhouse in a Hangchow monastery that serves as quarters for married Kuomintang air force trainees. Just as Helen bares her bottom during shared baths, she continues baring all in her seventies, forcing Winnie to be painfully exacting in her reminiscences. On first view of Helen's improprieties, Winnie criticizes her as a plump, unmannerly rural girl who lacks modesty and the refinement that comes from a good family and conservative upbringing. Winnie scorns Helen's indelicate scrubbing in front of other wives and her gullibility about local myth. The surprising factor in Helen's makeup is her sharp temper and henpecking of her husband, Captain Long Jiaguo, a strength that causes Winnie to envy her. Another strength is Helen's frank discussion of female bodies and reproduction, a subject that polite families withhold from ladylike girls like Winnie.

The shift in personal values that accompanies war turns Helen from suspect companion into Winnie's friend and rescuer. Helen's gift for hasty action saves Winnie during the panic in Nanking after the Japanese attack in November 1937. Helen guides her pregnant friend through the mob, then steals a pedicab to take them home. Helen's ready action with a stick suggests the doughty heart of a survivor who can improvise a means of escape from a desperate situation. Tan endears the character to readers through Helen's willingness to take blame for theft. In retrospect to her lawlessness, she admits that she is an example of "how bad the world has become" (p. 273).

As Winnie hardens and toughens during the war, she observes a perplexing alteration in Helen. Perhaps because she was born in the country and suffered famine in girlhood, Helen observes starving refugees in Kunming and begins eating ravenously. Winnie compares Helen's gluttony to a form of storage, like a thrifty person's bank account saved for hard times to come. At their parting in August 1945, Winnie clings to the loving sister and exchanges addresses so the two can remain in contact. After Helen's husband dies, she settles in Harbin to tend his grave and the plot of Danru, Winnie's son who died in the same epidemic. The acts of devotion and remembrance reflect a kind heart worthy of Winnie's life-long friendship.

Helen's return to Winnie's life finds Helen endowed with good fortune while Winnie struggles to attain a better future in America. Pregnant with the child of her second husband, Henry Kwong, Helen cooks Winnie's welcome-home-from-prison meal, aids her preparations for immigration to California, and witnesses the signatures on her divorce papers. Good luck smiles on Winnie while Wen Fu returns to rape and terrorize her with a gun. Helen ends the episode with laughter. She interrupts Wen Fu *in flagrante delicto* and helps Winnie humiliate him one last time by throwing his pants out the window and forcing him bare-bottomed into the street. The blend of anguish and humor softens the terrible crime against Winnie, which leaves her in doubt about the fatherhood of Pearl.

The vitality and *joie de vivre* of the Helen character remains alive into the last pages of the novel. At the wedding of her son Bao-bao, she reverts to wartime thinking by gobbling remaining tidbits at the banquet. Like a *nouveau riche* peasant, she proposes asking the bride's family to discount costs of a trip to China, where Helen will throw a dinner in her hometown to show off her American wealth. In one final secret shared with Pearl, Helen confesses that she and Winnie intend to take Pearl to China to shop for an herbal cure for multiple sclerosis. The confidence illustrates how Helen bobs in and out of respectability and why she gains the Louie family's constant gratitude.

See also **Kwong genealogy, sisterhood, women**

• *Further Reading*

McFadden, Cyra. "Amy Tan's Second Novel Is Rich and Satisfying Tale." *San Francisco Examiner*, June 17, 1991, p. C8.

Mendoza, Alice. "The Ink of Diverse Gods." *Quarterly Literary Review Singapore*, Vol. 2, No. 2, January 2003.

Wong, Sau-ling Cynthia. "'Sugar Sisterhood': Situating the Amy Tan Phenomenon," in *The Ethnic Canon: Histories, Institutions, and Interventions*. Minneapolis: University of Minnesota Press, 1995, pp. 174–210.

Kwong genealogy

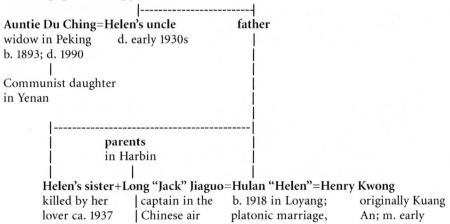

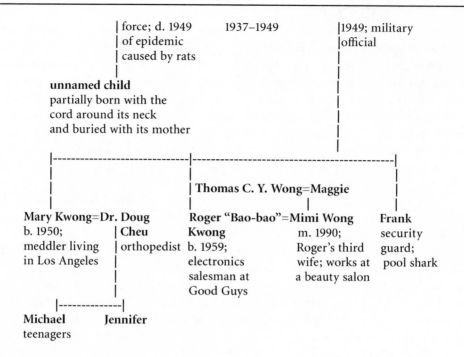

force; d. 1949	1937–1949	1949; military
of epidemic		official
caused by rats		

unnamed child
partially born with the
cord around its neck
and buried with its mother

Mary Kwong=Dr. Doug
b. 1950;   **Cheu**
meddler living   orthopedist
in Los Angeles

Thomas C. Y. Wong=Maggie

Roger "Bao-bao"=Mimi Wong   **Frank**
Kwong   m. 1990;   security
b. 1959;   Roger's third   guard;
electronics   wife; works at pool shark
salesman at   a beauty salon
Good Guys

Michael   Jennifer
teenagers

Li, Kwan

Kwan Li, the ghost-seer in *The Hundred Secret Senses* (1995), is one of Tan's mixed-bag characters. Kwan is born with generous helpings of good-heartedness, guile, and "yin eyes," a form of second sight (p. 3). Consequently, she lives in a fluid mental state that overlays dealings with living people with visitations from spirits and visions of former lives. To *Bookpage* interviewer Ellen Kanner, Tan described the character as "wacky" and "hard to live with" (Kanner, p. 3). In the novel, she "bounces from topic to topic," placing herself in multiple centuries and variant realities (p. 18). Tan based Kwan's strong individuality and gift for storytelling on Daisy Tan, the author's mother and source of some of Tan's most popular works. In the text, Kwan's American family considers her exasperating for clinging to Chinese beliefs and refusing to assimilate; yet, spirits of the dead value her advice like the words of Dear Abby. It takes many years and much maturity for Kwan's sister Olivia Yee Laguni to trust her visions and accept wisdom gained from a series of past lives. Tan implies that Amerasians use their skepticism as a shield against the primitivism of their ancestors' mythology.

Tan uses Kwan's experiences to explain how a person can overcome sorrow by visiting with the dead and viewing each life as a strand of an ongoing process of reincarnation. Born to market clerk Li Chen in Guilin, China, in 1944, Kwan is Jack Yee's first child. At age four, Kwan watches Chen wither and die in childbirth from Jack's disloyalty. The newborn child dies with her. Kwan remains in the care of her rough-spoken Aunt Li Bin-bin, called Big Ma, a child abuser who forces Kwan to gather kindling for sale to neighbors and who threatens to send her away for talking too much. The slight depicts women's despicable role in perpetuating the silencing of other women.

At a bizarre point in the story, Tan inserts magical realism by having Kwan switch bodies with her stocky friend Buncake after both girls drown. The confusing tale of a transmigrated soul results in Olivia's uncertainty about Kwan's identity: "Is Kwan — that is, this woman who claims to be my sister — actually a demented person who *believed* she was Kwan? Did the flesh-and-blood Kwan drown as a little girl? … Is she a ghost or just insane?" (pp. 233–234). On her way back to Changmian, China, to right old wrongs, Kwan loses an earthly opportunity to ameliorate the harsh foster parenting after Big Ma dies in a car-bus crash. Undeterred, Kwan resorts to spirit communication to settle disquieting memories of Big Ma's stern discipline. The ease with which Kwan slips from one dimension to another explains her equanimity and fearlessness.

Travel from one spiritual plane to another is also beneficial to Kwan for other reasons. By age eight, she begins seeing spirits with her "yin eyes" and later glides effortlessly between the real world and the ghostly beyond (p. 3). Contributing to her unusual skill is a parallel gift for storytelling, such as her explanation of the mountain named Young Girl's Wish for two lovers who became phoenixes and lived in an immortal white pine forest. The geographical fable accounts for young women in Changmian climbing to the mountaintop, releasing birds, then making wishes that ostensibly fly to heaven on the birds' wings. The fable illustrates the upbeat, optimistic side of Kwan. She concludes, "Everyone must dream. We dream to give ourselves hope," a recurrent theme in Tan's fiction (p. 217).

Tan puts Kwan to work in California as a solace to her younger sister, Olivia Yee Laguni. Two years after Jack Yee's death in 1960, eighteen-year-old Kwan undergoes a cultural shift when she arrives in the United States. Living on Balboa Street in San Francisco, she becomes Olivia's beloved, ever-faithful older sister. When Olivia's dog Captain is run over, Kwan conceals the truth by claiming that he ran away. Olivia remembers her as a surrogate parent who "bandaged my wounds, taught me to ride a bike, placed her hands on my feverish six-year-old forehead and whispered, 'Sleep, Libby-ah, sleep'" (p. 393). She mystifies the family with superstitions, charms, and prophecy. Following a year of her otherworldliness, Bob Laguni, her stepfather, signs her into a ward at Mary's Help, where psychiatric treatment consists of electroshock therapy. From that point on, Kwan develops bizarre traits— kinky hair and the ability to interfere with radios, televisions, and watches and to recharge telephone and flashlight batteries with a touch of the fingers. Tan wryly implies that attempts to silence Kwan result in an increase in her ability to communicate.

To normalize Kwan, Tan supplies her with a stable homelife, beginning with marriage to George Lew, grocery manager of Good-4-Less and father of Kwan's two stepsons, Timmy and Teddy. While working for twenty years at Spencer's drugstore in the Castro community, Kwan diagnoses musculo-skeletal ailments with a handshake and advises AIDS patients on health matters. When Olivia asks Kwan's help in exorcising the ghost of Elza Marie Vandervort, Simon's former girlfriend, Kwan abandons truth by rephrasing the spiritual message to further her sister's romance. The gesture attests to Kwan's love for Olivia and her wish to satisfy unrequited love by having Olivia marry Simon, who was Yiban Johnson, Olivia's suitor, in an earlier life. Thus, Tan exalts her eccentric character by having Kwan facilitate earthly love.

Tan illustrates how Olivia, the original narrator, gradually abandons skepticism of her irrepressible ghost-seeing sister's clairvoyance. In 1994, Kwan's obsession with visiting China results in a family journey retracing Jack Yee's original emigration route. After the two sisters join Simon in a two-week professional tour of Changmian to study peasant foodways, Olivia begins to visualize more clearly her sister's metaphysical viewpoint. To slow Rocky, a speeding tour driver, Kwan takes the Chinese tack: If his three passengers die in an accident, he will receive no pay and will owe them restitution in the afterlife. Kwan's eventual disappearance into the spirit realm grieves Olivia and Simon, but seems like a natural resumption of a former life for someone who is at home in past and present.

See also **doppelgänger**, ghosts, Yee genealogy

• *Further Reading*

Kanner, Ellen. "From Amy Tan, a Superb Novel of Two Sisters, Two Worlds, and a Few Ghosts." *Bookpage*, December 1995, p. 3.
Pavey, Ruth. "Spirit Levels." *New Statesman & Society*, Vol. 9, No. 390, February 16, 1996, p. 38.
Shapiro, Laura. "Ghost Story." *Newsweek*, Vol. 126, No. 19, November 6, 1995, pp. 91–92.

Livotny, Lena St. Clair

Just as competition shapes Waverly Jong's childhood in *The Joy Luck Club* (1989), a pervasive doom threatens her friend and contemporary Lena St. Clair. At age five, she begins suffering abnormal fears derived from the psychotic episodes of her mother, Ying-ying St. Clair. Lena claims to see menacing demons with her Chinese eyes, her term for slitted, nearly lidless orbs. The term suggests an Asian mindset instilled by a paranoid mother. Ying-ying's gradual retreat from reality after the birth of an anacephalic son terrorizes Lena, who awaits the worst that can happen. Her father's denial of Ying-ying's demented state and his false predictions of prosperity for the family worsen Lena's insecurity. In contrast to Teresa Sorci, the spunky Italian girl next door who sneaks back home via the fire escape, Lena has no guile or coping mechanism to ward off despair. In fantasy, she retrieves her mother from psychosis by performing the death of one thousand cuts, a pantomimed execution that assures her mother that she has survived the worst. The vision offers two benefits: it allows Lena to play the dual role of rescuer and militant heroine, a pose completely at odds with her actual persona.

In a mental dream chamber, Lena thrives on imagining the worst possible outcomes of real-life actions. At age eight, she misinterprets her mother's prediction that she will marry a pock-marked man and displaces her distaste on a local boy, Arnold Reisman, who dies of complications from measles five years later. In adulthood, Lena is vital, intuitive, and exuberant. She majors in Asian-American studies and weds Harold Livotny, a prosperous Hungarian restaurant designer at Hartned Kelley &

Davis who harbors a cynical attitude toward marriage. With her encouragement and aid, he opens his own firm, but fails to recognize her value as a wife or to reward her for supporting his career. The daily discounting gradually wears away Lena's optimism.

Tan depicts Lena as a confused individual lacking a clear perception of cause and effect. Although the Livotnys live in a modish remodeled barn outside San Francisco in Woodside and drive a Jaguar, she fails to feel deserving of the marriage or its material rewards. In her mother's opinion, Lena and Harold are shallow materialists spending their money for show rather than for personal pleasure. When their relationship founders, Lena perceives him as her comeuppance for avoiding marriage to Arnold, but she abandons childish guilt and struggles to put a mounting discontent into words. The effort parallels other struggles in Tan's parade of silenced women who must learn to speak for themselves if they are to prosper. The return of Ying-ying in *The Moon Lady* (1992), a children's story drawn from *The Joy Luck Club*, and the appearance of three granddaughters, June, Lily, and Maggie, implies that Lena has children, but the father is not named.

See also **The Moon Lady, mother-daughter relationships, Ying-ying St. Clair, St. Clair genealogy**

• *Further Reading*

Hamilton, Patricia L. "Feng Shui, Astrology, and the Five Elements: Traditional Chinese Belief in Amy Tan's *The Joy Luck Club*." *MELUS*, Vol. 24, No. 2, Summer 1999, pp. 125–145.

Louie, Jimmy

James Y. "Jimmy" Louie is one of Amy Tan's most admirable male characters. A translator for the United States Information Service and press relations office for the American consulate general in China, he occupies a valuable perch above the ethnic divide between American and Asian. During the Sino-Japanese War (1937–1945), he is valuable to the allies because of his facility with Cantonese, Mandarin, Japanese, tribal dialects, and English. To keep abreast of attitudes and rumors, he combs the post-war newspapers for articles significant to the occupation staff. Tan illustrates that communication separates Jimmy from patriarchal wives like Winnie, who rely on their husbands for an honest appraisal of the era and of their abilities to survive it.

Jimmy and Winnie meet at a pivotal point in the international conflict. At a victory celebration following an American foray on Japanese bombers in December 1941, Jimmy becomes Winnie's rescuer after she breaks the heel of a shoe, a symbol of stalled motion. The victim-rescuer roles dominate their life together, beginning five years later when they meet in Shanghai near a book and newspaper shop at the nadir of Winnie's marriage to Wen fu. Jimmy's sympathy for her family's sufferings impresses Winnie and becomes the basis of their love. He expresses devotion in small gestures, e.g., abandoning the photo of four potential wives on the teahouse table and waiting an hour and a half for Winnie at their next rendezvous at the bookshop. Critics charge Tan with providing sweeping, heroic roles to women like Winnie and with relegating men like Jimmy Louie to limited character development. Another way of assessing Jimmy Louie's character strength is Tan's intent to focus on the woman's hardships in fleeing patriarchal marriage and her good fortune in locating more promising husband material in a good-hearted male like Jimmy.

In the falling action, Tan illustrates how Jimmy becomes Winnie's life-long mate and how he cherishes his "Baby-ah" for strengths that she has yet to discover in herself (p. 469). His certainty lends courage to Winnie at a critical point in her self-liberation. To bolster her resolve, he promises to wait as long as it takes. To Winnie, they became "two people talking with one heart" (p. 457). The couple's intuitive trust in love gives Winnie a boost toward leaving Wen Fu. While living in Jimmy's two-room flat, she loses her fear of sex and becomes his sunshine, a happy face and loving mate that he frequently photographs. The pictures serve Tan as evidence of commitment after Jimmy's death, which leaves Winnie alone and forces her to express in word pictures a war-time love to her uninformed daughter. Through talk-story about Jimmy, she and Pearl form a more mature mother-daughter bond.

The hardship of returning to San Francisco and constant prayer for Winnie's release from jail turn Jimmy Louie toward religion, a spiritual refuge that Tan half-heartedly supports. As a minister at the First Chinese Baptist Church, he carries out a Christian mission. Still a committed husband and family man, he is devoted to Winnie. He displays his loyalty and affection after Winnie faints at the church steps, a second motif of stalled motion. In a romantic baptism, he tenderly carries her to safety and cools her with water. After Jimmy's death from stomach cancer, she ponders the Chinese notion of swallowing sorrow and blames the ministry for forcing him to ingest other people's troubles that devoured his abdomen. She treasures her romance with Jimmy so much that she buys shoes for Bao-bao's wedding similar to the ones she wore when she went to the American Volunteer Group Christmas dance in 1941. Shoes serve as symbols of her long journey from a miserable marriage and a reminder of the broken heel at her first meeting with her beloved rescuer Jimmy.

See also **autonomy, Pearl Louie Brandt, communication, confinement, fate and fortune, ghosts, journeys**

• *Further Reading*

McFadden, Cyra. "Amy Tan's Second Novel Is Rich and Satisfying Tale." *San Francisco Examiner*, June 17, 1991, p. C8.
Pate, Nancy. "'Wife' Is the Story of an Amazing Life." *Orlando Sentinel*, June 23, 1991, p. C11.

Louie, Winnie

Winnie Louie, the protagonist of *The Kitchen God's Wife* (1991), is one of many Chinese emigrants in Tan's fiction who try to forget hard times in the past. She describes herself as "pretty skin, foolish heart, strong will, scared bones," and born lucky, but gradually she believes herself abandoned by good fortune (p. 345). The daughter of Jiang Sao-yen, a wealthy textile manufacturer, she is shamed by her mother's disappearance and reared as an outsider in her uncle's house on Tsungming Island. Under the control of her uncle's two wives, Old Aunt and New Aunt, she lives a child's misery of longing for her absent mother and of alienation from family, which considers her second rate. At times, the pain of memory reduces her to the six-year-old who has no means to explain her mother's disappearance in 1924. Ultimately, Winnie grows up to wreak vengeance, a drive that Maureen Harrington of the *Denver Post* describes as "a universal female need for poetic justice" (Harrington, p. C9).

At the novel's beginning, Winnie and her daughter Pearl are locked into a love-hate relationship that reaches beyond the daughter into the mother's miserable past. In the estimation of *San Francisco Examiner* reviewer Cyra McFadden, the two "find loving each other easy, understanding each other hard" (McFadden, p. C8). Pearl sees her mother as a human container for perpetual regrets that she could not alter fate. Winnie blames herself for not finding a less stressful job for her husband, Jimmy Louie, a Baptist minister who died of stomach cancer in 1964. In her perverted understanding of disease, she carries guilt for hiring an electrician who may have infected the house with malignancy. The image of microbes leaking out of wall sockets is both deplorably ignorant and endearing.

The oral revelations in Winnie's unburdening are the result of Helen Kwong's insistence that the two old friends sweep their houses clean of lies and secrets before Chinese New Year. All that night, Winnie ponders the decades of lies as she changes sheets and cleans curtains, furniture, and a photo of her dead husband. Before revealing all to Pearl, Winnie strengthens her daughter with a serving of noodle soup, a loving mother-daughter scenario that dates to Pearl's childhood. To spare Pearl the aching uncertainty of family secrets and intergenerational gaps in understanding, Winnie narrates a detailed war-time saga of misery, exile, and separation from loved ones. She intends her lengthy talk-story to bridge the mental chasms that separate a young Amerasian from her native Chinese parents. Significantly, photographic evidence is absent because Winnie destroyed pictures of the worst years of her life. At a break in the telling, she offers tea and watermelon seeds, which Pearl prefers to remove whole from the husk, just as Winnie unwraps the whole truth of her girlhood and first marriage.

Winnie's long list of repressed memories and regrets concerns marriage and family more than war or material loss. She recalls the pure trust that she shared with her unnamed mother, a romantic who cultivated eclectic tastes in European luxuries and who impressed her young daughter by peeling an apple in one long curl, a symbol of the long matrilineal tradition that links girl to mother and grandmothers. Although educated in Western ideas, the mother agreed to a feudal marriage with Jiang Sao-yen as a replacement for his deceased second wife. At the sumptuous house on Julu Road, the bad-luck spot in the family earned her the unflattering title of Double Second. Spoiled and coddled, Winnie received whatever she demanded and, until age six, was carried in her mother's arms until those all-too-human arms could no longer stave off the ugly realities of polygyny.

After fortunes reverse with the disappearance of the mother, Winnie survives like a cast-off stepchild at her Uncle Jiang's house on Tsungming Island. In secret thoughts, she considers the possible fates of her mother, whom her aunts revile. Winnie's inward nature develops from sneaking off to be alone with her thoughts in the greenhouse, one of numerous alliances of Winnie with the color green, a symbol of hope represented by imperial jade earrings as a wedding gift and her green dress and coat. She later discerns that she suppressed feelings for so long that she is no longer sure of her own emotions. It is only after her return to Tsungming Island by flatboat in adulthood that she can look out on cheering relatives and realize that they treasure her for herself. The image uplifts her as a returning heroine in contrast to Wen Fu, the evil husband who falsely describes himself as a disabled war hero of the Kuomintang.

Confinement pocks Winnie's life with cheerless episodes of lovelessness. She completes her education in Shanghai at a Catholic boarding school, but receives no family from her father's mansion on Julu Road. In 1935, she rejects Lin, a mannerly, educated suitor who later crops up at Jimmy Louie's church as Dr. Lin, a successful Chinese-American professional. At age nineteen, she enters a period of fantasy that she can marry her way out of unhappiness into a contented household where the mother-in-law never chastises the young bride. Winnie accepts an arranged marriage to Wen Fu, who represents hope of ending her misery as the daughter of a woman immured in scandal for abandoning her family. Her father extends her expectations with return to her mother's old room, a formal welcome to his table, and a week of shopping with San Ma for a trousseau and household goods. Winnie is so hungry for father-love that she interprets his courtesy as proof that she is precious to him.

At the crux of Winnie's liberation from feudal ideas, she ponders her need for a father image. Her reliance on Wen Fu results in nightly battery, the deaths of two baby girls, Mochou and Yiku, and verbal abuse in public and private. She battles with Helen about the war and snips out a dress from cotton cloth while carrying on an internal monologue about how she will survive widowhood. At a defining moment, she realizes that she is wishing that Wen Fu would die in combat so she can choose her own second husband. Tan creates a metaphor for Winnie's hopeless marriage by picturing her getting stuck in the too-small dress she is making, a domestic image that precedes even graver concern for her survival against her abusive spouse.

Facing the exigencies of war changes Winnie. On the long truck ride southwest to Kunming, she abandons modesty and fastidiousness by coping with no toilets along the mountain road and bedbugs in a hotel. As combat alters Wen Fu, she conceals her brutal marriage until there is no way to hide the terrible fights, sexual abuse, and nightly threats. Perplexing Winnie is the duplicity of Helen, who lends her money for a rooming house, then leads the angry husband to his runaway wife and son. In January, Winnie retaliates against Wen Fu by aborting a baby and again in March and May ends the gestation of luckless children sired by Wen Fu. Out of love for children, Winnie prefers that they not live at all rather than suffer the fate of Mochou and Yiku, both killed by their father's evil. Tan takes this view of abortion as the choice of a desperate mother.

On return to Shanghai, where Wen Fu wastes her family's money and sells their heirlooms, Winnie displays a form of the decisiveness she once saw in her father. After the Wen family commandeers the Jiang mansion on Julu Road, she adopts passive aggression and retaliates with small, clandestine annoyances, like the removal of a mah jong tile from the set and infestation of Wen Fu's bedding with insects. Her trickery does not compare with the harm he does by raping her and leaving her in doubt as to the siring of her daughter Pearl. To ease the harm done by telling Pearl about those terrible last days in China, Winnie confers a touch of grace. With a tender pat to Pearl's cheek and a stroke of her hair, Winnie murmurs, "You looked like ... all the children I could not keep but could never forget" (p. 511). The remark indicates the ongoing hell of Winnie's thoughts, which never come to terms with Wen Fu's sadism.

See also **diaspora, Jiang Sao-yen, Kitchen God, love, religion, reunion, sisterhood, talk-story, women**

• *Further Reading*

Harrington, Maureen. "Tan's Immigrant Tale Top Quality." *Denver Post*, June 23, 1991, p. C9.
McFadden, Cyra. "Amy Tan's Second Novel Is Rich and Satisfying Tale." *San Francisco Examiner*, June 17, 1991, p. C8.
Pate, Nancy. "'Wife' Is the Story of an Amazing Life." *Orlando Sentinel*, June 23, 1991, p. C11.

Louie genealogy

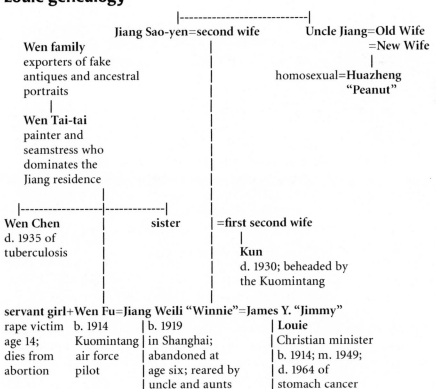

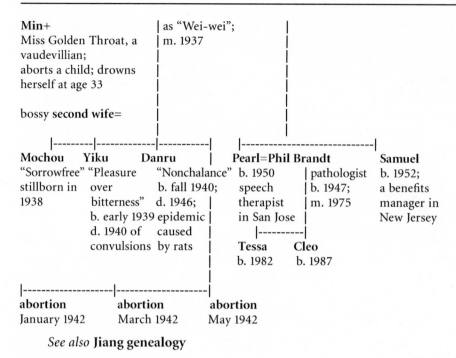

```
Min+                          | as "Wei-wei";          |
Miss Golden Throat, a         | m. 1937                |
vaudevillian;                 |                        |
aborts a child; drowns        |                        |
herself at age 33             |                        |
                              |                        |
bossy second wife=            |                        |
                              |                        |

|---------|------------|-----------|       |----------------------------|
Mochou    Yiku       Danru     |         Pearl=Phil Brandt           Samuel
"Sorrowfree" "Pleasure  "Nonchalance"  b. 1950   | pathologist    b. 1952;
stillborn in  over      b. fall 1940;  speech    | b. 1947;       a benefits
1938         bitterness" d. 1946;  |   therapist  | m. 1975       manager in
             b. early 1939 epidemic |  in San Jose |              New Jersey
             d. 1940 of  caused   |    |----------|
             convulsions  by rats |    Tessa     Cleo
                                  |    b. 1982    b. 1987
                                  |
|--------------------|------------------|
abortion          abortion        abortion
January 1942      March 1942      May 1942
```

See also **Jiang genealogy**

love

Tan cautiously sprinkles her texts with expressions of love, for example, a Christmas Eve dinner in the early short-short story "Fish Cheeks" (1987), where a Chinese father selects a succulent piece of soft steamed flesh from beneath the eye of a rock cod to offer his teenage daughter. In *The Joy Luck Club* (1989), Tan expresses the problematic mother-daughter relationships of Chinese mothers with their Amerasian daughters. A major literary coup is the abiding affection of Suyuan Woo for her grown twins Chwun Yu and Chwun Hwa Wang, whom she abandoned in 1944 near the end of the Sino-Japanese War (1937–1945). The power of love to reunite a family even after the mother's death is evident in the twins' eager letter to her. At their first view of June Woo in October 1987, they murmur "Mama, Mama" in acknowledgement of their parent's death and of the family resemblance in their younger sister, who arrives as her emissary (p. 331). The endearing features and affectionate behaviors that strengthen family bonds illustrate the depth of mother love and its survival into succeeding generations.

In expression of the difference between parental bonding and infatuation, the author introduces the cost of romantic love in *The Kitchen God's Wife* (1991). The sufferings of women escaping polygyny take shape in Winnie's mother, who chooses to marry Jiang Sao-yen, then leaves him seven years later, perhaps to flee with Lu, her Marxist lover. A more illustrative example of the Chinese view of romance occurs in Winnie's love for Gan, a tall, thin, awkward pilot who joins the other Kuomintang soldiers at Winnie's table. She pictures him as self-deprecating in his jokes and quick to lend a hand. His gracious compliments to her cooking causes her to compare Gan to Wen Fu and wish that her husband was less loud and caustic in his humor. She begins to wonder not just how she married so poor a mate, but why she didn't know that she had a choice.

The author develops a sweet and loving relationship between Winnie and Gan as part of her education about female autonomy. When Wen Fu is out of town, Gan and Winnie share evening walks, games of chicken-feather ball, and dinners of noodles. Their camaraderie gives her a new view of happiness as an equal to a male friend. She is pleased to know Gan's motivations and to feel less lonely in his company. To maintain an appropriate distance between herself and an unmarried male, she jokes and teases when she really longs for a soothing intimacy. Her restraint illustrates how thoroughly indoctrinated she is to respect her husband and avoid disrespect to her family.

Wartime loss puts Winnie's concealment to the test. When Gan confesses his terror of a prediction of death in 1938, she yearns to console him to relieve his fears and to receive his love. Still obedient to Chinese proprieties, she remains on the periphery of his friendship out of fear of a scandalous male-female entanglement. She envisions mutual affection as the sharing of inmost feelings and sorrows, resulting in "so much released until you overflowed with joy" (p. 254). At Gan's grotesque disembowelment and slow death after being shot down near Nanking, Winnie thinks of him as her ghost lover and of herself as his ninth fate. Her pathetic grasp at a fantasy romance indicates how starved she is for affection.

In Tan's third novel, *The Hundred Secret Senses* (1995), the plot branches out to more complex love relationships. A bittersweet mother-daughter tie develops between Kwan Li and her little Amerasian sister Olivia Yee Laguni. Although Kwan embarrasses and annoys Olivia with her countrified ways, the younger sibling admits that Kwan has become a substitute parent and protector. Olivia exaggerates that Kwan would "tear off the ear of anyone who said an unkind word about me" (p. 24). Despite proof of loyalty, Olivia resents Kwan's meddling in personal matters, especially Olivia's separation from Simon Bishop, who destroyed their marriage because he offered his wife only "emotional scraps" (p. 27). Kwan exerts her powers of persuasion to arrange a journey to Changmian, China, that includes the warring Bishops, who view the trip as a professional assignment rather than a romantic encounter.

Tan uses the journey as an opportunity to illustrate that love survives hardships, even death. To *Bookpage* interviewer Ellen Kanner, the author expresses the necessity of Kwan, Simon, and Olivia's jaunt to the rural village: "We're all looking for the meaning of love, looking for sense in our relationships, while still being unable to let go of our neuroses" (Kanner, p. 3). Of the two sisters, Kwan is the one who "believes the real power, the real secret sense is love, it's however you love, the qualities of love, of empathy, of the deepest form of empathy we can't even imagine" (*Ibid.*). In her past life in rural China near Thistle Mountain, she came to know and encourage Nelly Banner's yearning for love and recognized that women desperate for passion will take the rotten kind, any tenderness "to fill the hollow" (p. 71). In Kwan's opinion, such desperation eventually accepts false love in place of the real thing, a catastrophe that costs Nelly her life at the hands of the wicked General Warren Cape. A similar embrace of an unreliable romance ruins Olivia's seventeen-year marriage to Simon Bishop and proves that the motif survives from century to century.

Tan ponders the rhythms of interracial courtship in Yiban Johnson's wooing of Nelly Banner. Although she accepts nineteenth-century bigotry concerning intimacy between Caucasian women and mixed race men, she gives in to long conversations and sweet emotional exchanges. Told through the observations of Nunumu, a one-eyed Hakka laundress who speaks no English and understands little of their verbal relationship, the fervency of their tête-à-têtes and the touching of hands indicates a growing regard that requires no translation. Tan illustrates the contagion of romance by Nunumu's acceptance of Zeng, the one-eared jar seller, whose grease-spotted clothes she offers to wash. He reciprocates with gifts of rice and oil, staples in short supply at the mission kitchen. The gesture reprises numerous examples in Tan's fiction of food gifts as love messages.

After the Taipeng Rebellion of 1864, love spreads throughout the mission compound. It kindles the cooling marriage of the pastor and his wife and brings together Dr. Too Late with the timid Miss Mouse. The advance of Manchu death squads in search of God Worshippers prompts Zeng to volunteer to shelter Nunumu in a cave. To her, the statement has little in common with Western ideas of romance, yet, the offer to save her life reflects Zeng's intentions toward her. Rather than hurt his feelings, she tries to maneuver him into advancing from courtship to physical union by extending him the hospitality of a room at the compound. After he begins making decisions for her, she recognizes that they are truly man and wife in the spirit. He mentions marriage only after his death, when he returns to her as a ghost. His loyalty reflects the novel's theme of love that survives multiple reincarnations.

Tan relegates the most serious meditations on love to Olivia. During the two-week stay in Changmian at Big Ma's house, she, her estranged husband, and her big sister must share a four-poster bed, the only guest accommodation available. Olivia tries to remain aloof from Simon, but finds herself tormented by thoughts of snuggling and making love. She regrets that their former marital affection dwindled. In her opinion, the union was not to last their entire adult lives because Simon navigated her body better than he occupied her heart. She reveals bitter cynicism by portraying their former bliss as a physical surrender to endorphins. Like Nelly Banner, Olivia yearns for something better — a total union of body and spirit.

The multiple types of love that enfold Olivia in the novel's resolution stem from Kwan's meddling and her intent to complete unfinished business from a former life. After identifying Nelly and her lover Yiban in the living forms of Olivia and her estranged husband Simon, Kwan is driven to reunite the couple in their current incarnations. Through spiritual magic, Olivia ends seventeen barren years by conceiving in the old marriage bed and revives her relationship with Simon, father of their daughter Samantha Li. Olivia admits to learning from Kwan "vastness of soul" and the undying and inclusive nature of love that encompasses worry and sorrow along with bliss (p. 399).

Love returns to Tan's writing in *The Bonesetter's Daughter* (2001), which parallels two couples. The first, Precious Auntie and Liu Hu Sen, is a tender pairing that ends on their wedding day with Precious Auntie left groomless after a horse kicks her fiancé and kills him. Their abiding affection returns in the couple's illegitimate daughter LuLing Liu, who clings to Precious Auntie and flourishes under her mothering. When the mother's death parts them, LuLing lives a tenuous existence in an orphanage until her marriage to geologist Pan Kai Jing. The author expresses a gentle, nurturing love in Kai Jing as he rocks his wife and soothes away her fears of a ghost's curse. As though crooning a Zen love charm, he murmurs an elegant testimonial to love's immortality: "You are beauty, and love is beauty and we are beauty. We are divine, unchanged by time" (p. 230). The words echo in LuLing's head in the weeks following Kai Jing's execution by Japanese soldiers as a promise of reunion in the afterlife.

See also **assimilation, autonomy, mother-daughter relationships, Precious Auntie, racism, reunion, storytelling, women**

- *Further Reading*

Kanner, Ellen. "From Amy Tan, a Superb Novel of Two Sisters, Two Worlds, and a Few Ghosts." *Bookpage*, December 1995, p. 3.
Shapiro, Laura. "From China, with Love." *Newsweek*, Vol. 117, No. 25, June 24, 1991, pp. 63–64.
_____. "Ghost Story." *Newsweek*, Vol. 126, No. 19, November 6, 1995, pp. 91–92.

mah jong

Amy Tan uses casual games of mah jong, a common pastime based on the arrangement of tiles for competitive play, as a structural device and as commentary on the lives of characters who abandon the concept of luck to embrace self-actualization. In *The Joy Luck Club* (1989), the symmetry of a mah jong table imposes an artificial order in the lives of four Chinese women who seek their fortune in a new land. The women friends playing the game — An-mei Hsu, Lindo Jong, Ying-ying St. Clair, and Suyuan Woo—compete with determination and a will to win, an antidote to memories of coercive marriages, silencing, displacement, and the terrors and disruptions of the Sino-Japanese War (1937–1945). They bet *yuan*, the paper money that became worthless during China's hard times. Their choice illustrates the importance of the game itself and the camaraderie of people who share the same background and hopes.

There is more to games of mah jong than passing the time with friends. Before the women's emigration, conversation provides an outlet to Chinese females whom rigid patriarchy, polygyny, and male-centered feudal marriage stifled. While deliberately consuming luxuries in a time of famine, they confine speech to the action of sixteen rounds of their game, then talk all night about joys of the past and hopes for a bright future free from war. The game becomes a vital survival strategy. Suyuan explains through rhetorical questions: "What was worse, we asked among ourselves, to sit and wait for our own deaths with proper somber faces? Or to choose our own happiness" (p. 25). When the game resumes in the United States, Suyuan, a seriously traumatized survivor of wartime flight, speaks the belief of her peers that "you could be anything you wanted to be in America" (p. 132). In proof of her vision, the mah jong sessions picture female participants enjoying personal safety and gender freedoms as well as the financial equities of capitalism.

Pragmatically, the players assure luck by discussing wise investments of their winnings, a focus of newcomers to America. Their games cancel dreadful memories with an exuberance that refuses to give in to the terror they suffered from past atrocities. The death of Suyuan is Tan's method of passing along traditions and value systems to a first-generation Chinese-American girl, June Woo, who must navigate the tricky intergenerational differences that separate mothers from daughters. Born in a culture that exalts individuality, June ponders the native Chinese women's old-fashioned clothing, the silk dresses embroidered over the heart with a hopeful maternal symbol, a blooming branch. To cope with their conservatism, she and her peers— Waverly Jong, Rose Hsu Jordan, and Lena St. Clair Livotny — temper their American freedoms by accepting some of the maternal control expected of proper Chinese girls.

See also **Appendix B, materialism**

• *Further Reading*

Chong, Denise. "Emotions Journeys through East and West." *Quill and Quire*, Vol. 55, No. 5, 1989, p. 23.
Hamilton, Patricia L. "Feng Shui, Astrology, and the Five Elements: Traditional Chinese Belief in Amy Tan's *The Joy Luck Club*." *MELUS*, Vol. 24, No. 2, Summer 1999, pp. 125–145.
Ling, Amy. *Between Worlds: Women Writers of Chinese Ancestry*. New York: Pergamon Press, 1990.
Schell, Orville. "Your Mother Is in Your Bones." *New York Times Book Review*, Vol. 26, March 19, 1989, pp. 3, 28.

materialism

Discussions of material goods, bargains, and money and debts come naturally to the Asian characters in Amy Tan's fiction. In *The Joy Luck Club* (1989), which appeared during the hedonistic Reagan era, the prevalence of materialism in first-generation Asian-Americans contrasts the thrift of parents from the old country. One example, An-mei and George Hsu's new furniture, follows them from Chinatown to the Sunset district, but remains under yellowing plastic wrap to protect the upholstery. In another setting, Ying-ying St. Clair sizes up her daughter Lena's relationship with husband Harold Livotny by evaluating their waste of money on a showplace home and Jaguar convertible. While Suyuan Woo narrates her life story to her daughter June, Suyuan's strong pulls on old ski sweaters rip out yarn for salvaging on pieces of cardboard. In another scene, her refusal to buy June a transistor radio precedes a lengthy story worth much more to the daughter than tinny American music. These examples attest to the refugee's inability to waste goods or to squander money on transitory amusements.

In *The Kitchen God's Wife* (1991), the author perpetuates the pinchpenny logic of immigrant Chinese housewives who seem to march out of her first novel into the second. She stresses Winnie Louie's interest in bargain-hunting in everything from toilet paper and tofu to a female deity to replace the evil Kitchen God. After the reception for Bao-bao's wedding, a central event that reunites local Chinese families, attendees troll the table for leftovers, which they intend to eat at the next day's meals. The boxing of salvageable food reprises Helen's gluttony during the Sino-Japanese War (1937–1945), an unconscious attempt to stuff the body with food to stave off the famine and want that is sure to engulf China's peasants.

Crucial to the novel is the grasping nature of the Wen family, who negotiate Winnie's marriage to Wen Fu in good faith, then steal her dowry goods for sale or use in their own homes. The mercenary grabbing of other people's possessions worsens after the war, when Wen Fu and his parents take control of Jiang Sao-yen's home on Julu road in Shanghai and strip it of saleable antiques and art treasures. Tan creates dramatic irony out of the dying industrial magnate's trickery, which inspires Wen Fu to demolish the house in search of a non-existent treasure in gold. The author implies that the novel's villain loses his real treasures, his wife Winnie and their son Danru, whom he is too venal to value.

In Tan's third novel, *The Hundred Secret Senses* (1995), materialism intertwines with the theme of love. Kwan Li observes no decorum in discussing personal subjects, which extend to her sister's love life or the cost of vacations and oranges from the supermarket. A countrified native of Changmian village, she seems out of sync with behaviors and outlooks of refined Asian-Americans living in San Francisco. Tan illustrates the source of Kwan's material concerns after Kwan and Olivia and Simon Bishop travel back to her homeland. Surrounded by grim poverty, the outsiders return to medieval conditions and recognize in local waitresses and hair-trimmers their outsized hopes of earning a living from infrequent tourists. The extent of need in Changmian quickly divests the visitors of American materialism.

It is obvious that need shifts the thinking of the poor from owning luxuries to feeding hungry bellies. Because villagers survive in cold houses on wok cookery over a small fire, the family gathering for meals is a high point of their existence. The Bishops interview, take notes, and photograph the cooking of chicken broth and the serving of aromatic tea while attempting to record enough of local need to express to readers how food replaces material goods in worth and meaning. Because of their familiarity with skimpy meals and outright famine, the locals greet Kwan with cries of "Fat! You've grown unbelievably fat" (p. 231). To an American, the greeting seems rude; to Chinese peasants, the comment acknowledges that Kwan has found a good living in the promised land.

Drawing on disparities in material wealth, Tan describes a rift between sisters in her fourth novel, *The Bonesetter's Daughter* (2001). LuLing Young faults her sister GaoLing Young with flaunting wealth after the two marry brothers. LuLing weds the luckless medical student, who dies in a hit-and-run accident, and GaoLing unites with Edmund Young, the brother who becomes a prosperous dentist. Some of LuLing's unfounded imaginings charge GaoLing for extravagant living in her ranch-style California home with swimming pool. To maintain pride, LuLing becomes the miser who stacks soiled writing paper for use as blotters, practice sheets, and hot pads. In a scolding to the housekeeper that LuLing's daughter Ruth hires for her mother, LuLing declares, "You think you don't lift finger? No, America not this way" (p. 90). Near the end of LuLing's life, Ruth is surprised to learn that her mother's shrewd investments will pay for her stay in Mira Mar Manor, an expensive retirement home.

See also **Lena St. Clair Livotny, obedience**

• *Further Reading*

Palumbo-Liu, David, ed. *The Ethnic Canon: Histories, Institutions, and Interventions.* Minneapolis: University of Minnesota Press, 1995.

men

Critics have lambasted Amy Tan for a common feminist failing, the elevation of female characters and the vilification, abasement, or dismissal of males. A thorough examination of her canon proves otherwise, as in the case of the loving father in the short-short story "Fish Cheeks" (1987), who feeds his teenage daughter her favorite food, a soft piece of flesh from beneath the eye of a steamed rock cod, which he plucks with his own chopsticks. In *The Joy Luck Club* (1989), several husbands drift in and out of the story without making significant impact. Clifford St. Clair, as compared with his daughter Lena St. Clair, seems largely clueless about the mental aberrations of his depressed wife Ying-ying. Even less important to the story are George Hsu, who offers little comfort to his wife An-mei and daughter Rose after the drowning death of son Bing, and Tin Jong, an employee of the telephone company who, ironically, has almost no speaking role in the novel. Of the second tier of husbands, Marvin Chen is completely absent and Rich Schields and Harold Livotny nearly so. Only Ted Jordan seems important enough to shape motivation as he maneuvers his wife Rose toward divorce with a paltry bribe of ten thousand dollars.

One exception to the novel's discounted male roles is Canning Woo, a recent widower who offers his daughter June emotional support during their trip to China, but who has limited influence on her outlook, as compared with her relationship with his wife Suyuan. In a tender example of father-daughter talk-story, he helps June comprehend the war-time upheaval that left Suyuan hospitalized for dysentery and suicidal after she abandoned her baby daughters, Chwun Hwa and Chwun Yu, by the roadside. He downplays his part in accompanying Suyuan to Shanghai and Hong Kong in search of information about the twins' whereabouts. Because he defends his wife's actions, he perpetuates the value of oral stories as legacies of love and pillars of family honor. Although his strength does not cancel the numerous feeble male roles, he does disprove critical complaint that Tan is hostile toward husband and father figures.

With *The Kitchen God's Wife* (1991), Tan creates a major villain. Wen Fu, the abusive husband and father, first appears in the New Year's stage role of dragon, a foretoken of his gradual decline toward bestial menace. During the Sino-Japanese War (1937–1945), he breaches the bounds of the hostile husband and expands his evil from domestic battery and bullying of his fellow pilots to felonies. He is guilty of death by motor vehicle of one of his paramours and of terrorizing and neglect in the demise of his baby daughters Mochou and Yiku. These combat era crimes precede post-war instances of extortion, theft, rape, and threatening with a gun. Added to more mundane faults of lying under oath, intimidation, and deceit, these actions deny humanity in Wen Fu, whose death from coronary disease suits a man with no heart.

Tan makes no effort to balance the characterization of Jiang Sao-yen and Jimmy

Louie, Wen Fu's foils, with Winnie's wicked first husband. Jiang bears his own burden of guilt for ignoring Winnie during her education at a Shanghai boarding school and for failing to intercede at the time of her betrothal to a suitor from the questionable Wen family. Tan allows Jiang a brief redemption in the encouragement of her flight from Wen Fu by giving her gold ingots to finance her freedom. The scenes of Jimmy Louie's skill as an interpreter and friend-maker and his genuine love for Winnie and his stepson Danru are brief and lacking in dialogue. His absence during Winnie's trial and imprisonment requires the creation of a female supporter, Auntie Du Ching, who brings supplies and news to Winnie during visits to Shanghai's women's prison. Thus, Jimmy Louie seems more like a comic-book rescuer than a mate and equal of Winnie. When the action shifts to Pearl's failure to mourn her father's death, Winnie returns the gesture by rescuing her husband from ignominy to assure proper familial respect for his devotion to family and to God. These proofs of a stable, dependable husband come too late to revive a largely lifeless character.

In *The Hundred Secret Senses* (1995), the author continues pairing hapless women with faithless, evil men. Store clerk Li Chen, mother of the ghost-seer Kwan Li, is loyal to husband Jack Yee, but dies from grief after he deserts her before the birth of their second child. When Kwan backtracks to an earlier life, she becomes Nunumu, the friend of Nelly Banner, a lonely and unappreciated translator for a Christian mission of dubious repute. Nunumu knows the history of General Warren Cape, a despicable mercenary, and sinks into heart sadness when she hears Nelly leave her bedroom door open each night to him. Accompanying the general is Yiban "One-Half" Johnson, a stateless half-breed born in a coffin after his mother's death. Nunumu realizes the value of Johnson as compared to Cape, who doesn't deserve his translator's skill and loyalty.

Beyond the main characters, Tan adds to the story a variety of male boobs and lesser villains, including Rocky the cab driver, the witless servant-turned-ghost Lao Lu, and Bob Laguni, the stepfather who leaves Olivia in bed with flu and travels to Hawaii. In adulthood, Olivia tries to trace strange noises in her co-op and learns that Paul Dawson, her blind neighbor, uses electronic devices and dialers to terrorize the women he telephones. Olivia drops her sympathy for him after police locate bugging devices by which he monitors her third-floor quarters. Other one-dimensional males in the plot include George Lew, Kwan's husband, who marries his cousin Virgie from Vancouver soon after Kwan's disappearance, and Pastor Amen, a pathetic excuse for pulpit minister who sinks into idiocy as Manchu soldiers advance on the compound and roast a human leg over the fire.

At a turning point in the novel, Tan introduces surprising family history. Speaking in Chinese, Kwan tells Olivia about living in Liangfeng in 1948 with her mother, Li Chen, and father, whom she called Ba. After he locates immigration papers, visa, ticket to the United States, cash, and a certificate of paid tuition for a year at Lincoln University in San Francisco in a stolen coat, he adopts the name Jack Yee. The transformation kills his love for Li Chen and causes his survivors to conceal his real name from Kwan. Contributing to mystery is the absence of information about the coat's original owner. At the novel's resolution, the importance of Jack sinks to virtually zero as Tan turns her attention to Kwan's disappearance and Olivia's miracle daughter, Samantha Li, sired by Simon while the couple toured Changmian. Once more, female characters outweigh males in anticipation of fulfillment and a satisfying conclusion.

Instances of memorable human passion recur in *The Bonesetter's Daughter* (2001), which exalts Bonesetter Gu for his adoration of his intelligent, capable daughter and exonerates Liu Hu Sen for his impetuous love of Precious Auntie and the result of their coupling, LuLing Liu. Although her father and mother enjoy only a brief love affair, Precious Auntie thrives on memories of the kindness and affection of Hu Sen, the man her father once treated for injured toes. In her teen years, LuLing meets Pan Kai Jing, a man like her father in the strength of his passion and gentle treatment of his wife. The couple suit each other — LuLing providing acceptance and respect for a lame mate, and Kai Jing adoring his wife and applying his scientific training to ridding her of fears of a family curse. At his death during the Japanese occupation of China, LuLing has his moral strength and faith in love as a support during early widowhood. In both mother and daughter, Tan pictures man's love for woman as fleeting, but powerful in the afterglow.

See also **Phil Brandt, Jiang Sao-yen, Jimmy Louie, Simon Bishop, Wen Fu**

• *Further Reading*

Ho, Wendy. *In Her Mother's House — The Politics of Asian American Mother-Daughter Writing*. Walnut Creek, Calif.: AltaMira Press, 1999.
Nhu, T. T. "We Need More Movies That Portray Asian Men Realistically." *San Jose Mercury*, October 4, 1993.

The Moon Lady

Tan's first children's story, *The Moon Lady* (1992), is an adaptation of an episode in *The Joy Luck Club* (1989) that took place in 1918, when Ying-ying St. Clair was four years old. The author wrote the text to help children examine their yearnings and powers to attain them. She stated to reviewer Stephanie Loer of the *Boston Globe*: "I wanted kids to wonder about wishes: where they came from and who helps us fulfill those wishes" (Loer, p. E3). Set in Wushi in the years following the collapse of the Ching Dynasty (1644–1912), the story tells of Grandmother Ying-Ying's response to the wishes of her granddaughters June, Lily, and Maggie, who are immured indoors on a rainy day. The book received excellent reviews from *Publishers Weekly* and *School Library Journal*.

The text opens with an upbeat image of a tile-roofed festival boat in bright crayon colors. Drawing their "nai-nai" into the conversation, the three girls learn about how she told a secret wish to the Moon Lady (n.p.). At age seven, Ying-ying wrestles with her amah to avoid wearing a hot jacket to the Moon Festival on Tai Lake in mid-autumn. The child is eager to divulge a secret wish to Lady Chang-o, a mythic female who lives on the moon. Ying-ying has normal shortcomings, including not wanting to share her rabbit rice cake with her cousins and not staying clean while chasing a dragonfly. Both suggest that disobedience is her worst fault.

The author illustrates important concepts of Chinese life, particularly the participation of family in annual holidays. Essential to a day of fun is a noon spread of fruit, preserved meat and vegetables, crabs and shrimp, and moon cakes washed down with tea. Tan's story illustrates how boys catch fish by stealing the prey of a diving bird and how a servant cleans eels and fish for dinner. The action implies that Ying-ying is guiltless for getting her clothing mussed with eel blood and fish scales, symbols of the realities of the laboring class, but Amah is angry nonetheless and strips her down to her underthings. The removal of festal garb also strips Ying-ying of the marks of social class and equalizes her with peasants who share the annual holiday.

The encounter with the Moon Lady is the result of Ying-ying's pouting at the rear of the boat and her tumble into the lake. The story avoids terrorizing children with the fear of drowning by depicting the child rescued by lowly net fishers. The woman correctly identifies the child's social status by the softness of her feet, which are accustomed to wearing shoes. Left on shore, Ying-ying attends a shadow play that illustrates the importance of not meddling in others' belongings and of not being greedy or selfish. An identity crisis leads her to empathize with the Moon Lady for being banished and "lost to the world" (n.p.).

Tan concludes her story of the lost child with disillusion preceding a valuable coming to knowledge. As Ying-ying presses close to the shadowy player, she sees the stage illusion give place to an unattractive male acting the female role. Wishing only to be reclaimed, she races across a footbridge to her relatives, a scenario symbolizing the clear delineation of social classes. The moral depicts her drawing a sensible conclusion about the mystical nature of yearning: that the best wishes are those she can fulfill by herself. Tan's distillation of the original episode into a children's book won high marks from *Publishers Weekly*, both for the print and audio versions. Critic Sheng-Mei Ma dissents from these opinions with complaints of mythic "Orientalized images of China," which perpetuate false Western opinions based on "a timeless golden age of ritualistic festivity" (Ma, p. 95).

See also **Ying-ying St. Clair, storytelling, yin and yang**

• *Further Reading*

Loer, Stephanie. "Amy Tan Writes from a Child's Point of View." *Boston Globe*, November 10, 1992, pp. E3–E4.
Ma, Sheng-mei. *The Deathly Embrace: Orientalism and Asian American Identity*. Minneapolis: University of Minnesota Press, 2000
Philbrook, John. "Review: *The Moon Lady*." *School Library Journal*, Vol. 92, No. 38, September 1992, p. 255.
"Review: *The Moon Lady*." *Publishers Weekly*, Vol. 239, No. 50, November 16, 1992, p. 24.

morality tale

Tan resets traditional Chinese lore in her novels as a link to beliefs and customs of the Amerasian motherland. She introduces "The Twenty-Six Malignant Gates," the second part of *The Joy Luck Club* (1989), with a brief morality tale about a

Chinese-American girl who copes with an overly protective parent. The girl disobeys her mother and suffers a fall from a bicycle, just as the mother predicted. The story contains a deeper meaning than the surface details. The mother fears that her child will round the corner and incur harm out of the parent's sight. The mother draws wisdom from a Chinese source, which is inaccessible to a first-generation American girl. The failure of one generation to communicate with another dominates Tan's novel, which focuses on the tensions mothers and daughters experience in meeting each others' expectations.

The cautionary narrative, presented in talk-story, a common Asian form of parental instruction, is an oral reminder of the parent's knowledge of life's pitfalls. Like the suicide story in Maxine Hong Kingston's *The Woman Warrior* (1975) about the shame resulting from pregnancy out of wedlock, Tan's bicycle story relates a warning of misbehavior that may bring unnecessary pain or permanent harm, but the text lacks the European-style morality tag line common to Aesopic fables. In Tan's morality tale, the corner suggests a complete departure from Chinese teachings and a right angle into American ways, which allow more freedom for children than do Chinese parenting methods. The seven-year-old not only insults her mother's intelligence, but angrily departs on the actual path that the older woman warned of. The fall before the girl reaches the corner implies that the girl violates both Asian and American rules and suffers the consequences. Tan's talk-story omits the mother's response by focusing only on the younger generation's rebellion and pain.

See also **communication, talk-story**

• *Further Reading*

Heung, Marina. "Daughter-Text/Mother-Text: Matrilineage in Amy Tan's Joy Luck Club." *Feminist Studies*, Vol. 19, No. 3, Fall 1993, pp. 597–616.
Ho, Wendy. *In Her Mother's House — The Politics of Asian American Mother-Daughter Writing*. Walnut Creek, Calif.: AltaMira Press, 1999.
Pearlman, Mickey, and Katherine Usher Henderson. *Inter/view: Talks with America's Writing Women*. Lexington: University Press of Kentucky, 1990.

mother-daughter relationships

Amy Tan is noted for the delicious ironies that arise when her fictional mothers and daughters carry on a protracted scrimmage that produces no winners. It is the contention of critic Amy Ling that the source of familial combat is the possessiveness of Chinese mothers who fight the American-style liberation and autonomy that their daughters cultivate. According to Deirdre Donahue, reviewer for *USA Today*, "No contemporary writer has dug deeper and more effectively into the crucible of the mother-daughter bond: loving, claustrophobic, maddening, inescapable" (Donahue, p. 1D). Reviewer Susan Balee of the *Philadelphia Enquirer* compared Tan's handling of female archetypes to that of English novelist Jane Austen and predicted that Tan's works could remain a part of the literary canon for the next two centuries.

In Tan's four novels, the cause of life-long mother-vs.-child verbal strife is the result of assimilation and new identities. As critic Elaine H. Kim observes, mothers brandish not only old-world Chinese conservatism, but also a "fierce love, which makes them desire their daughters' freedom and selfhood as well as their own" (Kim, p. 83). One mother, Ying-Ying St. Clair, realizes that her Amerasian daughter, Lena Livotny, has moved steadily away from a Chinese upbringing from birth. The mother recalls that "she sprang from me like a slippery fish, and has been swimming away from me since" (p. 242). One explanation of maternal unrest is the placement of the Chinese father in business and citizenship and of the Chinese mother in directing and disciplining children and making decisions concerning their education and welfare. Thus, Chinese-born mothers' strict stance and ambitions for their children have as justification and support the weight of centuries of Chinese culture. When the mothers live in the freer social environs of the New World, their conservatism and poor language skills force them to the margin as outsiders, even intruders and outcasts, producing mother-daughter relationships based on alienation and imperfect expressions of love.

In a discussion of *The Joy Luck Club* and its film version, the author expressed a matrilineal purpose: "Mother-daughter relationships are at the heart of what I was writing" (Taylor, p. F1). The text dramatizes a complex, multifaceted series of relationships that wounds with honest appraisal and heals with generous love and acceptance of daughters who came of age during the civil rights and women's movements. Through courageous parenting and a nose-to-nose "I-Thou" interaction, mothers infuse in their daughters a subjective wisdom that comes from the older generation's war-time suffering. Like breastfeeding, the infusion is up-close and personal, a human bonding that requires the daughters' full cooperation.

The source of maternal strength is similar to nutrients. As three original club members— An-mei Hsu, Lindo Jong, and Ying-ying St. Clair — explain to June Woo shortly after Suyuan Woo's death, "Your mother is in your bones!" (p. 31). June recognizes that the women educate her while mentally picturing their own daughters, who are "just as unmindful of all the truths and hopes they have brought to America" (p. 31). When Rose Hsu attempts to shush her mother from asking personal questions during a funeral, An-mei condemns her daughter's confessions to a psychiatrist and exclaims: "A mother is best. A mother knows what is inside you" (p. 210). Ying-ying, who feels distanced from her daughter in part because of Lena's profession as an "arty-tecky" (architect), echoes mother wisdom by vowing to relate her past to Lena "to penetrate her skin and pull her to where she can be saved" (pp. 242, 274). There is a desperation in Ying-ying's mother love, which she brandishes in her daughter's face like an antidote to poison.

In the chapter "Double Face," Lindo Jong, a tough parent who recalls her own mother's rejection, attempts to understand the change in Waverly after she becomes a brilliant tax attorney. While Mr. Rory prepares to style Lindo's hair for Waverly's second marriage, he inadvertently alters the family power structure by commenting on the mother-daughter resemblance. To Waverly's rejection of the comment, Lindo conceals the fact that she, too, saw her mother's resemblance in her own face. Lindo's relationship is marred in girlhood after her betrothal, which causes her mother to view her as an outsider who will soon live under the supervision of a mother-in-law, Huang Tai-tai. Overall, Tan uses the mirror image to represent the historical perspective through which a chain of mothers and daughters looks at present and past and attempts to ally events in contrasting times and places. The motif recurs in An-mei's first view of her mother, who looks back with the same face as the daughter. The exchanged glance creates a bond that enables An-mei to rescue her mother from spiteful gossip, a reversal of the motif of parent saving child.

The Kitchen God's Wife (1991) reprises the mother-daughter tensions, but distills the mix to one pair, Winnie Louie and her adult daughter, Pearl Louie Brandt. Patti Doten, book reviewer for the *Boston Globe,* praised Tan's clarification of "the convoluted loops and holes of this relationship, not with a harsh Freudian microscope, but through the softly blazing metaphors of Asia" (Doten, p. 63). In telling her life story to Pearl, Winnie refers to relations with her own mother, the unnamed second wife of self-important Shanghai industrialist Jiang Sao-yen. In the private eden of her mother's room, Winnie enjoys constant attention and the bestowal of exotic tidbits from her mother's stash of English biscuits. As the loving relationship comes to an unexpected end, the mother reaches for self-actualization by reuniting with Lu, the Marxist journalist, at an afternoon movie. Foreshadowing Winnie's future ache for her mother is the delicacy called *wah-wah yu,* a fish that reaches and cries like an infant. The personified fish also foretells of the hapless infants that Winnie bears to the demonic Wen Fu and loses, one by one.

Tan uses physical distance to portray the lack of heart-to-heart familiarity. At a tender moment in the relationship between Winnie and Pearl, they sit at separate tables at Bao-bao's engagement party. Pearl, feeling guilty that she hasn't divulged her illness from multiple sclerosis, acknowledges the distance between them and their inability to share important life elements. She asks in a rhetorical question, "All these meaningless gestures, old misunderstandings, and painful secrets, why do we keep them up?" (p. 33). As Winnie cleans house a week later, she thinks of the polite distancing her daughter maintains, "Always trying not to bump into each other, just like strangers" (p. 95).

The author exulted over the success of her second novel, particularly its revelations about her own family. She marveled at the "way [the story's] transformed over time, yet always endures, and is passed on from mother to daughter" (Tan, p. 114). According to Assunta Ng, publisher of the *Seattle Chinese Post,* Tan's compulsion to write about woman-to-woman familial tension creates universality in her fiction. The author relates the cause of friction: "Every mother and daughter ends up holding a little bit of themselves from one another, and that can widen and widen into a deep gulf" (Doten, p. 63). The novel offers female readers insight into family alienation and proposes redress through confessional talk-story, a source of redemption.

With *The Hundred Secret Senses* (1995), the author expresses a more touching alienation, the pervasive sadness in motherless girls. She begins with Kwan Li, whose mother, Li Chen, died in 1948 after her husband, Jack Yee, deserted her during her second pregnancy. Kwan denies that the cause was tuberculosis and insists that heartsickness killed Chen as surely as cold wind could destroy a straw roof and blow away a family member. Similarly, in the exposition of Simon Bishop, Tan describes his passion for Elza, an orphan with no knowledge of her parentage. Simon substantiates the presence of Polish Jewry in Elza, who chants in Polish after encountering information about Holocaust victims at Auschwitz. Elza believes that "her mother's memories [passed] from heart to womb" and into Elza's brain (p. 82). The mystic communication epitomizes Tan's reverence for matrilineal linkage.

Tan uses a sad moment in the novel to comment on grown women's feelings for the mothers and surrogate parents who reared them. After the death of Big Ma, Kwan's aunt and foster mother, in a car-bus accident on the road to Guilin, Kwan grieves for the woman who treated her cruelly. Olivia, child of a neglectful mother, ponders the undeserved tenderness toward Big Ma: "Why do we love the mothers of our lives even if they are lousy caretakers?" (p. 236). Olivia posits that infants bear "blank hearts" on which mothers inscribe their own version of maternal love (*Ibid.*). The epiphany explains in part why Olivia has difficulty expressing wifely love to her husband Simon and why their child, Samantha "Sammy" Li, freshens their withering marriage.

Like mother-daughter detentes in Tan's first three novels, the line of communication in the fourth, *The Bonesetter's Daughter* (2001), between LuLing Liu and her daughter Ruth requires meticulous diplomacy. The mother's didactic aphorism explains the Chinese reverence for matrilineal wisdom: "A mother is always the beginning. She is how things begin" (p. 228). LuLing demands faultless obedience and constantly carps at her daughter for laziness. Ruth, who admires her mother's skill at classical calligraphy, chooses not to learn the art. Her reasoning is self-defeating: "Why even try? Her mother would just get upset that she could not do it right" (p. 48). The paradox of a mother who wants the best for her child and who stifles creativity with perfectionism justifies why Ruth avoids LuLing's artistic domain.

Elucidating LuLing's demands for filial love is the revelation that she failed her own mother, whom she knew as Precious Auntie, her nursemaid. At a major family upheaval over LuLing's betrothal to Fu Nan, a son of Chang the coffinmaker, Precious Auntie kills herself, leaving a threat to Chang's wife that Precious Auntie's ghost will haunt the family. LuLing's coming-to-knowledge arrives with fearful clarity after the woman she knows as Mother kicks the nursemaid's corpse and orders it carted away and dropped into a ravine called the End of the World. During an era of greed for valuable prehistoric bones, the girl searches the dreary dump, but finds no human remains. The subtext implies that the mother-daughter relationship is not valued on a material scale but through the sharing of endearments and advice and the passing of tender memories to the next generation of daughters.

See also **Waverly Jong, Rose Hsu Jordan, obedience, secrets, June Woo, Suyuan Woo, LuLing Liu Young, Ruth Luyi Young**

• *Further Reading*

Balee, Susan. "True to Form." *Philadelphia Enquirer*, February 18, 2001.

Chong, Denise. "Emotions Journeys through East and West." *Quill and Quire*, Vol. 55, No. 5, 1989, p. 23.

Cujec, Carol. "Excavating Memory, Reconstructing Legacy." *World & I*, Vol. 16, No. 7, July 2001, pp. 215–223.

Donahue, Deirdre. "Tan's Books Excavate Life's Joy and Pain." *USA Today*, February 19, 2001, pp. 1D–2D.

Doten, Patti. "Sharing Her Mother's Secrets." *Boston Globe*, June 21, 1991, p. 63.

Fry, Donna. "The Joy and Luck of Amy Tan." *Seattle Times*, July 7, 1991, pp. C3–C4.

Harrington, Maureen. "Tan's Immigrant Tale Top Quality." *Denver Post*, June 23, 1991, p. C9.

Heung, Marina. "Daughter-Text/Mother-Text: Matrilineage in Amy Tan's Joy Luck Club." *Feminist Studies*, Vol. 19, No. 3, Fall 1993, pp. 597–616.

Kim, Elaine H. "'Such Opposite Creatures': Men and Women in Asian American Literature." *Michigan Quarterly Review*, Vol. 29, No. 1, pp. 68–93.

Ling, Amy. *Between Worlds: Women Writers of Chinese Ancestry*. New York: Pergamon Press, 1990.

Palumbo-Liu, David, ed. *The Ethnic Canon: Histories, Institutions, and Interventions.* Minneapolis: University of Minnesota Press, 1995.

Tan, Amy. "Excerpt: *The Kitchen God's Wife.*" *McCall's*, July 1991, p. 114.

Taylor, Noel. "The Luck of Amy Tan." *Ottawa Citizen*, October 1, 1993, p. F1.

"Mother Tongue"

From growing up on the lingual borderland inhabited by Asian-Americans, Amy Tan has contributed to an understanding of bicultural communication. Her popular story "Mother Tongue" — first published in the fall 1990 issue of *Threepenny Review*, and reprinted in *Best American Essays, 1991* and in *The Opposite of Fate: A Book of Musings* (2003) — delves into the difficulties of assimilation and adaptation to a new language and alphabet. She explains in *The Opposite of Fate* that she wrote the piece "as an apologia the night before I was to be on a panel with people far more erudite than I" (p. 2). She exulted over an unforeseen honor, the inclusion of the essay on the Advanced Placement SAT in English.

Written from a daughter's point of view, the text stresses the pidgin English that colored family life for the Tans and for Amy and her husband, Lou DeMattei. She categorizes three layers of makeshift language — the simple English she spoke to her mother Daisy, the broken English Daisy spoke to her, and the watered down translation of Daisy's Chinese that Amy conveyed to others in person, in written correspondence, and on the telephone. Like a private and curiously intimate communication method, the makeshift phrasing served a small insular group. She remarked about her faithful reproduction of Daisy's pidgin English: "It was the language that I grew up with, and it was also a language that I didn't want to listen to. Like many people, I thought that because the language was imperfect that the thoughts were imperfect — that the person was imperfect" (Ruiz). In honor of the fractured English of Tan's extended family, Tan's named her story with a pun suggesting both the language of her homeland and of her mother.

Tan's essay reveals the complexities of translation as well as inappropriate evaluations of immigrant intelligence based on their spoken expertise with English as a second language. Daisy's limited diction and awkward sentence structure earned her denigration from store clerks, patronizing from restaurant staff, additional insults when people ignored her, misunderstandings during a medical examination, and her daughter's embarrassment and frustration. The situation places pressure on Amy and her brothers "to think like a Chinese person but ... always speak perfect English so we can take advantage of circumstances" (Woo). While serving as go-between for

Daisy, Tan is aware that Americans threaten Daisy's financial dealings with investors and terrify her by withholding details of a CAT scan and by failing to make the effort to converse with her. Tan also suspects that growing up in an immigrant family limited the reliability of intelligence and achievement tests to measure her capabilities.

See also **communication, mother-daughter relationships, secrets, silence, titles, LuLing Liu Young**

• *Further Reading*

Guy, David. "Wheel of Fortune: A Writer's Thoughts on Joy, Luck and Heartache." *Washington Post*, November 2, 2002, p. T4.
Ruiz, Sophia. "Amy Tan." http://www.ireadpages.com/archive/marapr01/amytan/amy tan.html.
Woo, Elaine. "Interview." *Los Angeles Times*, April 17, 1989.

names

Tan values genealogy to affirm self and reclaim belonging to an extended family. After she learned her mother and grandmother's birth names from documents, she explained to interviewer Jami Edwards of *Book Reporter* the issue of names: "It's more important to know what's behind a name, but a name is your first gift in life. It's your placemark in the world; it's what's left behind. Sometimes it's the only thing that's left behind, what people remember one hundred or two hundred years from now" (Edwards). The author's fervid honor of family identities influences the disclosure of matrilineage in much of her fiction. From another perspective, the absence of a name identifying An-mei Hsu's mother in *The Joy Luck Club* (1989) deepens the tragedy of her brief life and suicide. Such gaps in the family tree enhance mystery and imply a facelessness in a heroine who gives her life to increase her daughter's worth.

The marital quandary of Olivia Yee Laguni, the divorced protagonist of *The Hundred Secret Senses* (1995), surfaces in her consideration of dropping Bishop, her married name. In the midst of the debate, her intrusive sister Kwan Li interferes to press the case against divorce rather than offer an opinion on women's surnames. To rekindle her sister's relationship with husband Simon Bishop, a scion of a famous biracial Hawaiian clan, Kwan maneuvers the couple into a professional journey to Changmian, China, for a professional study of culinary customs. When the Bishops restore the physical side of their union, they produce a daughter. The addition of another female to her family line again forces Olivia to select a name. She chooses Samantha Li in honor of Kwan, who disappears during the trip, and also adds Li to her own given name. Thus, the name unites Kwan's grandmother Li Chen with Kwan, Olivia, and baby Sammy. Olivia describes the choice as a gesture toward genealogy: "What's a family name if not a claim to being connected in the future to someone from the past?" (p. 398).

In *The Bonesetter's Daughter* (2001), Tan presents one of her most complex examples of matrilineage. LuLing and her daughter Ruth both attempt to restructure the past to give meaning to their lives. LuLing relies on the manuscript of her birth mother, whom she knew as the nursemaid Precious Auntie. Tan explained a pivotal element in the creation of Precious Auntie, the nameless nursemaid: "The whole thing of missing a name was not in the story at first. Even though names are not important [to the plot], they are an anchor and have a sense of power to them.... And I needed to remember" (Cujec, p. 215).

As Alzheimer's clouds the present, LuLing retreats into the more familiar past and dredges up her servant-mother's surname and given names, Gu Liu Xin, which explain her connection with the pun "liu xing" (shooting star), an image suggesting a brief but brilliant existence (p. 301). Her life, snuffed out by suicide, left one sparkling memory of love and devotion to LuLing, the daughter she could not claim. The sudden revelation echoes an autobiographical detail that influenced the novel, the death of author Amy Tan's mother Daisy and the family's recovery of two names— Li Bingzi, Daisy's maiden name, and the birth name of Daisy's mother, Gu Jingmei. The additions to the Tan genealogy divulge family secrets at the same time that they provide closure to an honorable matrilineage.

See also **suicide, Tan genealogy, Yee genealogy, Young genealogy**

• *Further Reading*

Cujec, Carol. "Excavating Memory, Reconstructing Legacy." *World & I*, Vol. 16, No. 7, July 2001, pp. 215–223.
Edwards, Jami. "Amy Tan." http://www.bookreporter.com/authors/au-tan-amy.asp.

obedience

Crucial to husband-wife and parent-child relationships in Tan's novels is the pervasive tug-of-war over obedience. In *The Joy Luck Club* (1989), female protagonists attempt to balance longings for autonomy with society's demands that one gender and various kinships and classes of people deserve to rule over others. Just as the Chinese emperor once maintained full power over his empire, husbands require wives to honor the male-over-female dominance that constitutes a patriarchal marriage. Similarly, fathers and mothers control children and choose their mates in a perpetuation of feudal marriage that flourished during and after the Ching dynasty (1644–1912). In an early example of willful behavior, Ying-ying St. Clair causes her family grief by getting dirty at the Moon Festival, falling from the family's boat, and becoming separated from her amah and parents. Disobedience so unsettles the little girl that she believes she has lost her identity, a delusion that seriously impairs her self-esteem and future success as a wife and mother. The pitiful life story of Ying-ying illuminates the psychic trauma faced by the first wave of liberated Chinese women.

The gender-based power structure creates a more unbearable strife in An-mei Hsu's unnamed mother, causing her to return home to a merciless mother, Popo, who ousts her as a disgrace for violating the feudal code by remarrying. An-mei's mother commits suicide to escape the ogreish Wu Tsing, who rapes and dishonors her as his third wife. In a less tragic example, Lindo Sun Jong honors her parents' arranged marriage, which a matchmaker contracts when Lindo is a toddler. In compliance with her parents' instruction that she be a good wife, after the Fen River flood forces the Sun family to flee, she finds herself wedded to Huang Tyan-Yu, a petulant boy-child who is too immature to bed a wife. He commands that she sleep apart from him on a sofa. To satisfy the demands of both husband and domineering mother-in-law, Huang Tai-tai, Lindo must create a ruse to cause the Huang family to release her from a life-long marital commitment. Tan lauds a clever girl who not only escapes misery but acquires the funds to emigrate to America. In a new homeland, she recovers her sense of worth through materialism by buying herself twenty-four-karat gold jewelry, an emblem of self-love.

The Chinese diaspora elevates the question of dominance to a new importance in family relationships. As Asian husbands and wives attempt to rear Chinese-American offspring by old-country rules, outspoken children like Waverly Jong have no intention of following social and moral precepts that no longer apply in the United States. Tan, herself a wayward first-generation Amerasian, understands the ins and outs of demands for total obedience. She creates in Rose Hsu a miserable self-castigation for disobeying her parents by allowing her little brother Bing to wander down a reef and drown in the sea. Likewise rebelling against a totalitarian mother, June Woo regrets that she refused to become a musical prodigy and that she deliberately performed poorly at a talent contest, causing her parents to lose face before their friends. The public humiliation illustrates the cost to parents of enforcing traditional Chinese strictures on children who have no direct tie with the motherland.

On the flip side of the question of obedience, Tan applies the theme of autonomy and female liberation to *The Kitchen God's Wife* (1991). The plot illustrates the faulty husband-wife relationship established under a feudal marriage arranged by family or a matchmaker. The centrality of obedience in a patriarchal union deprives couples of an adult relationship and allows husbands to assume the role of all-powerful fathers and to subjugate womenfolk as perpetual children, a hierarchy evident in the household of Jiang Sao-yen. After his second wife disappears, ostensibly to join her Marxist lover Lu, shame falls on daughter Winnie, who carries the burden of an absentee mother into adulthood. The shame creates ambivalence in Winnie, who secretly loves and admires her mother, but who accepts medieval matchmaking and dowry arrangements by the very father who tormented her mother. Her compliance illustrates one of several examples in Tan's fiction of women who perpetuate paternal enslavement.

Patriarchy stalks Winnie as she forms her own family, created through the dealings of a corrupt matchmaker. Because Wen Fu treats his bride like a naughty child, he feels authorized to punish her, usually by abasement and sexual intimidation. After the loss of an eye from reckless driving worsens his maladjustment, Tan expresses the nightmare of the martinet husband turned into a vengeful psychopath and pursuer of other women. In tyrannic style, he thinks of Winnie as a possession that has escaped his grasp. To assure her obedience, he lies under oath in court about her wifely failings and returns after her release from prison to assault, rape, and hold her at gunpoint. His mania denotes the extreme demands on women for total obedience, even if it threatens their lives and the survival of their children.

See also **An-mei Hsu, Winnie Louie, patriarchy, suicide, Wen Fu**

• *Further Reading*

Hamilton, Patricia L. "Feng Shui, Astrology, and the Five Elements: Traditional Chinese Belief in Amy Tan's *The Joy Luck Club*." *MELUS*, Vol. 24, No. 2, Summer 1999, pp. 125–145.
Heung, Marina. "Daughter-Text/Mother-Text: Matrilineage in Amy Tan's Joy Luck Club." *Feminist Studies*, Vol. 19, No. 3, Fall 1993, pp. 597–616.

The Opposite of Fate

A collection of thirty-two disparate pieces dedicated to her husband, tax attorney Lou DeMattei, Tan's fifth adult publication, *The Opposite of Fate: A Book of Musings* (2003), surveys and elucidates many of the elements of her previous works. In reference to the title, she explained to her publisher the importance of fate to her life and canon: "I've only had one life and these are the aspects of my life that I continue to dwell upon. We as writers, when we talk about what our oeuvre is, we go back to the same questions and the same pivotal moments in our lives and they become the themes in our writing" (MacDonald). Thus, the workings of chance stand as route markers for the important passages of her life.

In the melange of thoughts and reflections, which extends back to 1960 and a prize-winning essay on the library, Tan covers much of her autobiography. In the words of *Time Asia* reviewer Bryan Walsh, the reminiscences "unweave the tangled web of family memory and ... trace those threads that span continents—Asia and North America—and generations" (Walsh). She describes her mother's emotional instability and her father's efforts to ameliorate the edgy homelife of his three children. She recalls living in Montreux, the Swiss town to which Vladimir Nabokov retired, and wonders if the two crossed paths. She addresses reading lists and the rigid classification of literary works under labels, particularly feminist and Asian-American, and declares self-proclaimed ethnic authority "a new and more insidious form of censorship" (p. 309). Her words justify a career in writing as a means of answering the humanistic conundrums she terms "questions about life" (p. 322). The force of those questions goads her to express her quandary or else "implode if I don't find the words" (*Ibid.*).

Central to Tan's fifth adult publication is candor, particularly about the death of best friend Peter, who was strangled by thieves, and about her travels to her parents' homeland. In answer to critics who question her representation of China, Chinese behaviors, and the residual Asian philosophy in emigrants to America, the author revisits the story of her family and insists that drawing plots and motivations from relatives negates any attempt at being spokesperson for all things Chinese. Painfully open about family dissonance, she lays bear the relationships that floundered in her immature years and that recovered validity and strength as she began to investigate and write about them. Reviewers credit her with turning self-definition into popular fiction and with having the courage to reveal her own shortcomings as examples of universal human weakness.

See also **autobiography, Amy Tan**

• *Further Reading*

Bertodano, Helene de. "A Life Stranger Than Fiction." *Daily Telegraph*, November 11, 2003.
Guy, David. "Hilarious and Terrifying: Chinese Mother Haunts Collection of Autobiographical Essays." *Houston Chronicle*, December 19, 2003.
MacDonald, Jay. "A Date with Fate." *BookPage*, November 2003.
Wald-Hopkins, Christine. "Amy Tan's Essays Allow a Peek Inside Her World." *Denver Post*, November 23, 2003.
Walsh, Bryan. "Family Phantoms." *Time Asia*, December 7, 2003.

otherness

In Amy Tan's fiction, the concept of otherness underlies the intergenerational squabbles of Asian-American families and menaces the patriarchal family. Examples arise frequently — Lindo Jong's humiliation as the outsider at Mr. Rory's beauty salon in *The Joy Luck Club* (1989), paid mourners who earn their living in California by wailing at Buddhist funerals in *The Kitchen God's Wife* (1991), the galloping, unassimilated Chinese sister Kwan Li in *The Hundred Secret Senses* (1995), and the combative LuLing Liu Young, who requires her daughter Ruth's translation of her arguments in *The Bonesetter's Daughter* (2001). The outsider's intrusions form the subtext of all of Tan's writings, beginning with the early short-short story "Fish Cheeks" (1987), in which a teenage girl sinks into embarrassed silence at her parents' choice of steamed rock cod, prawns, fungus, and squid for a Christmas Eve dinner with Caucasians. In Tan's depictions of feudal marriage in her four novels, disclosures about Chinese customs of arranging betrothals between toddlers and forcing women to accept their parents' choices explore barriers to intercultural understanding and raise reader disdain for the coercion of Chinese women. The emigration of self-liberated women like Lindo Sun Jong and Winnie Louie from miserable marriages rejects traditions, establishes a more liberal familial order in the new homeland, and affirm's America's cultural standards and equal treatment of professional women like Waverly Jong, June May Woo, Lena St. Clair Livotny, and Rose Hsu Jordan and of wives and mothers like Pearl Louie Brandt as the hope of the future.

As liberated Amerasians grasp at success, otherness contributes to antagonisms with their Chinese mothers. Out of compliance with the New World order, Amerasian children distance themselves from advice and discipline based on old world models. A testimony to the alienation of immigrant parents creates tension in June Woo, the motherless daughter in *The Joy Luck Club*. In mulling over the qualities of her dead mother, Suyuan Woo, June fears that she doesn't remember any particular traits, in part because the daughter's list of criteria for success excludes the mother's accomplishments. June's "aunties," who are Suyuan's former mah jong partners, begin listing her skill at the game, her kindness, intelligence, duty to family, and quality cooking. By stripping Suyuan's memory of oddities unsuited to her American life, June is able to think of her in the broad sense of mother, housewife, and cook rather than outsider Chinese emigrant. Gradually, June develops the courage to retrace the journey from Suyuan's homeland and to inform adult twin half-sisters, Chwun Hwa and Chwun Yu Wang, about their mother's good qualities. The sharing of her American life becomes a form of grieving for her loss and of establishing her place in June's proud matrilineage.

In *The Hundred Secret Senses*, perhaps Tan's weakest novel, the text turns to the supernatural to authenticate the shift in female autonomy from the 1860s to the 1990s. The author pictures Kwan Li as a sure-footed traveler between spiritual states of life and death. Because of her familiarity with ghosts and the ease with which she chats with both her contemporaries and spirits, she eases some of the perversity of otherness. The story becomes taut and perplexing in the falling action, when the ghost-seer gives up her earthly life to retrieve her sister Olivia's husband Simon from a tangle of cave passages. For some critics, the brevity of explanation fails to account for Kwan's sacrifice, which allows an old love match between Nelly Banner and the half-breed Yiban Johnson to reach fruition in the reunion of their subsequent lives as Olivia and Simon. For others, the fictional sleight of hand is appropriate to a protagonist whose love of her friend Nelly in a former life is based in part on class differences between a valued Caucasian translator and a devoted Chinese laundress. Still self-defined as the underling, Kwan Li negates racial barriers through reincarnation and elevates Olivia's happiness above her own, thus assuring her a second chance at a satisfying marriage blessed by a child.

With a fourth novel, *The Bonesetter's Daughter*, Tan moves more deeply into otherness by perusing memories and metaphysical events in the twentieth century. The text describes otherness as the fear of ghostly intervention in human life, a belief that dominates Tan's previous novel. She sets LuLing Liu apart from her American daughter by a family curse that threatens to overwhelm the mother in retaliation for rejecting her beloved amah. Ruth, who ignores her mother's bizarre talks with the spirit of Precious Auntie, manipulates LuLing's moments of terror by scribbling answers in a sand tray or with the plectrum of a Ouija board. Ruth later doubts that she answered of her own volition. She wonders if "nudges and notions" from a ghost influenced her replies (p. 290). The author leaves to the reader's interpretation LuLing's success in building a nest egg from investments in treasury bills and blue chip stocks based on guidance from Ruth's act as the go-between for the spirit world.

In reference to the superstitions of her mother that preceded the fictional LuLing, Tan remarked, "Why she believed that people on the other side would care about the Dow Jones, I don't know" (Strohm). Daisy was so convinced that ghosts visited the family that she had Amy set a place at the table for her father's spirit. Amy declared, "I could sense them. My mother told me I could" (Mason). The author added that her novels restructure "the chaos of [the] family's past," a reordering that both clarifies and places in context points of view that only spirits can provide (*Ibid.*). In explanation of otherness in Daisy Tan, the author stated that her mother viewed family history as a continuum that stretches into the ghost-honoring past. By delving into the motivations and achievements of ancestors, Tan accepts without question their beliefs and peculiarities.

See also **racism, silence, superstition**

• *Further Reading*

Mason, Deborah. "A Not-So-Dutiful Daughter." *New York Times*, November 23, 2003.
Palumbo-Liu, David, ed. *The Ethnic Canon: Histories, Institutions, and Interventions.* Minneapolis: University of Minnesota Press, 1995.
Ruiz, Sophia. "Amy Tan." http://www.ireadpages.com/archive/marapr01/amytan/amytan. html.
Strohm, J. Elizabeth. "University of Pittsburgh: Author Tan Discusses Writing, Ouija Board Labors." *Pittsburgh Pitt News*, December 5, 2003.

patriarchy

Amy Tan depicts the life of women in pre–Communist China as a parade of male possessions ranging in value from wives and sex toys to handmaidens and kitchen slaves. Jonetta Rose Barras, reviewer for the *Washington Times*, lauds the most resilient of Tan characters as the ones who got away from paternalism — the ones "who have seen their innocence stolen, blossomed despite hardships and shaped their destinies with hope where circumstances dictate none should exist" (Barras, p. C6). Their lives become one long re-negotiation of their place in the familial and social order. It is the struggle to escape the cellblock of male domination that marks Tan's mastery of feminist themes and her emergence as a major American feminist writer.

Tan describes the worst type of marriage as an arrangement that requires female courtesy, modesty, and forebearance in the face of a husband's self-indulgent tyranny and sadism. As critic Patricia Hamilton explains in a discussion of *The Joy Luck Club* (1989), Chinese women "inherited from their families a centuries-old spiritual framework, which, combined with rigid social constraints regarding class and gender, made the world into an ordered place for them" (Hamilton, p. 125). At the fall of the Ching dynasty (1644–1912), China's early twentieth-century social order required repression of untenable female revolt against subjugation. Tan portrays Lindo Sun Jong as a successful rebel who is brought up to think of herself as secondary in importance. She works out a ruse to end an unconsummated marriage with Tyan-yu and the in-laws' theft of her possessions. Because the Huang family robs her of jewelry, she buys herself gold bracelets, choosing only "twenty-four carats, all genuine" (p. 66). Her self-praise offsets an inflexible social order that considers her brash and unwomanly.

In *The Kitchen God's Wife* (1991), Tan gives pictorial accounts of women fleeing similar oppressive marriages of the past and embracing the Western concept of romantic love and mate choice. In one scene, a nameless concubine eludes the cruelties of feudal marriage. Unnoticed in her departure from a mansion on Julu Road, she tosses behind a symbol of patriarchal tethering — a lopped-off hank of hair. In the following generation, the author depicts Wen Fu's courtship of Peanut, a daughter of the wealthy Jiang family. His behavior suits the times, when men bettered themselves through marital alliances. Winnie, the protagonist, recalls that traditional Chinese courtship "was like buying real estate," a form of barter conducted by a go-between to work out details of dowry and bride price (p. 164). Such dollars-and-cents deals dehumanized women as chattel passed from one male owner to another.

Tan's fiction characterizes arranged marriage as unfulfilling to the husband and potentially disastrous to the wife, who is powerless and highly vulnerable in a hierarchical household. Winnie tries to be a dutiful, passive, obedient wife to Wen Fu, but his womanizing degrades their union and his sadism and sexual abuse crush her physically and emotionally. Dispirited by devaluation, she chooses to exit a dysfunctional marriage by illegal means, her only choice in a patriarchal society. The author parallels Winnie's courage and resourcefulness with the experiences of other outlaw women, notably the refugees at Peanut's shelter and Little Yu, a martyr to women's liberation who chooses to hang herself rather than live in misery. The desperation of such women in escaping unhappiness attests to the unfair burden that wives bear when yoked to insensitive, overbearing mates.

In her third novel, *The Hundred Secret Senses* (1995), Tan reduces patriarchy to a lesser theme. It recurs in the romance of the evil General Warren Cape and Nelly Banner, a man-hungry spinster who translates for a Christian mission, and in the tentative pairing of the laundress Nunumu with Zeng, the jar seller. After Zeng's offer to rescue her from Manchu mercenaries, Nunumu considers his words a pseudo-proposal of marriage. When he begins making decisions for her, his paternalism proves that they are already wed in the spirit. Another incident of patriarchy occurs at Big Ma's house, where Olivia quibbles over sharing the only guest bed with her sister and estranged husband. Their hostess, cousin Du Lili, defers to Simon with simple logic, "You're the husband" (p. 265). Her remark illustrates how women are unwittingly complicit in the subjugation of their own gender.

A defiance of patriarchy in *The Bonesetter's Daughter* (2001), Tan's fourth novel, expresses the dissenter's minority opinion. The unnamed Precious Auntie, recalling the coffinmaker Chang's proposal of marriage, reprises her refusal of a likely catch. She prefers no marriage to concubinage under the control of Chang and his first wife. With the spirit of Chinese folk heroine Fa Mu Lan, she retorts, "I'm not interested in being a slave in a feudal marriage" (pp. 150–151). Her rejection of Chang is so firm that, upon her daughter's betrothal to Chang Fu Nan, the coffinmaker's drug-addicted son, Precious Auntie chooses suicide rather than to live with the coming catastrophe to LuLing. Ironically, after LuLing rejects him, she falls rapidly from favored daughter to unmarriageable orphan. Fu Nan marries her sister and stalks LuLing to demand money to buy opium. To escape the Chang family's unstinting intrusion in her life, LuLing emigrates to California and suppresses the facts of her escape from patriarchy until old age and Alzheimer's disease release the bitter memories.

Though critically and financially successful in her depiction of male-female relations, Tan is not without literary detractors. Frank Chin, author of the diatribe "Come All Ye Asian American Writers of the Real and the Fake" in *The Big Aiiieeeee!: An Anthology of Chinese American and Japanese American Literature* (1991), launched a virulent campaign to discredit Tan's view of Chinese males, particularly batterers and wife and child abusers. In defiance of stereotypes, he declared, "Chinese culture is not any more misogynistic than Western culture. Amy Tan is attacking Chinese myth as teaching misogyny" (Chung, p. D4). Without hesitation, she riposted that she drew her themes not from myth but from her own mother's life. In subsequent interviews, she declared no interest in serving as an expert on China and things Chinese.

See also **abortion, disillusion, dismemberment, Kitchen God, men, Peanut, polygyny, silence, spousal abuse, storytelling, suicide, violence, women**

• *Further Reading*

Barras, Jonetta Rose. "'Kitchen' Provides Complex Look at Relations of Women." *Washington Times*, July 15, 1991, pp. C6–C7.

Chung, L. A. "Chinese American Literary War: Writers, Critics Argue Over Portrayal of Asians." *San Francisco Chronicle*, August 26, 1991, p. D4.

Craig, Paul. "More Luck for Amy Tan." *Sacramento Bee*, July 14, 1991, p. C5.

Hamilton, Patricia L. "Feng Shui, Astrology, and the Five Elements: Traditional Chinese Belief in Amy Tan's *The Joy Luck Club*." *MELUS*, Vol. 24, No. 2, Summer 1999, pp. 125–145.

Heung, Marina. "Daughter-Text/Mother-Text: Matrilineage in Amy Tan's Joy Luck Club." *Feminist Studies*, Vol. 19, No. 3, Fall 1993, pp. 597–616.

Pate, Nancy. "'Wife' Is the Story of an Amazing Life." *Orlando Sentinel*, June 23, 1991, p. C11.

Peanut

In *The Kitchen God's Wife* (1991), a novel about female bonding, Huazheng, whom the Jiang family calls Peanut, is an important literary foil to her cousin Winnie Louie. Plump and spirited, Peanut, who is the coddled daughter of Uncle Jiang and New Aunt, is only a year older than Winnie, but much more worldly and daring. She basks in the preferment of her family, who considers Winnie merely a visiting relative and the daughter of a disgraced women. Tan develops the cruel irony of Winnie's obedience and subservience and of Peanut's willfulness. Although Winnie assures her she needs no makeup, Peanut adorns her face in powder and lipstick and totters to the marketplace in a narrow hobble coat that was fashionable in the West in the 1920s. The crippling, though harmless and temporary, mirrors the horror of foot-binding, a custom that left women permanently maimed with broken bones and misshapen arches and incapable of defending themselves.

Tan advances the plot by replacing Winnie with Peanut in the suitor's intentions. Winnie serves as go-between during Wen Fu's secret visits to Peanut in the greenhouse, where he covers her face and neck with kisses. The upset in Peanut's plans occurs after Winnie develops the backbone to refuse ferrying her letters to and from Wen Fu. The surprise nuptial arrangement by Auntie Miao, the matchmaker, with the Wen family for Winnie throws Peanut into a pout "like a dragon whose tail had been stepped on" (p. 167). Winnie realizes that Peanut lacks one of Winnie's assets— the ability to hide her wish to have Wen Fu's attentions, love letters, and kisses for herself. As the sibling rivalry mounts, Peanut recovers by sneering at Winnie's dowry and by pressing her to choose a white Western-style wedding dress with suitable bridesmaid attire to adorn Peanut.

During the war, Peanut retains a sisterly attachment to Winnie. It is Peanut who withdraws money from Winnie's bank account and sends it to her to cover the rising cost of living in Kunming. Mature in her view of the growing independence of educated Chinese women, Peanut deserts her homosexual husband, outraging her father for scandalizing the family name. Her friend-making ability draws her into a web of women who aid each other during hard times. She opens a shelter in Shanghai for women and children escaping feudal marriage. New Aunt calls her daughter a bad influence and blames Communists for deceiving Peanut with propaganda about equality of the sexes. Old Aunt, a hard-line Chinese matron, claims that Peanut deserved more beatings in her youth to discipline her. These remarks are among many in Tan's novels that indicate women's acceptance of a punitive patriarchy dating into the early days of the Ching dynasty (1644–1912).

Tan draws the parted sisters into a mature sisterhood, a common motif in her novels. Winnie admires Peanut's courage and longs to find the backbone to divorce Wen Fu. New Aunt secretly visits her daughter and offers the address to Winnie. The clandestine nature of the mother-daughter relationship suggests that New Aunt harbors some of Peanut's daring and admires her spunk. Old Aunt surprises Winnie by passing along the same information, a suggestion that neither woman can cut ties to Peanut, yet neither can bring herself to embrace women's liberation or to acknowledge Peanut's heroism as a trendsetter. The duality in Jiang's two wives is typical of people living in a period of widespread social liberalization.

Tan reunites the sisters on ground unfamiliar to Winnie. Suited to Peanut's revolutionary lifestyle is her residence on the second floor of a ramshackle underground shelter for women and children in the seedy Japanese section of Shanghai. After hearing the sad story of Little Yu's suicide to escape a hopeless marriage to a retarded man, Peanut abandoned the prettified customs of the Chinese gentry to serve egalitarian Communist ideals. Assisting her is Little Yu's mother, who regrets that her daughter hanged herself in despair. Tan includes this model of martyrdom to the feminist cause as a gesture to women who made up the first wave of freedom fighters.

See also **Wen Fu**

• *Further Reading*

Huntley, E. D. *Amy Tan, A Critical Companion*. Westport, Conn.: Greenwood Press, 1998.

Peking Man

The human remains of *Homo erectus pekinensis*, Peking Man was the discovery of Canadian medical doctor and physical anthropologist Davidson Black in 1927 in a cave at Chou-k'ou-tien thirty miles southwest of China's capital city. Beginning with the unearthing of a single tooth from Dragon Bone Hill, the exploration of the Ice Age hominid remains produced jaws, arm and leg bones, fourteen skulls, and more teeth for a total of forty prehistoric hominids classed as Pithecanthropus or Sinanthropus. Study of anatomical structures in adult males and females and children characterized the hominid as flat-headed with a sturdy cranium, low forehead, heavy brow, powerful jaws, and a frame that enabled the species to walk upright. Dating placed the find as far back as 111,000 B.C. during the Middle Pleistocene age and indicated continuous human habitation in the region until 8,100 B.C. The hearths where Peking Man communed contained evidence of cooking with fire, flaking of weapons, and making bone tools for supplying small clans and hunting parties. In 1987, UNESCO named the site a world heritage center.

Amy Tan's *The Bonesetter's Daughter* (2001) views the scientific disclosure of early human life in China from the point of view of superstitious peasants and a geologist, Pan Kai Jing. After decades of folk belief that the hominid bones belonged to dragons, the remains take on near-magical qualities. Local bonesetters, a profession suited to treatment of workers injured in quarries, prize the bones and grind minuscule amounts of the tissue into medicines and potions to be placed on wounds. Greed for the valuable bones results in a disastrous antipathy between the family of Chang the coffinmaker and Precious Auntie, daughter of Bonesetter Gu.

See also **The Bonesetter's Daughter**

• *Further Reading*

Boaz, Noel T., and Russell L. Ciochon. *Dragon Bone Hill: An Ice Age Saga of Homo Erectus*. New York: Oxford University Press, 2004.
_____. "The Scavenging of 'Peking Man.'" *Natural History*, Vol. 110, No. 2, March 2001, p. 46.
"Peking Man Site of Further Research Value." *Xinhua News Agency*, December 13, 2002.
Schuster, Angela M. H. "Hominid Saga." *Archaelogy*, Vol. 57, No. 3, May/June 2004, p. 52.

polygyny

Amy Tan's interest in female liberation and self-actualization results in narrative strands picturing the one-sided patriarchal relationships common to the Ching dynasty (1644–1912), which crumbled in pre–Communist China. In *The Joy Luck Club* (1989), she recreates China's male-pleasing system of concubinage, a form of polygyny or marriage to multiple wives and sex slaves. This gender imbalance violates a basic male-female alliance, causing ambitious wives to compromise their integrity and to betray their fellow wives in efforts to co-exist or rise socially or economically in a male-privileged household. At a sumptuous three-story manor in Tientsin, Wu Tsing, a strutting cloth manufacturer with five wives, creates an unhealthy power struggle among his women. His arbitrary allotment of prestige, privilege, and goods perpetuates inequalities and keeps his family off balance from spying and jealousy. The first wife, elderly and dignified, absents herself from the fray by devoting her actions to propitiating Buddha on behalf of a crippled daughter and a second girl marked by a tea-colored birthmark. To appease the first wife and accommodate her religious fanaticism, Wu Tsing provides her with a separate dwelling.

The rise of the second wife, a former teahouse singer from Shantung, derives from her ability to manipulate Wu Tsing by feigning suicide attempts. Maliciously, she wield's the traitor's nefarious power by reminding her husband that his third wife is ungainly and incapable of producing sons. Second wife's plot to end Wu Tsing's philandering and wasting money on prostitutes results in the rape of An-mei's mother, a widow who innocently spends the night with second wife after a game of mah jong. In the estimation of critic Wendy Ho, the betrayal "paints a painfully problematic picture of women's complicity, not only in another woman's oppression, but in their own continuing oppression in, and maintenance of, a patriarchal culture" (Ho, p. 152).

As fourth wife, An-mei's mother incurs social and familial ostracism for breaking social decorum for widows. In the family's genealogy, she survives shamed and nameless in her daughter's memory, a narrative strategy that dramatizes the mother's debasement. Socially crippled and powerless over her own destiny, she is unable to halt second wife from stealing her contribution to the household, Wu Tsing's first son, Syaudi, whom he claims by patrilineal rights. The arrival of a simple country girl as fifth wife completes the household in which Wu Tsing enjoys sexual and financial dominance over five women, seven children, and their individual servants. Second Wife chooses suicide over the protracted misery of her family's disapproval and her own disinclination to be the sexual playmate of a fat, ungainly womanizer.

With *The Kitchen God's Wife* (1991), Tan takes a more detailed look at the polygynous household through a study of Jiang Sao-yen, a Shanghai industrial magnate. Although he holds supreme control of his six wives and offspring, he can't quell female power over his household, including wives, daughters, and female servants. He suffers a blow to the ego when his second wife disappears, perhaps in the company of her Marxist lover Lu. After a hiatus in family history, the story returns to Jiang in his declining years following a stroke, when San Ma and Wu Ma, his third and fifth wives, tend to the shambles of a mansion and protect him from harm. His lost wealth leaves the extended family vulnerable to Wen Fu, who fleeces the family compound of its saleable goods. After Jiang's death, the women have little choice of a future and retreat to Wu Ma's brother's home in Yentai for shelter. Their departure illustrates the system's creation of dependent women who cast their burdens on male relatives rather than make independent lives for themselves.

See also **patriarchy, Precious Auntie, suicide**

• *Further Reading*

Heung, Marina. "Daughter-Text/Mother-Text: Matrilineage in Amy Tan's Joy Luck Club." *Feminist Studies*, Vol. 19, No. 3, Fall 1993, pp. 597–616.

Ho, Wendy. *In Her Mother's House — The Politics of Asian American Mother-Daughter Writing*. Walnut Creek, Calif.: AltaMira Press, 1999.

Uslu, Didem. "Female Quest for Freedom Through Journey Into Past Heritage: The Turkish-American Guneli Gun and the Chinese-American Amy Tan." http://www.salzburgseminar.org/ASC/csacl/progs/amlit/didem.htm.

Precious Auntie

The mute and maimed nursemaid in *The Bonesetter's Daughter* (2001) earns the title of Bao Bomu or Precious Auntie, the servant of the Liu family whom circumstance silences from declaring her own motherhood. A native of Zhou's Mouth of the Mountain, she comes to the Liu household as the bride of Liu Hu Sen, who is killed before marriage can legitimize her pregnancy. She remains as a shamed servant who works in the Lius' inkstick business. By setting a professional example, she teaches daughter LuLing Liu classical calligraphy and extols its discipline as a basis for a balanced life. Precious Auntie is the most important person in LuLing's life, but she withholds from her charge the nature of their kinship. By tending to LuLing and supervising her dress, cleanliness, hair style, and deportment, Precious Auntie becomes vital to the girl's everyday activities and choices and colors vivid memories into LuLing's last days.

Precious Auntie's tragic story forms the heart of the novel. A beauty in her youth, she is hideously scarred. She maintains silent communication through wheezes, sniffs, snorts, and facial contortions. With graceful hands, she creates images and writes words on a chalkboard, which adds chalk-talk to hand- and face-talk for a more exacting expression of thoughts. She retells her young charge the unlikely story of cooking food in her mouth by swallowing fire and describes the accident that destroyed one side of her face, her tongue, and some of her teeth. The real cause is attempted suicide by swallowing a hot black ink resin, a symbol of a communication medium that ironically contributes to her silencing and LuLing's ultimate liberation.

The web of secrecy concerning the nursemaid's identity begins in the first chapter, in which an aged LuLing struggles to recall the name of Precious Auntie, whom she loves like a surrogate mother. At the family reunion for the Full Moon Festival, LuLing denies being GaoLing Liu's sister and pulls out a photo of Bao Bomu. While cleaning her mother's apartment, Ruth retrieves a photo of Precious Auntie in the family bible and discovers a manuscript inscribed with the Chinese character for "truth" (p. 130). Within, she reads about the Liu family's inkstick manufacture and discovers that Baby Uncle, Liu Hu Sen, was LuLing's real father. The genealogy clarifies LuLing's devotion to Precious Auntie, a scion of nine centuries of bonesetters, a professional family who passed along their skill patrilineally through apprenticeships limited to the family's sons.

Tan creates an anomaly in Precious Auntie, whose confessions of a privileged childhood stress the opportunities not usually offered to daughters and the paradox of an education that limits her choices. After her mother and older brothers die of an intestinal disease when Precious Auntie is four, she learns reading and writing, riddles, and haiku. Her doting father gives her license to wander the outdoors. Set at the collapse of the Ching dynasty (1644–1912), the text describes the price females paid for a liberal education and personal freedom in pre–Communist China. Unlike other girls, Precious Auntie walks on unbound feet, which scandalize local scolds. As she progresses in the knowledge of human anatomy and healing, her autonomy increases as her marriageability declines.

Tan uses Precious Auntie as a spokeswoman against spousal abuse. After aiding a woman with a broken jaw, the bonesetter's daughter recognizes a similar case of battery in the woman's baby son, Chang Fu Nan, who suffers a dislocated shoulder. Boldly, Precious Auntie upbraids the husband, the coffinmaker Chang, for assaulting his wife and child and rejects his subsequent proposal of marriage. Because she is more outspoken than polite Chinese women of her day, her candor initiates a series of catastrophes that cost her happiness, marriage, and the motherhood of her own daughter. Worsening the loss of both father and his associate are the theft of her dowry, valuable dragon bones used in healing, and the Chang family's betrothal of their son Fu Nan to LuLing, an untenable pairing.

The novel uses Precious Auntie's story to express the perversity of a gender-based power struggle. For Chinese women pushed to the limit of endurance, the only solution is suicide, an assertion of power through the threat of haunting. At Precious Auntie's death, LuLing's life careens from its stable round of girlhood activities into ignominy. Because Chang's wife fears ghosts, the family withdraws the marriage proposal. LuLing, realizing that Precious Auntie is her mother, regrets the ejection of the nursemaid's corpse into a rocky ravine and attempts to honor her with a formal burial. Although the girl fails to locate the body, she later learns that Old Cook performed what reverence he could by mounding rocks over the amah's remains. Nature completes the receipt of her bones after an escarpment collapses, covering the slope in tons of soil. Tan demonstrates through transmission of Precious Auntie's life story that the whereabouts of her bones is of minor importance compared to the example she set for her daughter and granddaughter.

See also **pride, secrets, silence, social class, storytelling, suicide, superstition**

• *Further Reading*

Cujec, Carol. "Excavating Memory, Reconstructing Legacy." *World & I*, Vol. 16, No. 7, July 2001, pp. 215–223.
McMillan, Stephanie. "Review: *The Bonesetter's Daughter*." *City Link*, March 2001.
Edwards, Jami. "Amy Tan." http://www.bookreporter.com/authors/au-tan-amy.asp.
Russo, Maria. "Review: *The Bonesetter's Daughter*." *Salon*, February 21, 2001.

pride

Pride in self, family, and nation is an essential, but problematic theme in Tan's fiction. In an early short-short story, "Fish Cheeks" (1987), she depicts the humiliation of a teenage girl during a Chinese Christmas Eve dinner, when Robert, a boy who has caught her eye, shares the Chinese family's unusual Asian delicacies rather than the standard menu of turkey and sweet potatoes. Worsening the scene of Caucasians unfamiliar with the reaching and poking of chopsticks into dishes is the father's loud belch to acknowledge his wife's cooking ability. The girl's pose of assimilation destroyed, she falls silent and wishes to disappear. Tan concludes with a knowing gesture of the mother, who takes a private moment to offer the daughter an American miniskirt as a holiday gift and to remind her that she can't change family or ethnicity. In the mother's opinion, "Your only shame is to have shame" (p. 99). The homily sets the tone of Tan's four novels, which center on the passage of Chinese customs from native-born mother to Amerasian daughter.

Tan's first novel, *The Joy Luck Club* (1989), depicts the uplifting memories of war brides, refugees, and immigrants that remind them of who they once were and what values they carry with them to new homes and marriages. A proud rebel from girlhood, Lindo Sun Jong rejects the secondhand Christmas gifts with broken or missing parts that do-gooders award children in San Francisco's Chinatown as an inducement to espouse Christianity. After her daughter Waverly becomes a chess whiz, Lindo begins posturing before Suyuan Woo by whining that the many trophies from chess competitions burden her with extra dusting. The offhand boast causes Suyuan to brag about daughter June Woo's natural talent for music, which Suyuan fabricates. The one-upmanship is detrimental to the girls' relationship and generates unnecessary competition that extends into their adulthood.

The author's presentation of pride in *The Kitchen God's Wife* (1991) perpetuates the theme as a potential for destructive relationships. Wen Fu, the self-important Kuomintang air force trainee, boasts about his value as a flying ace during dogfights with the Japanese, although he retreats from engagement via a list of flimsy excuses. Upon the return of the Wen family to Shanghai after war's end, Wen Fu has the opportunity to nettle Jiang Sao-yen, a former wealthy industrialist whom the Japanese coerced during their occupation of coastal cities. To retain his pride, Jiang tossed tea on a valuable heirloom panel on his office wall. Facing Wen Fu, Jiang is less able to express his indomitable spirit because a stroke leaves him partially paralyzed and speechless. Posing as a wounded war hero, Wen Fu takes advantage of the old man's handicap with threats to have the Kuomintang execute Jiang for collaborating with the enemy. The cruelty piques Jiang's guile, causing him to outfox Wen Fu with a deathbed mention of buried treasure, which lures the devious son-in-law into a destructive plundering of walls and flooring.

In *The Bonesetter's Daughter* (2001), Tan depicts LuLing Liu as a headstrong teenager who causes her own downfall by failing to understand the circumstances of her birth. Because she is the bastard of her amah, a servant who commits suicide, LuLing Liu falls out of favor and enters a family of Girls of New Destiny housed at a Christian orphanage. A staff member, Sister Yu, chastises Eurasian and Amerasian girls for their pride in physical beauty. She lectures them on taking pride in accomplishment, but urges the avoidance both of self-pity and "arrogance in what you were born with" (p. 200). The admonition stays with LuLing into old age, when she berates herself for failing to value her real mother, Precious Auntie.

See also **Jiang Sao-yen, Lindo Jong, silence, June Woo**

- *Further Reading*

Ng, Franklin, et al., eds. "New Visions in Asian American Studies: Diversity, Community, Power." *ERIC*, 1994.

racism

Amy Tan tinges her writing with the sufferings of Asians from overt bigotry, such as children's taunting cries to Olivia Yee in *The Hundred Secret Senses* (1995), "Hey, Yee! Yeah, you, yee-eye-yee-eye-oh" (p. 174). Upon the arrival of Olivia's sister, eighteen-year-old Kwan Li, to Daly City, California, Tan depicts her as wide-eyed and gullible, the perfect dupe for Caucasian racism. Some of her younger brothers' friends amaze Kwan by turning on the lawn sprinklers, then laugh at Kwan's amazement and call her a "dumb Chink" (p. 12). Instead of taking Kwan's side, Olivia, her six-year-old half-sister, denies their kinship and wishes Kwan would return to Changmian. Louise Yee Laguni, Olivia's mother, chides Olivia for expressing hate toward anyone. A later incident overturns Olivia's role in bigotry when kids urinate on her and call her the sister of a "retard" (p. 49). The assault depicts the power of racism to harm not only minorities but also those who associate with them.

Kwan's retreat into a former life pictures her as Nunumu, laundress at a Christian mission compound, and friend of a translator, Miss Nelly Banner. After Nunumu involves herself in her friend's love life, Nunumu is pleased that Nelly can recover from losing the disloyal General Warren Cape by loving Cape's translator, Yiban "One-Half" Johnson, a Chinese half-breed. Nelly recoils from Nunumu's romantic scenario by declaring that white American women can never involve themselves with mixed-race men. A tender courtship belies her racist upbringing. She eventually admits her illogic: with lyric clarity: "I am like a falling star who has finally found her place ... in a lovely constellation" (pp. 200–201).

Near the novel's end, Tan returns to nineteenth-century Caucasian racism, which infects even supposedly open-minded Christian missionaries. After Kwan locates Nelly Banner's music box left in the valley of caves during the Taiping Rebellion, Olivia finds a copy of Pennsylvania-born traveler James Bayard Taylor's *A Visit to India, China, and Japan* (1862), sixth in a set of eleven guidebooks, which belonged to Pastor Amen. The discovery of a link to Kwan's former life is even more startling in its revelations of the Quaker author and lecturer's bigotry toward Chinese peasants. The text comments on Asians: "Their crooked eyes are typical of their crooked moral vision" (p. 354). The racist aspersion belies the sincerity of American missions to China and casts doubt on other forms of Asian-Caucasian intimacy.

See also **otherness**

- *Further Reading*

Hoggard, Liz. "Death as a Source of Life" *Manchester Guardian*, November 23, 2003.
Romagnolo, Catherine. "Narrative Beginnings in Amy Tan's *The Joy Luck Club*: A Feminist Study." *Studies in the Novel*, Vol. 35, No. 1, Spring 2003, pp. 89–107.

religion

Religion is a lesser motif in Tan's writing, but it informs major themes, including marriage, customs, and superstitions. In an interview for BBC radio, she acknowledged the influence of her mother's beliefs, a multi-faceted faith blending ancestor worship and Buddhism with orthodox Christianity from her years at a Catholic boarding school. In a reflection on her mother's eclecticism, Tan recalled: "She was the ultimate pragmatist. She could look for miracles, she could look for curses, she could look for beliefs in an afterlife, she could look at heaven as a possibility for reward. And they were all there and they sort of co-existed in a way, rather mutually, without seeming contradiction for her" ("Amy Tan"). The syncretism of variant strands impacted the author's beliefs, which color her transcultural writings.

In *The Joy Luck Club* (1989), Tan describes the ancient faith that characters maintain before their emigration from China. She pictures sixteen-year-old Lindo Jong as a devout Buddhist who prays on her wedding night that the nuptial candle will blow out and rid her of an odious union with a man-child, Huang Tyan-yu, to whom she was betrothed in babyhood. In another marital scenario, An-mei Hsu describes Wu Tsing's first wife, who pursues Buddhist intervention to correct imperfections in two daughters, one with a short leg and the other with a tea-colored birthmark on her face. An-mei's mispronunciation of faith as "fate" subtly predicts her loss of trust in God. To her daughter Rose, the mother's previous declarations of faith constituted "an illusion that somehow you're in control" (p. 128). The collapse of An-mei's belief system after the drowning of her young son Bing in a seashore accident indicates that she adopted Western-style Christianity out of a naive belief that faith would protect her family from catastrophe.

At the outset of *The Kitchen God's Wife* (1991), Tan uses religious ritual as justification for a family reunion. She views Chinese Buddhism and superstition through the eyes of Pearl Louie Brandt, an educated first-generation Chinese-American. She recalls Auntie Du Ching's home altar, a miniature red temple revealing the framed image of a Chinese deity called the Kitchen God. Because of Auntie's gifts of incense, oranges, cigarettes, and whiskey at the small worship center to bribe the god into making a good report of her conduct to Jade Emperor, Pearl compares the small shrine to a Christian manger scene.

The motif of propitiation through bribes continues after Auntie Du's death. In fealty to ancient mourners' tradition, Pearl acquires one hundred million dollars in spirit money from Mr. Hong's shop to offer at Auntie Du's funeral to enable her to purchase a place in Chinese heaven. To Pearl's challenge of these outmoded funeral customs, Winnie avoids the question of belief and claims that she follows Chinese customs out of respect for the dead. Her practice reflects on semi-religiosity that shies away from zealous belief, yet hesitates to violate customs that might have some value.

At the ceremony honoring Auntie Du, events turn a Chinese-style farewell video-taped by Uncle Henry into tragicomedy. Tan emphasizes Tessie, Cleo, Phil, and Pearl's American skepticism about customary incense and foods arranged on the banquet table to feed the deceased during her long journey into the afterlife. Honoring the shrunken corpse is a good luck banner, paid mourners, clappers and bells, and a Buddhist monk and nun chanting cries to Amitaba, the Buddha of paradise. Phil quickly removes his terrified daughters from the unfamiliar obsequies, which include family members circling the casket with lighted sticks of incense. To Winnie, the old-style funeral is a necessary ritual to mark the passing of a valuable person who was loyal during a difficult time in Winnie's life. By participating in the procession, she and others achieve closure by relieving themselves of the obligation to mourn.

In *The Hundred Secret Senses* (1995), Tan's third novel, the Christian concept of redemption and heaven as seen by a child enlivens satiric passages. Six-year-old Olivia Yee Laguni, who battles the superstitions of her eighteen-year-old sister Kwan Li, lumps religious faith into conflicting beliefs about "Santa Claus, the Tooth Fairy, the Easter Bunny" (p. 57). To explain the merit system of good deeds, she pictures herself pasting S&H Green Stamps in booklets to earn "a one-way ticket to heaven, hell, or purgatory" (*Ibid.*). She imagines the afterlife as a place where she can meet movie stars, find lost objects, and get answers to puzzling questions, like the guilt or innocence of alleged ax murderer Lizzie Borden. Kwan, who is more sophisticated about the workings of religion, enjoys Catholic mass from the perspective of her multiple reincarnations extending into the mid–1800s. Of personal faith, she claims that she can't see Jesus because she looks with Chinese eyes. Of the shift in mariology over time, she exults, "I'm glad [Mary] got a promotion," Tan's snide commentary on the rise of the Virgin Mary in a patriarchal faith to a place of godhood (p. 64).

Additional satire continues to deflate the sincerity and value of Christian proselytizing in China. Kwan's memories of an earlier life as the laundress Numumu in the mid–1800s recalls hard servant labor and the required distribution of "The Good News" on Saturdays. Because of the pervasive illiteracy on Thistle Mountain, peasants accept the pamphlets, but turn them to practical use. The pages serve as clothing stuffing, coverings for rice bowls, and repair kits for cracked plaster. Numumu recycles the pages as wrappings for preserving duck eggs. After the Manchus overwhelm the mission compound, the winds scatter Pastor Amen's leaflets, an image suggesting the impermanence of Christian teachings to a largely unschooled and unreceptive peasant culture.

The inculcation of Christian virtues in an orphanage is a source of inspiration in *The Bonesetter's Daughter* (2001). LuLing Lui Young, orphaned about the time she was to be married to Fu Nan, the son of Chang the coffinmaker, takes hope from a syncretic view: "I believed that if I was respectful to both the Chinese gods and the Christian one, neither would harm me" (p. 209). This hedging of bets suggests a pragmatism in people who lose faith in outmoded theologies, yet who cling to early home training in deities and their powers. She passes on to her daughter Ruth Luyi the terror of relegation to the boneyard at the End of the World, an improper burial in a bottomless abyss where bad people go after they die. Later mention of the ravine as a community garbage dump called "land's end" relieves it of its mystic role in punishing evil souls (p. 292).

Tan extends her perusal of China's mixed beliefs by picturing LuLing Liu's experience at a Christian orphanage. While under the supervision of Sister Yu, LuLing observes the source of China's fascination with Communism. In discussing the gender inequities that brought her sister misery, Sister Yu explains why she, a Christian teacher, condones Communism: Even though Marxists are atheists, they further human equality. Sister Yu exults, "Share the fish and loaves, that's what they believe," a reference to Matthew 14: 15–20, which describes Christ's miraculous feeding of five thousand followers with two fish and five loaves of bread (p. 221). With surprising insight into syncretism, she proposes that the Communists "should form a united front with Jesus worshippers rather than with the Nationalists" (*Ibid.*). Despite Sister Yu's praise for Communist tenets, it is her steadfast Christian faith that stops LuLing from committing suicide in the early weeks of her widowhood and gives her hope of rejoining husband Kai Jing in eternity.

See also **fate and fortune, ghosts, Jimmy Louie, superstition**

• *Further Reading*

"Amy Tan" (interview). http://www.bbc.co.uk/religion/programmes/belief/scripts/amy_tan.
    shtml.
Ma, Sheng-mei. "'Chinese and Dogs' in Amy Tan's 'The Hundred Secret Senses': Eth-
    nicizing the Primitive à la New Age." *MELUS*, Vol. 26, No. 1, Spring 2001, pp. 29–
    44.

repression

Tan uses Chinese metaphor to restate the Freudian concept of repression. In *The
Joy Luck Club* (1989), Canning Woo fears that his wife Suyuan died suddenly of a
brain aneurysm after harboring secret longings and regrets that assailed her mind.
Similarly, Winnie Louie, protagonist of *The Kitchen God's Wife* (1991), represses
memories of her early marriage to the evil Wen Fu and the deaths of their three children. When she chooses a time to divulge her secrets and lies to daughter Pearl Louie
Brandt, Winnie describes the job of concealment as a pain of the heart, a metaphor
for the trials she hid from her American children. Ironically, it is heart disease that
kills the villainous Wen Fu, a suggestion of the burden of evil that he bears to the
grave.

In a flashback to childhood, Winnie recalls repression beginning in the early
1940s, when she tries to live among her Uncle Jiang and his two wives, who ignore
her mother's sufferings as Jiang Sao-yen's second wife. After Winnie's mother disappears, relatives give no thought to what caused her misery or why she fled, but
Winnie never stops turning over in her mind the scraps of clues to her mother's
repressed emotions. As a bride living in a pilots' compound in Kunming, Winnie
devotes herself to motherhood while trying to keep peace with an unpredictable husband. After Wen Fu despoils a fourteen-year-old servant, the vaudevillian Min, plus
unnamed local girls, prostitutes, and a teacher, Winnie gives up seeking a divorce
and swallows her anguish. Because of internal pressure, she feels forced to conceal
from the outside world her nightly sufferings from a sexual predator and child abuser.
The charade of a happy marriage works against her when she goes to friends Helen
and Auntie Du Ching and finds them unwilling to believe the extent of family battery. The subtextual message implies that women who are adept at repression have
a harder time making a case for divorce after they decide to reveal the emotional burden they carry.

A serious flaw in the marriage of Olivia Yee Laguni in *The Hundred Secret Senses*
(1995) contrasts the sadism of Winnie's hardships. Psychological insecurity grows
after Simon Bishop, her campus pal, reveals his sorrow at the death of his brilliant
soul-mate, Elza Marie Vandervort, from a skiing accident that precipitates an
avalanche. Olivia represses competition with Elza's ghost throughout the marriage,
but does not dispel the damage it does to her self-esteem. At an intimate moment
in the couple's making up in Changmian, China, Olivia explodes with anger that
Simon is unable to forget Elza and get on with adulthood and marriage. Simon counters with an accurate evaluation of Olivia's mental state — she scapegoats Elza as the
source of insecurities. His claim fails to blunt Olivia's anger or her hidden store of

hatred for Simon's dead girlfriend. Tan uses Olivia's repressed hostility as evidence that a hidden garden of emotional weeds can range out of control, choking the positive emotions of hope and love.

See also **secrecy, silence, Ying-ying St. Clair**

• *Further Reading*

Herbert, Rosemary. "'Fate' Accompli: Amy Tan Shares a Lifetime of Writings in Her New Book." *Boston Herald*, November 7, 2003.

Ma, Sheng-mei. "'Chinese and Dogs' in Amy Tan's 'The Hundred Secret Senses': Ethnicizing the Primitive à la New Age." *MELUS*, Vol. 26, No. 1, Spring 2001, pp. 29–44.

Souris, Stephen. "Only Two Kinds of Daughters: Inter-monologue Dialogicity in *The Joy Luck Club*." *MELUS*, Vol. 19, No. 2, Summer 1994, pp. 99–123.

reunion

Tan unites the Chinese diaspora and reunion as themes common to immigrant Chinese in America and their first-generation Amerasian children. A controlling image in *The Joy Luck Club* (1989), reunion soothes the surviving club members after the death of Suyuan Woo, a refugee from the Sino-Japanese War (1937–1945). The three original mah jong players invite June Woo to take her mother's place at the eastern corner of the game table. Crucial to closure for the members and for Suyuan's husband is her daughter's return to China to meet her long-lost twin sisters, Chwun Yu and Chwun Hwa Wang, whom Suyuan abandoned in 1944. The pivotal moment arrives when June and Canning Woo leave the plane to look for the daughters in Shanghai's airport to reclaim the mother's loss. In a scene of reciprocal completions, June fills in the twins' missing mother; the twins model the culture and language of Suyuan's homeland. The movie version of the novel skillfully portrays the scene with visible mother-want in the twins' eyes. Female viewers frequently cry during the scene, which pictures three women weeping because each bears a unique resemblance to Suyuan.

With less pathos, the lengthy account of Winnie Louie's life in *The Kitchen God's Wife* (1991) involves two reunions, one on the streets of Shanghai near a newspaper stand and the other in California. The first is filled with joy in Winnie's good luck in encountering Jimmy Louie once more, but hesitancy over the fact that she is still a married woman. The second reunion is so low key it seems anticlimactic. Having survived marriage to a sadist, courtroom humiliation as an adulterer, fifteen months in a women's prison, divorce, and rape at gunpoint by Wen Fu, Winnie is surprisingly calm and calculating in plotting her escape from China. Within days of the Communist takeover and the halting of emigration, she musters money, visas, and three tickets, a hedge against obstacles to her flight to California. Within a few sentences, Tan summarizes Winnie's reunion on May 15, 1949, with Jimmy, her second husband, who has become a Baptist minister. Clouding the joyous meeting is Winnie's awareness that Jimmy is still loving, but that his affection flows in two directions—to his wife and to God.

A different kind of reunion energizes *The Hundred Secret Senses* (1995). To the surprise of Jack Yee's family, he requests on his deathbed that they welcome eighteen-year-old Kwan Li, his daughter from a first marriage in China to Li Chen, a market clerk in Guilin. The reception for Kwan is awkward because of her ungainly size, countrified appearance, and bumptious manners, which bear no resemblance to Jack or her half-sister Olivia. Kwan's loyalty to family and her importance to their lives remain firm for thirty-two years. At age fifty, she convinces Olivia and Olivia's estranged husband Simon Bishop to accompany her to Changmian, her native village. The proposal offers an opportunity for a double reunion — Kwang with her relatives and neighbors and Olivia with Simon.

Preceding the long-awaited arrival in Changmian is a highway accident, which extends reunion from the present to the hereafter. Rocky, the cab driver, dismisses the car-bus smashup as a common occurrence in a crowded country. In the village center, a dozen people wait for Kwan with wide smiles. After the joshing and teasing, Kwan encounters the ghost of Big Ma, a victim of the wreck Kwan observed on the drive into Changmian. The meeting subdues the welcoming party at the community hall, where friends lay out food for the festivities. An official's report of Big Ma's death causes Kwan to give up her desire to release a white owl from the mountain top named Young Girl's Wish. The liberation of a bird reenacts a legend about a girl and her lover who turn into phoenixes and fly away together. Kwan sets the bird free, but lightens the moment by informing Olivia that Big Ma admitted regret for sending Kwan away to America. As though echoing the poignance of the complex arrival and leave-taking in Changmian, school children call out in English "Hello good-bye!" (p. 235).

In contrast to the rural Chinese meeting and its merger with a funeral, a family reunion at the Full Moon Festival in *The Bonesetter's Daughter* (2001) reflects a twenty-first century blended family. Differing levels of respect for the occasion arouse antagonism between the hostess, Ruth Luyi Young, and her lover Art Kamen. Ruth considers the gathering a Chinese Thanksgiving, even though Art's ex-wife Miriam horns in by demanding spaces for her family of four. Despite seating complaints and Caucasian dismay at Chinese dishes, guests enjoy the meal. Ruth concludes, "In spite of the uneasy moments, reunions were important, a ritual to preserve what was left of the family" (p. 81). The statement reflects Tan's pervasive theme of family renewal through the retracing of the Chinese diaspora and the thrashing out of past antagonisms to get at the heart of family love.

See also **diaspora, journeys, Kwan Li, June Woo, Suyuan Woo**

• *Further Reading*

Heung, Marina. "Daughter-Text/Mother-Text: Matrilineage in Amy Tan's Joy Luck Club." *Feminist Studies*, Vol. 19, No. 3, Fall 1993, pp. 597–616.
Ling, Amy. *Between Worlds: Women Writers of Chinese Ancestry*. New York: Pergamon Press, 1990.
Miner, Valerie. "The Daughters' Journeys." *Nation*, Vol. 248, No. 16, April 24, 1989, pp. 566–569.
Taylor, Noel. "The Luck of Amy Tan." *Ottawa Citizen*, October 1, 1993, p. F1.

Tseo, George K. Y. "The Perils of Transcultural 'Translation.'" *Literature/Film Quarterly*, Vol. 24, No. 4, 1996, pp. 338–343.

St. Clair, Ying-ying

In *The Joy Luck Club* (1989), Tan presents Ying-ying St. Clair as a Chinese woman out of balance from decades of repression. The text pictures her in 1918 as a willful four-year-old born under the sign of the tiger to the wealthy Gu family. She is a treasure to her mother and amah, but admits to taking for granted their daily intimacy. The one-sided relationship prefigures the haughtiness of LuLing Liu toward Precious Auntie, the devoted nursemaid and teacher who commits suicide in *The Bonesetter's Daughter* (2001). Fortunately for Ying-ying, she changes her attitude before she experiences a permanent separation from her sources of love and security.

The focus of the action is a celebration of the Moon Festival aboard a boat on Tai Lake, which Tan reprises in a children's book, *The Moon Lady* (1992). The scenario of preparations for a holiday meal reveal the cruelties of life. Ying-ying observes as two boys provide meat for dinner by girdling the throat of a long-necked bird and retrieving the fish it catches, but can't swallow. The child observes a female servant gutting and scaling the fish, then cleaning chickens and a turtle. Too late, Ying-ying realizes that a close observation of servant tasks has exposed her to bloody refuse and scales. As the evening progresses, she accepts her mother's admonition to stand still and discovers her shadow, a symbol of duality linking a picture-perfect little girl with an unruly nature.

For Ying-ying, the Moon Festival is an epiphany, a night of change. After tumbling into the lake, she undergoes an identity transformation and fears that she will never reunite with her family. Because rescuers identify her as a beggar child, she wonders if an abrupt disappearance from the family boat could transform her forever into a member of a lower class. The evening's events are so unsettling that her little-rich-girl confidence gives place to a more complex world view and to reliance on the family's good fortune rather than on self. The author uses her decline as evidence that happiness is temporary, even for members of the privileged class.

Vain and stubborn in her youth, Ying-ying bears a name meaning "clear reflection" in token of her resemblance to her mother, who indulges her wild recklessness. Ying-ying is slender, beautiful, and disdainful of marriage to boys her own age. Her gift for divining the future reveals that she will wed Lin Xiao, the vulgar, arrogant womanizer who splits a watermelon to imply his seizure of her virginity. Over the years of a self-alienating marriage, she erases her hopes and feelings "the same way carvings on stone are worn down by water" (p. 67). After aborting her son and ordering his corpse to be wrapped in newspaper and hurled into the lake, she sinks into depression and returns to her parents' home. For ten years, she lives near Shanghai in the crowded house of a poor second cousin as though atoning for her earlier willfulness by embracing poverty.

At age twenty-eight, Ying-ying moves to the city, dresses elegantly, and works in a women's clothing shop until Lin Xiao's death sets her free. In 1946, four years after meeting Clifford St. Clair, she marries him, but without a strong commitment, romantic attachment, or passion for life. She arrives in California at the Angel Island processing station as a fearful refugee under uncertain status. After three weeks, she emerges into American society as a displaced person, both historically and psychologically. The category presages a life of exaggerated fears, which she passes on to her daughter Lena.

The move from the old country requires learning new ways. Devoid of her girlhood spunk, Ying-ying lives a dispirited sham of love for "Saint" and a fake enthusiasm for marriage and motherhood. She later regrets having no *chi* (spirit) to pass on to her daughter. Lena recalls that Ying-ying sinks into paranoia, terrorized by the imaginary evil man who lives in her basement. She fears the steep hill on which the family settles in San Francisco and predicts that the angle will cause her unborn child to die, a self-fulfilling prophecy that threatens her life. After the death of the second child from anacephaly, she takes to her bed. Tan characterizes her near self-annihilation as a death of the spirit.

To her ten-year-old daughter Lena, the demoralized mother appears as lethargic as a corpse or living ghost, a persona deprived of volition. In later years, Ying-ying predicts catastrophes and awaits like a tiger the opportunity to restore spirit to Lena. The vehicle that revives consciousness and agency to Ying-ying is talk-story, a means of negating the sexist stories of a patriarchal homeland with honest accounts of her experiences. Speaking in first person, she gives strength and meaning to herself at the same time that she nurtures the disquieted inner being of her daughter. Tan's pairing of Ying-ying and Lena presages a similar pairing in *The Kitchen God's Wife* (1991), in which Winnie Louie, a demoralized mother, rescues herself and passes to her daughter Pearl the wisdom gained from liberation from patriarchal authority.

See also **The Moon Lady, mother-daughter relationships**

• *Further Reading*

Hamilton, Patricia L. "Feng Shui, Astrology, and the Five Elements: Traditional Chinese Belief in Amy Tan's *The Joy Luck Club*." *MELUS*, Vol. 24, No. 2, Summer 1999, pp. 125–145.

Ho, Wendy. *In Her Mother's House — The Politics of Asian American Mother-Daughter Writing*. Walnut Creek, Calif.: AltaMira Press, 1999.

Ling, Amy. *Between Worlds: Women Writers of Chinese Ancestry*. New York: Pergamon Press, 1990.

Tseo, George K. Y. "The Perils of Transcultural 'Translation.'" *Literature/Film Quarterly*, Vol. 24, No. 4, 1996, pp. 338–343.

St. Clair genealogy

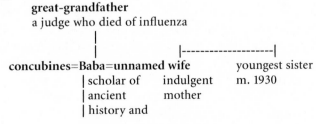

```
                        great-grandfather
                        a judge who died of influenza
                              |
                              |                   |-------------------|
          concubines=Baba=unnamed wife            youngest sister
                   | scholar of    indulgent      m. 1930
                   | ancient       mother
                   | history and
```

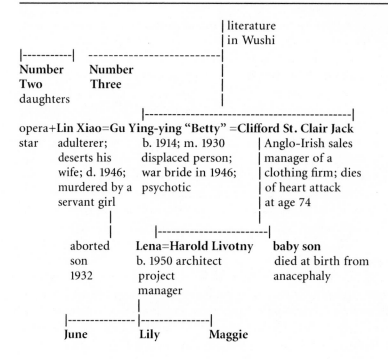

```
                                                | literature
                                                | in Wushi
|----------|  -------------------------|
Number      Number                      |
Two         Three                       |
daughters                               |
                    |--------------------------------------------|
opera+Lin Xiao=Gu Ying-ying "Betty" =Clifford St. Clair Jack
star     adulterer;      b. 1914; m. 1930    | Anglo-Irish sales
         deserts his     displaced person;   | manager of a
         wife; d. 1946;  war bride in 1946;  | clothing firm; dies
         murdered by a   psychotic           | of heart attack
         servant girl                        | at age 74
              |                               |
              |        |----------------------|
          aborted    Lena=Harold Livotny    baby son
          son         b. 1950 architect     died at birth from
          1932         project              anacephaly
                       manager
                          |
          |--------------|--------------|
          June          Lily           Maggie
```

secrets

   Secrecy pervades Amy Tan's life and fiction. In childhood, she concealed an interest in the past from her mother, Daisy Tan. In 1993, Daisy remarked, "I never knew she care about Chinese culture and history until much later in her life. She hide her interest from me, was very secretive" (Goodavage, p. 12D). Just as in life, secrets surface in Tan's fiction as inducements to learning and competition, the impetus in *The Joy Luck Club* (1989) that drives Waverly Jong to learn chess. The budding chess champ concludes from a careful study that "it is a game of secrets in which one must show and never tell" (p. 96). Study under chessmaster Lau Po increases her instinct for classic attack and defense strategies, which she performs beneath an emotionless mask. By the time that she reaches adulthood, subterfuge clouds her interpersonal relations, causing unrest and diffidence in old friend June Woo and soul-searching during Waverly's romance with Rich Schields. Her admission of dampered emotions hint that a second marriage may be more successful than the first.

   The hidden sufferings and evil deeds of the novel's previous generation prove more dramatic, more enveloping than Waverly Jong's chess maneuvers and love affair. Toxic secrets pass from Yan Chang, maid of Wu Tsing's fourth wife, to nine-year-old An-mei. She learns the seamy account of her mother's rape by Wu Tsing, the birth of their son Syaudi, and the boy's rearing as Second Wife's child. In retrospect, An-mei surmises that adults keep secrets like "a lid on top of the soup kettle, so they do not boil over with too much truth" (p. 268). The explanation suggests a parental wish not to overburden children with family events that may prove fearful or unmanageable in a child's mind. Another aspect of lidding the pot is adult repression of truths that cause pain and loss of self-esteem if they become common knowledge.

Tan's second novel, *The Kitchen God's Wife* (1991), deals more directly with secrecy as repression. The text peels away layers of deception, indirect aggression, and misrepresentation to reveal Winnie Louie's first marriage and three deceased children, Pearl Louie Brandt's concealment of multiple sclerosis from her mother, and Helen Kwong's pretense of being Pearl's aunt. At Bao-bao's engagement party, an obligatory family gathering, Helen uses her own benign brain tumor as an excuse to prod Pearl into telling all to Winnie before the dawning of Chinese New Year, a time of interpersonal forgiveness and fence-mending. Helen intrudes further on the Louie family's past to insist that Winnie spill her secrets to her daughter. More than a reverence for traditional New Year making up, the rush to spill wartime secrets suggests the tidying up of loose ends in the lives of two septuagenarians.

During the lengthy talk-story of Winnie's early life, deception and subterfuge inform an autobiography about feudal marriage and the silencing of women. The tissue of secrets that envelops the narrative billows up in numerous scenes, as with the Jiang family servants' refusal to tell young Winnie that her mother abandoned her and Peanut's sharing of sexual gossip she overhears while eavesdropping on males who attend Winnie's wedding. When Winnie begins to understand some of Helen's inexplicable behaviors, she realizes that a platonic marriage has deprived her friend both of marital passion and children. Winnie learns of Captain Long Jiaguo's sorrow at the empty relationship by reading his letter to Helen, a poser who conceals from her husband how little literacy she has acquired from his lessons in Chinese characters. The linkage of secrets forms a tottery house of cards that is certain to collapse with further revelations.

At first, the little secrets between Helen and Winnie reflect their evolving sisterhood. The concealments appear small, yet meaningful to their intimacy and eventual emigration from China. After Auntie Du Ching intimidates prison officials into releasing Winnie, Helen believes that her new husband, Henry Kwong, is responsible for coercing a former schoolmate into ending the two-year sentence after only fifteen months' incarceration. To spare the Kwongs humiliation, Auntie Du lets Helen keep the illusion of rescuing Winnie through Henry's connections. She justifies her cloaking the truth as gratitude for Henry's good intentions, even if they failed. Helen uses the rescue as a lever to pry favors from her old friend, causing Winnie to mull over a revelation that would put Helen in her place. The contretemps within their sisterhood develops into humor, which the author exploits at a tense moment in the falling action.

At the novel's end, Tan has expunged most of the secrets with a wide swipe of truth, leaving only one harsh deception unexplained. Pearl and Winnie discuss Pearl's rebellious teen years, which terrified Winnie that Wen Fu had sired her daughter and transferred his evil nature into her spirit. After thrashing out the past, Pearl divulges her hereditary illness, which Winnie blames on Wen Fu. The mother's immediate mobilization for a better diagnosis and herbal cures suggests that truth strengthens the mother-daughter relationship and confers hope. Helen continues the tradition of secrets by inveigling Winnie into going to China to locate an herbal treatment for

Pearl's multiple sclerosis. The possibility of a folk cure taps another form of secrecy, the traditional Chinese healer's knowledge of nature's secrets.

In another version of sisterhood, *The Hundred Secret Senses* (1995) presents secrets as the bond that grows between disparate half-siblings, Olivia Yee Laguni and Kwan Li. To her six-year-old sister Olivia, Kwan whispers the sad demise of her mother, market clerk Li Chen, from heartsickness. Kwan also discloses her supernatural powers, which she describes as "yin eyes" (p. 3). Although Olivia divulges the secrets to her stepfather, Bob Laguni, and causes him to send Kwan to a mental institution for electroshock therapy, Kwan remains devoted to her beloved "Libby-ah" (p. 3). In discussing the motivation for basing her third novel on secrets, Tan explained to *Bookpage* interviewer Ellen Kanner that secrets "have a power to them.... They could affect us profoundly. There's an ambiguity as to whether they will help or harm us. They are the ghosts of our past" (Kanner, p. 3).

The importance of late twentieth-century secrets to the narrative doubles with the inclusion of the Buddhist concept of reincarnation, a source of secrets that extend beyond a single lifetime. Kwan imparts memories of a previous life among the Christian missionaries of Changmian in the mid–1800s, when she is a laundress known as Nunumu. Her servant friend Lao Lu, the compound gatekeeper, spies through the windows on strange Caucasian behaviors, e.g., weeping over a Victorian locket that enshrines hair of the dead, stockpiling communion wafers for the endtime, and Pastor Amen's inflated headcount to mission headquarters of converts from only one to one hundred. Nunumu, who is more discreet, conceals her awareness that Nelly Banner still loves General Cape, a vicious mercenary whom she calls "Wa-ren," and that Nunumu is not really committed to Christianity (p. 70). These historical elements seem unrelated to the story of Olivia and Kwan until the past refuses to stay buried and rises up in the falling action to threaten Olivia's husband, Simon Bishop.

The web of secrecy grows more complex, more mendacious after Nunumu saves Nelly Banner from ignominy for plotting to elope with Cape, who robs the mission compound and its residents and skips out on Nelly. Nunumu simulates assault by sprinkling blood on her old friend; Yiban "One-Half" Johnson, Cape's half-breed translator, pretends that Cape left Miss Banner's travel bag in the pavilion by mistake. The end of the tangled plot occurs in 1864 during the Taiping Rebellion, when Manchu soldiers set a fire to the caves of Thistle Mountain and destroy almost all villagers who take refuge in subterranean passages. By revealing the final moments in the lives of Nunumu and Nelly, Kwan reaches catharsis by identifying Olivia as the reincarnation of Nelly and Simon as a new version of Yiban and by paying back Olivia's loyalty by reuniting her with Simon. In the identification of past lives in the resolution, Kwan is able to relieve Olivia of her distaste for Elza, Simon's former girlfriend, who used to be Louise Yee Liguni, Olivia's mother in another existence. The relinking of lives with past lives netted Tan numerous criticisms for relying too heavily on a pat conclusion constructed out of the supernatural and coincidence.

In Tan's fourth novel, *The Bonesetter's Daughter* (2001), secrets are integral to the story of a mother's inability to claim her child. In the narrative, the Liu family amah, Precious Auntie, is LuLing Liu's mute nursemaid. Precious Auntie communicates through physical nuance and written communications the words she can't say with her mutilated tongue, which she burned by swallowing boiling ink resin in a failed attempt to commit suicide. The motif of secrecy worsens LuLing's relationship with her daughter Ruth Luyi Young, who hides her diary in obscure places and chooses a multisyllabic vocabulary to conceal her thoughts from a snoopy Chinese mother who knows only rudimentary English. Ruth ponders, "Didn't Mom ever realize ... how her demands for no secrets drove me to hide even more from her?" (p. 122). Ruth, the third generation of a misinformed matrilineage, rightly concludes that the cycle of secrecy leads to dishonesty and betrayal.

The discovery of LuLing's photo of her nursemaid informs Ruth that the game of secrets works both ways. From the writings of Precious Auntie, Ruth unearths a greater network of lies that conceal the identity of her real grandmother, who is pregnant on her wedding day. Because a vengeful suitor, Chang the coffinmaker, murders Bonesetter Gu, Precious Auntie's father, shortly before the kick of a horse kills the groom, the bride, orphaned and husbandless, enters the care of Great-Granny Liu and accepts the cover story that Precious Auntie is the baby's nursemaid. A corrected genealogy explains much of LuLing's peculiarities to her daughter and helps Ruth cope with her mother's descent into senile dementia, which clouds the present while shedding new light on old memories. Contributing alterations to tone and fact are the additions of Ruth's Auntie Gal, who remarks on LuLing's revelations, "Ah, so she told you. Good, I'm glad. Better to tell the truth" (p. 285).

See also **Precious Auntie, repression, silence, women, Suyuan Woo, LuLing Liu Young**

- *Further Reading*

Barras, Jonetta Rose. "'Kitchen' Provides Complex Look at Relations of Women." *Washington Times*, July 15, 1991, pp. C6–C7.

Ganahl, Jane. "Amy Tan Gets Her Voice Back." *West Egg Communications*, January 2001, p. 40.

Goodavage, Maria. "'The Joy Luck Club' Is Born from Her Life of Hardship." *USA Today*, October 5, 1993, p. 12D.

Kanner, Ellen. "From Amy Tan, a Superb Novel of Two Sisters, Two Worlds, and a Few Ghosts." *Bookpage*, December 1995, p. 3.

Ling, Amy. *Between Worlds: Women Writers of Chinese Ancestry.* New York: Pergamon Press, 1990.

silence

Tan incorporates into her feminist fiction images of silent and silenced women who come of age in China after the collapse of the repressive Ching dynasty (1644–1912). She acquired an understanding of disenfranchised women from communion with the spirit of Jingmei, the maternal grandmother who killed herself in 1925 to escape concubinage under the rich industrialist who raped her. Of the spiritual relationship between Jingmei and her granddaughter, Tan remarked, "By looking at why she did this and her sense of both anger and despair in not having a voice, I'm saying to her: we have a voice now, we can give voice to this" (Bertodano). Out of devotion to a woman who died twenty-seven years before Amy was born, the author continues to honor her grandmother by bearing witness to her unvoiced struggles.

Like the archetypal figure of O-lan, the Chinese servant-wife in Nobel Prize-winning author Pearl Buck's classic *The Good Earth* (1931), the powerful image of women devoid of opportunities to speak their minds found its way into Tan's fiction from the first. In an early short-short story, "Fish Cheeks" (1987), the teenage protagonist stops talking during a Christmas Eve dinner of Chinese delicacies that embarrasses her before Robert, a Caucasian boy she wants to impress. The silence does not hide from her mother the reason for discourtesy to guests. Her mother later scolds her daughter for feeling shame at the family's Chinese menu and table manners, which allows the dipping of used chopsticks into platters of steamed fish and prawns and belching as a sign of pleasure and thanks to the hostess. The story prefigures Tan's use of silence/communication themes in more dramatic scenarios in her four feminist novels.

In the first, *The Joy Luck Club* (1989), Tan explains the distancing that grows between a mother and her daughter after the girl's betrothal. Because the child, Lindo Sun Jong, technically belongs to her future mother-in-law, Huang Tai-tai, the birth mother must defend her own sorrow at parting by biting back endearments and beginning the separation process. According to critic Amy Ling, the mother makes offhand remarks about the girl as though she were a stranger in the house and a guest at the family table: "The conventional words are not spoken with glibness and hostility but with difficulty, as bitter pills the mother herself must swallow and learn to like the taste of" (Ling, p. 136). Thus, silence between mother and daughter requires an unspoken acceptance of feudal marriage.

The author employs a mirror in the chapter entitled "Double Face" to explore the painful misalliance between Lindo and her daughter Waverly Jong, a smug Amerasian tax attorney at Price Waterhouse in San Francisco. When both women look into the mirror of Mr. Rory, the hairdresser, Waverly carries on a conversation with him as though her mother is incapable of understanding English or is hearing impaired. The scenario demeans Lindo, but leaves her free to judge the pseudo-familiarity of the toney haircutter and Waverly. Alternating a Chinese pose that Caucasians expect with her adopted American face, Lindo glimpses the duplicity in Waverly, who is embarrassed to be compared to her mother. As though the mirror could also reflect the past, Lindo envisions her own mother, but says nothing about her observations or humiliation from Waverly's attempt to discount her as an intelligent individual.

In the same novel, silence for Ying-ying St. Clair is a reminder of another arranged marriage to Lin Xiao, the first husband whom she pleases by saying only what he wants to hear. With womanly guile, she aborts his male child in a passive aggressive negation of his proud family tree. Her failure to reclaim a voice in a second marriage nearly extinguishes her, body and spirit, until she realizes that daughter Lena needs counsel. To keep Lena from retreating into the same silent abyss as wife of the self-important architect Harold Livotny, Ying-ying addresses the Livotnys' empty marriage that robs Lena of joy and hope. The verbal reprimand serves both parties, affirming the daughter's need for her mother and reclaiming Ying-ying's pride in the role of mentor to the next generation of the Gu family's women.

American society's choice of which women to silence provides *The Hundred*

Secret Senses (1995) with a New World taken on misogyny. Bob Laguni commits his Chinese stepdaughter, Kwan Li, to Mary's Help, a euphemistic name for an asylum that coerces the mentally ill with electroshock therapy. In a Catholic setting that implies loving, Christ-like care, psychiatrists attempt to strip Kwan of the Chinese otherness that sets her apart from assimilated Amerasians and makes her an embarrassment to her upscale California family. Diagnosed as a catatonic during a bout of the Chinese silent treatment, Kwan has no choice about submitting to therapy. Tan lightens the scenario with black humor by depicting Kwan returning home with kinky hair and the ability to revive dead batteries with a touch of the hand, a mystic form of communication that sets her apart from ordinary people.

Silence serves a rebellious Amerasian daughter in *The Bonesetter's Daughter* (2001), Tan's fourth novel, a narrative based on truncated communication lines. After a reckless tumble down a sliding board causes Ruth Luyi Young to bite her tongue and crush her lip, she remains silent while recuperating at home. During a visit from her Aunt Gal and Uncle Edmund Young, Ruth realizes that a sudden recovery of speech might lessen their attention to her injuries. During days of tender care, she admits to herself, "It was comforting to be a baby again, well loved, blameless" (p. 65). The silent treatment also works on Caucasian school friends, who had previously ostracized her. Her power grows after LuLing offers a sand tray and chopstick stylus for quick notes, which expand to Ouija board communication with both mother and spirits of the dead.

As Ruth reaches a difficult pass in her teens, silent second-hand communication continues to plague the mother-daughter relationship. By tormenting LuLing with cruel words in her diary, Ruth feels powerful and clever. Her mother typically retaliates by ignoring Ruth over dinner, a signal of rejection. When Ruth carries her manipulations too far, LuLing falls from a window to the cement below and damages skull, shoulder, and rib. Ruth chooses to apologize in writing in her diary, but cancels the gesture by hiding the text in a kitchen cabinet above her mother's reach. Tan uses the incomplete apology as an example of human abandonment of I-thou conversation as an underhanded means of saving face.

In adulthood, forty-six-year-old Ruth, a ghostwriter for authors of self-help manuals, undergoes a psychosomatic silencing every August 12. Only after learning the history of her mother and grandmother, a victim who muted herself by drinking boiling resin, can Ruth comprehend the mysterious laryngitis. The facts tumble out of a lengthy autobiography which her mother derives in part from her own mother's manuscript, written during her service to the Lius, a family of inkstick manufacturers. By picturing the mute grandmother as a woman forced to swallow her sorrows and by freeing her mother from depression by placing her in a nurturing retirement community of elderly people, Ruth frees herself from an inability to relate honestly and fully with Art Kamen, her long-term lover. In a move toward self-fulfillment, she migrates from a career of reshaping other people's words to writing fiction. The author confers on Ruth a special gift, the art of the storyteller.

See also **communication, fable, Precious Auntie, secrecy, storytelling, talk-story, women, June Woo**

• *Further Reading*

Bertodano, Helene de. "A Life Stranger Than Fiction." *Daily Telegraph*, November 11, 2003.
Heung, Marina. "Daughter-Text/Mother-Text: Matrilineage in Amy Tan's *Joy Luck Club*." *Feminist Studies*, Vol. 19, No. 3, Fall 1993, pp. 597–616.
Hull, Akasha. "Uncommon Language." *Women's Review of Books*, Vol. 18, No. 9, June 2001, p. 13.
Ling, Amy. *Between Worlds: Women Writers of Chinese Ancestry*. New York: Pergamon Press, 1990.

Sino-Japanese War (1937–1945)

The expansionism of Japan into choice Chinese territory as far north as Mongolia began with a preemptive strike to conquer the Chinese and expunge Western and Christian influence. The Japanese banked on fighting an enemy divided between loyalty to Nationalist leader Chiang Kai-shek and Communist organizer Mao Tse-tung. The outbreak of hostilities began in September 1936, when Chiang refused the secret demands of the Japanese emperor. Formal war erupted on July 7, 1937, with a clash at the Marco Polo Bridge outside Peking that advanced in three weeks' time to the occupation of Peking and Tientsin. To the surprise of the Japanese, Chiang and Mao united against the insurgents, who blockaded South Chinese ports and seized Shanghai in December 1937 at a high cost in civilian lives. Tan incorporates this period of the United Front in *The Bonesetter's Daughter* (2001), which describes the forced enlistment of geologist Pan Kai Jing, Chao, and Dong into the Communist patrol that guards a peasant village near Dragon Bone Hill.

The most brutal episode of an extended conflict was the Rape of Nanking, a savage assault in November 1937 that concluded with Japanese capture of the city on December 13. Chiang reorganized his government at Hangkow and began drawing the Japanese deeper into Chinese territory. After global condemnation of Japanese aggression, the Russians united with the Mongols to push the enemy out of the north. Chiang relocated his headquarters to Chungking in May 1939, when the Japanese bombarded the city. On July 29, 1939, U.S. President Franklin D. Roosevelt took a pro–Chinese stance by denouncing Japan's blatant land grab and slaughter of innocent citizens and by curtailing sale of supplies to Japanese defense plants. After the Japanese attacked Pearl Harbor, Hawaii, on December 7, 1941, world war decided the fate of the aggressors, whose emperor, Hirohito, surrendered aboard the American battleship U.S.S. *Missouri* on August 15, 1945.

At the height of the Japanese atrocities against the Chinese in *The Bonesetter's Daughter*, Tan outlines the privations of citizens from interrupted train service and loss of food markets as well as the terrorizing and murder of peasants. Among the Girls of New Destiny at the Christian orphanage near Dragon Bone Hill, Japanese insurgents shoot down a row of American flags and kill the mission's chickens. Adviser Ruth Grutoff protects the fifty-six female inmates and remaining staff by hiding gold and silver in statues of Jesus's apostles and by arranging for shelter of groups of girls with former pupils in Peking. Linking the mission compound with the outside world is the ham radio, which informs the inmates of incipient danger.

After inmates find new homes, LuLing Liu, a recent widow of Pan Kai Jing, remains behind. She prays to Buddha and Jesus, "whoever was listening," for protection from torture (p. 236). In the face of danger from Japanese soldiers, Tan depicts LuLing as skilled at guile by pouring chicken blood into her mouth and pretending to cough clots and by having the orphan girls fake the scratching of lice-ridden bodies. The depiction is typical of Tan, who chooses for prominence the types of women characters who rely on self and trickery to help them survive war. Thus, LuLing has much in common with Suyuan Woo, Lindo Jong, Winnie Louie, and Nunumu, all of whom fall back on wit in the face of danger.

See also **violence**

• *Further Reading*

Adams, Bella. "Representing History in Amy Tan's *The Kitchen God's Wife*." *MELUS*, Vol. 28, No. 2, Summer 2003, pp. 9–30.
Craft, Stephen G. "Peacemakers in China: American Missionaries and the Sino-Japanese War, 1937–1941." *Journal of Church & State*, Vol. 41, No. 3, Summer 1999, pp. 575–591.

sisterhood

Female bonding is an essential in Tan's fictional woman-to-woman relationships. The organization of mah jong tables in *The Joy Luck Club* (1989) illustrates the resilience of women during the Sino-Japanese War (1937–1945), when they exorcise fears of bombardment and rioting through friendly competition, conversation, humor, and snacks. After the diaspora sends survivors to new homes in the United States, Californian immigrants, led by Suyuan Woo, reinstate their club in peacetime as a means of discussing assimilation and investment in American markets. The sisterhood is valuable to Suyuan, whose heart is torn between contentment with her American family and regret that she left twin daughters, Chwun Hwa and Chwun Yu, behind on her flight to safety. Even though Suyuan dies before she can realize her dream of a family reunion, the three surviving club members welcome June Woo to her mother's place at the table and offer her twelve hundred dollars to travel to China and meet her sisters in Shanghai. The gesture elevates sisterhood to a form of interfamilial network powered by women's actions.

In *The Kitchen God's Wife* (1991), the author returns to wartime terrors to describe the camaraderie between pilots' wives, feudal wives, servants, and other women who bond as a sisterly support system. It is during the long intimacy with other young brides and female cooks and maids that Helen Kwong and Winnie Louie form a lasting friendship. The two manage to complement each other's faults—Winnie's naivete, refinement, and open-heartedness and her reliance on Helen's bald candor, homeliness, and pragmatism. Rather than chastise Helen for absentmindedness and for misidentifying a flock of birds as Japanese bombers, Winnie recognizes the problem and buys her glasses. As their outlook darkens with the advance of the Japanese into China, Winnie adds another close friend, Wan Betty, the widowed Nanking telegrapher who sends Winnie's message to her sister Peanut in Shanghai asking for a withdrawal of enough money to carry her through difficult times. Winnie and Wan Betty develop empathy for each other's trials after Winnie reveals how Wen Fu's family robbed her of her wedding furnishings and Betty describes how her husband's family stole his survivor's pay. Tan creates their bond out of adversity, the common element in women's lives in the years following the collapse of the Ching dynasty (1644–1912).

In November 1937, at the height of wartime danger to Nanking, Winnie seals her long friendship with Wan Betty. In a gesture that reveals Winnie's gratitude, she offers Betty clothes, a radio, and a sewing machine. Betty promises to earn a living by sewing and to repay her debt to Winnie. News of the Rape of Nanking fills Winnie with fears for Betty's safety. The two women do not reunite until another height of danger, the arrival of Communists in Shanghai in 1948. Betty, who still works for the telegraph office, helps Winnie word a telegram to Jimmy Louie in California and explains how she used Winnie's unclaimed four hundred dollars to flee from Japanese insurgents to safety in Shanghai. Like the linked silver chopsticks hidden in Winnie's suitcase lining, the tie between women bears sterling qualities that outlast marriages, invasions, and the foundering of Chinese patriarchy.

Winnie's complex needs precipitate another important bond with Wen Fu's concubine Min, a vaudeville actor with country manners. Out of pity for the girl's tenuous situation sharing quarters in the family apartment, Winnie befriends her and swaps lessons—instruction in manners and deportment in exchange for Min's dance lessons in tango, waltz, fox trot, and the lindy hop. To Helen's jibes about Min's opportunism with men, Winnie exonerates her friend and envies her for leaving Wen Fu, aborting their child, and finding a new mate. As the grim image of marriage to a sadist settles on Winnie, she pictures herself in the trick torture box that held Min in her stage performance. The metaphor suggests Winnie's fears for her life and her need for outside intervention to relieve her confinement.

Meanwhile, a loving relationship develops in Shanghai during the war between San Ma and Wu Ma, third and fifth wives of Winnie's father, Jiang Sao-yen. While surviving the Japanese occupation of the city, they manage to live on less as Jiang's fortune withers. When Winnie returns at war's end with her husband and son Danru, San Ma and Wu Ma welcome her and explain how Jiang lapsed from a paralytic stroke. The two wives tolerate Wen Fu and his bossy mother, Wen Tai-tai. After Wen Fu destroys the mansion on Julu Road in search of hidden gold, San Ma and Wu Ma leave for Yentai to live with the latter's brother. Like sisters, they take comfort in their friendship and cheer Winnie with Jiang's deathbed joke that convinces Wen Fu that the house holds a fortune. As Friedrich Nietzsche declared in the adage "That which does not kill us makes us strong," the spunk of feudal wives appears to grow from years of self-denial and repression, which toughen their spirits.

Four decades after the war, Winnie's ambivalence toward her old friend Helen Kwong parallels a normal human friendship, paradoxically fraught with doubt, annoyance, secrecy, and life-long love and trust. The author provides symbols of pairing—the opposite sides of scissors, Helen's gift of knitting needles, and the ten pairs of silver chopsticks that Winnie recovers from a panel in her luggage — as suggestions that the two women belong in an extended sisterhood, even when their natures appear at cross purposes. The loving union of female friends contrasts Winnie's wretched marriage, which Helen at first promotes. To express Winnie's long-hidden fear of Wen Fu, she claims to have developed a "bad heart," the same disease that kills her ex-husband on Christmas Day, 1989 (p. 98). The play on words illustrates the Chinese literal interpretation of abstract concepts, such as guilt and heartlessness. At novel's end, sisterhood prevails over fear after Helen admits that she knew all along that Wen Fu was a monster and that Winnie suffered unnecessarily.

See also **confinement, men, patriarchy, Peanut, storytelling, violence, women**

• *Further Reading*

Clarke, Stella. "More Secrets of the Mama Sisterhood." *Australian*, March 10, 2001.
Ma, Sheng-mei. "'Chinese and Dogs' in Amy Tan's 'The Hundred Secret Senses': Ethnicizing the Primitive à la New Age." *MELUS*, Vol. 26, No. 1, Spring 2001, pp. 29–44.
Wong, Sau-ling Cynthia. "'Sugar Sisterhood': Situating the Amy Tan Phenomenon," in *The Ethnic Canon: Histories, Institutions, and Interventions*. Minneapolis: University of Minnesota Press, 1995, pp. 174–210.

social class

The importance of social class in Amy Tan's fiction reflects a longstanding situation in Chinese history, extending from the early days of the Ching dynasty (1644–1912). In *The Joy Luck Club* (1989), social stratification affects the lives of adult females who grew up under China's paternal system of matchmaking and feudal marriage. An-mei Hsu inherits the disgrace of her mother, an unnamed widow whom Wu Tsing rapes and forces into concubinage as his third wife. In the upper echelons of society, Ying-ying St. Clair's holiday tiger costume, hovering amah, and pale, uncalloused skin attest to her upper-class upbringing. After her amah removes her soiled costume, Ying-ying falls into the hands of a fisher family that has limited clues to her identity or social prominence. Her soft feet are the only proof that she has led the easy, toil-free childhood of the privileged class. In each case, interaction with other classes hinges on a determination of where each fits in the social order.

In linking stories of four protagonists, Tan stresses the value of brains and ingenuity in defeating the rigid social stratification of Imperial China. In a feudal arrangement, Lindo Sun Jong marries above her family's social position to Huang Tyan-yu, a roly-poly mama's boy who lives higher up the Fen River valley in a pretentious manor housing four generations. Upon her arrival as future wife, being ushered into a second-floor kitchen clarifies Lindo's lowly status. She displays the spunk of a survivor by arranging a ruse that nets her both a divorce and seed money to start a new life.

The most terrifying of the novel's war stories is the downward spiral of Suyuan Woo's fortunes. Blessed with wealth and jewelry, she joins a mob fleeing the insurgent Japanese in Kweilin. As her strength gives way from fatigue, terror, and the debilitating effects of dysentery, she realizes that her real treasures, twin infant daughters Chwun Hwa and Chwun Yu, must remain behind if any of the trio is to survive.

She leaves with the babies jewelry and photos attesting to the family's prominence. Upon her recuperation in a hospital, she remarries and spends the remainder of her life attempting to recover her girls. Although the twins grow up in an illiterate family of Muslims, they are well cared for and bear no grudge against the mother who abandoned them. Upon their reunion with their sister June Woo, the twins murmur their abiding love of "mama" (p. 331).

Social class remains a complex element of character interaction in *The Kitchen God's Wife* (1991). Although Winnie Louie lives in the mansion of Jiang Sao-yen on Julu Road near Shanghai's Caucasian district, she belongs to a multi-layered pecking system that places men above women, first wives above concubines, mothers of sons above barren women, children of concubines below favored offspring, and servants beneath all of the above. In adulthood, as the only wife of Wen Fu, Winnie expects to enjoy the role. Because Wen Fu denigrates her with frequent womanizing and by bringing home other women, Winnie realizes that her fantasy of social status is a sham. She envies the vaudevillian Min, a short-term paramour of Wen Fu, who frees herself by aborting their child and moving on to a more promising affair. Winnie's embrace of women's liberation enables her to short-circuit China's elaborate elitist system by demanding a divorce, emigrating to America, and remarrying the man of her choice.

Tan returns to the issue of social rigidity in *The Hundred Secret Senses* (1995), in which Kwan Li attains fluid movement among classifications by living in the twentieth century while reminiscing about a past incarnation. Through mystic communion as a ghost-seer, she recalls the hardships of laundering clothes and bedding for a Christian mission compound in the mid-nineteenth century as Nunumu. After her friendship with gatekeeper Lao Lu ends with his decapitation at the hand of Manchu invaders, she reunites with him in the 1990s, when he pops up as jokester while she attends Catholic mass. Seemingly unconcerned about the rigors of social deference, she guides her California-born sister Olivia Yee Laguni through the terrors of the Taiping Rebellion of 1864, which Kwan recreates through storytelling. To assure Olivia's happiness, Kwan willingly sacrifices herself in the caves of Thistle Mountain, leaving no clue to her circumstances as a ghost.

Tan's fourth novel, *The Bonesetter's Daughter* (2001), expresses a painful between-the-classes situation with the story of Precious Auntie, a fallen woman. Reared as the daughter and apprentice of Bonesetter Gu, she masters reading, writing, and folk healing, an accomplishment that ostensibly prohibits her from the marriage pool. After Liu Hu Sen proposes, she permits premarital intimacy and departs to her wedding in the early stages of pregnancy. The accidental death of the groom plunges Precious Auntie from a promising position as daughter-in-law in the house of Liu to the mother of an illegitimate daughter. Because Great-Granny Liu realizes her dilemma, Precious Auntie remains in the household in a greatly diminished capacity, the grievous post as amah to LuLing, the daughter she is unable to claim as her own.

The author depicts LuLing's regrets for her mother's suffering and suicide not as a longing for higher social status, but as genuine sorrow that she did not recognize Precious Auntie's importance to her life. In a parallel diminution, LuLing exits the house of Liu, where she enjoyed favor as a daughter, and enters a Christian orphanage housing the Girls of New Destiny. Education as a calligrapher and reading teacher places her on a new horizon for women — the socioeconomic position as educated female and maker of her own destiny. By marrying a geologist, Pan Kai Jing, she rises once more from outcast and enjoys a brief respite from unfavorable comparison with her sister GaoLing Liu, the wife of Chang Fu Nan and daughter-in-law of Chang the coffinmaker. In widowhood, LuLing once more eludes the social trap by emigrating to the United States under a provision welcoming visiting artists and by marrying a pre-med student. In a second widowhood, she continues to elevate her position by managing rental property and by acquiring substantial wealth from investments in the stock exchange. The fluidity of her up and down movements on the social scale illustrate the value of learning and property to Chinese women as they flee the restrictions of the feudal past.

See also **autonomy, fate and fortune, *The Moon Lady*, Ying-ying St. Clair, Taiping Rebellion, women**

• *Further Reading*

Hamilton, Patricia L. "Feng Shui, Astrology, and the Five Elements: Traditional Chinese Belief in Amy Tan's *The Joy Luck Club*." *MELUS*, Vol. 24, No. 2, Summer 1999, pp. 125–145.

Ma, Sheng-mei. *Immigrant Subjectivities in Asian American and Asian Diaspora Literature*. Albany: State University of New York Press, 1998.

spousal abuse

The revelations of spousal abuse in *The Kitchen God's Wife* (1991) mark Amy Tan's feminist writing at its most poignant. In picturing eighteen-year-old Winnie Jiang in the second month of her marriage to Wen Fu, the author describes the difference between living with a mother-in-law, Wen Tai-tai, and moving into private quarters in a Hangchow monastery during Wen Fu's aviation training. At first, he demands daily sex and withholds tenderness and understanding. As his lovemaking departs from normality into assault and torture, he threatens his bride for refusing to say dirty words, then drags her, naked and fainting, into the corridor in full view of other residents. He abases her by forcing her to crawl on the cold floor and beg for sex in coarse language. The crude nature of his motivation indicates that he is sexually perverse, violent, and unsuited for marriage and fatherhood.

Tan echoes Winnie's sufferings in stories of other unlucky women. Her friend Helen describes trying to deliver the baby of a village girl whom a pilot spurned, then slapped, causing the victim to go into labor. Before she and the baby died, she placed a death curse on him. Helen reveals that the pathetic girl was her sister, whom their parents buried with their grandchild still undelivered. The abuser was Captain Long "Jack" Jiaguo, who sought expiation by marrying Helen. Their odd sexless marriage puzzles Winnie, who is unsure of the reason for the brother-sister relationship, but she admires the atonement and kindness in Jiaguo, who is a polar opposite of Wen Fu.

The escalating spousal abuse to Winnie endangers not only the wife, but also the couple's unborn child Mochou. When Wen Fu wastes Winnie's dowry money on the remains of a Fiat, he roars away before she can climb over the broken passenger door. She notes during their wild ride to the Purple and Gold Mountains that terrifying her delights him more than any other experience they have shared. The misery of his bullying and unpredictable outbursts worsens in Kunming after his bad driving results in an accident, loss of an eye, and brain damage. He calls Winnie a whore and slaps her in front of dinner guests, demanding that she kneel and repent for infractions she didn't commit. She states a fact about domestic abuse that prevails worldwide — the hesitation of outsiders to defend the browbeaten wife against a torrent of spite, sadism, and debasement.

In tandem with the Sino-Japanese War (1937–1945), the cat-and-mouse game the evil husband plays continues in 1941, when Wen Fu becomes more public with his womanizing. To Winnie's complaint of bitter cabbage, he has the same dish served fourteen consecutive nights as a display of patriarchal power. The meal symbolizes the everyday bitterness of marriage to a brute. At the Christmas dance, held in a warehouse, Wen Fu seethes because Winnie accepts a dance from Jimmy Louie, a self-assured translator for the United States Information Service and press relations office for the American consulate general in China. In the privacy of their quarters, Wen Fu denounces her, grabs her hair, and tosses her to the floor. He holds her at gunpoint and forces her to write out a divorce bill that will deny her Danru. With the gun to her head, he attacks her with carnal savagery.

Tan develops the most prominent villainy by picturing Wen Fu's ambivalence about ending his marriage. After testifying that Winnie deserted him, rifled family heirlooms, and stole their son Danru, Wen Fu smirks at the court and anticipates that his perjury will force her to beg for reinstatement. Winnie reveals the beginnings of self-assertion by choosing women's prison over marriage to a sadist. Before fleeing China to join Jimmy Louie in California, she precipitates more brutality from Wen Fu by forcing him to sign divorce papers in the telegraph office before jeering customers and staff. His retaliation again places Winnie in jeopardy as he stalks her, holds her at gunpoint, rapes her, and threatens to destroy the necessary exit papers and plane tickets. Helen's arrival at a pivotal moment stops Winnie from shooting Wen Fu and proposes instead the removal of his trousers. To his public embarrassment, he must depart Winnie's flat with his backside bare. The comeuppance is particularly gratifying for exposing his genitals.

See also **patriarchy, polygyny, Precious Auntie, violence**

• *Further Reading*

Barras, Jonetta Rose. "'Kitchen' Provides Complex Look at Relations of Women." *Washington Times*, July 15, 1991, pp. C6–C7.

Chung, L. A. "Chinese American Literary War: Writers, Critics Argue Over Portrayal of Asians." *San Francisco Chronicle*, August 26, 1991, p. D4.

Pate, Nancy. "'Wife' Is the Story of an Amazing Life." *Orlando Sentinel*, June 23, 1991, p. C11.

storytelling

One of Amy Tan's most successful modes of fictional expression is the internal story. She learned to value narrative in childhood and explained in *The Opposite of Fate: A Book of Musings* (2003) that, from age seven, she listened nightly to the reading of her father, John Tan, from a bedtime storybook. She recalled, "What I loved most was listening to his voice" (p. 336). Because of prodigious reading skills and impatience, she finished the book at one sitting and went to the library for works of her own choosing. Paramount to a departure from father-read stories was her wish to pace the events of narrative to suit her own thoughts and needs for closure. The decision prefaced an adult career built on voicing human stories in complex, many-layered novels.

Of narrative-within-narrative, Tan explained at the 1998 annual American Library Association convention in Washington, D.C., that storytelling is "a deliberate derangement of the mind," a reordering of logic and exorcism of past fears to reveal pertinent insights (Eberhart). From illustrative character anecdotes and fables, she concluded that life is neither planned nor totally random. She pictured life with a womanly image — "a crazy quilt of love, pieced together, torn apart, repaired over and over again, and strong enough to protect us all" (*Ibid.*). Kitty Benedict, a reviewer for the *Hartford Courant*, remarked that such narrative has special meaning for women in patriarchal marriages: "The way out of this bondage, imposed by man's need to subjugate and deny women their autonomy, is for the memories of mothers to be handed down honestly to their daughters" (Benedict, p. C10).

Such buoyant oral narrative is the source of *The Joy Luck Club* (1989), a mesh of fables and exempla that the author gleaned from her mother. The novel opens with the tale of a swan that used to be a duck, a fable about delayed ambitions. The story introduces the novel's psychological underpinnings of four Chinese mothers who maintain hopelessly high expectations of their Amerasian daughters. Critic Amy Ling notes that the daughters admire the mothers for their courage and ingenuity and are touched by the hardships of feudal marriage and silencing that the older generation of women encountered in China. Ling adds that, simultaneously, the Chinese-American daughters are "exasperated by their mothers' impossible demands; resentful of their mother's intrusions on their lives, and sometimes humiliated and ashamed of their stubborn, superstitious, out-of-place Old World ways" (Ling, p. 133). Thus, storytelling becomes a paradox of autobiographical gifts, history, and admonition.

The avian tale is the introit to the first episode, in which June Woo replaces her mother Suyuan at the mah jong table after the mother's death from brain aneurysm. The substitution is a significant intergenerational moment after the first loss of a club member and the rise of the initial first-generation Chinese-American into a parent's place. Canning Woo accounts for his wife's sudden death as the result of holding ideas inside and allowing them to exceed their limits and explode. Suyuan's peers — An-mei Hsu, Lindo Jong, and Ying-ying St. Clair — regret that she died like a rabbit, a quick-legged, but small-framed mammal that ceases to exist without completing its life's business. Subsequent anecdotes and vignettes serve as a reclamation of Suyuan's individuality and a re-creation of her strengths as an aid to her less-than-successful daughter.

At a dramatic moment in club member An-mei's life, the author interposes another story, an orderly fable of magpies and a turtle. Reunited with her unnamed mother, An-mei listens to the tale of her mother's seven tears that fall into the turtle's mouth. The turtle transforms the droplets into seven pearly eggs, which yield seven magpies. The birds fly away laughing, a symbol of exploiters who turn other people's sufferings into joy. On the duo's seven-day journey to Tientsin, the mother's stories are so entrancing that An-mei forgets her sorrow at leaving Ningpo. The stories continue in Wu Tsing's house, where An-mei falls asleep in her mother's arms to the sound of her voice, a form of reassurance that relieves the child of insecurity during the move from her former home.

The novel exalts storytelling as a prop during threatening times. When An-mei's mother lies dying of an overdose of bitter poison, the turtle story returns in a dream with An-mei in the place of the turtle and the magpies above drinking the pond dry of her tears. In adulthood, she rejects psychiatrists as birds drinking the sufferers' tears. She resets her mother's story in modern times by describing the peasant revolt against coercion and the shout from rebels that causes millions of birds to fall dead. For good reason, An-mei pictures herself in the role of a hard-shelled beast that moves slowly, carefully among dangers. The image expresses a subconscious choice of position in the fable as compassionate, tear-eating turtle rather than laughing magpie.

Tan earned critical regard for her ability to relate events and reflections from distinct voices. She took one episode as the source for *The Moon Lady* (1992), her first children's story, which contains myths about the marriage of the sun and moon and about the master archer's receipt of a magic peach, which his mate steals and eats in one gulp. Tan found that such storytelling for young readers requires discipline: "A story must go in direct line from beginning to end; it cannot afford to get sidetracked by long, descriptive passages.... There's also more freedom. The freedom has to do with the possibilities that can happen with a children's story" (Loer, p. E4). Her assessment destroys the illusion among non-writers that composing children's literature is easy.

In Tan's second novel, *The Kitchen God's Wife* (1991), Winnie Louie, the narrator within the framework, offers her life history as a sacred gift, much as Old Testament patriarchs prepared their sons for the future with a formal blessing. In a flashback to girlhood, she recalls how her own mother read her a story about a classic beauty who longed for friends who didn't envy her. The girl found a smiling face as she gazed at her reflection in a pond. Winnie's mother, who resembles the beautiful protagonist, ridicules the story as nonsense. Winnie, a member of China's emerging liberated women, questions the story's premise that the ideal woman should be lovely and graceful.

A second example of storytelling occurs at a crux in Winnie's mother's life. After she is widowed and agrees to a marriage with Jiang Sao-yen, Lu, a Marxist journalist who loves her, tells about a revolutionary village girl who refuses feudal marriage to an old man. Locked in a pig shed, she remains until her wedding day. During transportation to the groom in a sedan chair, she hangs herself with a loop of her hair. Lu exalts the girl as a martyr to the peasant revolt against outmoded Chinese thinking, a leftover of Confucianism and the Ching dynasty (1644–1912).

Winnie's loss of her mother and arrival at a marriageable age precedes her fantasy of a satisfying marriage unlike the one that killed her mother. In the early months of wedlock with Kuomintang air force pilot Wen Fu, Winnie and Helen use oral narrative as an escape from their long truck ride across China to wives' quarters at Kunming. Drawing on stories of celestial constellations they remember from childhood, the two women fill in with made-up patterns about the Separated Goose Lovers, the Drowned Woman with Her Hair Unbound, and the Lady with the Horse's Head. To Winnie, the reshaping of these stories into moralistic fables cultivates a lasting friendship with Helen. Winnie explains that, along the miserable drive, stars provided "signs of contentment in the world, a peace that would never change" (p. 290).

At war's end, Tan portrays an up-tick in the tone of women's storytelling. On return from Kunming, Winnie attempts to settle in her father's mansion on Julu Road and to recover from jaundice, which she may have contracted in Changsha from tainted river crabs. Old Aunt, who learns of her illness, tells a comic tale about Miao Tai-tai, the matchmaker, whose husband becomes so agitated at her illness and his inability to telephone a physician that he falls dead. By the time the doctor arrives, he finds the wife well and the husband stone cold. Old Aunt uses the story as justification for demanding telephone service, a symbol of restored communication and a rising demand for modern technology among families recovering from the Japanese occupation of China's east coast.

For her third novel, *The Hundred Secret Senses* (1995), Tan confers an unusual honor on the storyteller. Kwan Li, the Chinese ghost-seer, regales her little sister Olivia with sequential nights of memories and tales of her mother Li Chen's sadness and death, which Kwan confides as secrets. Although Olivia can't understand Chinese, she acquires respect for the spirits that populate her sister's mystic world. In addition, she absorbs the tales and gradually learns the language through narrative without voluntarily studying it, as though absorbing foreign words through hypnopedia or sleep-study. The acquisition of fluency without formal training suggests the power of stories to inform and to encourage sisterly communication.

The sibling relationship continues in adulthood with more titillating plots narrated by Kwan. At a difficult pass in Olivia's life, Kwan energizes her spiel of ghost lore with storytelling from dreams, which predict that Simon will return his heart to Olivia, his ex-wife. In a more engrossing tale, Kwan speaks of her death in a former life during the chaos of the Taiping Rebellion of 1864, when the Girl with the Dagger Eye made Kwan a messenger to the Hakka people. After a pleasant meal in Changmian, Kwan regales Olivia, Simon, and old friend Du Lili with familiar village stories of dragons and a huge cave that holds an ancient stone village. Only after Kwan's disappearance does Olivia have full proof that Kwan's stories were real memories of her life as Nunumu, the mission laundress who died in 1864 while attempting to rescue her friend, Nelly Banner, from Manchu invaders. The link to Chinese history elevates after-dinner storytelling in validity and significance.

Iain Finlayson's review of the novel for *Chinatown News* focuses on storytelling as the author's forte. He remarked that "The sheer buoyancy of Amy Tan's writing, her spirited genius for storytelling, the gutsy humor, the unsentimental expression of emotion, the sharp dialogue, and the sheer verve of the narrative as it bounces along from modern San Francisco to nineteenth-century provincial China, is entrancing" (Finlayson, p. 38). He neglects to mention the author's skillful pacing, the insertion of talk-story during the 1994 visit to Changmian, China. At important moments in the action, Kwan spans out the remainder of the story and proves its veracity through an insider's knowledge of Thistle Mountain and its myriad caves.

See also **autonomy, fable,** *The Hundred Secret Senses,* **Kwan Li, morality tale, talk-story**

- *Further Reading*

Benedict, Kitty. "Mother to Daughter: Here Is the Truth of My Life." *Hartford Courant,* June 30, 1991, p. C10.

Eberhart, George, et al. "ALA Thinks Globally, Acts Federally." *American Libraries,* Vol. 29, No. 7, August 1998, pp. 70–83.

Finlayson, Iain. "Chinese Whispers with Humour." *Chinatown News,* Vol. 43, No. 9, March 1, 1996, pp. 38–39.

Heung, Marina. "Daughter-Text/Mother-Text: Matrilineage in Amy Tan's Joy Luck Club." *Feminist Studies,* Vol. 19, No. 3, Fall 1993, pp. 597–616.

Ling, Amy. *Between Worlds: Women Writers of Chinese Ancestry.* New York: Pergamon Press, 1990.

Loer, Stephanie. "Amy Tan Writes from a Child's Point of View." *Boston Globe,* November 10, 1992, pp. E3–E4.

Marbella, Jean. "Amy Tan: Luck but Not Joy." *Baltimore Sun,* June 30, 1991, pp. B10–B13.

Shapiro, Laura. "Ghost Story." *Newsweek,* Vol. 126, No. 19, November 6, 1995, pp. 91–92.

suicide

Tan's fiction frequently portrays suicide as a woman's method of exiting a hopeless male-female relationship or feudal marriage. She introduces the theme in *The Joy Luck Club* (1989) through the threats of Suyuan Woo to kill herself after she abandons her twin girls by the roadside during the advance of the enemy into China during the Sino-Japanese War (1937–1945). A trivialized example of the power of suicide is the game-playing of a crafty concubine, a former Shantung teahouse chanteuse, who manipulates Wu Tsing, a lecherous womanizer, by faking deliberate overdoses of opium. According to Deirdre Donahue, writing for *USA Today,* the motif was common: some 25 percent of Chinese concubines killed themselves to escape polygyny. By playing on his fears of vengeful ghosts, the concubine wheedles an increase in her allowance, more luxuries, even amenities for her parents. The trickery epitomizes the extremes to which Chinese women go to wrest power from a male-dominated society.

In a more serious vein, Tan reprises the theme of suicide that permeated her own mother-daughter relationship. The author transfixes the memory of An-mei Hsu, a child deprived of parental nurturance because her unnamed mother killed herself by swallowing a bitter poison. Like Tan's grandmother Jingmei, the mother is a former widow and victim of Wu Tsing, who raped her and forced her into concubinage as his fourth wife. An-mei remembers the no-win situation that caused her mother to leave Grandmother Popo's house for a loveless marriage in Tientsin "to exchange one unhappiness for another" (p. 40). To soften the child's fears of sorrow, the mother tells An-mei a pleasant fable about a turtle that swallowed her tears.

The silencing of sorrows among Chinese women creates unbearable stress. After producing a son, Syaudi, An-mei's mother chooses suicide three days before New Year's day to liberate herself from disfavor in male-dominated feudal marriage and simultaneously to heap guilt on the man who must make amends with her spirit. The vision of the mother extending a swollen tongue and marching like a soldier in the grip of the poison fills the hours of waiting and disproves to An-mei the fable of the turtle swallowing sadness. The double purpose of the death frees the mother from in-house torment at the same time that it offers An-mei leverage in a family that denies her dignity and status. Because of the boost to An-mei's power, the suicide takes on the trappings of a posthumous love gift from her only surviving parent.

Although Tan reveals without details in *The Kitchen God's Wife* (1991) the suicidal death of Uncle Jiang on Tsungming Island in 1948 by walking in front of a truck, she reserves the power and drama of ending a wretched life for the characterization of despairing women. A notable example, Min, the vaudevillian who eludes Wen Fu to abort his child and form a new relationship, drowns herself at age thirty-three. Tan returns to the theme of self-murder out of desperation with the theatrical death of Precious Auntie, Gu Liu Xin, the silenced thirty-year-old mother in *The Bonesetter's Daughter* (2001), who serves as the nanny of the rebellious LuLing Liu. Precious Auntie tries to end her life on her wedding day, when the kick of a horse kills her fiancé, Liu Hu Sen. Already pregnant, the bride despairs and swallows boiling ink, but recovers to live as a hideous mute cripple. She accepts the offer of the family's aged great-granny to serve her own child as amah. Just as An-mei's mother attempts to survive wretchedness by swallowing sorrow, Precious Auntie lives in the shadows that occlude her motherhood.

The option to end life returns after Precious Auntie foresees LuLing's marriage to Fu Nan, the son of the evil coffin-maker Chang. Precious Auntie's death not only forestalls the wedding, but ends LuLing's illusion of being high born and results in her demotion to the orphan of a suicide. Ironically, the cruel death becomes, like the suicide of An-mei's mother, a posthumous love gift protecting LuLing from an evil she is too naive to suspect. The motif of self-murder recurs after LuLing loses her husband, geologist Pan Kai Jing, to invaders. It is the coaxing of Sister Yu to accept the promise of a Christian heaven that encourages the widow to live out her life and join Kai Jing in the hereafter. Into old age, LuLing retains the twisted power of Chinese women by threatening to end her life as a means of dramatizing her loss of control over her own daughter, Ruth Liu Young.

See also **autobiography, China, ghosts, patriarchy, polygyny, Precious Auntie, LuLing Liu Young**

• *Further Reading*

Cujec, Carol. "Excavating Memory, Reconstructing Legacy." *World & I*, Vol. 16, No. 7, July 2001, pp. 215–223.
Donahue, Deirdre. "Tan's Books Excavate Life's Joy and Pain." *USA Today*, February 19, 2001, pp. 1D–2D.

superstition

To shed light on the Asian-American mindset, Tan incorporates Chinese mythos and folk beliefs into narrative, such as the tying of chains to a child's ankles at her mother's funeral in "Lost Lives of Women" (1991) to keep her from flying away with the deceased. In the opening segment of *The Joy Luck Club* (1989), the author explains the first three of the five elements of human chemistry—fire for temper, wood for character strength, and water for perseverance. In a deathbed scene, Popo receives soup made from the flesh of her disgraced daughter, an ancient magic used as a last-ditch effort to cure the mortally ill. More complicated is An-mei Hsu's belief that children are in more danger on certain days, a zodiacal predisposition caused by their birth dates. Because she is unable to locate complementary dates on the American calendar, she worries about all possible catastrophes—dogbite, lightning, falling from a tree, slipping in the bathtub, and standing beneath a falling object. After the drowning of her young son Bing, she attempts to alter fate with Christian faith, which fails her.

Before the funeral of Auntie Du Ching, a significant family and community event at the opening of *The Kitchen God's Wife* (1991), superstition becomes a dominant motif. Pearl Louie Brandt recalls that her mother Winnie and Auntie Du both clung to Buddhist precepts and superstitious ritual, even though both women attended the First Chinese Baptist Church. The focus of their beliefs was the achievement of good fortune and the avoidance of ill luck. Winnie consciously strives to obtain luck rather than depend on inborn fortune. She further annoys her daughter by mentioning a belief in Nine Bad Fates, an accounting system that warns the victim of a fatal event that awaits after eight non-lethal occurrences. To Pearl, Winnie is "a Chinese version of Freud, or worse. Everything has a reason" (p. 27).

At a country funeral in *The Hundred Secret Senses* (1995), Tan returns to more arcane customs with the dressing of Big Ma's corpse. The purpose of placing seven layers on the torso and five layers below is muddled in survivors' quibbling. Even less rational is the tying of a rooster to the coffin. Kwan indicates that no one really believes that the spirit of the deceased can fly away in the rooster's body. She explains that old traditions continue to hold sway even when they have no sensible explanation. Rather than account for the spirit's whereabouts in the afterlife, folkways impart order to the chaos left by sudden death.

The unforeseen return of a spirit in *The Bonesetter's Daughter* (2001), Tan's fourth novel, terrifies Ruth Luyi Young, who becomes amanuensis for her mother, LuLing Liu. While scribbling in a sand tray with a chopstick after a sliding board accident wounds her tongue, Ruth draws the character for "mouth," leading LuLing to think that her nursemaid Precious Auntie has returned. Subsequent one-sided babblings to the ghost lead LuLing to believe that a family curse caused the accident. The onus of mediating between mother and ghost forces Ruth to reclaim her voice and assure her mother that all her past sins are forgiven. By serving as a medium in the bogus séance, Ruth gives voice to Precious Auntie, the grandmother who silenced herself by drinking boiling resin.

In a flashback of superstitions that LuLing learned from her nursemaid, she recalls examining a turtle bone and learning why they are called oracle bones. Precious Auntie relates that seekers inscribed on the bones in ancient script their questions to the gods. Diviners discovered the answers by cracking the bone with a hot nail, then interpreting the jagged surface. Such bones, retrieved from the Mouth of the Mountain, carried a high price at medicine shops, where dealers sold them as cure-alls. The link between communication and healing reflects Tan's pervasive theme of healing silenced women by retrieving them from patriarchy and encouraging them to tell their stories.

See also **fate and fortune, ghosts, religion**

- *Further Reading*

Bunce, Kim. "Review: *The Bonesetter's Daughter.*" *Guardian Unlimited*, March 18, 2001.
Hamilton, Patricia L. "Feng Shui, Astrology, and the Five Elements: Traditional Chinese Belief in Amy Tan's *The Joy Luck Club.*" *MELUS*, Vol. 24, No. 2, Summer 1999, pp. 125–145.
Ma, Sheng-mei. "'Chinese and Dogs' in Amy Tan's 'The Hundred Secret Senses': Ethnicizing the Primitive à la New Age." *MELUS*, Vol. 26, No. 1, Spring 2001, pp. 29–44.
Russo, Maria. "Review: *The Bonesetter's Daughter.*" *Salon*, February 21, 2001.

Taiping Rebellion (1864)

Tan contrasts milieus in *The Hundred Secret Senses* (1995) with the memories of Kwan Li, a late-twentieth-century ghost-seer who recalls her life in Changmian, Chinag, which ended violently in 1864 during the Taiping Rebellion, China's best documented upheaval. The lengthy turmoil, which began in 1850 during global Christian revivalism, spread over seventeen provinces, weakened the Ching dynasty (1644–1912), and killed some thirty million Chinese. Led by a Hakkanese visionary, Hung Hsiuch'uan, a demented Christian convert who believed himself to be Jesus's younger brother and God's son, the revolt targeted the God Worshippers' Society, a new religion organized by Feng Yun-shan among the poor peasants of Kwangsi province.

Hung attempted to launch a new anti–Confucian, anti-imperial dynasty with himself as ruler of a *taiping tianguo* (heavenly kingdom). The movement attracted over one million converts before breaking into splinter groups. In its heyday, the followers' social reform urged discipline, gender equality, communal land ownership, simplified language, and an end to rabid Confucianism and foot-binding, a grotesque form of child mutilation that increased patriarchal hold over young women. The movement's Communistic precepts, particularly the revocation of social class strictures, influenced Chinese Marxism, which took hold of the nation in 1949.

See also **violence**

• *Further Reading*

Fortuna, Diana. "Review: *The Hundred Secret Senses*." *America*, Vol. 174, No. 14, May 4, 1996, pp. 27–28.
Ma, Sheng-mei. "'Chinese and Dogs' in Amy Tan's 'The Hundred Secret Senses': Ethnicizing the Primitive à la New Age." *MELUS*, Vol. 26, No. 1, Spring 2001, pp. 29–44.
_____. *The Deathly Embrace: Orientalism and Asian American Identity*. Minneapolis: University of Minnesota Press, 2000.

talk-story

The tradition of passing family anecdotes, subjective narratives, testimonies, morality tales, and fables from parent to child tends to focus on warnings, confessions of bad conduct and poor applications of logic, and therapeutic dramatization of important life lessons. Amy Tan, Maxine Hong Kingston, Toni Morrison, Fae Myenne Ng, Leslie Marmon Silko, and other feminist authors have recovered the talk-story culture as a means of reclaiming women's history and of gauging how far women have come from the dark ages of patriarchy and feudal marriage. Texts honor the story-keepers, who preserve and convey past concealments, silencing of females, and the discounting of women's lives, sexuality, and aspirations. Tan claims that the courage of her own grandmother, Gu Jingmei, a dishonored concubine who killed herself in 1925 by swallowing raw opium, continues to infuse strength and autonomy to members of her family.

Through autobiographical fiction, Tan creates natural, familial instances of mother-to-daughter storytelling in which women seize an opportunity to speak freely without being censored or stifled. Their parables grow out of conversational opportunities in warm domestic settings. As described by critic Wendy Ho, author of *In Her Mother's House* (1999), an arrhythmic, fragmented telling is common, incorporating "a complicated vocabulary of rupture — heavy sighs, silences, trembling lips, downcast eyes, weeping, and wringing of hands" (Ho, p. 19). The end result requires patience on the part of the listener to deduce what each hiatus leaves unsaid and what emerges after false starts and hesitations reveal significant life passages. From these disjointed, sometimes contradictory efforts come the roots of more refined written folklore, memoir, annotated genealogy, and autobiography.

The organic flow and uneven cadence of talk-story invest mother-daughter relationships in Tan's novels, beginning with the Chinese immigrant. In *The Joy Luck Club* (1989), mah jong–playing mothers An-mei Hsu, Lindo Jong, and Ying-ying St. Clair divulge Suyuan Woo's early life and marriage to her daughter June, who takes Suyuan's place in the club. In the aftermath of the mother's death, the revelation of serious wartime privations, widowhood, flight, illness, and suicidal urges over the abandonment of twin daughters Chwun Hwa and Chwun Yu informs June that she is not an only child and that her mother suffered inwardly from sad memories of emigrating from her homeland. The transmission of stories about loss and social upheaval produces what critic Marina Heung calls "parables of self-affirmation and individual empowerment" (Heung, p. 607). Because of the dominant female point of view, talk-story aids both the teller and the hearer in understanding shifts in the social and familial assessment of women's worth that followed the collapse of the Ching dynasty (1644–1912).

Another survivor of the Sino-Japanese War (1937–1945), Ying-ying St. Clair, undergoes a gradual erasure of self after years of pleasing her first husband Lin Xiao by play-acting his ideal of the perfect wife. Through talk-story, she regains her lost self and builds a stronger relationship with her daughter, Lena Livotny. The oral mode increases in length and detail in *The Kitchen God's Wife* (1991), in which Winnie Louie, a woman similar to Ying-ying in past suffering, discloses to daughter Pearl Brandt the terrors of an early marriage during the Japanese invasion and occupation. Because the number of female points of view is limited in the second novel, Winnie's long narration surpasses talk-story to become war memoir and apologia.

The variety of talk-stories in *The Bonesetter's Daughter* (2001), the author's fourth novel, represents Precious Auntie's numerous explanations to LuLing Liu of how the speaker, her nursemaid, was seriously burned and muted. From fanciful stories of a falling star and a meal of hot coals, she segues to another untruth, a hapless busker performing fire tricks in the market square. Additional talk-story is necessary to fill in these years in LuLing's past to Ruth, who is Precious Auntie's grand-daughter. Goading Ruth to make time to listen to LuLing's regrets and griefs is Dr. Huey's diagnosis of senile dementia, a medical explanation of LuLing's peculiar behaviors and confusion. To fill in essential gaps, Ruth queries her Aunt GaoLing, LuLing's sister, who resets the tone of the fearful descent into the boneyard, the End of the World, by referring to it as a garbage dump. The puzzling out of matrilineal truth prepares Ruth for fiction-writing, another form of female self-expression.

See also **The Kitchen God's Wife**, morality tale, Ying-ying St. Clair

• *Further Reading*

Heung, Marina. "Daughter-Text/Mother-Text: Matrilineage in Amy Tan's Joy Luck Club." *Feminist Studies*, Vol. 19, No. 3, Fall 1993, pp. 597–616.

Ho, Wendy. *In Her Mother's House — The Politics of Asian American Mother-Daughter Writing*. Walnut Creek, Calif.: AltaMira Press, 1999.

Pearlman, Mickey, and Katherine Usher Henderson. *Inter/view: Talks with America's Writing Women*. Lexington: University Press of Kentucky, 1990.

Tan, Amy

Amy Tan has earned a well-deserved place among American fiction writers for the creation of engaging Chinese and immigrant Asian-American characters. Key to her success is the ability to energize pidgin English and to squeeze dramatic irony and humor from the miscommunications between native-born Chinese and their first-generation American offspring, e.g., Winnie and Helen's attempt to mislead potential robbers during a "stick-'em-up" at their Ding Ho Flower Shop and Winnie's description of "that Randy boy," Pearl's lover in college during her freshman year (pp. 15, 194). Tan, whom *Newsweek* literary critic Laura Shapiro calls "one of the prime storytellers writing fiction today," responds to two strong strands of nationalism, her mother's China and her own United States (Shapiro, p. 63). Of American freedoms, she states in "Watching China" (1993) of the expectations of U.S. citizens: "We put those rights in writing, carry them in our back pockets all over the world, pull them out as proof. We may be aliens in another country, but we still maintain that our rights are inalienable" (p. 303). While empathizing with Chinese citizens dreaming of democracy, she imagines the longing for liberty as a "feeling in the chest, one that has been restrained for so long it grows larger and more insistent, until it bursts forth with a shout" (*Ibid.*).

In *The Joy Luck Club* (1989), Tan's skill at dialogue and motivation derive from telling a story in a voice that only that character could relate. She captures the irony of social progress that allows a man to escape arranged marriage and choose his own wife, "with his parents' permission of course" (p. 45). Left unsaid is the fact that women have no choice under either system. She earned the praise of bicultural novelist Michael Dorris, who admired the authenticity of her fictional casts and the universality of their human situations. He noted that her first novel "leaves the reader changed, more aware of subtleties, anxious to explore the confusions of any parent's motivations, any child's rebellion" (Dorris, p. 11).

Of the importance of fiction to her self-awareness as a woman, Tan expressed strong approval of feminism and matrilineal connections. She explained, "I believe in self-determination and I believe there are experiences that filter down from generation to generation. It has to do with who we are as women, not who we are married to" (Taylor, p. F1). The experience of composing *The Joy Luck Club* was crucial to the author's wholeness and to the end of intergenerational animosities. She noted that writing her grandmother's story as fiction produced a satisfying intellectual fusion of past with present.

By the time that Tan published a second novel, *The Kitchen God's Wife* (1991), she was adept at differentiating characters and expressing conflicting opinions and beliefs. More subtle in delineating human feelings, she carefully created the character Winnie Louie as a voice for her own mother, Daisy Tan. Tan depicts the girl's precarious position in the Jiang household by picturing Winnie's mother holding her and peering down a long staircase to the floors below. By age eighteen, Winnie has spent twelve years as a guest in her paternal uncle's house on Tsungming Island, where she withdraws to a greenhouse for private meditation, a symbolic promise of the eventual greening of Winnie Louie. Tan describes her respect for the inanimate glass structure with the act of wiping a glass pane "as carefully as if it were the eye of a waking child" (p. 139). The image suggests Winnie's own slow awakening from naivete to independence. The description of the greenhouse as a storage shed for discarded oddments creates a more poignant picture of Winnie as a superfluous family member relegated to the scrap pile.

Tan cleverly inserts suspense, sense impressions, and symbolic parallels to lend meaning to Winnie's fearful autobiography. As described by Emily Ellison, reviewer for the *Atlanta Journal*, every scene teems with smells, tastes, sights, sounds, and textures that reveal China as it was at the end of the Ching dynasty (1644–1912) and before the Communist takeover in 1948. Winnie ends twelve years in virtual exile on Tsungming Island to begin another dozen as the wife-prisoner of the brute Wen

Fu. Just as she retreated to the greenhouse into discarded furniture and household goods in girlhood, in adulthood, she and Helen spend afternoons in another getaway, a gazebo where they sew and enjoy time without the burden of husbands. The blossoming of sisterhood foretells a satisfying late-in-life camaraderie with Helen as United States citizens.

A literary device that Tan shares with Toni Morrison's *Beloved* (1987) is the use of shoes as symbols of adventure, escape, and hard traveling. Winnie meets Wen Fu while escorting Peanut, who is hobbled by the latest Western fashions. Because of the disruption of Peanut's betrothal plans, it is Winnie who is ultimately hobbled with Wen Fu. At the victory dance on Christmas 1941, Wen Fu slings Winnie about, breaking the heel of her shoe. The discourtesy offers Jimmy Louie an opportunity to display courtliness and to catch her before she is hurt. Significantly, he repeats the rescue in 1955 after Winnie recognizes Dr. Lin, her former suitor, and faints on the steps of the First Chinese Baptist Church. Tan turns other ordinary objects into signposts, e.g., a pair of scissors, silver chopsticks, games of mah jong, a household icon, and photographs elucidating the past.

Tan manipulates suspense in the resolution of the plot, leaving the reader curious about how Winnie escapes from Wen Fu and the approaching Communists and about how she resolves the question of Pearl's paternity. The uncertainty of Pearl's emotional makeup hovers until Winnie confides one last story, the rebellion of Pearl and her brother Samuel. Winnie saw inklings of Wen Fu in Pearl's use of "bitch" to describe her mother. The mother was terrified of further development of Wen Fu's influence until Samuel went through the same teen phase of denouncing his mother as a bitch. Because Samuel is certainly Jimmy Louie's son, Winnie began to relax her watch for evidence of Wen Fu's psychosis in her daughter. Tan's careful remission of suspense eases the novel into a wholesome conclusion with the indestructible mother-daughter relationship and the sisterhood of Winnie and Helen assured.

The polish of the next two novels attests to a maturity in Tan's later fiction. In *The Hundred Secret Senses* (1995), she is expert at dramatic irony, e.g., the scattering of "The Good News" after Manchu mercenaries attack. She pictures atavistic warfare in the beheading and roasting of a haunch of gatekeeper Lao Lu over a cookfire. The image of fire and smoke follows the Manchus to the caves of Thistle Mountain, where they accidentally immolate themselves while smoking peasants out of the caves. Fire reverts once more into a cleansing element that scours signs of violence off the landscape.

In *The Bonesetter's Daughter* (2001), Tan's fourth novel, she devises a believable framework to support the telling of LuLing's family history. Within the saga, she creates memorable imagery, for example, the disease that eats the Immortal Tree, a symbol of the Ching dynasty (1644–1912), which collapses before revolution destroys China's ancient traditions and forces the nation into the modern world. Fine details relate the sense impressions of inkstick-making, beginning with grinding fragrant additives and mixing glue. By depicting the finished inksticks as properly dyed and hardened, the author contrasts the insubstantial imperial family, which weakens simultaneously as the Liu clan's industry is gaining strength and reputation. At a turning point in the story-within-a-story, Tan creates tension in the matchmaker's description of the coffinmaker Chang's furnishings, which are "purple like a fresh bruise" (p. 150). Tan's final image of Ruth Young writing away at her home office reveals something of the author's love for the life of a writer, for whom "happiness lies ... in love and freedom to give and take what has been there all along" (p. 308).

See also **chronology, humor, titles**

• *Further Reading*

Davis, Emory. "An Interview with Amy Tan: Fiction — The Beast That Roams." *Writing-on-the-Edge*, Spring 1990, pp. 97–111.

Dorris, Michael. "Mothers and Daughters." *Chicago Tribune*, March 12, 1989, pp. 1, 11.

Ellison, Emily. "Tragic Story Dazzles and Awes." *Atlanta Journal*, June 16, 1991, pp. C12–C13.

Guy, David. "Wheel of Fortune: A Writer's Thoughts on Joy, Luck and Heartache." *Washington Post*, November 2, 2002, p. T4.

Ma, Sheng-mei. *The Deathly Embrace: Orientalism and Asian American Identity*. Minneapolis: University of Minnesota Press, 2000.

Shapiro, Laura. "From China, with Love." *Newsweek*, Vol. 117, No. 25, June 24, 1991, pp. 63–64.

Taylor, Noel. "The Luck of Amy Tan." *Ottawa Citizen*, October 1, 1993, p. F1.

taonan

To flesh out the social upheaval in *The Kitchen God's Wife* (1991), Tan depicts a large cast of characters trapped by hunger, disease, loss, confusion, and terror at the outbreak of the Sino-Japanese War (1937–1945), a general trauma that the Chinese call *taonan*. Dazed by the consuming need to escape certain death and find sanctuary from invasion and falling bombs, the wives of the Kuomintang air force pilots console each other with wise counsel as they plot how to save their families. The scared-to-death phenomenon of *taonan* seizes protagonist Winnie Louie during the strafing and bombing of the Kunming marketplace, sending her in a panic to find her son Danru. Her reaction, multiplied by the heart-terrors of millions of Chinese peasants, describe a segment of World War II that receives little historical recognition.

It is significant that the protagonist's emigration from China occurs under similar *taonan*. After exiting women's prison in Shanghai for child theft and flight from a feudal marriage, in 1948, Winnie survives a brutal rape at gunpoint by her ex-husband Wen Fu. Before she can heal from the experience, she must telegraph Jimmy Louie, her future husband, and plan a departure date and method while most of Shanghai quakes in fear of the advancing Communists. Upon the withdrawal of the Kuomintang, leaving Shanghai open for grabs, Winnie once more mobilizes her assets, accepts the craziness of visa requirements that alter by the day, and leaves China for good by plane. Only after her reunion with Jimmy Louie does she feel safe from *taonan*.

See also **Sino-Japanese War**

• *Further Reading*

Ellison, Emily. "Tragic Story Dazzles and Awes." *Atlanta Journal*, June 16, 1991, pp. C12–C13.

Ma, Sheng-mei. "'Chinese and Dogs' in Amy Tan's 'The Hundred Secret Senses': Ethnicizing the Primitive à la New Age." *MELUS*, Vol. 26, No. 1, Spring 2001, pp. 29–44.

titles

Amy Tan sets the mood and manipulates reader expectation through evocative titles of stories, novels, and chapters of novels, for example, a short-short story about shame entitled "Fish Cheeks" (1987), which makes the lingual tie between a meal of steamed rock cod and the inflamed cheeks of a girl who is ashamed of her family's Chinese heritage. With *The Joy Luck Club* (1989), she establishes a mythic mode for her novel of four Chinese mothers and their four Amerasian daughters with internal narrative about "Feathers from a Thousand Li Away" and "The Twenty-Six Malignant Gates." The first suggests a light, wispy substance wafted on the breeze, a subtextual reference to the fragility of human stories. The second title poses menacing obstacles, the thematic thrust of hard times and escape from impossible human relationships. From "American Translation," the task of the Asian-American daughters, the stories of their mothers surface once more in a new, more propitious setting that, paradoxically, works against the mother-daughter bond by establishing the younger generation as experts and their mothers as linguistically inhibited.

Tan's final chapter title, "Queen Mother of the Western Skies," suggests the triumphs that females achieve through communicating their stories over a bicultural divide. After June Woo embraces her mother's life-long task and meets her twin half-sisters, Chwun Hwa and Chwun Yu Wang, the trio reflect the qualities they inherited from their mother. Like little children, they form a mystic chorus babbling "Mama, Mama," a tribute to Suyuan, the queen mother who gave them life (p. 331).

See also **"Mother Tongue"**

• *Further Reading*

Heung, Marina. "Daughter-Text/Mother-Text: Matrilineage in Amy Tan's Joy Luck Club." *Feminist Studies*, Vol. 19, No. 3, Fall 1993, pp. 597–616.

violence

To contrast causes and results, Tan blends the violence of warfare and banditry with natural disasters and domestic aggressions. In *The Kitchen God's Wife* (1991), she covers a litany of sufferings: "barbaric living conditions, a first marriage to a sadistic and sexually abusive husband, rape, routine torture, murder, primitive abortions, starving, and bloody attacks by the invading Japanese" (Link, p. C3). During the rise of Winnie Louie's husband Wen Fu to full villainy, the author inserts his reckless driving in a beat-up Fiat only days before Japanese planes bomb and strafe Nanking, an historic event of November 1937 preceding the Nanking Massacre, which began in December. Too heavy to run at the end of her second trimester of pregnancy, Winnie recalls the roar of planes, the shouts of people in the marketplace, and the cries of survivors to Amitaba, the Buddhist god of paradise. In terror of the panic that seizes the crowd, Winnie cries out for her mother, an instinctive act that connects her with childhood innocence at a time when she is about to advance from daughter to parent of her own child.

To portray the dangers of Winnie's home life, Tan uses violence to illustrate Wen Fu's penchant for grandstanding. His casual shooting of a pig and threat to a farmer on the drive to Changsha causes the fleeing pilots and their wives concern. He continues his bullying behavior by terrorizing isolated mountain people with false reports that the Japanese are coming. After a blow to the head and loss of an eye triggers psychotic outbursts, he terrorizes the cooks at the hospital where his daughter is born, chops up walls and furnishings, and dumps food on the stove. Lacking an understanding of megalomania, Winnie blames the explosive temper tantrums on her mother-in-law, who pampered Wen Fu, stoking his choler and making him "hungry to feed his own power" (p. 325).

Tan's running commentary on Winnie's home dilemma minimizes the war as Wen Fu becomes less stable and more dangerous. The battery increases with Winnie's accusation that he impregnated a nameless servant girl who later died of self-abortion. To express his anger at Winnie's boldness, Wen Fu strikes Yiku, who is only six months old. Persistent blows to her head cause her to retreat to a fetal position and suck her fingers rather than cry. In terror of more punishment, she pulls her hair, beats her head against the wall, tiptoes, and avoids looking at people's faces or at her father. The author's descriptions of Yiku's bizarre behavior are so real they appear to grow from actual events from Daisy Tan's memory as she revealed her predicament to the author.

After Wen Fu's departure with other pilots, Tan relieves Winnie of domestic strife, then ends the peaceful hiatus with Japanese bombs falling southeast of the Kunming market. The author muses on the behavior of people who have faced death from the clouds, then found themselves delivered from harm. Celebrating their good fortune, they return to the marketplace and treat themselves to shoes, meat, or luxury items. As the bomb runs extend into three forays a week, there is less jubilance at survival that could end within hours when the planes return with more explosives. Winnie congratulates herself on continuing to select the safest evacuation route until she encounters strafing and bombs, which shatter homes and the people trapped inside. Tan returns to an examination of human frailty by describing Winnie's bargains with deities to be a better parent to Danru, an uncomplaining wife, and a truer friend to Helen if only Danru survives the attack.

At war's end, Tan focuses on the continuing hell of domestic chaos, which is a greater threat to Winnie and her son than the bombing of Nanking. Wen Fu remains the repository of hostility and aggression, even in the eyes of Jiang Sao-yen, Winnie's crippled, mute old father, who has survived similar tactics from Japanese forces occupying his house in Shanghai. After Winnie leaves her incorrigible husband, he takes out his spite on her attorney by sending two goons to destroy his law office on Nanking Road and to tear up the divorce papers. As is often true with Wen Fu's malice, the attack is successful: it ends the attorney's aid to Winnie's case. Tan uses the event to illustrate a feminist theme — Winnie's reliance on a formidable network of supportive women.

Violence is a constant subtext of Tan's third novel, *The Hundred Secret Senses* (1995), which jockeys between two worlds, past and present. During Kwan Li's sisterly relationship with six-year-old Olivia Yee Laguni, she introduces the child to the power of "yin eyes," which see ghosts from the past (p. 3). The years of confided secrets and tales prepare Olivia in adulthood for the bulk of Kwan's lore, which derives from Manchu raids on a Christian mission in Changmian, China, during the Taiping Rebellion of 1864. To explain why Kwan wants Olivia to reunite with husband Simon Bishop, the storyteller departs from simple village anecdotes and fables to the terror that grips the mission staff and their servants as a strike force advances on the compound of the God Worshippers. Led by mercenary General Warren Cape, their predations extend to cannibalism.

As Kwan and Olivia wait out a tense night during their search for Simon, Kwan departs from the 1990s and completes the last episodes of her previous life in 1864. The story reaches a height of savagery after the beheading of Lao Lu, a faithful gatekeeper at the mission compound. Tan salts in details of Nunumu's search for her loyal friend, Nelly Banner, whose leg a mercenary breaks with a single blow. Because the story ends with the women's retreat to a maze of mountain caves, there is brief hope that some of the villagers will escape with their lives. The Manchus overextend themselves by setting lethal fires that whip out of control, killing both the villagers and most of the soldiers. The reincarnation of major characters relieves the story of much of its horror and assures Olivia that she can requite Nelly's love for Yiban Johnson by returning to Simon, Yiban's twentieth-century persona.

The chaos that disturbs the peasantry in *The Bonesetter's Daughter* (2001) returns to the motif of spousal abuse and child battery, which disorders the home of Chang the coffinmaker. Because Precious Auntie, a precocious female, charges him with harming his wife and baby, she wounds his pride, earning for herself a life-long enemy. After Chang's bandits raid her bridal party and kill her father, the Bonesetter Gu, the groom-to-be suffers a tragic accident when his horse kicks him. Chang's barbarity lodges in Precious Auntie's heart, causing her to rave in mute frenzy when his name is mentioned. A peculiar scene occurs at the ladder to the root cellar, where LuLing confronts Precious Auntie with the fact that the girl intends to marry into the Chang family. Tan uses the location to illustrate that LuLing strikes at the root of her amah's disquiet. Unable to speak since swallowing boiling resin and withering her tongue, she rages at LuLing, beating and slapping as though fighting Chang himself. As Precious Auntie's misdirected fury further alienates LuLing from her beloved nurse, Tan portrays the tragedy of silenced, suicidal women.

See also **abortion, dismemberment, spousal abuse, Taiping Rebellion**

• *Further Reading*

Edwards, Jami. "Amy Tan." http://www.bookreporter.com/authors/au-tan-amy.asp.
Link, Tom. "Revisiting Tangled Mother-Daughter Ties." *Los Angeles Daily News*, June 2, 1991, pp. C2–C3.
Ma, Sheng-mei. *The Deathly Embrace: Orientalism and Asian American Identity*. Minneapolis: University of Minnesota Press, 2000.
"Tan's Memoirs of a Tragic Life." *BBC News*, December 13, 2003.

Wen Fu

Degenerating from narcissism to a lethal psychosis, Wen Fu, a Kuomintang air force pilot-in-training in *The Kitchen God's Wife* (1991), is an unredeemable demon and Tan's most grotesque villain. In his role in a village New Year's performance, he plays the tail of a dragon and earns tips from the audience for his bold self-confidence. Winnie Louie recalls his elegant Western clothes, meticulous grooming, and straight teeth. Cagily, he curries favor with her cousin Peanut by entertaining the young male cousins, Little Gong and Little Gao, and carries the girls' purchases. Like a gentlemanly Sir Walter Raleigh, he stretches his jacket over the interior of a rented wheelbarrow and sings to Peanut as he pushes her home. On a visit to the Jiang household, he courts the aunts with baskets of fruit, flamboyant mannerisms, and cajolery. Tan stresses his opportunism to prepare for the revelation of the real Wen Fu, who resembles a dragon more than a courtier.

Wen Fu's success with Winnie is serendipitous—he meets her at a nadir in her life, when she struggles for self-esteem in a milieu where relatives discount her worth while pampering Peanut. After Peanut rejects him, he marries Winnie as second-best. Like Mr. Albert in Alice Walker's *The Color Purple* (1982), Wen Fu is too unstable, too depraved to live a normal life with a wife and small children. The chase complete, he regresses into a martinet and quickly establishes an adversarial relationship while winning the friendship of other pilots with his bluster, bullying, and recklessness. In retrospect, Winnie blames the philosopher Confucius (ca. 551–478 B.C.) for corrupting Chinese society by devaluing women's lives and leaving them vulnerable to physical and emotional battery by cruel, self-indulgent husbands.

Although Wen Fu is what *Atlanta Journal* reviewer Emily Ellison terms "one of the vilest characters in modern literature," Tan relieves him of total villainy through a pleasant conversation with Winnie in which he describes flying (Ellison, p. C12). After their party travels southwest toward Kunming and inches up the mountains through thick haze, he compares the experience to the joy of rising above clouds, then dipping in and out of them. He startles Winnie by breaking into the song he performed the day she met him. He is capable of cheery camaraderie with fellow mah jong players, but fights insecurity by controlling them with exhibitionism and the bully's whip, a lacerating temper that can burst through merriment at any time.

The author describes the jeep accident that costs Wen Fu his eye as the impetus to unbridled blowups, assaults on nurses, cursing, and petulant behavior. Upon visiting his second child, Yiku, for the first time, he roughly dandles her and bellows a drinking song. He grows angry because Winnie comforts and quiets the infant. After showing no compassion to Yiku during her illness from tainted food, he displaces responsibility for the child's worsening condition by berating Winnie. As Yiku sinks toward death, Winnie finds the strength to praise her for escaping an inhumane father. Wen Fu's sins escalate to womanizing, lying about being a war hero, threatening with a pistol, and fortune hunting. Repulsive in his cowardice and Dickensian in his lack of redeeming qualities, Wen Fu expresses extreme sexism in failing to mourn his stillborn daughter Mochou or to allow the doctor to treat Yiku because they are only girls. Winnie represses her rage at Wen Fu by storing up loving memories of her dead children, whom she describes to daughter Pearl a half century later. The exchange exemplifies the importance of talk-story to matrilineage.

Tan illustrates the emergence of self-empowerment in battered women as instinctive. The mounting barbarism in Wen Fu's domestic behavior galvanizes Winnie from subservient wife to survivor and protector of Danru, her only living child. After the family returns to Shanghai, she must suffer the supervision of Wen Tai-tai, her mother-in-law, who takes charge of the Jiang mansion on Julu Road and, along with her son, quickly squanders Jiang Sao-yen's wealth on luxuries, entertaining, and gambling. Wen Fu, like Chang Fu Nan in *The Bonesetter's Daughter* (2001), takes craven refuge in pretending to be a disabled war hero, a pose that suits his deceit and strutting. Out of impatience with a buyer, he demolishes the legs of a table that had been in the Jiang family for two centuries. The public battle between Wen Fu and Winnie brings her to the most trying time in the Chinese phase of her life. He stalks her, terrorizes her attorney, sneers at her in court, and rejoices in her sentence of two years in women's prison for leaving him and taking Danru.

Wen Fu is incapable of perceiving the effect of his torment on Winnie until the dramatic moment in court when she chooses a prison term over living with him. After his death on December 25, 1989, Helen breaks her silence to revive Winnie's memories. She recalls his clever lies and volatile demeanor. Fantasizing an opportunity to lean over his deathbed and spit in his face, she marvels at the resilience of his evil, which is still strong in 1990 as she confronts Helen's demand to tell the truth about her first marriage. Eating away at Winnie's peace of mind is the fear that Wen Fu fathered Pearl and passed along to his daughter a potential for evil. After learning of Pearl's sufferings from multiple sclerosis, Winnie stops grasping at amorphous evil and sets her itinerary to include Chinese herb markets, where she and Helen will shop for the right antidote to a real disease.

See also **patriarchy, spousal abuse, wisdom**

• *Further Reading*

Adams, Bella. "Representing History in Amy Tan's *The Kitchen God's Wife*." *MELUS*, Vol. 28, No. 2, Summer 2003, pp. 9–30.

Ellison, Emily. "Tragic Story Dazzles and Awes." *Atlanta Journal*, June 16, 1991, pp. C12–C13.

Young, Pamela. "Mother with a Past: The Family Album Inspires a Gifted Writer." *Maclean's*, Vol. 104, No. 28, July 15, 1991, p. 47.

wisdom

Tan laces her texts with the types of aphorisms common to Chinese people, e.g., "If you can't change your fate, change your attitude," "Lose control, lose your life," "Fall in love, fall into disgrace," and "Throw away family values, throw your face away" (*The Kitchen God's Wife*, pp. 361, 433–434). She chooses the mother figure to deliver the weightiest advice, as in the short-short story "Fish Cheeks" (1987), in which a mother reminds her Asian daughter, "Inside you must always be Chinese" (p. 99). In *The Bonesetter's Daughter* (2001), the mother figure, fearing financial ruin, cautions her daughters, "Want less, regret less," an indication that the family will suffer poverty in the near future (p. 195). These models fall into the black-white category of instruction common to parents who simplify the consequences of wrongheadedness.

Tan uses wise counsel at more complex character interaction, where the extremes of a black-or-white adage are inappropriate. At the brutal domestic coming-to-knowledge in *The Kitchen God's Wife* (1991) when Winnie Louie realizes that Wen Fu is an evil rapist of their fourteen-year-old servant girl, Winnie recalls her Old Aunt's saying, "Don't strike a flea on a tiger's head," a reminder to the wise to pick the most important battles rather than lesser troubles (p. 329). Winnie's decision to let the servant return home results in the girl's self-abortion with a broom straw and her subsequent death from hemorrhage. Tan uses the event to point up a dilemma that precipitates suffering, regardless of the choice.

The author illustrates the potential for injustice after the Sino-Japanese War (1937–1945), when loyal Chinese apply arbitrary wisdom to traitors. Upon her family's return to Jiang Sao-yen's mansion on the Julu Road in Shanghai, Winnie discovers the terrors of her father's war years, when he accommodated the Japanese in order to keep his Five Phoenixes Textile Trading companies in operation. The reinstatement of the Kuomintang after the surrender of Japanese Emperor Hirohito on August 15, 1945, releases the anger of the Chinese against collaborators with the enemy. They demean Jiang Sao-yen with rock throwing and painted slogans. Above filth smeared on the walls they inscribe a coarse folk truism: "He who pats the horse's ass deserves the dung of a donkey" (p. 417). It requires the intervention of San Ma, Jiang's third wife, to stave off a plenary judgment and execution to save Jiang's life, but there is nothing she can do to restore his dignity.

As the protagonist's fortunes improve, Tan verbalizes hope through aphorism. Upon reuniting with her foster family on Tsungming Island after New Year 1946, Winnie sees evidence of Uncle Jiang's failure in business during the war. The loss of family wealth forces her cousins to ferry metal by wheelbarrow on the docks. New Aunt, a former schoolmate of Winnie's mother at a Catholic missionary academy in Shanghai, explains the decline of mansion, grounds, and household with an adage from nature: "When the tree dies, the grass underneath withers" (p. 428). The loss hits home after Winnie sees the greenhouse, her girlhood retreat, splintered and glassless. Wisdom accompanies Winnie's new romance and enables her to plot escape from Wen Fu. She and Jimmy Louie settle on a secret telephone code, an optimistic Chinese proverb: "Open the door, you can already see the mountain" (p. 457).

In *The Hundred Secret Senses* (1995), Tan uses similar verbal idealism as an indicator of personal traits and beliefs. Kwan Li, the exuberant Chinese ghost-seer who immigrates to Daly City, California, offers pithy observations and "crackpot advice" to her six-year-old sister Olivia, with whom she shares a bedroom (p. 110). Throughout their adult lives, Kwan continues to mother Olivia with admonitions, for example, the obvious simile "Rumors trickle down the mountain like a roof leak" and the more philosophical nuggets "Between life and death, there is a place where one can balance the impossible" and "Truth lies not in logic but in hope, both past and future" (pp. 378, 380, 398). Kwan's intrusions on Olivia's privacy escalate from annoying to unbearable after Olivia weds, then parts from Simon Bishop, after a marriage of seventeen years. To nurture a reconciliation, Kwan asks, "Why not forgive? ... Stubborn and anger together, very bad for you" (p. 26). Tan depicts Olivia's mounting frustration in trying to refute an obvious truism.

In their early courtship, Olivia recalls Simon's revelation of his lover Elza Marie Vandervort's death in an avalanche in Utah in December 1977 and the letter she wrote the previous November. Rather than a standard missive, the text is an essay on love. In her description of passion's power, she warns that people can flee love, but "never say no" to it (p. 102). Ironically, Elza's metaphor of an overpowering wave prefigures her suffocation under mounds of snow and debris. Illustrating Olivia's maturity is her own understanding that the heart can be willful: like creeping ivy, it embraces the emotions and refuses to let go. The thundering avalanche returns again as Olivia ponders overwhelming questions about the validity of her relationship with Simon. At the novel's end, Olivia reframes Kwan's wisdom with a mature vision of love as "limitless, endless, all that moves us toward knowing what is true" (p. 399).

See also **communication, talk-story, LuLing Liu Young**

- *Further Reading*

Benedict, Kitty. "Mother to Daughter: Here Is the Truth of My Life." *Hartford Courant*, June 30, 1991, p. C10.
Hamilton, Patricia L. "Feng Shui, Astrology, and the Five Elements: Traditional Chinese Belief in Amy Tan's *The Joy Luck Club*." *MELUS*, Vol. 24, No. 2, Summer 1999, pp. 125–145.

women

Amy Tan has dedicated her career to recreating the loves, losses, and liberation of women and to the unorthodox families they form during dire circumstances. To reviewer George Gurley of the *Kansas City Star*, she explained: "I think women are less inhibited about some things. They can write about things men find it hard to write about, such as weaknesses and embarrassing moments, frailties, vulnerabilities. Women are willing to be a little more critical of themselves, more self-revealing" (Gurley). These revelations form the warp and woof of her expert storytelling, for example, the evolution of a female chess player's secret strategies in "Endgame" (1986) and a girl's revelation in the short-short story "Fish Cheeks" (1987) of embarrassment at her Chinese family's foodways and table manners on Christmas Eve in front of Caucasian company. Tan explains the importance of disclosing hidden responses as she views her grandmother's photo in "Lost Lives of Women" (1991), "This is the picture I see when I write. These are the secrets I was supposed to keep. These are the women who never let me forget why stories need to be told" (p. 91).

The structure of Tan's first novel, *The Joy Luck Club* (1989), involves a double strand of women, four to a strand, each with a unique story to tell. To reveal the desires and failings of two generations—one Chinese-born and the other American—the author pits mothers and daughters in life-long strife that is both universal and peculiarly Chinese. Critic Sheng-Mei Ma refers to this pairing as a "formula of opening the story with a 'naive' Asian American and then switching to one who is older and capable of revealing the ethnic roots" (Ma, p. 108). The narrative method alters in *The Hundred Secret Senses* (1995) with the pairing of Olivia Bishop, the first-generation Amerasian, with Kwan Li, her older half-sister and surrogate mother, who remains stubbornly Chinese during thirty-two years of residency in California. Tan returns to a double mother-daughter paradigm in *The Bonesetter's Daughter* (2001) to express LuLing Liu Young's regrets for slighting her birth mother, Precious Auntie, and additional chagrin that daughter Ruth Luyi Young discounts her own mother. Through double pairing, Tan implies that a full appreciation of daughter for mother requires concerted effort and cooperation by both parties.

The author's focus on female aspirations limits the development of males to what *New York* magazine reviewer Rhoda Koenig terms "tyrants or simpletons," a criticism echoed by *Newsweek* critic David Gates (Koenig, p. 82). With men conveniently shuffled to one side in *The Joy Luck Club*, Tan develops the keen edges of Lindo Sun Jong, the mental instability of Ying-ying St. Clair, An-mei Hsu's submissiveness, and Suyuan Woo's burden of guilt for failing her first daughters, Chwun Hwa and Chwun Yu. Like cripples aiding cripples, mothers instruct their daughters in traditional Chinese values and try to save them from the pitfalls of a capitalist society, which tends to promise more freedom and contentment than it can deliver. Because of faulty communication, Lindo can't prevent Waverly from developing into a legal shark, An-mei can't save Rose from a life of guilt for her little brother Bing's drowning, Ying-ying can't inject backbone into Lena Hsu Livotny, and Suyuan can't unite her abandoned twins with June, their half-sister. In the molding of these complex characters, Tan all but ignores the personal strengths and growth of husbands and fathers or the wisdom they might impart to their daughters.

In *The Kitchen God's Wife* (1991), a story-within-a-story on the themes of exile and redemption, Amy Tan attempts a more incisive view of womanhood by focusing on a single mother-daughter pair. She sets the telling at the traditional female confessional, the kitchen table. Before Winnie Louie decides to reveal her secret past to her daughter, Pearl Louie Brandt, Winnie works all night at cleaning house, a womanly symbol of the spiritual cleansing that precedes Chinese New Year and presages a purification of the heart. From a cache of treasures in Pearl's old room, Winnie finds the clue she needs—a funeral card honoring Jimmy Louie, the father that Pearl could not mourn in public. Like stains on the gold carpet, the blots on Winnie's past refuse to wipe clean. The extended metaphor of housework precedes the gradual unburdening that brings mother and daughter closer over their emotional divide. To ease the passage, Winnie offers Pearl tea and noodle soup, the little-girl treat that mothers save for wintry days and runny noses.

In Winnie's account of her childhood, she comes to grips with the lot of the trophy wife. Her own mother, second wife of Jiang Sao-yen, a wealthy industrialist, gazes at her reflection every night and takes stock of her beauty, in particular, unbound feet, a mark of modernity that emerged in China following the collapse of the Chings (1644–1912), the nation's last feudal dynasty. Winnie realizes that her father chose his second wife as a boost to his prestige. Her education and beauty merit the scorn of Old Aunt, a woman raised in the feudal way to believe that women are second rate handmaidens to males. Old Aunt declares that girls should use their eyes for sewing rather than reading, their ears to hear orders rather than ideas, and their lips to give thanks or elicit praise. In Old Aunt's opinion, Winnie's mother suffers a debilitating mental ferment from Western concepts inappropriately lodged in a Chinese mind.

Winnie ignores Old Aunt's criticism and surmises that women at the forefront of female liberation face alienation and disillusion by being in a minuscule vanguard. By way of explanation, Winnie exalts her own mother for bravery and condemns Confucianism for promoting a caste system that imposes second-class citizenship on women. In reflecting over the power of Auntie Miao, a gossipy local matchmaker on Tsungming Island, Winnie realizes that Miao disdains Winnie's betrothal to Lin because of an old grudge she bears against a Lin family member who jilted her. The character name, Miao, suits her penchant for prowling the village for gossip and displaying petty cat behavior unsuited to a professional go-between. She is one of a number of female characters who conspire with males to uphold the sexist status quo.

Before Winnie achieves full liberation from gender prejudice, her evolving womanhood echoes the Chinese attitude toward women as wives and mothers. She contrasts the independence of American girls with a girlish powerlessness as Auntie Miao arranges a union with Wen Fu, a social climber and fortune hunter eager to marry into the wealthy and prestigious Jiang clan. After San Ma, Jiang's third wife, takes the role of honorary mother and helps Winnie purchase furnishings, luggage, and intimate needs for her marriage, she teaches Winnie the rudiments of female hygiene, a before- and after-sex washing that implies that women appeal to men only if they remove natural secretions. Wen Tai-tai, Winnie's mother-in-law, contributes to her understanding of self-abasement by ordering her to burn her finger testing hot soup as a loving sacrifice to Wen Fu. The image prophesies the physical pain and emotional martyrdom that threatens Winnie's survival.

The lack of education for Chinese women proves detrimental to Winnie, who has no idea of the physical demands of intercourse or the mechanics of conception. In the first months of her marriage, she accepts an ignorant description of body lice (or possibly scabies) in women as a groin itch that causes them to demand sex as a relief. She describes such coarse misinformation as "common knowledge among young women about to be married" (p. 212). Similar faulty knowledge of human sexuality ruins the marriage of her cousin Peanut, who weds a homosexual, and of Little Yu, a schoolmate betrothed to a retarded man whom her mother hopes is able to father children. The lid on the seething pot of disillusion is silence, a social dictate that hinders women from demanding their rights to suitable mates or to divorces from unworthy husbands.

Tan credits Winnie with the wise use of a single empowerment — her dowry, a sum of four thousand yuan that her father deposits in Shanghai under her name alone. At various times in her marriage, she relies on money, beginning in 1937 after the pilots arrive at Yangchow, where she treats them to dinner. After harrowing combat generates extensive change in Wen Fu, Winnie has only the network of women as emotional support. At war's end, she realizes that she must part from Helen, her friend and mainstay, as Winnie goes east to Shanghai and Helen and Auntie Du

Ching go north to Harbin. The old friends retreat to their rooms and return with similar gifts—two pairs of knitting needles from Helen to Winnie and a blue sweater that Winnie knitted for Helen. Tan's fiber-work imagery suggests the web of women who continue to enfold Winnie as she slowly liberates herself and her five-year-old son from a monster.

Tan's stories-within-stories repeat and substantiate the experiences of disillusioned wives. Just as Little Yu's mother assists Peanut in escaping a failed marriage, the safety net of congenial runaway wives accepts Winnie as she flees Wen Fu. The idealistic women's refuge, which reviewer Constance Casey calls a "Sorrow Luck Club," offers sanctuary from patriarchal ogres until each new arrival can set a new course (Casey, p. C5). After Winnie develops a lasting love for Jimmy Louie, a translator for the United States Information Service and press relations office for the American consulate general in China, she expresses her feelings in womanly fashion during their rendezvous at the unsanitary teahouse by washing his tea cup twice in hot tea to cleanse it and protect his stomach. The act foretells her tender care after he contracts stomach cancer and dies in 1964 at age fifty. In typical feudal fashion, she blames herself for not being more careful of his health.

Tan saves her most sincere womanly encounters for mothers and daughters. She presents Winnie as a world-wise mom who wants to spare her only daughter the pain of marrying the wrong man. Winnie maintains skepticism about boyfriends and warns that Randy, Pearl's first beau, considers himself more important. His self-aggrandizement and evocative name flash warning signs of the self-indulgent Wen Fu, a sexual predator who made her life wretched. She justifies interference in Pearl's life by declaring her daughter too innocent and good-hearted to protect herself in a life-long commitment. Tan stresses the harm of silence to both women. Because Pearl doesn't know about Winnie's past, she can't value her mother's meddling as a gift of love.

In the author's third novel, *The Hundred Secret Senses* (1995), women again dominate the action and themes. The pairing of unlike sisters gives Tan an opportunity to develop Kwan Li's Chinese traits in contrast to Olivia Yee Laguni's California values and behaviors. Above their marital loyalties—Kwan with George Lew and Olivia with Simon Bishop—the author elevates sisterhood, the link that lives on from one incarnation to another. Kwan, who is called Nunumu in her previous life, establishes a caring a tie with Nelly Banner that Kwan revives in the 1960s in the incarnation of Nelly as Olivia. Kwan's self-sacrifice at the end of the novel enables the unrequited love of Nelly and Yiban Johnson to continue in the lives of Olivia and Simon. The final blessing on their union is the birth of Samantha Li, another female to carry matrilineal love into the next generation.

An unusual assortment of women in *The Bonesetter's Daughter* (2001) broadens the author's interest in the female role in world history. She depicts Precious Auntie as the bold, well-educated daughter of the Bonesetter Gu, who teaches her calligraphy, a skill she develops in her daughter LuLing Liu. After LuLing passes from the hands of foster parents to a Christian orphanage, she comes to admire the female missionaries for their education of young women and for their courage in the face of the Japanese occupation of China. Ruth Grutoff, the staff member with the most

foresight, anticipates danger to the fifty-six orphan girls and conceals in pagan statues individual caches of gold and silver along with names of former pupils who will
provide shelter in Peking. After Miss Grutoff's departure to a prisoner-of-war camp,
LuLing appreciates her sacrifice for the welfare of powerless girls.

Into the late twentieth century, sacrifice and empowerment mark the relationships of the Liu family's women. As LuLing loses touch with reality from the effects
of Alzheimer's disease, dementia forces her into past memories, where she is more
at home than with her present life. Through translation of valuable Chinese manuscripts, Ruth recognizes the strengths of her grandmother and mother and begins to
rethink the wisdom of a long relationship with linguist Art Kamen and a career in
nursemaiding mediocre self-help writers toward publication. Ruth, like her doughty
female ancestors, devotes more effort to caring for her mother and for herself. She
reclaims the admonitions that were "passed down, not simply to scare her" (p. 308).
As though gathering up a legacy, she retreats to her cubbyhole to compose her own
thoughts into stories "for her grandmother, for herself, and for the little girl who
became her mother" (*Ibid.*).

See also **communication, patriarchy, silence, storytelling, talk-story, wisdom**

• *Further Reading*

Casey, Constance. "Amy Tan's Second Book Focuses on the Overlooked Woman." *San
    Diego Union*, June 16, 1991, pp. C4–C5.
Gates, David. "A Game of Show Not Tell." *Newsweek*, Vol. 113, No. 16, April 17, 1989,
    pp. 68–69.
Gurley, George. "Amy Tan: The Ghosts and the Writer." *Kansas City Star*, April 22,
    1998.
Harrington, Maureen. "Tan's Immigrant Tale Top Quality." *Denver Post*, June 23, 1991,
    p. C9.
Koenig, Rhoda. "Heirloom China." *New York*, Vol. 22, No. 12, March 20, 1989, pp. 82–83.
Ma, Sheng-mei. *The Deathly Embrace: Orientalism and Asian American Identity*. Min-
    neapolis: University of Minnesota Press, 2000.

Woo, June

The daughter of Canning and Suyuan Li Woo, June May Woo, originally named
Jing Mei, is the appropriate focus of *The Joy Luck Club* (1989). In the opinion of critic
Zenobia Mistri, "She alone has a story in each of the four sections, thus forming the
central axis of the book" (Mistri). The mother attempts to shape the daughter into
a Chinese Shirley Temple by curling her hair into ringlets. June dreams of being a
prodigy — a ballerina or Cinderella, the type of dainty fairy princess image that idealistic American girls cultivate. Tan turns the mother-daughter dream of fame into
humor as Suyuan quizzes June on a melange of shallow subjects — global capitals, mul-
tiplication, card tricks, gymnastics, and predictions of temperatures in world cities.
The helter-skelter approach to grooming a genius provides comic relief as well as
insight into the parental tug-of-war with a rebellious child.

Suyuan substitutes a mother's pride for a rational understanding of giftedness.
Settling on piano, she orders June to take lessons from Mr. Chong and to practice

daily from four until six. Because the teacher is deaf, June makes little effort to correct mistakes. After Suyuan begins boasting of June's talent to Lindo Jong, June resolves to halt the bragging. Gazing into a mirror, she declares, "I won't let her change me.... I won't be what I'm not" (p. 134). In a talent contest, she botches a performance of Robert Schumann's "Pleading Child," then refuses to obey her mother's command to practice. The tension in June is so unbearable that she lacerates her mother with the wish to be dead like Suyuan's first two daughters. The hurtful outcry ends the struggle as the mother withdraws in defeat. The dramatic moment illustrates Tan's belief that communication is the only way to neutralize the harm caused by an unhealthy silence.

By age thirty-six, June has spent most of her life quitting, a mental self-crippling that is foreign to her success-minded mother. June's reasoning shifts blame to Suyuan, who "hoped for something so large that failure was inevitable" (p. 154). June leaves art and biology degrees only half completed and is typically tardy on the first night at her mother's place at the mah jong table. Tan creates irony from the fact that June, the eldest of the club's offspring, once tended the younger children while their mothers played and gambled. Now seated in Suyuan's place, June becomes like a small child among An-mei Hsu, Lindo Jong, and Ying-ying St. Clair, all Chinese natives, who catechize her and arrange for her trip to China to reclaim Chwun Yu and Chwun Hwa, the mother's abandoned twin daughters. The action implies that June still lacks volition and maturity when in the presence of the surviving three aunties and allows herself to be their pawn in a reverent gesture toward the first of the club to die.

A womanly legacy is June's salvation. As an unimaginative copywriter for an ad agency, she makes limited progress at her career. At the mah jong table, she takes her mother's seat at the East "where things begin," a suggestion of Tan's intent to develop June through the new experience as Suyuan's replacement (p. 22). To protect herself from insidious comparisons, June moves cautiously among leading questions about her education and comments about Lena St. Clair Livotny's new home in Woodside. At a Chinese New Year dinner at her mother's house, she allows herself to be cornered by Waverly Jong, who criticizes June's beautician as gay and possibly infected with AIDS. Waverly implies that her own beautician, Mr. Rory, is better, but probably too expensive for June. The barbs mount, threatening to topple June at a vulnerable moment in the grieving process.

Tan pictures June as making tentative stabs at self-assertion. The contest gets out of hand after her attempt to insult Waverly for failure to pay for ad copy. Waverly explains that the work was too unsophisticated for use in an upscale brochure. On withdrawing to the kitchen, June realizes that she is good at mediocre ad copy, "succeeding at something small" (p. 233). Suyuan soothes her daughter's hurt feelings with a gift of jade. The color of hope, the green pendant becomes a talisman after Suyuan's death. The author reveals June's evolving self-confidence in an initial meeting with a Chinese cousin, Li Gong, whom June enchants with a Polaroid photo. Without breaking out of character, June wins over Auntie Aiyi and "Lili" and envelops the twins with a sisterly welcome. Tan expresses June's mature strength in valuing family and in re-assessing the worth of her mother's example.

See also **competition, Waverly Jong,** *The Joy Luck Club*

• *Further Reading*

Heung, Marina. "Daughter-Text/Mother-Text: Matrilineage in Amy Tan's Joy Luck Club." *Feminist Studies*, Vol. 19, No. 3, Fall 1993, pp. 597–616.

Ling, Amy. *Between Worlds: Women Writers of Chinese Ancestry*. New York: Pergamon Press, 1990.

Mistri, Zenobia. "Discovering the Ethnic Name and the Genealogical Tie in Amy Tan's *The Joy Luck Club*." *Studies in Short Fiction*, Vol. 35, No. 3, Summer 1998, pp. 251–257.

Schell, Orville. "Your Mother Is in Your Bones." *New York Times Book Review*, Vol. 26, March 19, 1989, pp. 3, 28.

Tseo, George K. Y. "The Perils of Transcultural 'Translation.'" *Literature/Film Quarterly*, Vol. 24, No. 4, 1996, pp. 338–343.

Woo, Suyuan

One of the eight main characters of *The Joy Luck Club* (1989) and the first club member to die, Suyuan Li Woo leaves old business for her survivors and friends to settle. In the telling of her life history to daughter June May, Suyuan narrates growing up submissive and obedient, her first marriage, nursing study in Shanghai, and life in Kweilin during the Sino-Japanese War (1937–1945). While Wang Fuchi, her first husband, moves on to Chungking with the Kuomintang staff, she becomes aware that China is losing to Japanese invaders. Amid a mix of people, she tolerates the lack of hygiene, body odors, and diarrhea, but hates most the "habba-habba sounds" of American air force personnel (p. 9). Shut in caves during air raids, she describes the dampness as "dripping bowels of an ancient hill," an image suggesting the oppressive feudal customs that bind China to the past (p. 9).

Crucial to the novel is Suyuan's response to a brief warning that she must flee Kweilin before the Japanese can inflict cruelty on her and other officers' families. On the road to Chungking, she pushes her twin infant girls, Chwun Yu and Chwun Hwa, in a stolen wheelbarrow, then carries them in scarf slings until dysentery saps her strength. To save their lives, she has to abandon the babies and leaves them with valuable jewelry and photos with messages identifying them. Widowed in recovery, she meets journalist Canning Woo at a hospital, marries him, and initiates a search for her children. Upon arrival in the United States in 1949, she adopts a simplistic optimism that anything is possible in the new land. To spare her embarrassment, Canning does not discuss her missing daughters. The burden that she carries for nearly four decades defines her hopes until death ends the possibility for a reunion.

Like Kwan Li in *The Hundred Secret Senses* (1995), Suyuan Woo must die to pass on the matrilineal mantle to her daughters, who complete Suyuan's aspirations and fulfill her hopes. June, Suyuan's thirty-six-year-old Amerasian daughter, remembers her mother as hypercritical because "something was always missing…. Something was not in balance" (p. 19). Canning blames his wife's death from brain aneurysm on the mounting fear that the twins are dead. From An-mei Hsu, June learns that Suyuan was the most skillful mah jong player, a suggestion of quiet strength. The other two players, Lindo Jong and Ying-ying St. Clair, chime in that Suyuan was kind, intelligent, dutiful, hopeful, and clever at cookery. The list suggests the Chinese ideal of the perfect wife.

Suyuan's story, like a Polaroid photo, takes shape slowly and deliberately. After the first club session following her death, the surviving three members fill in parts of her past for June, their new player, to help her understand and accept painful family secrets. Their offer of twelve hundred dollars to pay for a trip to China allows June to reverse the diaspora that her mother began during World War II. In the novel's resolution, June recalls her mother's detailed image of the family's house crushed and burned, with only a twisted bed frame, ash-filled cup, and singed and limbless doll as proof that everyone died at once, "because that's how our family was" (p. 314). At a time when the other Chinese-born mothers of the story await fulfillment in their daughters, Suyuan dies suddenly, leaving to June the task of reuniting a scattered family.

See also **diaspora, imbalance, June Woo**

• *Further Reading*

Schell, Orville. "Your Mother Is in Your Bones." *New York Times Book Review*, Vol. 26, March 19, 1989, pp. 3, 28.

Tseo, George K. Y. "The Perils of Transcultural 'Translation.'" *Literature/Film Quarterly*, Vol. 24, No. 4, 1996, pp. 338–343.

Wong, Sau-ling Cynthia. *Reading Asian American Literature: From Necessity to Extravagance*. Princeton, N.J.: Princeton University Press, 1993.

Woo genealogy

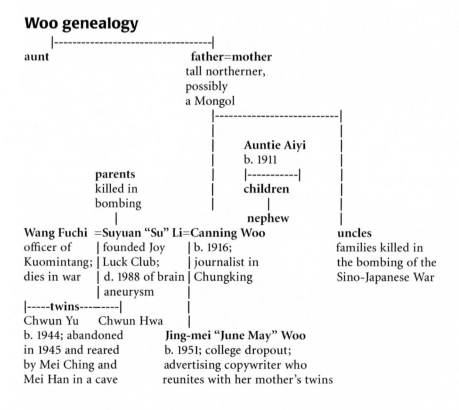

Yee genealogy

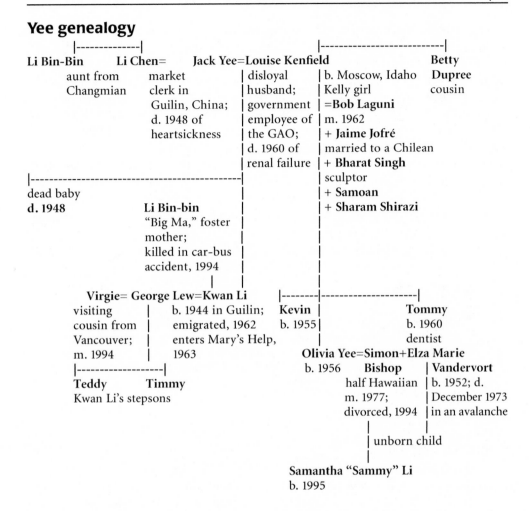

yin and yang

Tan applies the Chinese concept of opposites in her description of women's rise from oppression in pre–Communist China. As represented in *The Joy Luck Club* (1989), society, in obedience to Confucian teachings, weights the paradigm to favor males. Working against women is the view of the yin or female personality as dark, unruly, and enslaved to passion. In contrast, men profit from a yang nature that controls the mind through truth and logic. The instinctive rule of reason prevents them from making fools of themselves by allowing whim to override sense or ignore self-discipline. In *The Moon Lady* (1992), a children's story excerpted from the novel, the gender inequity of Chang-o and Hou Yi in the Moon Lady's myth concludes with females suffering for their emotional yin nature and with males earning rewards for the rationality of their controlled yang thinking. A cruel dramatic irony pictures the character as no lady. Rather, a male player tricks himself out in women's garb to act the part by imitating the trivial thinking and fluttery femininity of Chang-o.

Repeatedly, Tan's scenarios chip away at the yin-yang gender stereotype. Lindo Sun Jong, married to child-husband Huang Tyan-yu, discovers that he is too immature, too petulant to fulfill the role of mate. Exercising female yang thinking, she deludes the whole Huang clan by plotting a family crisis that will give them the bride and grandchild they want and still allow her to leave her marriage honorably. By playing on their superstitions about dreams, she acts the part of the yin-thinking bride and carries out her strategem, withdrawing from the household with both integrity and enough cash to start another life. The drama of Lindo's triumph over patriarchal marriage foretells the success of *The Kitchen God's Wife* (1991), a more detailed study of how the yang-thinking wife escapes a violent, yin-obsessed mate. Although Winnie Louie struggles longer and suffers more under marital oppression, like Lindo, she defeats Wen Fu, a vicious, psychopathic husband, and applies yang-type survival logic to escape the destructive marriage.

See also **disillusion, men, women**

• *Further Reading*

Heung, Marina. "Daughter-Text/Mother-Text: Matrilineage in Amy Tan's Joy Luck Club." *Feminist Studies*, Vol. 19, No. 3, Fall 1993, pp. 597–616.
Ho, Wendy. *In Her Mother's House — The Politics of Asian American Mother-Daughter Writing.* Walnut Creek, Calif.: AltaMira Press, 1999.
MacDonald, Jay. "A Date with Fate." *BookPage*, November 2003.
Reid, E. Shelley. "'Our Two Faces': Balancing Mothers and Daughters in *The Joy Luck Club* and *The Kitchen God's Wife*," *Paintbrush*, Vol. 22, No. 42, 1995, pp. 20–38.

Young, LuLing Liu

The protagonist of *The Bonesetter's Daughter* (2001), LuLing Liu Young captures in written commentary an autobiography that enables her daughter Ruth to break free from self-defeat. LuLing grows up in Immortal Heart and recalls from age six how her amah, Precious Auntie, compiles a running narrative of her life. Because the nursemaid superintends daily aspects of behavior and learning, LuLing enjoys safety and contentment. By the time she reaches adolescence, she grows careless of her servant and travels to Peking without her. In meditative moments, LuLing recalls the lessons that her nursemaid taught, e.g., "You can never be an artist if your work comes without effort" (p. 172). Unfortunately, emerging womanhood makes the girl long for autonomy, the wonders of Peking, and marriage to a citified man, far from the servant that LuLing views as "a sleepy-headed greasy-hat from the country" (p. 179). The rude pejorative haunts LuLing into old age, when she confesses to her daughter the sin of ingratitude.

After a run of ill luck follows LuLing's betrothal to a son of the self-important Chang the coffinmaker, she suffers in silence from her own foolishness. The author describes her as a headstrong fifteen-year-old who spurns her nursemaid and chooses not to read the mute woman's autobiography, which substitutes for her failed voice. Because the Liu family's Peking shop is destroyed in a fire, LuLing loses the love of the woman she had known as Mother. Within days, the family relegates the girl to an orphanage on Dragon Bone Hill, a parallel to the dumping of her nursemaid's corpse into a ravine at the End of the World. Tan carefully reduces LuLing to ignominy before portraying her rise to the good life in America.

The author establishes LuLing's strength of character through her foil, GaoLing Liu, her cousin and foster sister. While LuLing grieves for her birth mother at the orphanage, GaoLing expresses sibling love. The reunion of the two at the orphanage pictures her as tough and resilient and LuLing as well educated at Precious Auntie's skill of calligraphy. As the war years reduce hope in the inmates, LuLing's star rises through a clever survivalism that outpaces GaoLing's drive. Increasing LuLing's disillusion with her cousin-sister is a long tenure in Hong Kong because of GaoLing's failure to secure a visa for her. LuLing thinks of GaoLing as pampered and declares that she could have completed necessary embassy paperwork within weeks of arriving in America. LuLing alters her opinion after GaoLing arranges for her to immigrate as a visiting artist. The up-and-down rhythms of their relationship continue into old age after eighty-two-year-old GaoLing offers to care for LuLing after she sinks into senile dementia. Their sisterhood, which dates to infancy, expresses the normal human faults and strengths that Tan revealed in Joy Luck Club members and in Winnie Louie's relationship with Helen Kwong.

More troubling than the siblings' unsteady friendship is LuLing's relationship with her daughter Ruth Luyi Young, which is frequently derailed by the manipulative devices common to familial dysfunction. The mother insists that her daughter learn to write Chinese characters, but relents from the brush and ink method to chopsticks on sand, a compromise that delights Ruth with the Etch-A-Sketch ease of writing and obliterating mistakes. Less amenable in her early eighties, LuLing squabbles, hints at dire outcomes of secrets, threatens suicide, and pelts Ruth with guilt for neglecting her mother. With a child's logic, LuLing erupts in self-pity: "You wish no mother tell you what to do? Okay, maybe I die soon!" (p. 44). Lamely, her daughter chalks up the spats to LuLing's poor English, self-taught in China and Hong Kong before her immigration in 1951. Numerous miscommunications substantiate the author's belief, as expressed in the essay "Mother Tongue" (1990) and her first three novels, that lack of a common language inhibits mother-daughter love and trust.

In decline, LuLing reverses roles with Ruth by behaving like a recalcitrant daughter. At home in San Francisco's Sunset District in 1998, she exhibits perplexing symptoms of neural damage by becoming careless, interchanging words only peripherally alike, accusing her tenant Francine of not paying her rent, letting valuable calligraphy brushes dry with ink in them, confusing dates and times, and rear-ending a truck with her car. At Dr. Huey's office, she claims to have witnessed the murder of O. J. Simpson's wife. An M.R.I. confirms the diagnosis of senile dementia. Nightly dinners with Ruth's family pall from LuLing's frequent outbursts and "non sequiturs, as free-floating as dust motes" (p. 87). To Ruth's delight, the loss encourages memories of the past, which ameliorate the mother-daughter impasse by filling in their matrilineage.

See also **Precious Auntie, secrets, silence, Sino-Japanese War, talk-story, women**

• *Further Reading*

Cujec, Carol. "Excavating Memory, Reconstructing Legacy." *World & I,* Vol. 16, No. 7, July 2001, pp. 215–223.
Mones, Nicole. "China Syndrome." *Washington Post Book World,* February 11, 2001.
Zipp, Yvonne. "A Life Recalled from China." *Christian Science Monitor,* Vol. 93, No. 57, February 15, 2001, p. 20.

Young, Ruth Luyi

One of Amy Tan's first-generation Chinese-American females, Ruth Luyi Young suffers embarrassment by her mother's failure to assimilate to American language and customs. At age six, Ruth recoils from a child who ridicules her mother's Mandarin: "What's that gobbledy-gook-gook she's saying?" (p. 62). To distance herself from derision, Ruth claims not to know LuLing. Like her mother's rejection of her attentive amah, the denial comes back instantly to haunt Ruth, who belly-flops on the sliding board, breaking her glasses, fracturing an arm, and crushing her lip. Like a slap to the face, the latter injury suits the sin of verbally dishonoring her mother. Surprisingly, LuLing admires Ruth's courage and credits the spirit of the child's grandmother, Precious Auntie, as its source, an example of matrilineal influence that the author commends.

Complex communication problems create a multi-layered understanding between generations. Like Lena St. Clair in *The Joy Luck Club* (1989), Ruth becomes her mother's translator, making up for LuLing's failure to abandon Mandarin in favor of English. Like Waverly Jong, LuLing sees her mother as emotionally and spiritually strong, but bodily frail and vulnerable. Ambivalence makes it difficult for Ruth to defend LuLing against family complaints of increasingly peevish behaviors and outbursts. After the elderly woman's confusion develops into an identifiable dementia, Ruth takes the role of mother and assumes responsibility for LuLing's care and protection, including rephrasing for Dr. Huey what LuLing means by her puzzling answers to medical questions as simple as her age.

Interceding for other people is a way of life for Ruth. At work, she edits the self-help manuals published by inept authors and becomes adept at cajoling poor writers into accepting revamped texts. Each year on August 12, her voice mysteriously vanishes in what *World & I* reviewer Carol Cujec calls, "a metaphor for the passive role she has assumed in her relationship with her partner Art and his two teenaged daughters, who take her endless caregiving for granted" (Cujec, p. 215). Tan ties the event to the Perseid meteor shower and to Gu Liu Xin, the real name of Precious Auntie, which resembles "liu xing," the Mandarin for "shooting star." In achieving autonomy as writer, dutiful daughter, and wife to Art Kamen, Ruth achieves the personal growth that Tan ascribes to a matrilineal legacy from strong women.

See also **autobiography, LuLing Liu Young**

• *Further Reading*

Cujec, Carol. "Excavating Memory, Reconstructing Legacy." *World & I,* Vol. 16, No. 7, July 2001, pp. 215–223.

Mones, Nicole. "China Syndrome." *Washington Post Book World*, February 11, 2001.
Zipp, Yvonne. "A Life Recalled from China." *Christian Science Monitor*, Vol. 93, No. 57, February 15, 2001, p. 20.

Young genealogy

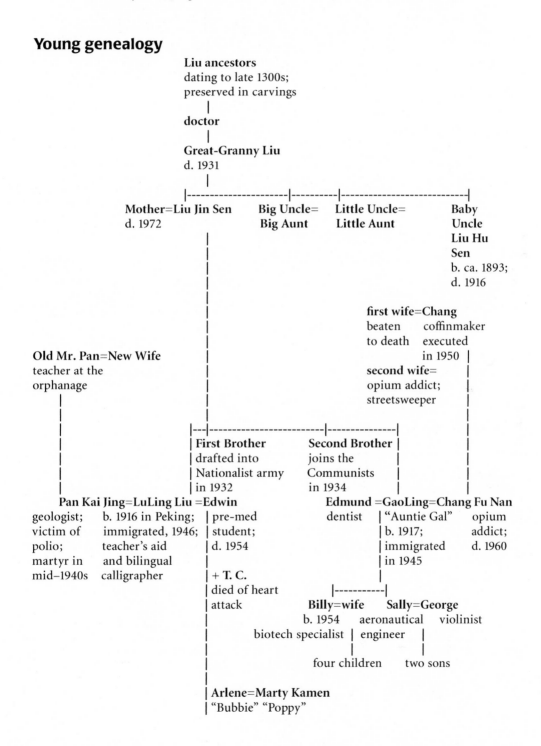

Liu ancestors
dating to late 1300s;
preserved in carvings
|
doctor
|
Great-Granny Liu
d. 1931
|
|--------------------------|----------|------------------------------|
Mother=Liu Jin Sen   **Big Uncle=**   **Little Uncle=**   **Baby**
d. 1972   **Big Aunt**   **Little Aunt**   **Uncle**
                                                                      Liu Hu
                                                                      Sen
                                                                      b. ca. 1893;
                                                                      d. 1916

                                                            first wife=Chang
                                                            beaten   coffinmaker
                                                            to death   executed
                                                                        in 1950
Old Mr. Pan=New Wife   **second wife=**
teacher at the   opium addict;
orphanage   streetsweeper

|---|------------------------|---------------|
| **First Brother**   **Second Brother** |
| drafted into   joins the |
| Nationalist army   Communists |
| in 1932   in 1934 |

Pan Kai Jing=LuLing Liu =Edwind   **Edmund =GaoLing=Chang Fu Nan**
geologist;   b. 1916 in Peking; | pre-med   dentist | "Auntie Gal"   opium
victim of   immigrated, 1946; | student; | b. 1917;   addict;
polio;   teacher's aid | d. 1954 | immigrated   d. 1960
martyr in   and bilingual | | in 1945
mid–1940s   calligrapher | + T. C.
                                | died of heart |----------|
                                | attack   **Billy=wife   Sally=George**
                                | b. 1954   aeronautical   violinist
                                | biotech specialist | engineer |
                                | | |
                                | four children   two sons
                                |
                                | **Arlene=Marty Kamen**
                                | "Bubbie" "Poppy"

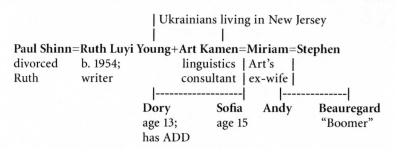

```
                              | Ukrainians living in New Jersey
                              |                 |
     Paul Shinn=Ruth Luyi Young+Art Kamen=Miriam=Stephen
     divorced    b. 1954;         linguistics | Art's  |
     Ruth        writer           consultant  | ex-wife|
                            |-------------------|    |--------------|
                            Dory          Sofia    Andy      Beauregard
                            age 13;       age 15               "Boomer"
                            has ADD
```

See also **the Bonesetter's genealogy**

Appendix A: Chronology of Historical and Fictional Events in Tan's Works

Each entry contains an abbreviated title for identification of the source of each event. Key: BD = *The Bonesetter's Daughter*; CSC = *The Chinese Siamese Cat*; HSS = *The Hundred Secret Senses*; JLC = *The Joy Luck Club*; KGW = *The Kitchen God's Wife*; LLW = "Lost Lives of Women"; ML = *The Moon Lady*; MT = "Mother Tongue"; OF = *The Opposite of Fate*

960–1279	During the Sung dynasty, the bonesetters of Mouth of the Mountain discover valuable dragon bones in a cave called Monkey's Jaw (BD, p. 143).
late 1300s	The Liu clan settles in Immortal Heart outside Peking and manufactures inksticks (BD, p. 137).
1851	A rock crushes Nunumu's eye (HSS, p. 34).
1858	Nunumu saves Nelly Banner from drowning and becomes her companion (HSS, pp. 33, 41).
1864	Nelly Banner gives Nunumu a music box (HSS, p. 32). Villagers flee from Changmian, China, and hide from the invading Manchus (HSS, p. 245). Invaders lop off the head of gatekeeper Lao Lu (HSS, p. 28).
ca. 1888	Bonesetter Gu's wife gives birth to Precious Auntie (BD, p. 141).
1889	
January 17	An earthquake levels much of San Francisco (HSS).
1890	Winnie Louie's mother is born (KGW, p. 122).
ca. 1892	Bonesetter Gu's wife and older sons die from drinking impure water (BD, p. 145).
1893	Auntie Du is born (KGW, p. 5).

1897   Gung-gung sends Winnie's mother to a Catholic missionary school in Shanghai (KGW, pp. 120–121).

1903   Wu Tsing claims as second wife a famous sing-song girl from Shantung (JLC, p. 264).

1905   The Ching government abolishes imperial examinations (BD, p. 148).

1906   The co-op that Olivia and Simon Bishop buy in Pacific Heights survived San Francisco's major earthquake of 1906 (HSS, p. 127).

1911   Rebels end the Ching dynasty and oust the Manchus from China (KGW, p. 122; BD, p. 136).
The death of a sacred pine tree ends the luck of LuLing's village of Immortal Heart (BD, p. 136).
During the revolution, Gung-gung loses his job at the bureau of foreign affairs and falls dead (KGW, pp. 122–123).
Canning Woo's Auntie Aiyi is born (JLC, p. 315).

1912

January 1   China becomes a republic under the leadership of Sun Yat-sen (BD, p. 136).
Wen Fu is born (KGW, pp. 98, 167).

1914   An-mei Hsu is born to an unnamed mother and scholarly father (JLC, p. 242).
Ying-ying St. Clair is born (JLC, pp. 65, 107, 282).

April 14   Jimmy Louie is born (KGW, p. 97).

ca. 1915   Liu Hu Sen breaks three toes in a riding accident and meets Precious Auntie at Bonesetter Gu's shop (BD, p. 148).

1916   Japan gains control of Inner Mongolia, Manchuria, and Shantung.
Suyuan Li and Canning Woo are born (JLC, p. 307).
An-mei's father, an intellectual and devout Buddhist, dies (JLC, p. 266).
Winnie Louie's mother meets Lu (KGW, p. 123).
Ha-bu betrothes Winnie Louie's mother to Jiang Sao-yen (KGW, p. 126).
Great-Granny Liu concocts a lie passing LuLing to Liu Jen Sen and his first wife, but leaves the child in care of her birth mother, Precious Auntie (BD, pp. 56, 154).

1917   Russian Marxism influences the philosophy of the Kuomintang, China's main political party.
LuLing's sister-cousin GaoLing Liu is born (BD, p. 154).
Wu Tsing rapes An-mei's mother and forces her to become his concubine (JLC, p. 267).

1918   An-mei is burned on hot soup, which spills from a table brazier (JLC, p. 38).
Hulan "Helen" is born in Loyang (KGW, pp. 90–91).

March 11   Lindo Jong, a member of the Sun clan, is born in Taiyuan, China (JLC, pp. 183, 203, 294).

fall   Ying-ying falls off a boat during the Moon Festival (JLC, p. 65; ML, unpaginated).

ca. 1919   Jiang Weili, later named Winnie, is born to the unnamed second wife of Jiang Sao-yen, a wealthy textile manufacturer in Shanghai (KGW, pp. 35, 81).

1920	Lindo is betrothed to Huang Tyan-yu (JLC, p. 43). Jiang Huazheng, called Peanut, is born to New Aunt (KGW, p. 137). Men of the Liu clan go to Peking to sell inksticks (BD, p. 137).
1923	Chinese Communists join the Kuomintang. An-mei's mother, who ran away to marry Wu Tsing, reclaims her daughter and takes her to Tientsin (JLC, p. 36). Although An-mei's mother offers a strip of flesh for a healing soup, Grandmother Popo dies (JLC, p. 34).
1925	Sun Yat-sen dies. Chiang Kai-shek heads the Kuomintang.
early summer	Winnie's mother abandons her and disappears (KGW, p. 102).
two weeks later	Winnie travels to Tsungming island to live with her uncle and his two wives, Old Aunt and New Aunt (KGW, p. 117). Winnie returns to Shanghai to enter a Catholic boarding school (KGW, pp. 133, 170).
1926	Lindo meets Huang Tyan-yu, her future husband, for the first time (JLC, p. 46).
1927	Davidson Black identifies remains of *Homo erectus* as Peking Man, found in a cave outside China's capital city (BD, p. 143).
1928	Lindo Jong observes in a mirror her resemblance to her mother, who believes Lindo will be even more clever than she (JLC, p. 292).
1929	Scientists buy dragon bones at Mouth of the Mountain (BD, p. 155).
1930	The Kuomintang decapitates Kun, Winnie's half-brother, for selling cloth to rebels (KGW, pp. 79, 82). Lin Xiao, Gu Ying-Ying's future husband, rips open a watermelon as a gesture of ravishment (JLC, p. 277). Ying-ying marries Lin Xiao, a vulgar, arrogant man (JLC, p. 278).
ca. **1930**	Because of the Fen River flood, Lindo Jong goes to live with the Huangs, her future in-laws (JLC, pp. 47, 293).
1931	After Precious Auntie commits suicide, Old Cook ejects her corpse into the ravine at the End of the World (BD, p. 185). The Liu family remands LuLing to a Christian orphanage in an old monastery (BD, p. 196). GaoLing Liu marries Chang Fu Nan, an opium-addicted groom formerly intended for LuLing (BD, p. 216).
1932	Lindo leaves the Huangs' house and settles in Peking (JLC, pp. 47, 62). After her husband takes up with an opera star, Ying-ying aborts her son and orders his corpse thrown into the lake (JLC, p. 281). Nationalists conscript GaoLing's older brother (BD, p. 216).
1933	American and Chinese scientists take quarters at the orphanage at Dragon Bone Hill (BD, p. 207). GaoLing learns that Old Cook piled rocks on Precious Auntie's corpse (BD, p. 218).
1934	Japanese troops overrun Shansi province (JLC, p. 257).

	GaoLing's second brother joins the Communists, followed by her three cousins (BD, p. 216).
October	Mao Tse-tung leads one hundred thousand Communists on the Long March, which covers five thousand miles from Hunan to northeast China.
1935	Wen Chen, an honor graduate of merchant seaman school, dies of tuberculosis (KGW, p. 210).
	On the advice of Old Aunt, Winnie rejects Lin as a suitor (KGW, p. 71).
1937	At the outbreak of the Sino-Japanese War, the Japanese overrun Shanghai (KGW, p. 80).
	Americans remain neutral toward the Japanese and the Chinese Nationalists and Communists (BD, p. 219).
early January	Winnie accompanies Peanut and her brothers to the market to seek a prediction of Peanut's fortune (KGW, pp. 137–138).
	Peanut earns the attention of an actor, Wen Fu, the spoiled son of wealthy parents (KGW, p. 153).
February	Wen Fu begins courting Peanut, but Auntie Miao, the matchmaker, makes a match between Wen Fu and Winnie, who comes from a wealthier family than her cousin (KGW, p. 166).
April	Claire Chennault becomes air training adviser to the Chinese government (KGW, p. 203).
	Winnie marries Wen Fu about the time that her best friend Hulan, called "Helen," weds Long Jiaguo, Wen Fu's commanding officer (KGW, pp. 187, 211).
	Wen Fu passes himself off as his dead brother, Wen Chen (KGW, p. 211).
Spring	Winnie and Helen live in an old monastery at Hangchow near the American-style air force school where Wen Fu learns to fly (KGW, p. 203).
	Winnie conceives Mochou, her first child (KGW, p. 218).
July 7	Japanese insurgents attack Peking near the Marco Polo Bridge over the Yungting River (BD, p. 215).
	GaoLing reunites with LuLing at the orphanage (BD, p. 216).
	Lindo's marriage to Huang Tyan-yu is postponed because of the invasion (JLC, p. 52).
July 28	The Japanese capture Peking.
August	Chiang Kai-shek's forces ally with Chinese Communists in the United Front to fight Japanese invaders in Shanghai (BD, p. 217).
late summer	Pilots' wives travel one hundred sixty miles north by boat from Hangchow to Yangchow northwest of Shanghai (KGW, pp. 242–243).
September	After Gan's plane is shot down, Winnie fantasizes that he is her ghost lover (KGW, p. 256).
November	Japanese forces slaughter one hundred thousand people in Nanking, which the Chinese abandon (KGW, pp. 268, 295).
December	Shanghai falls to Japan.
winter	Kuomintang pilots move west to Nanking (KGW, p. 258).
	Wen Fu drives recklessly and overturns his Fiat in a village graveyard (KGW, p. 266).

Winnie survives a stampede after Japanese planes drop leaflets on the Nanking marketplace (KGW, pp. 272–273).

Long Jiaguo loads eight people into a truck bound for Kunming (KGW, pp. 277–279).

LuLing Liu marries Pan Kai Jing in a winter wedding (BD, pp. 222–223).

1938   Japan controls north and central China and supplants the Kuomintang (KGW, p. 360).

Kuomintang pilots and their wives flee by truck on a two-month journey fourteen hundred miles to Kunming in southwest China on the Burma Road (KGW, p. 297).

October   Chinese officials set up a new capital in Chungking (KGW, p. 294).

Winnie gives birth to Mochou, a stillborn daughter, and buries her in the hills outside Kunming (KGW, p. 305).

Wen Fu suffers head injuries and the loss of an eye in a jeep accident that kills a female passenger (KGW, pp. 312–314).

1939

ca. July   Winnie's fourteen-year-old servant leaves after Wen Fu impregnates her (KGW, pp. 326–328).

Winnie gives birth to Yiku, a second daughter, in a Kunming hospital (KGW, p. 322).

1940   Because of Wen Fu's neglect and cruelty, Yiku dies of convulsions resulting from food poisoning (KGW, p. 338).

early fall   Winnie gives birth to a son, Danru (KGW, p. 339).

After Wen Fu impregnates Min, a beautiful dancer, Winnie determines to divorce him (KGW, p. 353).

1941   The bones of Peking Man disappear after they are packed in a wooden truck for transport from China (BD, p. 302).

summer   The British close the seven-hundred-mile Burma Road (KGW, p. 359).

Japanese planes bomb Kunming (KGW, p. 376).

Japanese officials seize Jiang Sao-yen's Five Phoenixes Textile Trading Companies and force him to support Emperor Hirohito (KGW, p. 415).

December 7   Japanese bombers attack Pearl Harbor, Hawaii (KGW, p. 213; BD, p. 234).

December 8   The United States declares war on Japan (BD, p. 234).

several days
later   Ruth Grutoff and the orphanage staff take hope that, because the United States has joined the war, China will overcome the Japanese (BD, p. 234).

that night   Ruth Grutoff announces the loss of the Peking Man remains, which were packed in a trunk (BD, pp. 234, 302).

Christmas   Winnie dances with Jimmy Y. Louie, an Asian-American interpreter, at the American Club (KGW, pp. 382, 391).

Wen Fu rapes Winnie at gunpoint, signs divorce papers, then demands custody of Danru, his only son (KGW, pp. 392–394).

December

26   Helen and Auntie Du Ching help Winnie and Danru escape to a rooming house (KGW, p. 396).

morning of December 27	Helen leads Wen Fu to Winnie's room (KGW, p. 397).
1942	Claire Chennault leads his Flying Tigers into China's war against Japan (KGW, p. 360).
	Clifford St. Clair begins courting Ying-ying after her first husband's death (JLC, p. 284).
January 1942	Winnie aborts a child (KGW, p. 397).
March 1942	Winnie aborts a second child (KGW, p. 397).
May 1942	Winnie aborts a third child. She considers suicide and aborts subsequent children fathered by Wen Fu over the next three years (KGW, pp. 397–398).
1944	Japan launches a major offensive in Kweilin (JLC, p. 13).
	Japan weakens after defeat in Burma.
	Suyuan Li gives birth to twin girls, Chwun Yu and Chwun Hwa (JLC, pp. 308, 322).
	After Suyuan abandons her infants on her way north to Chungking, Mei Ching and Mei Han find the girls and rear them in a stone cave (JLC, pp. 13–14, 223, 308).
	Suyuan's first husband, Wang Fuchi, dies during the Sino-Japanese War two weeks before she is hospitalized for dysentery (JLC, p. 326).
	Winnie receives a last letter from Peanut (KGW, p. 303).
	Li Chen gives birth to Kwan, Jack Yee's first child (HSS, p. 6).
1945	Suyuan and Canning Woo search for the twins (JLC, p. 328).
late January	Winnie depletes her savings and lives on Jimmy Louie's salary (KGW, p. 467).
July 25	Claire Chennault completes his role in China.
August 6	The *Enola Gay* drops an atom bomb on Hiroshima.
August 8	The Americans drop a second atom bomb on Nagasaki.
August 15	After Emperor Hirohito surrenders, the war ends (KGW, pp. 80, 402; BD, p. 239).
	Winnie, Helen, and the pilots learn of the surrender and celebrate (KGW, p. 402).
next day	Wen Fu's family departs from Kunming (KGW, p. 403).
	After Japan withdraws from China, the Kuomintang returns to power (KGW, p. 416).
September	Wen Fu, Winnie, and Danru return to Jiang Sao-yen's house in Shanghai (KGW, p. 403).
	Because Jiang Sao-yen has been shamed and suffers a paralytic stroke, Wen Fu seizes control and sells the family's wealth (KGW, pp. 416, 420).
	Helen, Jiaguo, and Auntie Du travel northeast to Harbin (KGW, p. 406).
	GaoLing immigrates from Hong Kong to California (BD, p. 244).
1946	Communist leaders under Mao Tse-tung fight Nationalist forces for control of China (BD, 255).
	Ying-ying marries Clifford St. Clair (JLC, p. 285).

New Year	After recovering from jaundice contracted from river crabs, Winnie and Danru visit relatives on Tsungming Island for two weeks (KGW, pp. 424–425).
three weeks later	On a visit to Peanut in Shanghai's Japanese section, Winnie encounters Jimmy Louie on the street five years after their first meeting (KGW, p. 434).
	Winnie leaves Wen Fu and, with her father's blessing and three gold ingots, settles in Jimmy's residence with Danru (KGW, p. 462).
1947	The Woos search for the twins in Hong Kong (JLC, p. 328).
	Lindo Sun flies from China to America, where she meets Tin Jong (JLC, p. 295).
	Winnie sends Danru to the north, where he and Jiaguo die of an epidemic disease (KGW, p. 471).
spring	Winnie grows thin from grief (KGW, p. 472).
	Police arrest Winnie for kidnapping Danru, stealing from the Wen family, and deserting her husband (KGW, pp. 472–473).
	When Jimmy's government post ends, he emigrates to San Francisco (KGW, p. 479).
1948	Jack Yee, a student at National Guangxi University, terrifies a thief into abandoning a rich man's coat containing the immigration papers of Yee Jun and an enrollment letter to Lincoln University (HSS, pp. 177–179).
	After Li Chen, Jack's first wife, dies of tuberculosis, he leaves daughter Kwan with Aunt Li Bin-Bin and seeks work in Hong Kong (HSS, p. 6).
January	After a trial, Winnie chooses a two-year sentence to a women's prison rather than return to Wen Fu (KGW, p. 477).
	Auntie Du supplies Winnie with clothes and newspaper accounts of her affair with an Asian-American (KGW, pp. 477, 478).
	San Ma and Wu Ma visit Winnie at the prison and report the death of her father, Jiang Sao-yen (KGW, pp. 484, 486).
	Jimmy Louie, who studies for the ministry, telegraphs a marriage proposal to Winnie (KGW, p. 488).
	After marrying Tin Jong, Lindo gives birth to Winston, her first son (JLC, p. 302).
1949	
January	Communists take Peking and control the People's Republic of China; Nationalists hold Taiwan (KGW, pp. 80, 496; HSS, p. 6).
February	Auntie Du tells Winnie that Helen is remarried and pregnant (KGW, p. 489).
	Winnie's uncle falls into depression, walks in front of a truck, and is killed (KGW, p. 72).
	After losing everything, Suyuan immigrates from China to San Francisco with her husband, Canning Woo (JLC, p. 141).
	Suyuan Woo launches the Joy Luck Club, comprised of An-mei Hsu, Lindo Jong, and Ying-ying St. Clair, all friends from the First Chinese Baptist Church (JLC, p. 6).
	Lindo Jong gives birth to Vincent, her second son (JLC, p. 303).
March	Henry Kwong is unable to influence an old friend to get Winnie out of jail (KGW, p. 495).

April	Citing court error, officials release Winnie from prison after Auntie Du divulges that Winnie is well connected to a Communist official (KGW, p. 491).
May 10	Lured by greed for a valuable package, Wen Fu signs divorce papers in the telegraph office on Quanshi Road (KGW, p. 501).
May 14	Sneaking up to Winnie's apartment, Wen Fu destroys the divorce papers and rapes her at gunpoint (KGW, pp. 501–502).
May 15	Winnie lies about being married to Jimmy Louie and boards a plane for California (KGW, p. 99).
May 21	Winnie arrives at Jimmy Louie's home in Fresno, where he is associate minister of the First Chinese Baptist Church (KGW, p. 76).
May 26	The Communists end all flights from Shanghai (KGW, p. 504).
August	Helen gives birth to Mary, her first child and only daughter (KGW, p. 20).
1950	Ying-ying St. Clair gives birth to Lena, her only surviving child (JLC, pp. 105, 286).
	Communists jail Chang the coffinmaker and execute him for cheating people and trading in opium (BD, p. 288).
February	Winnie gives birth to Pearl Louie, but doesn't know whether Wen Fu or Jimmy Louie is her father (KGW, pp. 20, 99).
1951	Jing-Mei "June May" Woo is born (JLC, pp. 14, 221, 307, 312).
March 17	Lindo Jong gives birth to her third and last child, Waverly "Meimei" Jong (JLC, pp. 92, 183, 303).
1952	Mei Han dies, leaving the twins in the care of Mei Ching, their adoptive mother, who searches for their birth parents (JLC, p. 327).
	Winnie Louie gives birth to Samuel (KGW, p. 99).
	Elza Marie Vandervort is born to Polish parents who are killed in an auto accident (HSS, p. 117).
1953	Posing as Winnie's half-sister, Helen immigrates from Formosa to California (KGW, pp. 78, 82, 496).
1954	Ruth Luyi is born to LuLing Liu and Edwin Young (BD, p. 58).
1955	Winnie recognizes Dr. Lin and faints on the steps of the First Chinese Baptist Church (KGW, pp. 73, 75).
1956	Olivia is born to Jack and Louise Kenfield Yee (HSS, p. 5).
1957	Waverly learns the "art of invisible strength" that helps her win arguments without exerting effort (JLC, p. 89).
1958	Waverly learns to play chess from Lau Po, who teaches her at sessions in the park (JLC, p. 97).
ca. 1959	Simon Bishop is believed sterile after his testicles descend late (HSS, pp. 128–129).
	Helen gives birth to Roger "Bao-Bao" Kwong (KGW, p. 84).
1960	Waverly becomes national chess champion (JLC, p. 99).
	Jimmy and Winnie move from San Francisco's Chinatown west to the Richmond district (KGW, pp. 11, 92).
	After confessing to having a daughter in China, Jack Yee dies of renal failure (HSS, p. 6).

1961	The St. Clairs move to an Italian neighborhood in San Francisco (JLC, p. 110). Ying-ying gives birth to a stillborn son (JLC, p. 116). Waverly stops playing chess (JLC, p. 188).
1962	Louise Kenfield Yee marries Bob Laguni (HSS, p. 9). Kwan Li emigrates from China to live with her stepmother (HSS, p. 10).
1963	Through nightly talks, Kwan Li teaches Olivia Chinese (HSS, p.13).
1964	Winston Jong dies in a car accident (JLC, p. 303). Pearl represses grief for Jimmy Louie after he dies from stomach cancer (KGW, pp. 48, 93). Helen and Winnie open the Ding Ho Flower Shop on Ross Avenue in Chinatown (KGW, pp. 7, 16). Bob Laguni enters Kwan Li at Mary's Help, a mental hospital, where she undergoes shock treatment (HSS, p. 16).
1965	Waverly loses a chess tournament and abandons the game a second time (JLC, p. 190). Ruth Luyi Young tries to commit suicide (BD, p. 117).
1966	June Woo denies her Asian ethnicity (JLC, p. 306).
1968	An-mei and George Hsu move from Chinatown to the Sunset district of San Francisco (JLC, p. 15).
December 25	Olivia Yee Laguni gives Kwan Li a Ouija board (HSS, pp. 107–108).
1969	Waverly elopes with Marvin Chen, her high school sweetheart (JLC, pp. 191–192).
1970	LuLing falls from a window shortly before Ruth's sixteenth birthday (BD, p. 126).
1972	Rose Hsu marries Ted Jordan, a dermatologist (JLC, p. 125). The house of the Liu family crumbles and sinks into the earth (BD, p. 292).
1973 December	Elza Vandervort and her unborn child die in an avalanche in Utah (HSS, p. 101).
1974	Mary Kwong Cheu introduces Pearl Louie to Phil Brandt, a medical student (KGW, p. 4).
March	Olivia Yee Laguni meets Simon Bishop (HSS, p. 103).
1975	Pearl Louie marries Phil Brandt and settles in San Jose, California (KGW, p. 7). Olivia Yee Laguni and Simon Bishop move in together (HSS, p. 121).
1978 June	Olivia Yee Laguni marries Simon Bishop (HSS, p. 121).
1981	Pearl has a miscarriage (KGW, p. 29).
1982	Pearl gives birth to Tessa Brandt (KGW, p. 9).
1983	Shoshana is born to Waverly Jong and Marvin Chen (JLC, p 193). Pearl suffers fatigue and begins taking aerobics with Mary Cheu (KGW, p. 22).

1983	June Woo quits college (JLC, p. 26).
	Pearl develops symptoms of multiple sclerosis (KGW, p. 22).
1984	Doug Cheu's colleague diagnoses Pearl's disease at the San Francisco Medical Center (KGW, p. 22).
1986	Lindo Jong visits China (JLC, p. 304).
1987	Pearl gives birth to Cleo Brandt (KGW, p. 10).
	Waverly hesitates to tell her mother that she is going to marry Rich Schields (JLC, p. 195).
	Ted Jordan leaves Rose, his wife of fifteen years (JLC, pp. 127, 208).
	Two months before her death, Suyuan gives her daughter June a jade pendant (JLC, p. 221).
	Three months later, June Woo learns the whereabouts of her two half-sisters in Shanghai (JLC, p. 308).
October	Canning Woo and his daughter June travel to China to meet Suyuan's twin daughters in Shanghai (JLC, pp. 30, 331).
1989	A San Francisco earthquake cracks the walls of Winnie and Helen's flower shop in Chinatown and the house that Olivia and Simon Bishop look at in Pacific Heights (KGW, p. 16; HSS, p. 127).
	Ruth Luyi Young meets Art at a yoga class (BD, p. 295).
November	Helen falls on the stairs and is diagnosed with a benign brain tumor (KGW, p. 34).
December	
25	Wen Fu dies of heart disease (KGW, pp. 89, 98).
	Wan Betty writes Helen the news that Wen Fu died of heart disease (KGW, p. 509).
1990	Pearl Louie Brandt works in speech and language therapy for retarded children (KGW, pp. 8, 94).
early	
January	Chinese-American mourners gather in San Francisco for the engagement party of Mimi Wong and Roger "Bao-bao" Kwong and for the funeral of Auntie Du Ching, who dies of a brain concussion at age ninety-seven following a bus accident (KGW, pp. 3, 6, 39).
	Auntie Du leaves to Pearl an altar to the Kitchen God (KGW, p. 58).
mid–January	Winnie learns from Helen about Wen Fu's death (KGW, pp. 89–90).
February	Bao-bao marries Mimi Wong, his third wife (KGW, pp. 4, 515).
February 20	Simon Bishop begins writing a novel (HSS, p. 146).
1991	Olivia and Simon Bishop's co-op in Pacific Heights emits ghostly sounds that Kwan Li identifies as human in origin (HHS, pp. 133–136).
ca. **1991**	LuLing Liu begins compiling an autobiography (BD, p. 286).
ca. **1992**	LuLing Liu gives Ruth some handwritten pages containing biographical data (BD, p. 130).
1994	
end of January	Olivia reads the first chapter of Simon's novel before attending Kwan's fiftieth birthday party (HSS, p. 146).

that night	Olivia quarrels with Simon and tosses the diskette version of his novel out the window (HSS, pp. 146, 149).
first of February	Simon moves out (HSS, p. 146).
November	Kwan, Olivia, and Simon arrive in Changmian, China, on the day that Big Ma dies in a car-bus accident (HSS, pp. 184–184, 231).
two weeks later	After Kwan's disappearance, villagers hold a funeral for Big Ma (HSS, p. 393).
1996	George Lew and Virgie marry and honeymoon in Changmian (HSS, p. 397).
1998	Dr. Huey diagnoses LuLing's mental confusion as dementia (BD, p. 60).
August	Olivia gives birth to Samantha "Sammy" Li (HSS, p. 398).
1999	Ruth leaves Art and moves in with LuLing on the pretense of collaborating on a children's book about animals (BD, p. 263). Art and Ruth celebrate the tenth anniversary of their meeting (BD, p. 295).

Appendix B:
Foreign Terms
in Tan's Works

Each entry contains an abbreviated title and page number for identification of the term in context. Some words appear in variant forms, e.g. *hulihudu* and *huli-hudu*; *pochai* and *po chai*. Source: *Concise English-Chinese Chinese-English Dictionary*, ed. Martin H. Manser, Oxford University Press, 2001.

Key: BD = *The Bonesetter's Daughter*; CSC = *The Chinese Siamese Cat*; HSS = *The Hundred Secret Senses*; JLC = *The Joy Luck Club*; KGW = *The Kitchen God's Wife*; LLW = "Lost Lives of Women"; ML = *The Moon Lady*; MT = "Mother Tongue"; OF = *The Opposite of Fate*

ah-vuh-gee (n.) AVG for American Volunteer Group (KGW, p. 382)

ai or **ai ya** (interj.) exclamation of dismay (JLC, p. 201; KGW, pp. 47–48, 149, 239, 311, 377, 410, 422, 427–428, 450, 503, 512, 515, 518, 521, 528; HSS, pp. 65, 84, 115, 118, 160, 176, 183, 227, 240, 252, 271, 278, 284, 339, 355, 366–367, 374, 394; BD, pp. 4, 49, 51, 55, 63–64, 79, 93, 110, 117, 166, 168–169, 237, 272, 282, 293, 294; OF, pp. 9, 70, 175, 280, 284)

aiyi (n.) auntie (JLC, pp. 314–322; KGW, p. 410; OF, pp. 100, 161–173)

amah (n.) nursemaid (JLC, pp. 65, 79, 327–328; ML, unpaginated)

Amitaba (n.) the Buddha of paradise (KGW, pp. 45, 269)

Andaru (n.) the Apostle Andrew (BD, p. 235)

anh (pron.) what? (KGW, p. 443)

ba or **baba** (n.) daddy (KGW, p. 358; HSS, p. 176; BD, pp. 224, 253)

Bai (n.) northern Chinese tribe (KGW, p. 361)

bao (adj.) precious (BD, p. 48)

bao (v.) protect (BD, p. 291)

bao-bao (n.) precious baby (KGW, pp. 3–4)

baobei (n.) treasure (LLW, p. 90)

bao-bing (n.) pancake (HSS, p. 277)

bao mu (n.) nursemaid (BD, pp. 291, 293)

bao-zi (n.) buncake (HSS, p. 278)

bomu (n.) auntie (BD, p. 48)

bu (adv.) no (HSS, pp. 264, 290–291, 296, 354; BD, p. 130)

Budalomu (n.) the Apostle Bartholomew (BD, p. 235)

bu-shr (v.) don't say (OF, p. 165)

butong (n.) "the better half of mixed intentions" (JLC, p. 6)

B'yao, zhen b'yao! I don't want it, really I don't! (OF, p. 280)

catty (n.) approximately one and one-third pounds (KGW, p. 247)

chabudwo (n.) soup (JLC, pp. 5–6)

chang (adj.) long (HSS, p. 308)

chang (n.) lucky pendant (JLC, p. 47)

chang (n.) singing (HSS, p. 308; OF, p. 261)

Changmian (n.) never-ending songs; long sleep, eternal rest; death (HSS, p. 43; OF, p. 261)

chaswei (n.) coin-sized slices of sweet barbecued pork (JLC, p. 20)

chi (n.) spirit (JLC, p. 285; HSS, p. 301; BD, pp. 43, 205)

ching (v.) "please eat" (JLC, p. 38)

chin wubing (n.) common soldier (KGW, pp. 244–245)

chipao (n.) dress (KGW, pp. 188, 473; BD, pp. 50, 170)

chiszle (adj.) "mad to death" (JLC, p. 24)

chiu ke (n.) checkers (KGW, p. 105)

cho (interj.) exclamation of disgust (BD, p. 180)

choszle (adj.) "stinks to death" (JLC, p. 184)

cho tofu (n.) bean curd (KGW, p. 400)

chr fan (v.) eat (JLC, p. 289)

chrle (v.) eaten already (OF, p. 288)

Chu Jung (n.) god of fire (JLC, p. 137)

chuming (n.) inner knowledge (JLC, p. 282)

chunwang chihan (adage) Without lips, teeth will be cold. (JLC, pp. 161, 178)

chwun (n.) spring (JLC, p. 322)

da bien (n.) excrement (OF, p. 174)

da bing (n.) round piece of flat bread (KGW, p. 485; OF, pp. 169–171)

dajya (n.) an entire family (JLC, p. 67, ML, unpaginated)

dan-dan (n.) a heavily spiced noodle dish (KGW, p. 283)

dang! (interj.) attention! (KGW, p. 368)

dangsying tamende shenti (verb and direct object) take care of them (JLC, p. 130)

danru (n.) nonchalance (KGW, p. 339)

danwei (n.) work units (OF, p. 160)

daomei (n.) negative thoughts that eventually come true (KGW, pp. 187, 239)

dim sum (n.) dumplings, called "potstickers" in English (JLC, p. 90)

ding-ngin (adj.) itchy (KGW, p. 74)

dong (adj.) east (JLC, p. 296)

dong lu (n.) hotel (JLC, p. 318)

duan (n.) stone found near the Duanxi River at the base of Mount Fuke (BD, pp. 225, 308)

dwei (adv.) correct (OF, p. 288)

dyansyin (n.) foods that confer good luck on diners (JLC, p. 10)

dunsyi (n.) child (JLC, p. 239)

er (adj.) younger (BD, p. 235)

ermei (n.) second or younger sister (HSS, pp. 189–192, 202, 238)

Fang pi bu-cho, cho pi bu-fang (adage) There's more power in silence. (Literally, "Loud farts don't stink, and the really smelly ones don't make a sound.") (OF, pp. 9, 295)

fantou (n.) a stupid or retarded person (HSS, p. 49)

fatsai (n.) black-hair fungus (KGW, pp. 247–248)

fen (n.) one-tenth of a cent (KGW, pp. 419–420; HSS, p. 210)

feng shui (n.) balance (literally "wind and water") (HSS, p. 301; OF, p. 233)

Filipa (n.) the Apostle Philip (BD, p. 235)

ganbei (slang) bottoms up (KGW, p. 180; HSS, p. 299)

gei wo kan (verb and direct object) show me the doll (HSS, p. 56)

ge-ti hu (verb and prepositional phrase) store in an outdoor stall (OF, p. 159)

goo (n.) bone (BD, p. 101)

gu (n.) bone (BD, p. 301); gorge (BD, p. 304)

gung-gung (n.) grandfather (KGW, p. 120)

guoyu (n.) Mandarin Chinese (BD, p. 56)

gwan deng shweijyau (verbs) close light sleep (JLC, p. 289)

ha-bu (n.) grandmother (KGW, pp. 10, 94–95, 123, 518)

Hakka (n.) northern Chinese tribe (HSS, pp. 33, 239, 365)

ha pi (adj.) exhaling farts (KGW, pp. 139–140)

hau (adj.) okay, good (KGW, p. 16; OF, p. 165)

haule (interj.) hurray (JLC, p. 159)

heimongmong (adj.) foggy (JLC, pp. 210, 220)

hong mu (n.) fine wood used in crafting furniture (JLC, p. 11)

houche (n.) choo-choo train (JLC, p. 289)

houlu (n.) small coal stove (JLC, p. 253)

huang do-zi (n.) bean sprout (HSS, p. 162)

huanshi (n.) garden (JLC, p. 318)

Hui (n.) northern Chinese tribe (KGW, p. 361)

hulihudu (adj.) confused (JLC, pp. 210, 219; BD, p. 109)

hwa (n.) flower (JLC, p. 322)

hwai (adj.) bad (JLC, p. 239; HSS, p. 148)

hwai dan (n.) bad egg (HSS, p. 148)

hwai dunsyi (n.) You bad child (JLC, p. 239)

Jaime er (n.) the Apostle James the younger (BD, p. 235)

Jaime yi (n.) the Apostle James the Elder (BD, p. 235)

jandale (adj.) grown up (JLC, pp. 315, 331)

jang (v.) speak or talk (HSS, p. 50)

jang Zhongwen (v.) talk Chinese (HSS, p. 50)

jiaoban (adj.) tough (HSS, p. 211)

jiao-zi (n.) steamed dumplings (KGW, p. 44)

jing (adj.) excellent or pure essence (JLC, p. 323)

jook (n.) thick rice soup (KGW, p. 517)

jou jin-shan (n.) Old Gold Mountain (San Francisco) (OF, p. 170)

jrdaule (slang) I already know it. (JLC, p. 200)

Judasa (n.) the Apostle Judas (BD, p. 235)

jyejye (n.) sister (JLC, p. 310)

jye shiang ru yi (phrase) all the kinds of luck that you wish (KGW, p. 58)

kai gwa (verb and direct object) open the watermelon (JLC, pp. 277, 278)

k'ang (n.) heated bed made of bricks (BD, pp. 3, 151, 158, 161, 167, 180, 183–187)

kaoliang cake (n.) seed cake (KGW, p. 362)

kechi (adj.) overly polite (JLC, p. 284)

koutou (v.) bow with deep respect (JLC, p. 268)

ku-ku (adj.) crying (BD, p. 253)

kuli (n.) laborer (HSS, pp. 41, 42, 44, 369)

kung fu (n.) Chinese martial arts (literally, skill) (OF, p. 382)

kunjing Kunming (phrase) stuck in Kunming (KGW, p. 277)

Kuomintang (n.) Nationalist People's Party (KGW, pp. 79, 205, 360, 412, 416, 418, 478)

Kwan Yin (n.) goddess of mercy (KGW, p. 58)

la-la (adj.) hot-hot (BD, p. 33)

laoshu (n.) mouse (HSS, p. 68)

la-sa (n.) garbage, cast-offs (KGW, p. 191)

La-sa hau chr (phrase) The garbage tastes good. (OF, p. 106)

lau tai po (n.) old lady (KGW, p. 466)

li (n.) a measure of length equal to 0.6 kilometers (JLC, p. 3; KGW, pp. 266, 291; HSS, p. 285)

lihai (adj.) wild and stubborn (JLC, p. 275)

liu xin (phrase) remain true (BD, p. 304)

liu xing (n.) shooting star (BD, p. 301)

lou (n.) building (JLC, p. 296)

louyi (slang) an insult comparing people to insects (KGW, p. 298)

luyi (n.) all that you wish (BD, p. 289)

mah jong (n.) a game of chance and strategy played with 144 small tiles (JLC, pp. 10 ff., 22–23, 30, 267; KGW, pp. 247, 251, 301, 335, 359, 420, 421; HSS, p. 152; OF, pp. 37, 82, 95, 102)

mai (n.) wheat (JLC, p. 296)

majie (n.) uniformed maid (BD, p. 252)

Maku Polo (n.) Marco Polo (BD, p. 215)

maodo (n.) sweet greens (KGW, p. 372)

maotai or **maotei** (n.) liquor (KGW, p. 198; HSS, p. 390)

Matu (n.) the Apostle Matthew (BD, p. 235)

mei gwansyi (phrase) It doesn't matter. (JLC, p. 117)

meigwo-ren (adj.) American (OF, p. 170)

meimei (n.) younger sister (JLC, pp. 323, 331)

mei-po (n.) matchmaker (HSS, p. 73)

meiyou (v.) have not (OF, p. 288)

membao che (slang) a van nicknamed a "bread truck" (OF, p. 157)

mian (adj.) silky, endless; also (n.) sleep (HSS, p. 308; OF, p. 261)

Miao (n.) northern Chinese tribe (KGW, p. 361)

mieyou wenti (phrase) don't worry (HSS, p. 343)

ming yuan (n.) fate (KGW, p. 435)

mochou (adj.) sorrowfree (KGW, pp. 306, 511)

momo meiyu (v.) rub sink gone (BD, p. 292)

moxa (n.) medicinal artemisia (KGW, p. 198)

mu (n.) one-sixth of an acre (KGW, p. 281; BD, p. 140)

mu (n.) mother (BD, p. 291)

Nai-nai (n.) grandma (ML, unpaginated)

nala (v.) take it (JLC, p. 235)

nale (interj.) there it is (JLC, p. 137)

nangko-ning (n.) foreigner (OF, p. 163)

nao (adj.) noisy (KGW, p. 203)

nengkan (n.) self-confidence; a can-do spirit (JLC, pp. 128, 132, 134, 135, 138)

ni (n.) a traitor to family and ancestors (JLC, p. 36)

nian gao (n.) sticky rice cakes (KGW, p. 157)

ni hau (phrase) how are you (HSS, pp. 323, 328)

ni kan (v.) you watch (JLC, pp. 142, 145; TK, pp. 53, 54)

nu (n.) girl (HSS, p. 34)

nuli (n.) slave girl (HSS, pp. 248, 250)

numu (n.) fierce stare (HSS, p. 34)

nunu (adj.) precious (OF, p. 100)

nu-pei (n.) original wife (LLW, p. 91)

nuwu (n.) witch (HSS, p. 249)

nuyer (n.) daughter (JLC, p. 37)

Nyah-nyah (n.) nickname for "grand-mother" (OF, pp. 69, 9495)

Old Mr. Chou (n.) the sandman (JLC, pp. 207, 210, 216, 219, 220)

oyo (interj.) exclamation of surprise (KGW, pp. 448, 486, 512)

Pa (n.) the Apostle Paul (BD, p. 235)

pah (interj.) exclamation of disgust (KGW, p. 486)

pai (n.) a tile used in the playing of mah jong [q. v.] (JLC, p. 11)

pai gar (n.) a brand name of wine (BD, p. 188)

pao (adj.) gone (HSS, p. 377)

pian pao (n.) firecracker (OF, p. 172)

pichi (n.) temperament (JLC, p. 44)

Pida (n.) the Apostle Peter (BD, p. 235)

ping (n.) peace (HSS, p. 357)

pochai (n.) herbal medicine (KGW, p. 88; BD, p. 60)

putong (n.) east side of the Yangtse River (MT; OF, p. 273)

ren (n.) man (HSS, p. 36)

renmenbi (n.) coins equal to a little more than twelve and one-half cents each (OF, pp. 171–172, 198)

rji-ji (slang) penis (KGW, pp. 195, 200)

sagwa silly (CSC, unpaginated)

sam fook (n.) triple blessing (KGW, p. 13)

san (adj.) third (KGW, p. 128)

sau nai-nai (n.) wetnurse (KGW, p. 326)

Shaimin (n.) the Apostle Simon (BD, p. 235)

shan (n.) lightning (KGW, p. 203)

shaoping (n.) flaky sesame seed buns (BD, p. 226)

shemma (pron.) what? (JLC, p. 200)

shemma yisz (phrase) what is the meaning (JLC, p. 109)

shou (n.) respect for family and ancestors (JLC, pp. 35, 41)

sh-sh (slang) pee-pee (JLC, p. 289)

shu-shu (n.) urination (KGW, p. 195)

shwo buchulai (idiom) words fail me (JLC, p. 108)

si (adj.) four (OF, p. 372)

si (n.) death (OF, p. 372)

siqing (n.) situation (BD, p. 251)

suanle or **swanle** (adj.) finished (JLC, p. 245)

suanle or **swanle** (phrase) forget it (KGW, p. 240); too late (HSS, p. 68)

suyuan (n.) long-cherished wish or (adj.) never forgotten (JLC, p. 322)

syaujye (n.) miss, girl (JLC, p. 297)

syaumei (n.) a small dumpling (JLC, p. 47)

syau ning (n.) little person (KGW, pp. 57, 352–353, 395–396, 470)

syau yen (n.) little wild goose (JLC, p. 314)

syen do jang (n.) soy-milk soup (KGW, p. 115)

syin ke (n.) heart liver, a precious tidbit (KGW, pp. 109, 129, 131)

syin yifu (n.) your new clothes (JLC, p. 70)

sz (adj.) fourth (KGW, p. 128)

sz (v.) die (JLC, pp. 258, 273)

sz tai (n.) fourth wife (JLC, p. 258)

Tadayisu (n.) the Apostle Thaddeus (BD, p. 235)

tael (n.) a unit of weight used to evaluate silver (HSS, p. 39; BD, p. 156)

tai (adj.) great (HSS, p. 357)

tai chi chuan (phrase) a physical exhibit of Taoist philosophy (HSS, p. 221)

taitai or **tai-tai** (n.) wife; ma'am (JLC, pp. 43–44 ff., 251; KGW, pp. 245–246, 327, 340, 419, 425)

tang jie (n.) sugar sister (KGW, pp. 190, 446)

Tao (n.) a philosophy based on the concept of "the way" (JLC, pp. 98, 170)

Taoist (n.) a follower of Taoism (BD, pp. 192, 209–210)

taonan (adj.) in the path of terrible danger (KGW, pp. 258–260, 267, 270, 273, 275, 497)

Tomasa (n.) the Apostle Thomas (BD, p. 235)

tounau (n.) a tonic soup that promises longevity for mothers (JLC, p. 57)

tyan (n.) sky (JLC, p. 44)

tyandi (n.) spiritual marriage (JLC, p. 262)

uni (n.) sea urchin (BD, p. 295)

wah-wah yu (n.) a rare fish that cries and gestures like a baby (KGW, pp. 111, 129)

waigoren (n.) foreigner (JLC, pp. 124, 224)

waipo (n.) an honorific for "grandmother" (BD, pp. 61, 86, 88, 127, 267, 294)

waixiao (n.) expatriate (OF, p. 280)

wan (adj.) beautiful (KGW, pp. 260–263)

wenmipo (n.) clairvoyant (BD, p. 246)

wenti (n.) worry (HSS, p. 343)

wonton (n.) noodle dough shaped in pockets, filled with flavorings, and either fried or served in broth (KGW, p. 146; HSS, pp. 147, 168; OF, p. 163)

wu (adj.) fourth (KGW, p. 128)

Xian Xin (n.) Immortal Heart (BD, p. 292)

xiao loong bao (n.) Shanghai dumplings (OF, pp. 168–169)

xin (n.) truth (BD, p. 304)

xing (n.) star (BD, p. 304)

yadan (n.) duck egg (HSS, pp. 188–189)

yamen (n.) police (HSS, p. 193)

yang (n.) the bright, truthful masculine realm equated with aggression, heat, activity, brightness, and dryness (JLC, pp. 82, 125; KGW, pp. 199, 200, 511; ML, un-

paginated; HSS, pp. 276–277; BD, pp. 26, 36; OF, p. 109)

yangfang (n.) foreign-style house (KGW, p. 299)

yangsele (slang) itching for sex (KGW, p. 74)

yen (n.) wild goose (JLC, p. 314)

Yi (n.) northern Chinese tribe (KGW, p. 361)

yi-ba-liu-si (idiom) translation of the year 1864 into "lose hope, slide into death" or "take hope, the dead remain" (HSS, pp. 32, 357)

yiban (adj.) one-half (HSS, p. 163)

yiban ren (n.) one-half man (HSS, p. 36)

yidafadwo (pron.) everything (JLC, p. 70)

yiding (n.) an obligation (JLC, pp. 130–131)

yiku (n.) sorrow over bitterness (KGW, pp. 326 ff., 511)

yin (n.) the dark, emotional feminine realm equated with coolness, receptivity, inactivity, moisture, and darkness; also, (adj.) invisible or shadow, a descriptive of spirits of the dead (JLC, pp. 82,125; KGW, pp. 187, 199, 201, 511; ML, unpaginated; HSS, pp. 3, 15 ff., 34, 85, 110 ff., 129, 135, 140, 157 ff., 181, 227, 234, 237, 254, 258, 267, 270, 276–277, 288, 307–308, 327, 351–352, 363, 375, 380; BD, pp. 26, 36, 163; OF, p. 109)

ying-gai (phrase) I should have (KGW, pp. 26–27; BD, p. 130)

ying-ying (n.) clear reflection (JLC, p. 276)

yinnang (n.) scrotum (HSS, p. 24)

yin-yang tou (n.) half-bald head (HSS, p. 17)

yinyuan (n.) the fate that unites lovers (HSS, p. 158)

yi (adj.) elder (BD, p. 235)

yisz (n.) meaning (JLC, p. 109)

yi tai (n.) first wife (JLC, p. 258)

yi wan (adj.) ten thousand (KGW, p. 104)

yu (n.) leftovers (JLC, p. 44)

yu (n.) rain (JLC, p. 322)

yuan (n.) Chinese paper money worth fifty American cents (JLC, p. 12l; KGW, pp. 175, 189, 247, 310, 325, 419, 492–493; HSS, pp. 210–211, 215, 222, 261, 279, 393; OF, pp. 162, 166)

Yuhan (n.) the Apostle John (BD, p. 235)

ywansyau (n.) sticky sweet dumpling served to celebrate the lunar new year (JLC, pp. 270–271)

zemma zaogao (slang) what a mess (HSS, p. 63)

Zhongwen (adj.) Chinese (HSS, p. 50)

zibuyong (n.) homosexual (KGW, pp. 447–448)

zong zi (n.) sticky rice and flavorings wrapped in lotus leaves (JLC, p. 71)

Appendix C:
Writing and Research Topics

1. Create a scenario in Amy Tan's *The Joy Luck Club* or *The Kitchen God's Wife*, Isabel Allende's *The House of the Spirits*, Meira Chand's *A Choice of Evils*, Nien Cheng's *Life and Death in Shanghai*, Anita Diamant's *The Red Tent*, Malika Oufkir's *Stolen Lives: Twenty Years in a Desert Prison*, Rosamunde Pilcher's *The Shell Seekers*, Anchee Min's *Katherine*, Julie Shigekuni's *A Bridge Between Us*, or Gail Tsukinama's *Women of the Silk* in which independent females discuss the value of a female network in supporting women's drive for autonomy and self-actualization.

2. Summarize dilemmas of biculturalism in Amy Tan's novels and either Frank Chin's *Donald Duk*, Michael Dorris's *Yellow Raft in Blue Water*, Jeanne Wakatsuki Houston and James Houston's *A Farewell to Manzanar*, Gus Lee's *China Boy*, Andrea Louie's *Moon Cakes*, or John van Druten's *I Remember Mama*. Describe incidents in which cultural demands clash, forcing young hyphenated Americans to honor the family's motherland or the customs of the United States. Note the value of compromise in settling bicultural dissonance.

3. Analyze elements of hope and ambition that inform Amy Tan's *The Joy Luck Club* and one of these novels: Pearl Buck's *The Good Earth*, Isabel Allende's *The House of the Spirits*, Jane Campion's *The Piano*, Peter Carey's *Oscar and Lucinda*, E. M. Forster's *A Passage to India*, Garrett Hongo's story "Kubota," Gish Jen's *Typical American*, Barbara Kingsolver's *The Poisonwood Bible*, Ruthann Lum McCunn's *Thousand Pieces of Gold*, Jean Rhys's *Wide Sargasso Sea*, or Sam Watson's *The Kadaitcha Sung*.

4. Explain the value of composing a novel to express racial and gender issues and conflicts caused by historical upheaval as revealed in Carlos Fuentes's *Old Gringo*, Jumpha Lahiri's *Interpreter of Maladies*, Amy Tan's *The Kitchen God's Wife* or *The Hundred Secret Senses*, and Mary Yukari Waters's *The Laws of Evening*. Outline controversies that *The Kitchen God's Wife* or *The Hundred Secret Senses* omitted, downplayed, or overlooked, particularly women's place in the communist hierarchy, Chinese religious rights, bureaucratic corruption, and the destruction of ancient Chinese monuments and esthetics.

5. Outline aspects of Western-style romance that inform the behaviors and expectations of characters in Amy Tan's *The Kitchen God's Wife* or *The Hundred Secret Senses* and David Wong Louie's story collection *Pangs of Love* or Ruthann Lum McCunn's *Thousand Pieces of Gold*.

206

6. Survey the collapse of folk values after emigrants abandon a homeland culture to come to the United States. Choose examples from Amy Tan's *The Joy Luck Club* or *The Bonesetter's Daughter* and one of the following: Johan Bojer's *The Emigrants*, Sandra Cisneros's *The House on Mango Street*, Laura Esquivel's *Like Water for Chocolate*, or Elie Wiesel's *All Rivers Run to the Sea*.

7. Summarize the political milieu that causes the displacement of refugees like Winnie and Helen in Amy Tan's *The Kitchen God's Wife* or LuLing Liu and GaoLing Liu in *The Bonesetter's Daughter* and similar figures in Barbara Kingsolver's *The Bean Trees*, T. Coraghessan Boyle's *The Tortilla Curtain*, Esther Hautzig's *The Endless Steppe*, Elie Wiesel's *Night*, or August Wilson's *Joe Turner's Come and Gone*. Compare historical conflicts to the situations producing the Long Walk, Trail of Tears, Underground Railroad, Holocaust, Great Migration of Southern blacks to industrialized cities in the North, Okie migration during the Dust Bowl, and murder of Americans by Nicaraguan kidnappers.

8. Identify and explain feelings of cultural and socioeconomic displacement in Amy Tan's *The Hundred Secret Senses*, Harriette Arnow's *The Dollmaker*, and Upton Sinclair's *The Jungle*. Consider examples of neighborliness, urban danger, economic opportunity, religious bigotry, self-respect, bad fortune, family disruptions, poverty and hunger, sickness, and violent death.

9. Account for the domination of self-serving mothers in Amy Tan's *The Joy Luck Club*, Laura Esquivel's *Like Water for Chocolate*, Lillian Hellman's *The Little Foxes*, Marsha Norman's *'night, Mother*, or Tennessee Williams's *The Glass Menagerie*. Chart the damage that accrues to each family member.

10. Contrast the disillusion of newlywed Winnie Louie in Amy Tan's *The Kitchen God's Wife* with that of Celie, the bartered bride in Alice Walker's *The Color Purple*, or Janie Mae Crawford, the runaway wife in Zora Neale Hurston's *Their Eyes Were Watch-ing God*. Depict elements of patriarchal marriage that burden these unions.

11. Select poems that portray a diaspora's disruption of family, such as Cathy Song's "Lost Sister" from the collection *Picture Bride*. Analyze emotions, ambitions, losses, and frustrations that weigh heavily on love relationships, for example, Suyuan Woo's grief over her missing twin daughters in *The Joy Luck Club* and Winnie's fear that Jimmy Louie has found new girlfriends in his folk dancing class in *The Kitchen God's Wife*.

12. Summarize common elements in Amy Tan's favorite works by Asian-American authors: Jessica Hagedorn's *Dogeaters*, Gish Jen's *Typical American*, Maxine Hong Kingston's *The Woman Warrior*, Gus Lee's *Honor and Duty*, Ben Fong Torres's *The Rice Room*, Beth Yahp's *Crocodile Fury*, and Bell Yang's *Baba: Odyssey of a Manchurian*.

13. Chart similarities between the misogyny and repression of women in Tsao Hsueh-chin's *Dream of the Red Chamber* with devaluation and mistreatment of women in Amy Tan's short stories and novels. Stress the victimization of Lindo Jong, Peanut, Winnie Louie, Little Yu, Jiang Sao-yen's second wife, Ying-ying St. Clair, GaoLing Liu, the first wife of Chang the coffinmaker, Wan Betty, Hulan's sister, Li Chen, and Nelly Banner.

14. Compare the role of the older generation in aiding married children and educating grandchildren in Rudolfo Anaya's *Bless Me, Ultima*, Esther Hautzig's *The Endless Steppe*, Amy Tan's *The Kitchen God's Wife* and *The Bonesetter's Daughter*, and Elie Wiesel's *Night*.

15. Describe supernatural qualities in Nunumu, Nelly Banner, Kwan Li, and Olivia Yee bishop in *The Hundred Secret Senses* that reflect similar qualities in the child ghost in Toni Morrison's *Beloved* or the hovering presence of Ruth May Price in Barbara Kingsolver's *The Poisonwood Bible*.

16. Compare scenes of marital discord in Beth Henley's *Crimes of the Heart*, Arthur Miller's *Death of a Salesman*, Lillian Hellman's *The Little Foxes*, Tennessee Williams's *Cat on a Hot Tin Roof*, or August Wilson's *Fences* to the disjointed marriages in Tan's fiction. Note insights and epiphanies that damn patriarchal marriage for its abasement of women, such as the disappearance of Winnie Louie's mother from a polygynous marriage to Jiang Sao-yen, GaoLing Liu's flight from Chang Fu Nan, Peanut's separation from a homosexual husband, Little Yu's suicide, Precious Auntie's rejection of a proposal from Chang the coffinmaker, and the overdose of bitter poison that frees An-mei's mother from the cruel rapist Wu Tsing.

17. Explore examples of maiming and dismemberment in fiction, including images of beheadings and burning deaths in Amy Tan's *The Hundred Secret Senses*, the loss of a child's arm in a train accident and the murder of a stalker in Fannie Flagg's *Fried Green Tomatoes at the Whistlestop Cafe*, the blinding of a child in Allan Gurganous's *The Oldest Living Confederate Widow Tells All*, a husband killed in a trucking accident in Barbara Kingsolver's *Prodigal Summer*, the lopping of a musician's finger in Jane Campion's *The Piano*, and the slicing of a child's throat in Toni Morrison's *Beloved*. Note in particular attitudes toward healing, sharing, secrecy, dedication, and the judgments of relatives and other people. Explain how women provide humor as well as wisdom to the text.

18. Summarize elements of LuLing Liu's life in *The Bonesetter's Daughter* with her foster parents, in the orphanage, and after her marriage to Pan Kai Jing that compare with the rise of Jane Eyre from rejection to self-fulfillment in Charlotte Brontë's *Jane Eyre*. Add commentary about similarities in the life of the unnamed wife in Daphne du Maurier's *Rebecca*, Victoria Holt's *Mistress of Mellyn*, or Jean Rhys's *Wide Sargasso Sea*, all of which display the influence of Brontë's Gothic masterwork.

19. Contrast the struggles of the sisters in Yoko Kawashima Watkins's autobiographical *So Far from the Bamboo Grove*, Anita Diamant's *The Red Tent*, or Suzanne Staples Fisher's *Shabanu: Daughter of the Wind* with the differences that separate Kwan Li and Olivia Yee Bishop in *The Hundred Secret Senses* or LuLing Liu and Gaoling Liu in *The Bonesetter's Daughter*. Determine how local customs, violence, secrets, silence, and unavoidable events impact the lives of these pairs of siblings.

20. Select contrasting scenes and describe their pictorial qualities, for example:

- confinement and the burning deaths of Manchu invaders at the caves outside Changmian, China, in *The Hundred Secret Senses*
- Precious Auntie's burned face, teeth, and tongue in *The Bonesetter's Daughter*
- the site of the accident that wrecks a Fiat in *The Kitchen God's Wife*
- Winnie's shopping trips for a trousseau and scissors in *The Kitchen God's Wife*
- the meeting of June Woo and her twin sisters Chwun Hwa and Chwun Yu at a Shanghai airport in *The Joy Luck Club*
- discovery of Nelly Banner's bag in the gazebo in *The Hundred Secret Senses*
- Rich Schields's dinner at the Jong residence in *The Joy Luck Club*
- Simon Bishop's photographic studies at a Changmian market in *The Hundred Secret Senses*
- Helen's stolen pedicab and defensive stick in *The Kitchen God's Wife*
- practice brush strokes of calligraphy in *The Bonesetter's Daughter*
- the procession that concludes Auntie Du Ching's funeral in *The Joy Luck Club*
- LuLing's fall from a window in *The Bonesetter's Daughter*.

21. Discuss the role of youthful self-discovery and autonomy in mother-daughter alienation in *The Joy Luck Club*. Contrast these scenarios with similar scenes in Jamaica Kincaid's *Annie John*, Paule Marshall's *Brown Girl, Brownstones*, Terri McMillan's *Mama*, Toni Morrison's *Beloved*, and Alice Walker's *Meridian*.

22. Compare the courtships and sexual relationships in *The Joy Luck Club*, *The Kitchen God's Wife*, or *The Bonesetter's Daughter* to similar male-female matchups in Isabel Allende's *Daughter of Fortune*, Olive Ann Burns's *Cold Sassy Tree*, Virginia Renfro Ellis's *The Wedding Dress*, Charles Frazier's *Cold Mountain*, Ernest J. Gaines's *The Autobiography of Miss Jane Pittman*, David Guterson's *Snow Falling on Cedars*, or Margaret Walker's *Jubilee*. Contrast obstacles to each couple's happiness, including war, separation, racial and cultural differences, and male dominance.

23. Write an extended definition of *confinement* using examples from *The Kitchen God's Wife*. Compare Winnie Louie's situation in a women's prison to the imprisonment of Hester Prynne in Nathaniel Hawthorne's *The Scarlet Letter*, the immurement of the Wakatsuki family in a detention camp in Jeanne Wakatsuki Houston and James Houston's *A Farewell to Manzanar*, Dana Franklin's time-tripping back to a Maryland slave quarters in Octavia Butler's *Kindred*, Olivia Rivers's unhappiness in a colonial compound in Ruth Prawer Jhabvala's *Heat and Dust*, or the wife locked in an asylum in Charlotte Perkins Gilman's "The Yellow Wallpaper."

24. Compare the urgency of overturning injustice in *The Kitchen God's Wife* with the same theme in Adrienne Rich's "Snapshots of a Daughter-in-Law," Sylvia Plath's "Daddy," and Anne Sexton's "Her Kind."

25. Describe elements of Joy Harjo's poem "For Alva Benson, and For Those Who Have Learned to Speak" that reflect similar condemnation of enforced silence in *The Bonesetter's Daughter*.

26. Improvise a discussion between Amy Tan, Cathy Song, and Rita Dove on the subject of female role models as depicted in *The Joy Luck Club* or *The Bonesetter's Daughter*, Song's images of female authority in "The White Porch," and Dove's description of teenage girls in "Adolescents—I, II, III."

27. Summarize the resources of strong women in Barbara Kingsolver's *Prodigal Summer*, Kaye Gibbons's *Charms for the Easy Life*, and Amy Tan's *The Joy Luck Club*. Note the reliance on education and hard work in folk healer and midwife Miss Charlie Kate Birch and her granddaughter Margaret, orchard keeper Nannie Land Rawley, forest ranger Deanna Wolfe, cancer victim Jewel Widener Walker, farmer and goatherd Lusa Maluf Landowski, refugee Suyuan Woo, shopgirl Ying-ying St. Clair, divorcee Lindo Jong, and abandoned child An-mei Hsu. Express efforts to pass worthy virtues to the younger generation.

28. List and describe a variety of narrative forms and styles in Amy Tan's writings, including talk-story, personal essay, dialogue, anecdote, satire, genealogy, fable, folklore, comic relief, pun, morality tale, myth, malapropism, irony, and ghost story.

29. Compare the roles of Lindo Jong, An-mei Hsu, Suyuan Woo, Ying-ying St. Clair, Winnie Louie, Helen Kwong, Kwan Li, Nunumu, LuLing Liu Young, and Precious Auntie as advisers and bearers of wisdom. Explain how the author uses compromise and nonviolence as strategies to neutralize hostility, for example, Winnie's efforts to placate Wen Fu and Nunumu's rescue of Nelly Banner from certain death at the mission compound.

30. Choose two characters from Amy Tan's works to compare in terms of religious beliefs, for example, An-mei Hsu's prayers to Jesus and Buddha, Winnie Louie's respect of Buddhism, Nunumu's rejection of Christianity, Sister Yu's departure from Christianity to Communism, Jiang's wife's fanaticism, and Kwan Li's cultivation of spirits.

31. Hypothesize the attitudes and roles of peripheral characters in Amy Tan's short stories and novels. Include Robert in "Fish Cheeks," Pastor Amen, Big Ma, Rocky, Dr. Huey, Bonesetter Gu, Elza Marie Vandervort, Min, Canning Woo, Bing Hsu, San Ma and Wu Ma, Little Yu's mother, Zeng, Uncle Jiang, Shoshana Chen, Mei Ching, Yiku,

Miriam, Bob Laguni, Du Lili, Buncake, and Rich Schields.

32. Characterize the importance of setting to significant scenes in Amy Tan's works, for example, Sagwa's marks on the parchment, Kwan Li's disappearance in a cave at Thistle Mountain, Lindo Jong's haircut in Mr. Rory's salon, Ruth Luyi's visit to Mira Mar Manor, Winnie's eavesdropping at the porch before her wedding, LuLing's examination of a battered child, Gan's death in the hospital from disembowelment, June Woo's first game of mah jong with the Joy Luck Club, LuLing's first trip to Peking, Ying-ying's tumble into the lake, and Jack Yee's deathbed confession and request.

33. Summarize the Chinese values of the mother in "Fish Cheeks." Compare her devotion to traditional foodways and courtesy with the beliefs of An-mei Hsu's mother, Rose Hsu Jordan, Lena St. Clair Livotny, Old Aunt, Auntie Aiyi, Nelly Banner, Du Lili, GaoLing Liu Young, and LuLing Liu Young.

34. Using characters from Amy Tan's novels and stories, outline a screenplay about pre–Communist China that explains why so many of her characters emigrate, particularly GaoLing Liu, Canning and Suyuan Woo, Lindo Jong, Winnie Louie, LuLing Liu, Dr. Lin, Helen Kwong, and Kwan Li.

35. Locate examples of racism, scapegoating, and exclusion in Jeanne Wakatsuki Houston and James Houston's *A Farewell to Manzanar*, James Michener's *Hawaii*, Barbara Kingsolver's *The Poisonwood Bible*, August Wilson's *Ma Rainey's Black Bottom*, David Guterson's *Snow Falling on Cedars*, Jerry Bock's *Fiddler on the Roof*, Conrad Richter's *The Light in the Forest*, or Forrest Carter's *The Education of Little Tree* that compare with Kwan Li's or LuLing Liu's sufferings in urban California.

36. Compare the ambitions, regrets, and yearnings of Art Kamen, Precious Auntie, Waverly Jong, Simon Bishop, Helen Kwong, Pan Kai Jing, Rose Hsu Jordan, and Ruth Liyu Young with those of characters in

Gary Paulsen's *Nightjohn*, Robin Lee Graham's *Dove*, John Updike's "The Ex-Basketball Player," Laurel Thatcher Ulrich's *A Midwife's Tale: The Life of Martha Ballard*, Richard Bach's *Jonathan Livingston Seagull*, Maya Angelou's *Now Sheba Sings the Song*, Jesse Stuart's *The Thread That Runs So True*, or Irving Stone's *Lust for Life*.

37. Account for the images that Amy Tan chooses for titles: "Two Kinds," "Fish Cheeks," "Mother Tongue," "The Shop of the Gods," "Fisher of Men," "The Valley of Statues," "Lost Lives of Women," "American Translation," "Watching China," "A Pair of Tickets," "In the Canon for all the Wrong Reasons," "Best Quality," "The Best Time to Eat Duck Eggs," and "Truth." What do these choices reveal about her major themes?

38. Contrast parental strengths in Tan's fictional mothers and fathers, particularly Winnie's mother and Jiang Sao-yen, Canning and Suyuan Woo, Precious Auntie and Liu Hu Sen, Winnie and Wen Fu, Li Chen and Jack Yee, Louise and Bob Laguni, Olivia and Simon Bishop, Ying-ying and Clifford St. Clair, Jimmy and Winnie Louie, and the parents in "Fish Cheeks." Mention the courage of Bonsetter Gu for leaving his daughter's feet unbound and for teaching her about healing and herbalism.

39. List and describe the drama of realistic elements from "Fish Cheeks," "Mother Tongue," *The Joy Luck Club*, *The Kitchen God's Wife*, *The Moon Lady*, *The Hundred Secret Senses*, *The Chinese Siamese Cat*, and *The Bonesetter's Daughter*. Stress the wreck of the Fiat, falling overboard at a festival on the lake, preserving eggs, making inksticks, hiding in the caves of Thistle Mountain, settling a divorce, interpreting for a non–English-speaking parent, jettisoning a body at the End of the World, honoring Auntie Du with a Buddhist funeral, photographing Changmian, retrieving gold ingots, viewing Lady Chang-o, searching for Bing Hsu's body, preparing a Christmas Eve meal, and reading new laws to the public.

40. Summarize universal themes in Amy Tan's fiction, particularly wartime

separations, spousal abuse, social upheaval, loss of wealth and family heirlooms, disillusion, and difficulties of parenthood. Contrast these to Chinese themes, particularly feudal marriage, silenced females, foot-binding, Confucian traditions, and unquestioned obedience to parents.

41. Analyze Amy Tan's storytelling style. Discuss stories-within-stories, fables, recovered manuscripts, aphorisms, dreamscapes, and story-talk along with dialogue, circular narrative, and personal narrative. Determine why particular combinations of methods suit *The Hundred Secret Senses* and *The Bonesetter's Daughter*.

42. Create a role for an outsider in Amy Tan's China scenes, for example, a Caucasian anthropologist aiding geologist Pan Kai Jing in surveying Peking Man, an American telegrapher typing messages for Wan Betty, an immigrant replacing stock at the inkstick shop in Peking, and a European journalist covering wartime traffic along the Burma Road. Comment on views of outsiders at dramatic moments, particularly the bombing of Nanking, search for a missing woman in the caves of Thistle Mountain, return of the Kuomintang to power in Shanghai, treatment of a child for burns, identification and burial of victims of the Taiping Rebellion, retrieval of an infant from his mother's dead body, and a meeting of three sisters at the Shanghai airport.

43. Act out an interview with new arrivals to California. Question Winnie Louie about the conditions in Shanghai as Communists approach the city. Ask LuLing Liu how she plans to display her talents at calligraphy. Counsel Canning Woo on methods of searching for twin daughters that Suyuan left behind in China. Interview Helen Kwong about the panic that followed the Japanese bombing of Nanking.

44. Summarize Amy Tan's method of composition and self-editing as described in *The Opposite of Fate*. Explain how she incorporates autobiographical events and details by reshaping them into fiction, for example, her mother, Daisy Tan, as Winnie Louie.

45. Discuss Tan's use of medical details as character motivation, for example, brain aneurysm, suicide, and depression in *The Joy Luck Club*, Alzheimer's disease, addiction to opium, and facial trauma in *The Bonesetter's Daughter*, infertility, insanity, and depression in *The Hundred Secret Senses*, mental illness, depression, and brain tumor in *The Opposite of Fate*, and stroke, multiple sclerosis, cranial trauma, stomach cancer, disembowelment, suicide, stillbirth, heart disease, and brain tumor in *The Kitchen God's Wife*.

Bibliography

A Chronology of Primary Sources

"Endgame." *FM*, 1986; reprinted in *Seventeen*, November 1986 as "Rules of the Game," pp. 106–108; *Norton Anthology of Contemporary Fiction* (Norton, 1987); *Growing Up Ethnic in America* (Penguin, 1999); *Norton Anthology of Short Fiction* (Norton, 2000).

"Fish Cheeks." *Seventeen*, December 1987, p. 99; reprinted in *The Opposite of Fate: A Book of Musings* (2003).

The Joy Luck Club. New York: Putnam, 1989.

"The Joy Luck Club." *Ladies' Home Journal*, March 1989; *Granta Book of the American Short Story* (Penguin, 1998).

"Two Kinds." *Atlantic Monthly*, Vol. 263, No. 2, February 1989, pp. 53–57; *Harper Anthology of Fiction* (Longman, 1991); *Growing Up Female* (Mentor, 1993); *Fiction: A Longman Pocket Anthology* (Addison-Wesley, 1998); *Scribner Anthology of Contemporary Short Fiction* (Scribner, 1999).

"Watching China." *Glamour*, 1989, pp. 302–303.

"Amy Tan and *The Joy Luck Club*." *California State Library Foundation Bulletin*, Vol. 31, April 1990.

"The Language of Discretion." *The State of the Language*. Berkeley: University of California Press, 1990, pp. 25–32; reprinted in *The Opposite of Fate* (2003).

"Mother Tongue." *Threepenny Review*, Fall 1990; reprinted in *Best American Essays, 1991* and in the *Canadian Reader's Digest*, December 1999, p. 48.

"Angst and the Second Novel." *Publishers Weekly*, April 5, 1991, pp. 4–7; reprinted in *The Opposite of Fate* (2003).

"Excerpt: *The Kitchen God's Wife*." *McCall's*, July 1991.

The Kitchen God's Wife. New York: Putnam, 1991.

"Lecture for Asian American Student Union." Van Hise Hall, Madison, Wisconsin, April 11, 1991.

"Lost Lives of Women: My Grandmother's Choice." *Life*, Vol. 14, April 1991, pp. 90–91; reprinted in *The Opposite of Fate* (2003).

A Closer Look: The Writer's Reader. New York: McGraw-Hill, 1991.

"Peanut's Fortune." *Grand Street*, Vol. 10, No. 2, Winter 1991, pp. 10–22.

The Moon Lady. New York: Macmillan, 1992.

"Alien Relative," in *Charlie Chan Is Dead*. New York: Viking Penguin, 1993.

"Amy Tan," in *Writers Dreaming*. New York: Carol Southern, 1993.

"Half and Half." *Worlds of Fiction*. New York: Macmillan, 1993.

"Joy Luck and Hollywood." *Los Angeles Times*, September 5, 1996, p. 6.

The Joy Luck Club (screenplay). Hollywood: Hollywood Pictures, 1993.

The Chinese Siamese Cat. New York: Macmillan, 1994.

"Introduction." *You've Got to Read This*. New York: HarperPerennial, 1994.

"Midlife Confidential," in *Mid-Life Confidential*. New York: Viking, 1994.

"A Pair of Tickets." *Oxford Book of Modern Women's Stories*, Oxford University Press, 1994; *An Introduction to Fiction*, New York: Longman, 1999; *Short Fiction*, New York: Prentice Hall, 1999; *Longman Anthology of Short Fiction*, New York: Longman, 2000.

The Hundred Secret Senses. New York: Putnam, 1995.

"Biting Mother Tongue" (poem). *Paintbrush*, Vol. 22, 1995, p. 67.

"The Voice from the Wall." *Points of View*. New York: Mentor, 1995.

"Young Girl's Wish." *New Yorker*, October 2, 1995, p. 80; *Fiction 100: An Anthology of Short Stories*. New York: Prentice Hall, 2000.

"Required Reading and Other Dangerous Subjects." *Threepenny Review*, Fall 1996; reprinted in *The Opposite of Fate* (2003).

"In the Canon for all the Wrong Reasons." *Harper's*, Vol. 293, December 1996, pp. 27–31.

"Amy Tan's Personal Best: *Lolita*." *Salon*, September 30, 1996; reprinted in *The Opposite of Fate* (2003).

"Required Reading and Other Dangerous Subjects," in *Threepenny Review*, Fall 1996; reprinted in *Out of the Mold: Independent Voices Breaking Out of the Mold*, Tarrytown, N.Y.: American Booksellers Association, 1997.

"Amy Tan on Writing, Setting the Voice." *An Introduction to Fiction*, New York: Longman, 1999; *The Longman Anthology of Short Fiction*, New York: Longman, 2000.

"The Best Stories." *Best American Short Stories 1999* (editor). Boston: Houghton-Mifflin, 1999; reprinted in *The Opposite of Fate* (2003).

"Best Quality." *A Web of Stories: An Introduction to Short Fiction*. Prentice Hall, 1998.

"Two Vignettes." *Many Californias*. Reno: University of Nevada Press, 1999.

"Why I Write." *Literary Cavalcade*, Vol. 99, No. 51, March 1999, pp. 10–13.

The Bonesetter's Daughter. New York: Putnam, 2001; excerpted in *Literary Cavalcade*, April 2001, Vol. 53, No. 7, p. 4; *World & I*, July 2001, Vol. 16, No. 7, p. 207; and *Faith: Stories*, Myrtle Point, Ore.: Mariner, 2003.

Sagwa: The Chinese Siamese Cat (PBS-TV). Los Angeles: Kids' Station, 2001.

"Writers on Writing: Family Ghosts Hoard Secrets That Bewitch the Living." *New York Times*, February 26, 2001; reprinted in *The Opposite of Fate* (2003).

Mother (contributor). New York: Pocket Books, 2002.

Classic Chinese Cuisine (foreword). Boston: Houghton Mifflin, 2003.

"Five Writing Tips," commencement address at Simmons College, Boston, 2003; reprinted in *The Opposite of Fate* (2003).

"How We Knew," in "Most Romantic Moments." *Harper's Bazaar*, February 2003, pp. 207–212; reprinted in *The Opposite of Fate* (2003).

The Opposite of Fate: A Book of Musings. New York: G. P. Putnam, 2003.

"Without Wood," in *Lives in Two Languages: An Exploration of Identity and Culture* (University of Michigan Press, 2003).

Secondary Sources

Adams, Bella. "Representing History in Amy Tan's *The Kitchen God's Wife*." *MELUS*, Vol. 28, No. 2, Summer 2003, pp. 9–30.

Allen, Moira. "@Deadline." *Writer*, Vol. 114, No. 6, June 2001, pp. 12–14.

Amry, Shireem. "Review: *The Bonesetter's Daughter*." *New Straits Times*, April 11, 2001.

"Amy Tan (interview). http://www.bbc.co.uk/religion/programmes/belief/scripts/amy_tan.shtml.

"Amy Tan (interview)." Phoenix *Arizona Republic*, October 5, 1993.

"Amy Tan Faces Her Fears." *BBC World Service*, May 10, 2001.

Angier, Carole. "Chinese Customs." *New Statesman & Society*, Vol. 2, No. 95, June 30, 1989, p. 35.

Anschel, Eugene Homer Lea. *Sun Yat-sen and the Chinese Revolution*. Westport, Conn.: Greenwood, 1984.

Archer, Jules. *Mao Tse-Tung*. New York: Hawthorn Books, 1972.

Avins, Mimi. "How to Tell the Players in 'The Joy Luck Club.'" *New York Times*, September 5, 1993.

Bacalzo, Dan. "All Over the Map." http://www.theatermania.com/content/news.cfm?int_news_id=2976, January 9, 2003.

Baker, John F. "Fresh Voices, New Audiences." *Publishers Weekly*, August 9, 1993, pp. 32–34.

Balee, Susan. "True to Form." *Philadelphia Enquirer*, February 18, 2001.

Bannister, Linda. "Three Women Revise: What Morrison, Oates, and Tan Can Teach Our Students About Revision," paper delivered to the Conference on College Composition and Communication, March 31–April 3, 1993, ERIC.

Bard, Nancy. "Adult Books for Young Adults." *School Library Journal*, Vol. 37, No. 12, December 1991, p. 149.

Barras, Jonetta Rose. "'Kitchen' Provides Complex Look at Relations of Women." *Washington Times*, July 15, 1991, pp. C6–C7.

Bauers, Sandy. "*The Bonesetter's Daughter* Is Amy Tan's Best." *Philadelphia Inquirer*, March 20, 2001.

Beason, Tyrone. "Tan's Musings Blend Dark and Light, Past and Present." *Seattle Times*, October 31, 2001.

Behe, Regis. "Writer Amy Tan Relies On 'The Opposite of Fate' to Get By." *Pittsburgh Tribune-Review*, December 3, 2003.

"Beijing Determined to Censor Outside Voice." *American Libraries*, Vol. 27, No. 5, May 1996, p. 28.

Benedict, Kitty. "Mother to Daughter: Here Is the Truth of My Life." *Hartford Courant*, June 30, 1991, p. C10.

Benjamin, Susan J. "Review: *The Joy Luck Club*." *English Journal*, October 1990, p. 82.

Bennett, Elizabeth. "The Joy and Good Luck of Amy Tan." *Houston Post*, July 14, 1991, pp. C1–C2.

Bernikow, Louise. "Review: *The Kitchen God's Wife*." *Cosmopolitan*, Vol. 210, No. 6, June 1991, p. 36.

Bertodano, Helene de. "A Life Stranger Than Fiction." *Daily Telegraph*, November 11, 2003.

"Bestselling Author Amy Tan Is a Wonder-ful Storyteller." *Chinatown News*, Vol. 43, No. 8, February 18, 1996, pp. 22–23.

Boaz, Noel T., and Russell L. Ciochon. "The Scavenging of 'Peking Man.'" *Natural History*, Vol. 110, No. 2, March 2001, p. 46.

Braendlin, Bonnie. "Mother/Daughter Dialog(ic)s In, Around, and About Amy Tan's *The Joy Luck Club*." *Synthesis: An Interdisciplinary Journal*, Vol. 1, No. 2, Fall 1995, pp. 41–53.

Briggs, Tracey Wong. "'Hundred Secret Senses': Tan's Nimble Trip into the Spirit World." *USA Today*, October 26, 1995.

Brownstone, David M. *The Chinese-American Heritage*. New York: Facts on File, 1988.

Bruckner, D. J. R. "For These Bonded Souls, Some Luck but Little Joy." *New York Times*, April 27, 1999.

Bunce, Kim. "Review: *The Bonesetter's Daughter*." *Guardian Unlimited*, March 18, 2001.

Caesar, Judith. "Patriarchy, Imperialism, and Knowledge in *The Kitchen God's Wife*." *North Dakota Quarterly*, Vol. 62, No. 4, 1994-1995, pp. 164–174.

Caldwell, Gail. "Review: *The Hundred Secret Senses*." *Boston Globe*, October 22, 1995, p. B37.

Cardozo, Erica L. "The Spirits Are with Her." *Entertainment Weekly*, No. 298, October 27, 1995, p. 84.

Carlin, Margaret. "Writing for Herself." *Rocky Mountain News*, September 26, 1992, p. E1.

Casey, Constance. "Amy Tan's Second Book Focuses on the Overlooked Woman." *San Diego Union*, June 16, 1991, pp. C4–C5.

Chambers, Vernica. "Surprised by Joy." *Premiere*, Vol. 7, No. 2, October 1993, pp. 80–84.

Chang, Jeff. "Up Identity Creek." *Color Lines*, Vol. 1, No. 3, Winter 1999.

Chang, Joan Chiung-Heiu. *Transforming Chinese American Literature: A Study of History, Sexuality, and Ethnicity*. New York: Peter Lang, 2000.

Chang, Margaret A. "Review: *The Chinese Siamese Cat*." *School Library Journal*, Vol. 40, No. 11, November 1994, p. 91.

"Charity Ends at Home." *Economist*, Vol. 339, No. 7,960, p. 39.

Chatfield-Taylor, Joan. "Cosmo Talks to

Amy Tan: Dazzling New Literary Light." *Cosmopolitan*, Vol. 207, November 1989, p. 178–180.

Cheung, King-Kok. *An Interethnic Companion to Asian American Literature*. New York: Cambridge University Press, 1997.

Chin, Frank. "Come All Ye Asian American Writers of the Real and the Fake." *The Big Aiiieeeee!: An Anthology of Chinese American and Japanese American Literature*. New York: Meridian, 1991, pp. 1–92.

Chiu, Christina. *Lives of Notable Asian Americans: Literature and Education*. New York: Chelsea House, 1996.

Chong, Denise. "Emotions Journeys through East and West." *Quill and Quire*, Vol. 55, No. 5, 1989, p. 23.

Chua, C. L. "Review: *The Kitchen God's Wife*." *Magill's Literary Annual*. Englewood Cliffs, N.J.: Salem Press, 1992.

Chung, L. A. "Chinese American Literary War: Writers, Critics Argue Over Portrayal of Asians." *San Francisco Chronicle*, August 26, 1991, p. D4.

Clarey, Kathey. "Amy Tan's Literary Concerns." *Fresno Bee*, October 5, 1994, p. B1.

Clarke, Stella. "More Secrets of the Mama Sisterhood." *Australian*, March 10, 2001.

Condini, Ned. "Saints, Histories, Carnal Acts: Best Reads in 1991." *National Catholic Reporter*, Vol. 28, No. 5, November 22, 1991, p. 36.

Cooperman, Jeannette Batz. *The Broom Closet: Secret Meanings of Domesticity in Postfeminist Novels by Louise Erdrich, Mary Gordon, Toni Morrison, Marge Piercy, Jane Smiley, and Amy Tan*. New York: Peter Lang, 1999.

Craft, Stephen G. "Peacemakers in China: American Missionaries and the Sino-Japanese War, 1937–1941." *Journal of Church & State*, Vol. 41, No. 3, Summer 1999, pp. 575–591.

Craig, Paul. "More Luck for Amy Tan." *Sacramento Bee*, July 14, 1991, p. C5.

Cujec, Carol. "Excavating Memory, Reconstructing Legacy." *World & I*, Vol. 16, No. 7, July 2001, pp. 215–223.

Davis, Emory. "An Interview with Amy Tan: Fiction — The Beast That Roams." *Writing-on-the-Edge*, Spring 1990, pp. 97–111.

Davis, Robert Murray. "West Meets East: A Conversation with Frank Chin." *Amerasia Journal*, Vol. 24, No. 1, Spring 1998, pp. 87–103.

Davis, Rocio G. "Amy Tan's *The Kitchen God's Wife*: An American Dream Come True — in China," in *Notes on Contemporary Literature*, Vol. 24, No. 5, 1994, pp. 3–5.

_____. "Identity in Community in Ethnic Short Story Cycles: Amy Tan's *The Joy Luck Club*, Louise Erdrich's *Love Medicine*, Gloria Naylor's *The Women of Brewster Place*," in *Ethnicity and the American Short Story*. New York: Garland, 1997.

_____, and Sami Ludwig. *Asian American Literature in the International Context: Readings on Fiction, Poetry and Performance*. London: Lit Verlag, 2002.

Del Negro, Janice. "Review: *The Chinese Siamese Cat*." *Booklist*, Vol. 91, No. 3, October 1, 1994, p. 335.

Denbi, David. "Review: The Joy Luck Club." *New York*, September 2, 1993, p. 64.

Denison, D. C. "Amy Tan." *Boston Sunday Globe*, June 28, 1991, p. 63.

Dew, Robb Forman. "Pangs of an Abandoned Child." *New York Times Book Review*, June 16, 1991, p. 9.

Dixler, Elsa. "Our Holiday Lists." *Nation*, Vol. 253, No. 23, December 30, 1991, pp. 851–852.

Donahue, Deirdre. "Tan's Books Excavate Life's Joy and Pain." *USA Today*, February 19, 2001, pp. 1D–2D.

Donovan, Mary Ann. "Review: *The Joy Luck Club*." *America*, Vol. 163, No. 15, November 17, 1990, p. 372.

Dooley, Susan. "Mah-Jongg and the Ladies of the Club." *Washington Post Book World*, March 5, 1989, p. 7.

Dorris, Michael. "Mothers and Daughters." *Chicago Tribune*, March 12, 1989, pp. 1, 11.

Doten, Patti. "Sharing Her Mother's Secrets." *Boston Globe*, June 21, 1991, p. 63.

Durrant, Sabine. "Review: *The Kitchen God's Wife*." *London Times*, July 11, 1991, p. 16.

Eastman, Lloyd, et al. *The Nationalist Era in China, 1927–1949*. New York: Cambridge University Press, 1991.

Eberhart, George, et al. "ALA Thinks Globally, Acts Federally." *American Libraries*, Vol. 29, No. 7, August 1998, pp. 70–83.

Edwards, Jami. "Amy Tan." http://www.book reporter.com/authors/au-tan-amy.asp.

Ellison, Emily. "Tragic Story Dazzles and Awes." *Atlanta Journal*, June 16, 1991, pp. C12–C13.

Erdrich, Louise. "What Writers Are Reading." *Ms.*, Vol. 2, No. 1, July/August 1991, pp. 82–83.

Feldman, Gayle. "*The Joy Luck Club:* Chinese Magic, American Blessings, and a Publishing Fairy Tale." *Publishers Weekly*, Vol. 236, July 7, 1989, p. 24.

_____. "Spring's Five Fictional Encounters of the Chinese American Kind." *Publishers Weekly*, Vol. 238, No. 8, February 8, 1991, pp. 25–27.

Fenster, Bob. "Singing Author's Luck Holds in Bringing Book to Film." (Phoenix) *Arizona Republic*, October 5, 1993.

"A Fiery Mother-Daughter Relationship." *USA Today*, October 5, 1993, p. D12.

Finlayson, Iain. "Chinese Whispers with Humour." *Chinatown News*, Vol. 43, No. 9, March 1, 1996, pp. 38–39.

Fisher, Ann H. "Review: *The Kitchen God's Wife*." *Library Journal*, Vol. 116, No. 10, June 1, 1991, p. 198.

Fong, Yem Siu. "Review: *The Joy Luck Club*." *Frontiers*, Vol. 6, No. 2–3, 1990, pp. 122–123.

Fong-Torres, Ben. "Can Amy Tan Do It Again?" *San Francisco Chronicle*, June 12, 1991, pp. B3, B4.

Foran, Charles. "Review: *The Kitchen God's Wife*." *Toronto Globe and Mail*, June 29, 1991.

Fortuna, Diana. "Review: *The Hundred Secret Senses*." *America*, Vol. 174, No. 14, May 4, 1996, pp. 27–28.

Frostchild, Daphne. "Reading the Past." *Wag*, March 2001.

Fry, Donna. "The Joy and Luck of Amy Tan." *Seattle Times*, July 7, 1991, pp. C3–C4.

Ganahl, Jane. "Amy Tan Gets Her Voice Back." *West Egg Communications*, January 2001, p. 40.

Gates, David. "A Game of Show Not Tell." *Newsweek*, Vol. 113, No. 16, April 17, 1989, pp. 68–69.

Giles, Gretchen. "Ghost Writer." *Sonoma Independent*, December 14–20, 1995.

Gillen, Marilyn A. "The Rock Bottom Remainders." *Billboard*, Vol. 104, No. 44, October 31, 1992, p. 51.

Gillespie, Elzy. "Review: *The Kitchen God's Wife*." *San Francisco Review of Books*, Summer 1991, p. 33.

Golding, William. *Asian-American Women Writers*. New York: Chelsea House, 1998.

Goodavage, Maria. "'The Joy Luck Club' Is Born from Her Life of Hardship." *USA Today*, October 5, 1993, p. 12D.

Gray, Paul. "The Joys and Sorrows of Amy Tan." *Time*, February 19, 2001, pp. 72–74.

Guixia, Liang. "Complex Relationships Between Chinese-Born Mother and American-Born Daughters as Reflected in Amy Tan's *Joy Luck Club*." *International Review*, 2001.

Gupta, Himanee. "Novelist's Efforts Led to Her Own True Voice." *Seattle Times*, January 10, 1991, p. E4.

Gurley, George. "Amy Tan: The Ghosts and the Writer." *Kansas City Star*, April 22, 1998.

Guy, David. "Hilarious and Terrifying: Chinese Mother Haunts Collection of Autobiographical Essays." *Houston Chronicle*, December 19, 2003.

_____. "Wheel of Fortune: A Writer's Thoughts on Joy, Luck and Heartache." *Washington Post*, November 2, 2002, p. T4.

Hajari, Nisid. "Luck Is What You Make It." *Entertainment Weekly*, September 24, 1993, pp. 30–33.

Hamilton, Patricia L. "Feng Shui, Astrology, and the Five Elements: Traditional Chinese Belief in Amy Tan's *The Joy Luck Club*." *MELUS*, Vol. 24, No. 2, Summer 1999, pp. 125–145.

Hansen, Liane. "Author Amy Tan Discusses Her Latest Book, Her Mother, Her Supposedly Cursed Life, and Her Participation in the Rock Bottom Remainders." *Weekend Edition Sunday* (NPR), November 9, 2003.

Harleman, Ann. "Destiny's Runaway." *Boston Globe*, November 30, 2003.

Harrington, Maureen. "Tan's Immigrant Tale Top Quality." *Denver Post*, June 23, 1991, p. C9.

Haskell, Molly. "Movie of the Month — *The Joy Luck Club* Based on the Book by Amy Tan." *Ladies' Home Journal*, Vol. 110, No. 10, October 1993, p. 54.

Hawley, John C. "Assimilation and Resistance in Female Fiction of Immigration: Bharati Mukherjee, Amy Tan, and Christine Bell," in *Rediscovering America 1492–1992: National, Cultural and Disciplinary Boundaries Re-Examined.* Baton Rouge: Louisiana State University Press, 1992, pp. 226–234.

Herbert, Rosemary. "'Fate' Accompli: Amy Tan Shares a Lifetime of Writings in Her New Book." *Boston Herald,* November 7, 2003.

Heung, Marina. "Daughter-Text/Mother-Text: Matrilineage in Amy Tan's Joy Luck Club." *Feminist Studies,* Vol. 19, No. 3, Fall 1993, pp. 597–616.

Hicks, Ann. "Plot Luck." *Cincinnati Enquirer,* May 18, 1992, p. C14.

Ho, Wendy. *In Her Mother's House — The Politics of Asian American Mother-Daughter Writing.* Walnut Creek, Calif.: Alta-Mira Press, 1999.

Hoggard, Liz. "Death as a Source of Life." *Guardian Unlimited,* November 23, 2003.

Holt, Patricia. "Amy Tan Hits the Jackpot with Her First Novel." *San Francisco Chronicle,* March 27, 1989, p. C3.

_____. "Between the Lines— Students Read a Lot Into Amy Tan." *San Francisco Chronicle,* August 18, 1996.

_____. "The Shuffle Over 'Joy Luck.'" *San Francisco Chronicle Review,* July 16, 1989, p. 2.

Howe, Joyce. "Chinese in America: Telling the Immigrant Story." *East Bay Express,* October 1991, pp. 1, 14–15.

Hubbard, Kim. "*The Joy Luck Club* Has Brought Writer Amy Tan a Bit of Both." *People Weekly,* Vol. 31, April 10, 1989, pp. 149–150.

Hughes, Kathryn. "Sweet-Sour." *New Statesman and Society,* Vol. 4, No. 159, July 12, 1991, pp. 37–38.

Hull, Akasha. "Uncommon Language." *Women's Review of Books,* Vol. 18, No. 9, June 2001, p. 13.

Humphreys, Josephine. "Secret Truths: Amy Tan Writes of Fate and Luck." *Chicago Tribune,* June 9, 1991, pp. 1, 5.

Hunt, Adam Paul. "Audio Review: *The Kitchen God's Wife.*" *Library Journal,* Vol. 116, No. 12, July 1991, p. 154.

Huntley, E. D. *Amy Tan: A Critical Companion.* Westport, Conn.: Greenwood Press, 1998.

"Interview: Amy Tan." http://www.achievement.org/autodoc/page/tan0int-1, June 28, 1996.

Ishizuka, Kathy. *Asian American Authors.* New York: Enslow, 2000.

Iyer, Pico. "The Second Triumph of Amy Tan." *Time,* Vol. 137, No. 22, June 3, 1991, p. 67.

Jacobs, Alexandra. "Eight Day Week." *New York Observer,* May 7, 2001.

James Caryn. "Relax, but Don't Leave Your Mind Behind." *New York Times,* May 31, 1991, pp. C1, C5.

Jasmin, Ernest A. "Amy Tan Will See Play Based on 'Joy Luck Club.'" *Tacoma News Tribune,* February 13, 2004.

Kakutani, Michiko. "Sisters Looking for Ghosts in China." *New York Times,* November 17, 1995, p. C29.

Kanner, Ellen. "From Amy Tan, a Superb Novel of Two Sisters, Two Worlds, and a Few Ghosts." *Bookpage,* December 1995, p. 3.

Kepner, Susan. "Imagine This: The Amazing Adventure of Amy Tan." *San Francisco Examiner Focus,* May 1989, pp. 58–60, 161–162.

Kester-Shelton, Pamela, ed. *Feminist Writers.* Detroit: St. James Press, 1996.

Keung, Nicholas. "Writer Found Role as 'Alienated Narrator.'" *Toronto Star,* June 10, 2003.

Kidder, Gayle. "Giving Up Ghosts." *San Diego Union,* June 16, 1991, pp. C6–C7.

Kim, Elaine H. *Asian American Literature: An Introduction to the Writings and Their Social Context.* Philadelphia: Temple University Press, 1982.

_____. "'Such Opposite Creatures': Men and Women in Asian American Literature." *Michigan Quarterly Review,* Vol. 29, No. 1, pp. 68–93.

Klawans, Stuart. "Review: *The Joy Luck Club.*" *Nation,* October 4, 1993, p. 364.

Koenig, Rhoda. "Heirloom China." *New York,* Vol. 22, No. 12, March 20, 1989, pp. 82–83.

_____. "Nanking Pluck." *New York,* Vol. 24, No. 24, June 17, 1991, pp. 83–84.

Kropf, Joan. "Finding Her Voice." Longview, Washington, *Daily News*, January 11, 1991.

"Lady Luck." *Richmond Times-Dispatch*, September 26, 1993.

Law-Yone, Wendy. "Review: *The Kitchen God's Wife*." *Washington Post Book World*, June 16, 1991, pp. 1–2.

Lelyveld, Niva. "Mother as Muse: Amy Tan Had to Unravel the Mystery of Li Bingzi, Who Had Become the Voice of Her Novels." *Philadelphia Inquirer Magazine*, February 18, 2001.

Leonard, George, ed. *The Asian Pacific American Heritage: A Companion to Literature and Arts*. New York: Garland, 1998.

Lew, Julie. "How Stories Written for Mother Become Amy Tan's Bestsellers." *New York Times*, July 4, 1989, p. 23.

Ling, Amy. *Between Worlds: Women Writers of Chinese Ancestry*. New York: Pergamon Press, 1990.

Link, Tom. "Revisiting Tangled Mother-Daughter Ties." *Los Angeles Daily News*, June 2, 1991, pp. C2–C3.

Lipson, Edna Ross. "The Wicked English-speaking Daughter." *New York Times Book Review*, March 19, 1989, p. 3.

Liu, Edward. "Chinese Supermoms." *Chinatown News*, Vol. 41, No. 10, February 3, 1994, p. 2.

Loer, Stephanie. "Amy Tan Writes from a Child's Point of View." *Boston Globe*, November 10, 1992, pp. E3–E4.

Long, Judith. "Finding Invisible Strength." *Newsday*, November 9, 2003.

Longenecker, Donna. "Relationship with Mother Helped Tan Hone Writing Skills." *University of Buffalo Reporter*, March 27, 2003.

Lorber, Helen. "Review: *The Bonesetter's Daughter*." *Detroit Free Press*, February 28, 2001.

Lowe, Lisa. "Homogeneity, Hybridity, Multiplicity: Marking Asian American Differences." *Diaspora*, Vol. 1, No. 1, pp. 24–44.

Lucey, Rose Marciano. "Favorite New and Old Books of Certain Avid NCR Readers." *National Catholic Reporter*, November 19, 1993, p. 33.

Lyall, Sarah. "In the Country of the Spirits." *New York Times*, December 28, 1995, pp. C1, C6.

Ma, Sheng-mei. "'Chinese and Dogs' in Amy Tan's 'The Hundred Secret Senses': Ethnicizing the Primitive à la New Age." *MELUS*, Vol. 26, No. 1, Spring 2001, pp. 29–44.

_____. *The Deathly Embrace: Orientalism and Asian American Identity*. Minneapolis: University of Minnesota Press, 2000.

_____. *Immigrant Subjectivities in Asian American and Asian Diaspora Literature*. Albany: State University of New York Press, 1998.

MacDonald, Jay. "A Date with Fate." *BookPage*, November 2003.

Macedo, Ana Gabriela, and Ana Maria Macedo-Chaves. "Amy Tan's *The Joy Luck Club*: Translation as a 'Trans/Cultural' Experience." *Hitting Critical Mass*, Vol. 4, No. 1, 1996, pp. 69–80.

Mandell, Jonathan. "Interview." *New York Newsday*, July 15, 1991.

Mandell, Phyllis Levy, and Leah Hawkins. "Review: South Recording of *The Chinese Siamese Cat*." *School Library Journal*, Vol. 41, No. 5, May 1995, p. 66.

Marbella, Jean. "Amy Tan: Luck but Not Joy." *Baltimore Sun*, June 30, 1991, pp. B10–B13.

Maryles, Daisy. "Behind the Bestsellers." *Publishers Weekly*, Vol. 242, No. 44, October 30, 1995, p. 16.

Maslin, Janet. "Intimate Generational Lessons, Available to All." *New York Times*, September 8, 1993, p. C15.

Mason, Deborah. "A Not-So-Dutiful Daughter." *New York Times*, November 23, 2003.

Mathews, Laura. "More 'Joy Luck'." *Glamour*, Vol. 89, No. 6, June 1991, p. 106.

Maynard, Joyce. "The Almost All-American Girls." *Mademoiselle*, Vol. 95, July 1989, pp. 70, 72, 180.

McAlister, Melani. "(Mis)Reading The Joy Luck Club." *Asian America: Journal of Culture and the Arts*, Vol. 1, 1992, pp. 102–118.

McCoy, J. J. "Novelist Lives Dramatic Struggle with Lyme Disease." *Washington Post*, August 13, 2003.

McFadden, Cyra. "Amy Tan's Second Novel Is Rich and Satisfying Tale." *San Francisco Examiner*, June 17, 1991, p. C8.

McMillan, Stephanie. "Review: *The Bonesetter's Daughter*." *City Link*, March 2001.

Mendoza, Alice. "The Ink of Diverse Gods." *Quarterly Literary Review Singapore*, Vol. 2, No. 2, January 2003.

Merina, Anita. "Joy, Luck, and Literature: Meet Amy Tan." *NEA Today*, Vol. 10, No. 3, October 1991, p. 9.

Mesic, Penelope. "Review: *The Hundred Secret Senses*," *Chicago Tribune*, November 9, 1995, p. 16.

Messud, Claire. "Ghost Story." *New York Times Book Review*, October 29 1995, p. 11.

_____. "What's Safe to Say." *Daily Telegraph*, November 17, 2003.

Michael, Franz. *The Taiping Rebellion*. Seattle: University of Washington Press, 1971.

Miner, Valerie. "The Daughters' Journeys." *Nation*, Vol. 248, No. 16, April 24, 1989, pp. 566–569.

_____. "Review: *The Bonesetter's Daughter*." *Los Angeles Times*, February 18, 2001.

Mistri, Zenobia. "Discovering the Ethnic Name and the Genealogical Tie in Amy Tan's *The Joy Luck Club*." *Studies in Short Fiction*, Vol. 35, No. 3, Summer 1998, pp. 251–257.

Mones, Nicole. "China Syndrome." *Washington Post Book World*, February 11, 2001.

Moody, Lori. "Culture Clash." *Los Angeles Daily News*, June 6, 1992, pp. A6–A7.

Morrison, Mark. "Joy, Luck — and a Movie Deal." *USA Today*, September 10, 1993, pp. 4–6.

Mundow, Anna. "Tan Without a Plan." *New York Daily News*, November, 1, 2003.

Murray, Madeleine. "Stephen & Amy Go Rapping." *Sydney Morning Herald*, December 21, 2002.

Nadeau, Frances A. "The Mother/Daughter Relationship in Young Adult Fiction." *ALAN Review*, Vol. 22, No. 2, Winter 1995.

Naversen, Laurel, and Catherine Hong. "Write Guard." *Harper's Bazaar*, Vol. 134, No. 3,475, June 2001, pp. 116–117.

Needham, Nancy R. "By Their First Lines You Shall Know Them." *NEA Today*, May 1993, p. 27.

Nelson, Emmanuel S. *Asian American Novelists*. Westport, Conn.: Greenwood Press, 2000.

Nelson, Sara. "Picks and Pans." *People Weekly*, Vol. 36, No. 2, July 22, 1991, pp. 21–22.

Ng, Franklin, et al., eds. "New Visions in Asian American Studies: Diversity, Community, Power." *ERIC*, 1994.

Nguyen, Lan N. "The Next Amy Tan." *A Magazine*, February/March 1997, pp. 46–51, 55.

Nhu, T. T. "We Need More Movies That Portray Asian Men Realistically." *San Jose Mercury*, October 4, 1993.

Nishimuru, Scott. "More Tan Than Most Really Want." *Fort Worth Star-Telegram*, December 14, 2003.

Nurse, Donna. "House of the Spirits." *Maclean's*, Vol. 108, No. 45, November 6, 1995, p. 85.

"Obituary." *Washington Post*, November 26, 1999, p. B7.

O'Brien, Catherine. "What Does Life Tell Us About Love." *London Times*, December 24, 2003.

Oh, Seiwoong. "Review: *Transcultural Reinventions: Asian American and Asian Canadian Short-Story Cycle*." *MELUS*, Vol. 28, No. 1, Spring 2003, pp. 176–180.

Ong, Caroline. "Re-writing the Old Wives' Tales." *Times Literary Supplement*, No. 4,605, July 5, 1991, p. 20.

Painter, Charlotte. "In Search of a Voice." *San Francisco Review of Books*, Summer 1989, pp. 15–17.

Palumbo-Liu, David, ed. *The Ethnic Canon: Histories, Institutions, and Interventions*. Minneapolis: University of Minnesota Press, 1995.

Patchett, Ann. "Review: *The Joy Luck Club*." *Seventeen*, Vol. 48, August 1989, p. 126.

Pate, Nancy. "Review: *The Bonesetter's Daughter*." *Orlando Sentinel*, February 21, 2001.

_____. "'Wife' Is the Story of an Amazing Life." *Orlando Sentinel*, June 23, 1991, p. C11.

Patterson, Troy. "The New Age Club." *Entertainment Weekly*, February 23, 2001, p. 154.

Pavey, Ruth. "Spirit Levels." *New Statesman & Society*, Vol. 9, No. 390, February 16, 1996, p. 38.

Pearlman, Mickey, and Katherine Usher Henderson. *Inter/view: Talks with America's Writing Women*. Lexington: University Press of Kentucky, 1990.

"Peking Man Site of Further Research

Value." *Xinhua News Agency*, December 13, 2002.

Perrick, Penny. "Daughters of America." *Times Book Review*, July 14, 1991, p. 6.

Perry, Donna. *Backtalk: Women Writers Speak Out*. New Brunswick, N.J.: Rutgers University Press, 1993.

Peter, Nelson, and Peter Freundlich. "Women We Love: Nine Women Who Knock Us Out." *Esquire*, Vol. 112, August 1989, p. 86.

Philbrook, John. "Review: *The Moon Lady*." *School Library Journal*, Vol. 92, No. 38, September 1992, p. 255.

Powell, Sian. "Unravelling Amy." *Australian*, March 10, 2001.

Reid, E. Shelley. "'Our Two Faces': Balancing Mothers and Daughters in *The Joy Luck Club* and *The Kitchen God's Wife*." *Paintbrush*, Vol. 22, No. 42, 1995, pp. 20–38.

"Review: *The Kitchen God's Wife*." *Kirkus Reviews*, April 1, 1991.

"Review: *The Moon Lady*." *Publishers Weekly*, Vol. 239, No. 50, November 16, 1992, p. 24.

"Review: *The Opposite of Fate: A Book of Musings*." *Kirkus Reviews*, Vol. 7, No. 19, October 1, 2003, p. 1216.

Romagnolo, Catherine. "Narrative Beginnings in Amy Tan's *The Joy Luck Club*: A Feminist Study." *Studies in the Novel*, Vol. 35, No. 1, Spring 2003, pp. 89–107.

Romano, Nancy Forbes. "The Disorientation of Pearl and Kai." *Los Angeles Times Book Review*, June 26, 1991, p. 2.

Ross, Val. "Interview." *Toronto Globe and Mail*, June 25, 1991.

Rothstein, Mervyn. "A New Novel by Amy Tan, Who's Still Trying to Adapt to Success." *New York Times*, June 11, 1991, pp. 13–14.

Rowland, Penelope. "American Woman." *Mother Jones*, July/August 1989, p. 10.

Ruiz, Sophia. "Amy Tan." http://www.iread pages.com/archive/marapr01/amytan/amy tan.html.

Russo, Maria. "Review: *The Bonesetter's Daughter*." *Salon*, February 21, 2001.

"Sagwa, the Chinese Siamese Cat." http://pbs kids.org/sagwa/.

"Scenes from a Distance: 'The Joy Luck Club' Tour Beijing." *TIME/ International Edition*, November 18, 1993.

Schecter, Ellen. "Girl Overboard." *New York Times Book Review*, November 8, 1992, p. 31.

Schell, Orville. "Your Mother Is in Your Bones." *New York Times Book Review*, Vol. 26, March 19, 1989, pp. 3, 28.

Schneider, Katie. "The Novelist Tells (Almost) All in Her First Nonfiction Book." *Oregonian*, November 9, 2003.

Schueller, Malini Johar. "Theorizing Ethnicity and Subjectivity: Maxine Hong Kingston's *Tripmaster Monkey* and Amy Tan's *The Joy Luck Club*." *Genders*, Vol. 15, Winter 1992, pp. 72–85.

Schwartz, Gil. "…and Women of the Dunes." *Fortune*, Vol. 124, No. 5, August 26, 1991, p. 116.

Scott, Robert L., Jr. *God Is My Co-Pilot*. Reynoldsburg, Ohio: Buckeye Aviation Books, 1988.

Seaman, Donna. "Quick Bibs." *American Libraries*, Vol. 22, No. 7, July 1991, p. 688.

See, Carolyn. "Drowning in America, Starving for China." *Los Angeles Times Book Review*, March 12, 1989, pp. 1, 11.

Shapiro, Laura. "From China, with Love." *Newsweek*, Vol. 117, No. 25, June 24, 1991, pp. 63–64.

_____. "Ghost Story." *Newsweek*, Vol. 126, No. 19, November 6, 1995, pp. 91–92.

_____. "The Generation Gap in Chinatown." *Newsweek*, Vol. 122, No. 13, September 27, 1993, p. 70.

Shear, Walter. "Generational Differences and the Diaspora in *The Joy Luck Club*," *Critique*, Vol. 34, No. 3, Spring 1993, pp. 193–199.

Shen, Gloria. "Born of a Stranger: Mother-Daughter Relationships and Storytelling in Amy Tan's *The Joy Luck Club*," in *International Women's Writing: New Landscapes of Identity*. Westport, Conn.: Greenwood Press, 1995, pp. 233–244.

Shilling, Jane. "What the Memory Box Holds." *Daily Telegraph*, November 17, 2003.

"Short Takes on Beliefs and Behavior." *San Diego Union-Tribune*, January 8, 2003, p. E3.

Simon, Clea. "Amy Tan Explores the Interweaving of Fate, Fact and Fiction." *San Francisco Chronicle*, December 7, 2003.

Simon, John. "Review: The Joy Luck Club." *National Review*, November 15, Vol. 45, 1993, p. 61.

Simpson, Janice C. "Fresh Voices Above the Noisy Din." *Time*, Vol. 137, No. 22, June 3, 1991, pp. 66–67.

Singh Gee, Alison. "A Life on the Brink." *People*, Vol. 55, No. 18, May 7, 2001, pp. 85–88.

Sit, Elaine. "Taking 'My Mother's Place ... On the East, Where Things Begin.'" *East/West News*, April 13, 1989, p. 6.

Skow, John. "Tiger Ladies." *Time*, Vol. 133, March 27, 1989, p. 98.

Smith, Craig S. "A Rare Shot at Screen Stardom for Asians." *Wall Street Journal*, September 1, 1992, p. 12.

Snodgrass, Mary Ellen. *Literary Treks: Characters on the Move*. Westport, Conn.: Libraries Unlimited, 2003.

Solovitch, Sara. "Finding a Voice." *Mercury News*, June 30, 1991.

Somogyi, Barbara, and David Stanton. "Interview with Amy Tan." *Poets & Writers Magazine*, Vol. 19, No. 5, September-October 1991, pp. 24–32.

Souris, Stephen. "Only Two Kinds of Daughters: Inter-monologue Dialogicity in *The Joy Luck Club*." *MELUS*, Vol. 19, No. 2, Summer 1994, pp. 99–123.

Span, Paula. "The Lush Flowering of Asian American Drama." *Washington Post*, March 2, 1997, p. G1.

Stanley, Don. "Amy Tan Is Having Fun." *Sacramento Bee*, July 14, 1991.

Steinberg, Sybil. "Fiction Review." *Publishers Weekly*, Vol. 238, No. 17, April 12, 1991, p. 45.

_____, and Genevieve Stuttaford. "Review: *The Joy Luck Club*." *Publishers Weekly*, Vol. 234, No. 26, December 23, 1988, p. 66.

Street, Mike. "Review: *The Opposite of Fate*." *Asian Reporter*, January 20, 2004, p. 24.

Streitfeld, David. "Authors Rock 'em at Booksellers Convention." *Washington Post*, May 27, 1992

_____. "The 'Luck' of Amy Tan." *Washington Post*, October 8, 1989, pp. F1, F9.

Strohm, J. Elizabeth. "University of Pittsburgh: Author Tan Discusses Writing, Ouija Board Labors." *Pittsburgh Pitt News*, December 5, 2003.

Su, Suocai. "Orientalism in Popular Culture and New Orientalism in Asian American Literature." *Jouvert*, Vol. 7, No. 1.

Sweeting, Paul, and John Zinsser. "Review: *The Joy Luck Club*." *Publishers Weekly*, July 7, 1989, p. 37.

Takahama, Valerie. "Riding Amy Tan's Success, Wave of Asian-American Writers Hits Mainstream." *Orange County Register*, June 14, 1995.

Talbot, Stephen. "Talking Story: Maxine Hong Kingston Rewrites the American Dream," *Image*, Vol. 24, June 1990, pp. 6–8.

Tan, Amy. "Excerpt of 'Kitchen God's Wife.'" *McCall's*, July 1991, p. 115.

"Tan Meets Hollywood on Her Own Terms." *Boston Globe*, September 19, 1993.

"Tan's Memoirs of a Tragic Life." *BBC News*, December 13, 2003.

Tauber, Michelle, et al. "A New Ending." *People*, Vol. 60, No. 18, November 3, 2003, pp. 89–90.

Taylor, Noel. "The Luck of Amy Tan." *Ottawa Citizen*, October 1, 1993, p. F1.

Terrell, Ross. *The White-Boned Demon: A Biography of Madame Mao Zedong*. New York: Morrow, 1984.

Truzzi, Gianni. "'Joy Luck Club' Mirrors Their Own Generational Conflicts, Actors Say." *Seattle Post-Intelligencer*, January 3, 2003.

Tseo, George K. Y. "The Perils of Transcultural 'Translation.'" *Literature/Film Quarterly*, Vol. 24, No. 4, 1996, pp. 338–343.

Tyler, Patrick E. "Joint Production Takes 'The Joy Luck Club' to China's Stages." *New York Times*, November 27, 1993.

Uslu, Didem. "Female Quest for Freedom Through Journey Into Past Heritage: The Turkish-American Guneli Gun and the Chinese-American Amy Tan." http://www.salzburgseminar.org/ASC/csacl/progs/amlit/didem.htm.

Vogel, Christine. "A Remarkable Life Controlled by Gods' Whims." *Chicago Sun Times*, June 30, 1991, p. C14.

Wald-Hopkins, Christine. "Amy Tan's Essays Allow a Peek Inside Her World." *Denver Post*, November 23, 2003.

Walsh, Bryan. "Family Phantoms." *Time Asia*, December 7, 2003.

Wang, Dorothy. "A Game of Show Not Tell." *Newsweek*, Vol. 113, No. 16, April 17, 1989, p. 69.

Warren, Tim. "Write-On Rock — Best-Selling Authors Put Their Talents to Another Sort of Creativity: Music." *Baltimore Sun*, May 27, 1993.

Watkins-Goffman, Linda. *Lives in Two Languages: An Exploration of Identity and Culture*. Detroit: University of Michigan Press, 2003.

Wigston, Nancy. "Amy Tan's Latest Examination of Generation Gap and Culture Clash Is Her Most Engaging Since *The Joy Luck Club*." *Globe and Mail*, April 29, 1989.

Wilkinson, Joanne. "Review: *The Hundred Secret Senses*." *Booklist*, September 15, 1995.

Willard, Nancy. "Talking to Ghosts." *New York Times*, February 18, 2001.

_____. "Tiger Spirits." *Women's Review of Books*, Vol. 6, No. 10–11, July 1989, p. 12.

Witke, Roxane. *Comrade Chiang Ch'ing*. Boston: Little, Brown, 1977.

Wong, Gerrye. "Amy Tan Takes Her Book Tour to Old Hometown, San Jose." *Chinatown News*, Vol. 42, No. 5, November 3, 1994, pp. 15–16.

Wong, Sau-ling Cynthia. *Reading Asian American Literature: From Necessity to Extravagance*. Princeton, N.J.: Princeton University Press, 1993.

_____. "'Sugar Sisterhood': Situating the Amy Tan Phenomenon," in *The Ethnic Canon: Histories, Institutions, and Interventions*. Minneapolis: University of Minnesota Press, 1995, pp. 174–210.

Woo, Elaine. "Interview." *Los Angeles Times*, April 17, 1989.

Wordsworth, William. *The Works of William Wordsworth*. Ware, Herts.: Cumberland House, 1994.

Wu, Esther. "In Latest Book Amy Tan Keeps Focus on Family." *Dallas Morning News*, February 26, 2001.

Wu, Kelvin, trans. "'Fabricated Chinese Culture' and the Continuation of Tradition." *Singtao Daily*, September 15, 2002.

Xiaojing, Zhou. "Denaturalizing Identities, Decolonizing Desire: Videos by Richard Fung and Ming-Yuen S. Ma." *Jouvert*, Vol. 4, No. 3, Spring/ Summer 2000.

Xu, Ben. "Memory and the Ethnic Self: Reading Amy Tan's *The Joy Luck Club*." *MELUS*, Vol. 19, No. 1, 1994 Spring, pp. 3–19.

Yang, Vivian. "Asian-Am Writer Defined." *Asian Wall Street Journal*, February 15–17, 2002.

Yglesias, Helen. "Review: *The Kitchen God's Wife*." *Women's Review of Books*, Vol. 8, No. 12, 1991, pp. 1, 3–4.

Young, Pamela. "Mother with a Past: The Family Album Inspires a Gifted Writer." *Maclean's*, Vol. 104, No. 28, July 15, 1991, p. 47.

Yuan, Yuan. "The Semiotics of China Narratives in the Con/Texts of Kingston and Tan." *Critique*, Vol. 40, No. 3, Spring 1999, pp. 292–303.

Zia, Helen. "A Chinese Banquet of Secrets." *Ms.*, Vol. 2, No. 3, November/ December 1991, pp. 76–77.

Zinsser, John. "Audio Reviews: *The Kitchen God's Wife*." *Publishers Weekly*, Vol. 238, No. 25, June 7, 1991, p. 44.

Zipp, Yvonne. "A Life Recalled from China." *Christian Science Monitor*, Vol. 93, No. 57, February 15, 2001, p. 20.

Zura, Gregory. "Mahjong Epic." *The Stranger*, Vol. 12, No. 18, January 16, 2003.

Index